# Assessing Student Learning in Higher Education

There is no doubt about the importance of assessment: it defines what students regard as important, how they spend their time and how they come to see themselves – it is a necessary part of helping them to learn.

This text provides background research on different aspects of assessment. Its purpose is to help lecturers to refresh their approach to student assessment in order to create more efficient teaching and learning situations and encourage the foundations of life-long learning.

It explores the nature of both conventional assessment such as essays and projects and less widely used approaches that are often based on self- and peer-assessment. There are also chapters devoted to the use of IT, the role of external examiners and the introduction of different forms of assessment.

Containing guidelines, suggestions, examples of practice and activities that are designed to encourage reflection upon the nature and processes of assessment and learning, this book will become a springboard for action, discussion and even more active learning.

**George Brown** is Visiting Professor in the Faculty of Health and Social Sciences at the University of Ulster and Course Tutor for the M.Med.Sci in Clinical Education at the Queen's Medical Centre, University of Nottingham. He is the author (with Madeleine Atkins) of *Effective Teaching in Higher Education*.

**Joanna Bull** is Research Officer in the Unit for Learning, Teaching and Assessment at the University of Luton. **Malcolm Pendlebury** is the Trent Regional Adviser in Postgraduate Dental Education and Course Director for the M.Med.Sci in Clinical Education at the Queen's Medical Centre, University of Nottingham.

# Assessing Student Learning in Higher Education

George Brown with Joanna Bull and
Malcolm Pendlebury

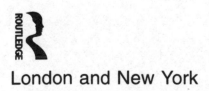

London and New York

First published 1997
by Routledge
11 New Fetter Lane, London EC4P 4EE

Simultaneously published in the USA and Canada
by Routledge
29 West 35th Street, New York, NY 10001

Typeset in Garamond by Keystroke, Jacaranda Lodge, Wolverhampton
Printed and bound in Great Britain by Mackays of Chatham PLC, Chatham, Kent

*British Library Cataloguing in Publication Data*
A catalogue record for this book is available from the British Library

*Library of Congress Cataloging in Publication Data*
Brown, George, 1935–
    Assessing student learning in higher education/George Brown with
Joanna Bull and Malcolm Pendlebury.
        p.   cm.
    Includes bibliographical references.
    1. Universities and colleges—Great Britain—Examinations.
    2. College students—Rating of—Great Britain.  3. College teaching—
Great Britain—Evaluation.  4. Education, Higher—Aims and
objectives—Great Britain.  5. Education, Higher—Great Britain—
Evaluation.  I. Bull, Joanna.  II. Pendlebury, Malcolm.
    III. Title.
    LB2367.G76B76    1996
    378. 1′662—dc20    96-43134
                        CIP
ISBN 0–415–16226–2 (hbk)
ISBN 0–415–14460–4 (pbk)

For Jessica, who persuaded us to write this book
For Emma and all other students entering universities
in the next decade

We must not expect more precision than the subject admits of.
Aristotle: *Nicomachean Ethics*

# Contents

List of figures     viii
Acknowledgements     xi
List of abbreviations     xii

1   Introduction to the text     1
2   What is assessment?     7
3   Student learning     21
4   Methods and strategies: an overview     40
5   Assessing essays     59
6   Multiple choice questions     84
7   Assessing practical work     98
8   Assessing projects     120
9   Assessing problem-solving     141
10   Assessing oral communication     154
11   Peer- and self-assessment     170
12   Self-assessment: some related approaches     185
13   Using computers in assessment     202
14   Changing assessment procedures     222
15   Reliability, validity and examining     233
16   Quality, standards and underlying issues     250

Appendix: examples of examination questions in arts, law and social sciences     265

Notes and comments on activities     276

Some further reading     291

Bibliography     295

Index     310

# Figures

2.1    Some influences on student learning    8
2.2    Some common weaknesses in assessment systems    9
2.3    Assessment and development    10
2.4    Purposes of assessment    11
2.5    The meaning of assessment    11
2.6    Trends in assessment    13
2.7    Examinations in Ancient China    15
3.1    Some students' conceptions of learning    22
3.2    Orientations to learning    24
3.3    Forms of understanding developed during revision    25
3.4    Characteristics of the context of learning associated with deep and surface approaches    28
3.5    When is effective learning most likely to occur?    29
3.6    Perry's stages of development    29
3.7    The process of learning    31
3.8    A model of learning skills    34
3.9    Hierarchy of the cognitive domain    36
3.10    Skills expected of graduates    37
4.1    Sources, instruments and methods of assessment    41
4.2    Modifying existing assessments    45
4.3    Which methods of assessment?    46
4.4    Course delivery and assessment plan    48
4.5    Marking efficiently for summative purposes    52
4.6    Some tactics for modular assessment    54
4.7    A letter from a student    55
4.8    Some coping strategies    56
5.1    Essays on railways in Victorian Britain    64
5.2    Suggestions on marking essays    66
5.3    Fair marking    67
5.4    A structured approach    68
5.5    A semi-structured approach    69
5.6    The beginnings of some criteria    70

| | | |
|---|---|---|
| 5.7 | Student checklist | 71 |
| 5.8 | Tutors' comments on first-year essays | 72 |
| 5.9 | Table for the conversion of literal grades into marks | 75 |
| 5.10 | 'Sunken Treasure' | 76 |
| 5.11 | 'Prang' | 79 |
| 5.12 | Extract from an MEQ | 80 |
| 6.1 | Some common terms in MCQs | 85 |
| 6.2 | Guidelines for preparing MCQs | 86 |
| 6.3 | Favoured wrong responses | 96 |
| 7.1 | Objectives, content and assessment | 101 |
| 7.2 | Levels of experiment I | 101 |
| 7.3 | Levels of experiment II | 104 |
| 7.4 | Laboratory report sheet | 105 |
| 7.5 | Laboratory report sheet | 106 |
| 7.6 | Designing a PEG | 106 |
| 7.7 | An example of a PEG | 107 |
| 7.8 | Alternative approaches to laboratory work | 112 |
| 7.9 | Checklist for setting up apparatus | 114 |
| 7.10 | Demonstrator skills | 115 |
| 8.1 | Examples of objectives | 123 |
| 8.2 | Stages in a project tutorial | 124 |
| 8.3 | Timetabling a project | 125 |
| 8.4 | Assessing an experimental project | 128 |
| 8.5 | Assessing a dissertation | 129 |
| 8.6 | Reading a report or dissertation | 132 |
| 8.7 | Some issues when considering poster sessions | 133 |
| 8.8 | Example of poster assessment sheet | 134 |
| 8.9 | Poster assessment | 135 |
| 8.10 | Some objectives of group projects | 136 |
| 8.11 | Suggestions for marking group projects | 137 |
| 8.12 | Some issues for discussion in a department | 138 |
| 9.1 | Some suggestions on marking | 147 |
| 10.1 | Making explanations clear | 155 |
| 10.2 | Making explanations interesting | 156 |
| 10.3 | Explanations evaluated | 158 |
| 10.4 | Seminar presentation and discussion | 159 |
| 10.5 | BIAS: an interaction system | 162 |
| 10.6 | ASKIT: analysing questions | 163 |
| 10.7 | Levels of discussion | 164 |
| 10.8 | Assessing structures and vocabularies | 165 |
| 10.9 | Common errors made by young doctors in consultations | 166 |
| 10.10 | The well-ordered consultation | 167 |
| 11.1 | Some uses of peer feedback and assessment | 172 |
| 11.2 | Criteria for self- and peer-assessment of group processes | 175 |

| 11.3 | Peer-group assessment: a global approach | 176 |
| 11.4 | How our group worked | 177 |
| 11.5 | Getting started with self- and peer-assessment | 182 |
| 11.6 | Lecturer: know thyself | 183 |
| 12.1 | Example from a portfolio | 188 |
| 12.2 | Guidelines for effective assessment | 199 |
| 13.1 | Computer-assisted assessment and teaching | 207 |
| 13.2 | Levels of CAL and assessment | 208 |
| 13.3 | Advantages of computerised MCQs | 211 |
| 13.4 | Checklist for the implementation of computerised self-assessment systems | 212 |
| 13.5 | Evaluation of computer-assisted assessment | 219 |
| 14.1 | Thirty ways of avoiding change | 224 |
| 14.2 | Reducing resistance to change | 225 |
| 14.3 | Some pointers to persuasion | 226 |
| 14.4 | Your assessment of our assessment | 227 |
| 14.5 | Student comments | 228 |
| 15.1 | A grade score scale | 237 |
| 15.2 | Effects of a wide range of marks in one module | 239 |
| 15.3 | Effects of scaling and rank ordering | 240 |
| 15.4 | 'Dentonia': a case study in invalid assessment? | 245 |
| 15.5 | A compulsory examination for all examiners | 247 |
| 16.1 | Observations on quality-assurance systems in universities | 261 |

# Acknowledgements

We wish to thank Pat Partington, Director of the CVCP Universities and Colleges Staff Development Agency (UCoSDA) for her encouragement and support. The book grew out of the UCoSDA projects on Effective Teaching and Learning and Altering Learning through Efficiency and Rigour (ALTER).

We also wish to thank Madeleine Atkins, University of Newcastle, Celia Boscolo, University of Birmingham, Chris Butcher, University of Leeds, Sir Colin Campbell and Kate Exley, University of Nottingham, Dai Hounsell, University of Edinburgh, Nancy Falchikov, Heriot Watt University, Don Mackenzie, University of Derby, Malcolm Shaw, Leeds Metropolitan University and Andrew Wilson, University of Loughborough for providing information and comments. Thanks are given to Faber and Faber Limited for permission to quote from 'Choruses from "The Rock"' by T.S. Eliot.

Thanks are also given to Victoria Hallam for assistance in checking the manuscript and for providing an undergraduate's view, to Trina Medlicott for assistance in preparing the final version of the manuscript, to Alison Kelly for her invaluable work as copy editor and to Helen Fairlie of Routledge for her comments and for steering the text through the labyrinth of printing processes.

Last but not least, we wish to thank participants of our workshops on assessment. It was their comments and observations that led us to write a text on assessment that contains practical advice underpinned by research.

July 1996

# Abbreviations

| | |
|---|---|
| AAC | Association of American Colleges |
| ABGDP | Advisory Board of General Dental Practice |
| AGR | Association of Graduate Recruiters |
| ALTER | Altering Learning through Efficiency and Rigour |
| APA | Accreditation of Prior Achievement |
| APAL | Assessment of Prior Assessed Learning |
| APEL | Assessment of Prior Experiential Learning |
| APL | Assessment of Prior Learning |
| APLA | Accreditation of Prior Learning Achievement |
| ASSHE | Assessment Strategies in Scottish Higher Education |
| BTEC | Business and Technical Education Council |
| CAA | Computer Assisted Assessment |
| CAI | Computer Assisted Instruction |
| CAL | Computer Assisted Learning |
| CALM | Computer Assisted Learning in Mathematics |
| CBI | Confederation of British Industry |
| CBL | Computer Based Learning |
| CBT | Computer Based Teaching |
| CEILIDH | Computer Environment for Interactive Learning in Diverse Habitats |
| CNAA | Council for National Academic Awards |
| CVCP | Committee of the Vice Chancellors and Principals |
| DIADS | Derby Interactive Assessment Delivery System |
| ED | Employment Department (now the Department for Education and Employment) |
| EEG | Electroencephalogram |
| EHE | Enterprise in higher education |
| GCSE | General Certificate of Secondary Education |
| GNVQ | General National Vocational Qualification |
| HEFC | Higher Education Funding Council |
| HEFCE | Higher Education Funding Council of England |
| HEQC | Higher Education Quality Council |

| | |
|---|---|
| IETI | Innovation in Education and Training International |
| LMU | Leeds Metropolitan University |
| LUISA | Leeds University Italian Software |
| MCQ | Multiple choice question |
| MEQ | Modified essay question |
| NCVQ | National Council of Vocational Qualifications |
| NFER | National Foundation of Educational Research |
| NUS | National Union of Students |
| NVQ | National Vocational Qualification |
| OHP | Overhead projector |
| OHT | Overhead transparency |
| OMR | Optical mark reader |
| OSCE | Objective Structured Clinical Education |
| PEG | Performance Evaluation Guide |
| RISE | Research in Sandwich Education Committee |
| RoA | Record of Achievements |
| SAMS | Self-Assessment Manual of Standards |
| SCED | Standing Conference on Educational Development |
| SCOTVEC | Scottish Vocational Education Council |
| SEDA | Staff and Educational Development Association |
| SOLO | Structure of Observed Learning Outcomes |
| SRHE | Society of Research in Higher Education |
| *THES* | *Times Higher Education Supplement* |
| UCoSDA | Universities and Colleges Staff Development Agency |

# Chapter 1

# Introduction to the text

## WHAT THIS TEXT IS ABOUT

This text provides background research on different aspects of assessment and learning in higher education together with guidelines, suggestions, examples of practice and activities that are designed to encourage reflection upon the nature and processes of assessment and learning. Its purpose is to help colleagues to refresh and develop their approach to the assessment of student learning. The task of assessing student learning involves knowledge, understanding and skills of assessment and of student learning. Hence we begin the text (Chapter 2) by considering what assessment is, what its purposes are and the emerging trends in assessment in higher education. We then (in Chapter 3) consider briefly the nature of student learning and its assessment. Subsequent chapters (4–12) are concerned with ways of assessing student learning through conventional approaches such as essays, multiple choice questions and problems and less widely used approaches that are often based on self- and peer-assessment. Chapter 13 is devoted to the various uses of IT in assessing, recording and reporting assessments. Chapter 14 is concerned with introducing different forms of assessment into a course and Chapter 15 with some of the assumptions underlying approaches to reliability and validity. The final chapter addresses issues of quality and standards. It is followed by an appendix containing sample examination questions; notes and comments on the activities provided for each chapter; suggestions for further reading and a bibliography.

Throughout the book, there are three main themes: effectiveness, efficiency and enablement. *Efficiency* is a primary concern for lecturers who are overloaded with teaching, assessment and related administration and who at the same time may be being urged to create stronger links with industry and to generate research. *Effectiveness* is concerned with ensuring that student learning matches course objectives – a knotty issue because one needs to know how students learn, how to express objectives in forms that guide the learners and course designers and how to create teaching and learning situations that move the students towards the learning outcomes, the objectives of the course. Effectiveness ties in with the notion of fitness for purpose and so has implications for the Higher

Education Funding Councils' assessment of the quality of educational provision in subject departments. The deepest and probably most challenging theme is *enablement*: how one uses assessment as well as teaching and learning to develop understanding and expertise and lay the foundations of life-long learning. Its primary objective is to enable students to cope with changes in knowledge, systems of working and new materials and methods. Graduates are likely to change their jobs at least five times during their careers; even if they do not change jobs, their jobs will change. So in a sense one has to prepare them for the unknown or, at best, the dimly known. The best way of doing that is to provide experiences and assessments for students which enable them to become autonomous, self-motivated learners who have a large repertoire of problem-solving strategies for working with materials, concepts and people. Enablement, then, is concerned with the longer reach, with what graduates might be doing in 20 years' time. It goes beyond the issue of fitness *for* purpose to that of fitness *of* purpose for the 21st century. Assessment of students' understanding of these themes is important in its own right and it also may provide students with strategies for thinking about other deep issues that they may encounter in their working lives.

## HOW TO USE THIS BOOK

How you use this text is, of course, dependent upon your purpose in reading it. As a broad strategy, we suggest that you browse through the contents list and skim the chapters before choosing your pathway through them.

The book may then be used in at least five different ways. First, it may simply be read. This approach will certainly refresh your knowledge of assessment. Second, you may read it, tackle some of the activities and check the notes and comments. This approach will deepen your reading and help you reflect upon your approaches to assessment. The notes and comments on the activities are provided so that readers can match their thoughts and observations against those of others who have tried the activities and against the views of the authors. Readers may find the notes and comments helpful and, perhaps, interesting. We expect that some people will disagree with the comments some of the time and a few may disagree with the comments all of the time. Third, the book may be used as a guide for a series of meetings between a less experienced teacher and a senior colleague who is acting as a mentor during the probationary period. Fourth, you may use the book as a source for a series of lunchtime meetings with colleagues in your department or other departments. Used in this way the text will, we hope, become a springboard for action, discussion and even more active learning. Fifth, the book may be used as the recommended text for a short course on assessment. If it is used in this way it is hoped that the course will be based upon the principles of reflective learning rather than those of effective lecturing.

## REFLECTIVE LEARNING

Readers of this book will be aware of the importance of reflecting upon what one reads and relating one's reading to one's practice. The activities in the chapters are designed to prompt those reflections. It is not proposed to rehearse in this chapter all the arguments from Dewey (1933), Kolb (1984), Boud *et al.* (1985), Schon (1983, 1988), and Hatton and Smith (1995) on the importance of reflective learning. That theme is discussed in Chapter 3. It is sufficient here to say that reflective learning is essential to the research work of any self-respecting academic. All we ask is that the same degree of understanding, expertise and responsibility is applied to the problems of assessing students. After all, we may be marking students for life.

Whilst reading this text you may wish to use an assessment logbook or file to record your thoughts on assessment and your responses to the chapters and activities that you tackle. This approach is widely used by Open University students and is one that other undergraduates are being asked to use in portfolios, learning diaries and records of achievement (Bull and Otter, 1994). The inside experience that you gain by keeping a log may help you to guide students in their log-keeping.

You may want to keep your assessment log in the form of a commonplace notebook or you may prefer a more formal structure, such as:

- your initial thoughts on aspects of assessment
- your existing methods of assessment and feedback
- your responses to the activities in this book
- your subsequent thoughts on aspects of assessment
- any plans for reviewing approaches to assessment in your courses
- any plans and strategies for modifying assessment in your courses
- any useful references or quotes
- any random thoughts on assessment and its deeper implications.

A structured assessment notebook will help you to reflect systematically, to plan, to act and to reflect again.

## GETTING GROUPS TO WORK ON ASSESSMENT

Given the challenging nature of assessment it seems sensible to work with a group of colleagues or, if that is not possible, then with a colleague. Colleagues of ours who have been involved in the Enterprise in Higher Education programme (ED 1991; Gray, 1995) and the Effective Engineering Education Project (Brown *et al.*, 1994) as departmental or school coordinators valued highly the mutual support and shared thinking on assessment which was engendered in their group meetings. A group of interested colleagues within the same department or school can build upon their common knowledge of the subjects involved and they may have a greater impact than any one individual upon course design, course delivery and the quality of student learning.

In essence, the group needs to establish its framework of purposes and procedures. These should include the frequency of meetings, a programme of activities and any allocation of tasks. For example, the group might discuss methods of organising an assessment log or it might use its first meeting to establish its priorities. The purposes of the working group should be reviewed after a few meetings.

Groups usually go through the phases of *forming*, *storming* and *norming* before they get to the stage of *performing* a task. As readers will know, some working groups do not get beyond the storming phase and some regress to that phase and disintegrate. To maximise effectiveness of task performance, one has to attend to personal details, including the physical as well as the psychological comfort of the group. In concrete terms, that means a comfortable, well equipped and well ventilated meeting room which has easy access to food and drink. It is also useful, after a few meetings, to review the workings and achievements of the group. Again this task is not only valuable in its own right, it will also help you to understand the processes of group assessment that you may want your students to attempt.

## WORKING WITH A MENTOR

'Mentor' is a fashionable term for a senior colleague whose task is to help a newly qualified or less experienced colleague to develop his/her expertise. A similar notion was advocated in universities in the 1970s but infrequently put into practice. The essentials of a good mentor–colleague relationship are mutual rapport, a structure of regular meetings and a series of jointly agreed tasks. An assessment log provides a useful framework for developing expertise in assessment and for reviewing progress. Such an approach is used successfully in dentistry, medicine and nursing (Morton-Cooper and Palmer, 1993) as well as in higher education.

### Giving feedback

Giving feedback is a central skill of assessment so it may be wise to get it right in a mentor–colleague relationship or in a group that meets to discuss assessment.

The purpose of feedback is to help a person to improve what he or she is doing. It follows that the feedback has to be useful and acceptable to the receiver. To meet these criteria, feedback has to be specific, accurate, timely, clear, focused upon the attainable and expressed in a way which will encourage a person to think and, if he or she thinks that it is necessary, to change.

The strategy of *Ask, Listen, Respond* and *Tell* – if it is necessary – is usually better than the strategy of *Telling*. Three useful questions to ask when providing feedback are:

- What were you trying to do?
- How did you do it?
- Why did you do it in that way?

These questions enable a person to provide his or her own assessment as a preliminary to any feedback that you may need to give. In using this procedure you are helping a person to develop his or her own self-assessment skills.

Three common errors in feedback are:

- Not allowing the speaker or presenter the opportunity to comment on his/her work.
- Saying what you would do rather than listening to what the person says he or she did.
- Saying what was done is totally useless.
- Attacking the person rather than analysing the actions.

These errors rarely lead to improvement or trust. When people are trying out new approaches, they may be insecure and vulnerable. Supportive, constructive feedback is particularly important in these circumstances. However, one does, occasionally, have to give bad news. As with all forms of communication it is not just a matter of what you say but how and when you say it. (See Nelson-Jones, 1986, 1988 for further suggestions on providing and receiving feedback.)

### Receiving feedback

Receiving feedback is also a central skill of assessment. There is a range of reactions to feedback. At one end is passive, uncritical acceptance of advice. At the other is uncritical aggressive rejection of feedback. Interestingly, these reactions fit the early stages of Perry's developmental model referred to in Chapter 3 (Perry, 1970). A more mature response is to accept the feedback graciously and then consider it in the light of one's values and experience.

## ACTIVITIES

1.1 Jot down your reasons for reading this module. If possible compare your reasons with those of a few colleagues.

1.2 Think of the time when you were an undergraduate and select either a good or a bad experience of being assessed or given feedback. What lessons can you draw from the experience? Discuss the experiences and their implications with a few colleagues.

1.3 Two mini-problems:
    In a few minutes' time you are meeting with a shy first-year student to

discuss that student's first assignment in the course. It was awful. How will you approach the tutorial?

In the next tutorial you are meeting an aggressive, overconfident first-year student to discuss that student's first assignment. The student has plagiarised large chunks of a little-known textbook. How will you approach that tutorial?

1.4 What aspects of assessing students' work in a course do you find the most distressing?

1.5 Imagine that you are in your first post as a lecturer. You have a choice of a mentor from one of three.

A is a young, dynamic, abrasive Reader who is cold, ruthless but very well informed about assessment.

B is the Head of Department. B is rarely present in the department, forgetful and given to sudden bouts of activity followed by torpor.

C is a jolly person who enjoys teaching and who is popular with students. C is not very well informed about assessment but willing to learn.

On the basis of the evidence given, who would you choose and why?

1.6 If you were to join a group of colleagues to explore some topics in assessment, what suggestions would you offer to the group?

# Chapter 2

# What is assessment?

This chapter provides a framework for considering assessment. It indicates the importance of assessment and it outlines the nature of assessment and its purposes. Key terms in assessment are introduced and the trends in assessment procedures are identified.

## THE IMPORTANCE OF ASSESSMENT

There is no doubt about the importance of assessment. It is a legitimate concern of those who learn, those who teach and those who are responsible for the development and accreditation of courses. In a sense, assessment is the cash nexus of learning. As Brown and Knight (1994) point out, 'assessment is at the heart of the student experience'. Assessment defines what students regard as important, how they spend their time and how they come to see themselves as students and then as graduates. Students take their cues from what is assessed rather than from what lecturers assert is important. Put rather starkly: *If you want to change student learning then change the methods of assessment.*

This assertion may seem bold but there is plenty of evidence to support it. For example: Newble and Jaeger (1983) describe how changing the clinical assessment from a pass/fail, based on ward reports, to a clinical practical examination increased the amount of time spent by medical students on the wards. Watkins and Hattie (1985) showed that the type of assessment influences styles of learning. The use of multiple choice questions and other forms of tests promoted reproductive styles of learning whereas projects and open-ended assessments promoted independence and deeper strategies of understanding. Perhaps the most disquieting findings are that deeper approaches to study and independent learning declined during many undergraduate courses (Biggs, 1987; Harper and Kember, 1989). Furthermore some students reject deeper approaches to study on the grounds that the assessment of their courses involves so much reproductive learning that deeper approaches are not worth learning (Ramsden, 1988). Fortunately, there is some evidence that the use of problem-based approaches and appropriate forms of assessment can promote deeper styles of learning (e.g. Thomas and Bain, 1984; Newble and Clarke, 1987; Vernon

Institutional climate
Course climate and°
Course design
Management
Face to face

STUDENT LEARNING

Teaching
Assessment subjects
Course resources
Institutional resources

*Figure 2.1* Some influences on student learning

and Blake, 1994). Further evidence on the effect of assessment on learning may be found in Entwistle (1987, 1992) and Ramsden (1992).

## WHAT IS ASSESSMENT?

*Before reading this section, some of you may wish to try Activity 2.2.*

Assessment consists, essentially, of taking a sample of what students do, making inferences and estimating the worth of their actions. The sample may include the use of computers, writing essays, completing tests or checklists, solving problems and reporting their solutions, carrying out practical procedures, or recalling and reporting orally, or in writing, actions, thoughts and feelings. The behaviours sampled may be specific to a course or they may be more general. They may be related to explicit or implicit criteria. The sampling may be undertaken by the students themselves, their peers, their tutors or employers with whom they are working. On the basis of the sample that is taken, inferences are made about a person's achievements, potential, intelligence, aptitudes, attitudes, motivations and, perhaps, personality and an estimate of worth in the form of grades, marks or recommendations is made.

Each of the three aspects of assessment may suffer from weaknesses. The sample may not be representative of the student's capabilities or may not match the learning objectives of the course. It may draw on too narrow a domain – such as only written examinations – and it may be over-weighted towards particular skills or methods. The inferences drawn about a student's assignment may vary widely from assessor to assessor, particularly if they are not using explicit criteria or marking schemes. Estimates of worth in terms of marks or grades may vary, so too may degree classifications. Figure 2.2 lists some of the common weaknesses of assessment systems. By implication, more effective assessment systems are relatively free of these weaknesses.

1 Overload of students and staff.
2 Too many assignments with the same deadline set in the department/school.
3 Insufficient time for students to complete the assignments in the time available.
4 Insufficient time for staff to mark the assignments before the next semester.
5 Inadequate or superficial feedback provided to students.

6 Wide variations in assessment demands of different modules.
7 Wide variations in marking across modules.
8 Wide variations in marking within a module.
9 Wide variations in marking by demonstrators.

10 Fuzzy or non-existent criteria.
11 Undue precision and specificity of marking schemes or criteria.

12 Students do not know what is expected of them.
13 Students do not know what counts as a good or bad assignment/ project.

14 Assessment viewed by some departments/schools as an extra rather than a recognised use of staff time.
15 Project supervision seen as an extra or the real time involved is not recognised.

*Figure 2.2* Some common weaknesses in assessment systems

All forms of assessment provide estimates of the person's *current* status. The results of assessment may be used for judgmental and for developmental purposes. The simple model given in Figure 2.3 captures the main characteristics of a continuum extending from the judgmental to the developmental. The continuum is not a pure diagonal for even the most judgmental of assessments, the award of a degree, has developmental implications. Similarly developmental assessment, such as feedback on a group task, requires judgement.

Developmental assessment is concerned with improving student learning and is founded on trust between individuals and in the system of assessment. Judgmental assessment is concerned with licences to proceed to the next stage. It is allied to accountability and marketing strategies. Consistency, uniformity and fairness are the hallmarks of judgmental procedures. If judgmental and developmental assessment are totally conflated, then trust is likely to diminish, concealment of developmental needs is likely to occur; risk taking and creativity may be reduced and compliance increased. Unfortunately, the emerging system of student assessment in higher education is forcing both students and staff towards a strongly judgmental approach.

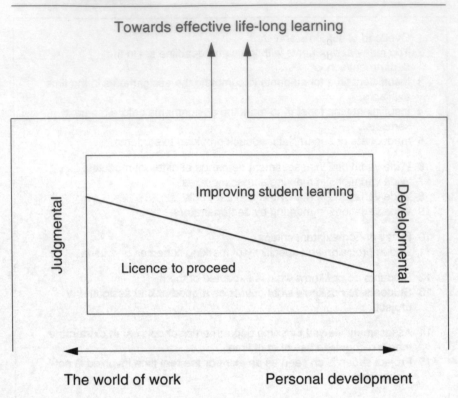

Figure 2.3 Assessment and development

## THE PURPOSES OF ASSESSMENT

Figure 2.4 provides a list of the common purposes of assessment. Clearly all the purposes are related and they can become confused. A common error is to use an assessment task for one set of purposes and then assume that the results from it are appropriate for other purposes. What is appropriate for helping a student to learn may not necessarily yield appropriate information to give to an employer. For example, reflective diaries or detailed records of achievement can be useful during the process of learning but they may be inappropriate for a prospective employer's selection purposes. If students anticipate that such material may be submitted to an employer they may be reluctant to report their true feelings and thoughts.

## KEY TERMS

The first ever assessment of learning was probably undertaken by *Homo Australopithecus*. He said to his son: 'Now go out and kill your first bear.' This task is an example of *criterion-referenced* assessment in which certain criteria have

- To provide feedback to students to improve their learning.
- To motivate students.
- To diagnose a student's strengths and weaknesses.
- To help students to develop their skills of self-assessment.
- To provide a profile of what a student has learnt.

- To pass or fail a student.
- To grade or rank a student.
- To licence to proceed.
- To select for future courses.
- To licence to practice.
- To predict success in future courses.
- To predict success in employment.
- To select for future employment.

- To provide feedback to lecturers.
- To improve teaching.
- To evaluate a course's strengths and weaknesses.
- To make the course appear 'respectable' and creditworthy to other institutions and employers.

*Figure 2.4* Purposes of assessment

The term assessment is derived from *ad sedere* – to sit down beside. The implication of its etymology is that it is primarily concerned with providing guidance and feedback to the learner. Arguably, this is still its most important function.

There is much debate about the precise relationships and meanings of the terms assessment, appraisal, audit and evaluation. For the purpose of this book the term assessment will be used to refer to any procedure used to estimate student learning for whatever purpose.

*Figure 2.5* The meaning of assessment

to be met in order to succeed and, strictly speaking, only the pass/fail point is important.

If the assessment task had been changed to: 'Go out and kill as many bears as you can', and if it had been given in order to grade all the sons in the tribe, then the test would have been a *norm-referenced* task which yields a rank order of candidates based on a distribution of scores.

If this task had been used to measure the extent of learning at the end of a hunting training course then the assessment would have been described as *summative* – or even as *terminal.* However, if it had been given during the training and used to provide feedback to the sons of the tribe on how well their hunting skills were developing, then the task would have been described as *formative* assessment.

Finally, if the test had included observation and measurement of which hunting skills were and were not used, then the assessment would have been *diagnostic.*

The terms 'criterion referenced' and 'norm referenced' refer to the *type* of test or examination, while the terms 'summative', 'formative' and 'diagnostic' refer to the *function* of assessment or examination.

In practice, the relationships between the above terms are not as clear-cut as one might think. Criterion-referenced tests are based on a pass/fail system yet a high level of performance may be used to select a candidate for a course or a job. This could be a misuse of the test since an assumption is being made that a high level of performance on that test is a reliable predictor of future success in the job. This misuse of criterion-referenced tests is exacerbated when the grading system is merit/pass/fail. Norm-referenced tests and examinations do have criteria – if only to establish the norm. They also have a pass/fail cut-off point. Unfortunately, the criteria, particularly for pass/fail, may be unclear even to the lecturers using them and consequently students may not know the standards against which they are being judged and compared. A useful compromise is the use of *criteria-graded assessment* in which the broad criteria for each grade level (such as First, Upper Second and so on in degree classifications) are specified.

Formative and summative assessment may, in practice, be confused. The essence of formative assessment is that it provides feedback to students during the course so that they have opportunities to improve. Clearly formative assessment overlaps with feedback in learning. Strictly speaking, formative assessment does not contribute to the marks for a module, year or degree. In practice, outside of Oxford and Cambridge, few courses contain purely formative assessments. Within other universities, because of the workload of marking and other commitments, the amount of feedback given to students on some courses may be small and they may get little guidance in how to use it to improve their future performance. Coursework assessment is usually both summative and formative. It is intended as feedback and it counts towards the final profile of marks. When this happens, in-course assessment becomes part of a multiple-point summative assessment and it may sometimes cease to provide useful feedback to the student. Sometimes a spurious reason given is that 'marks and comments are confidential to the Board of Examiners'. At other times the burden on staff precludes them from devoting the necessary time to providing useful feedback. Finally, the diagnostic function of an assessment is often lost in the administrative machinery of the system. For example, composites or aggregates of marks may prevent identification of a student's particular strengths and weaknesses.

At this stage we do not want to discuss the technical aspects of reliability and validity. These are covered in Chapter 15 and are touched on in Chapter 5 on assessing essays. In the meantime, it is sufficient to note that the reliability, or consistency, and validity, or accuracy, of assessment procedures are deep practical issues which involve values, the prioritising of purposes, concepts of assessment and an examination of traditional practices.

Finally it is worth noting that assessment, together with face-to-face teaching, course design, course management and course evaluation, is part of the generic task of teaching. The phrase 'teaching, learning and assessment' often makes assessment look like an afterthought or at least a separate entity. In fact, teaching and feedback (formative assessment) merge and assessment is a necessary part of helping students to learn.

## TRENDS IN ASSESSMENT

It is over 20 years since there was a dramatic shift in assessment in higher education (see Cox, 1986). At the time the cry was 'Down with exams. Up with coursework.' A few writers even advocated the abolition of all forms of assessment or degrees (see Klug, 1974). Looking back over the past 20 years one can also detect other shifts in assessment. For convenience, these trends are summarised in Figure 2.6. Each of them is discussed briefly in this section. The trends overlap and interweave but, for convenience, they are discussed separately.

### Written examinations and coursework

At first sight, written examinations and coursework are but the popular names of summative and formative assessment. A moment's reflection should convince you that the terms are not identical. Written examinations *can* be used as

| From | Towards |
|------|---------|
| Written examinations | Coursework |
| Tutor-led assessment | Student-led assessment |
| Implicit criteria | Explicit criteria |
| Competition | Collaboration |
| Product assessment | Process assessment |
| Objectives | Outcomes |
| Content | Competencies |
| Course assessment | Modular assessment |
| Advanced levels | Assessed prior learning |

*Figure 2.6* Trends in assessment

summative or as part of formative assessment. The condition is that the results are provided to the student in a way which will help him or her to improve performance. Coursework may be summative – it often is. The marks and comments on coursework may not be provided at all or provided in a perfunctory form to students, thereby reducing their formative value.

The key characteristics of a written examination are claimed to be that:

- All students are given the same tasks and time allocation.
- The precise nature of the task is not revealed before the examination.
- The work examined is solely that of the candidate.

At least two of these three conditions are rarely met in written examinations. Students are usually given a choice of examination questions. They are sometimes provided, quite rightly, with hints and suggestions on the structure and nature of the examination paper. Even the notion that the work is solely that of the candidate is questionable – but we leave you to discuss that point.

Examinations suffer from the defect of being one-shot measures. A bad day or a couple of bad days can make the difference between a 2.1 and a First or a 2.1 and a 2.2. Attacks on written examinations in the late 1960s led to the introduction of examinable coursework. The advantage of such an approach, from the standpoint of reliability and validity, is that one obtains multiple points of assessment. Evidence against one approach however is not necessarily evidence in favour of another. Whereas previously some students may have suffered from acute stress because of written examinations, the advent of coursework assessment may increase the prevalence of chronic stress. This remark applies particularly to modular-based courses.

The debate concerning written papers and coursework is still alive in many faculties. There appears to be no substantial research that estimates the abilities tested in different forms of examination and coursework. Such research would be most challenging. Our view is that written papers and coursework sample overlapping sets of abilities. Written papers measure recalled knowledge, familiar problem-solving strategies, recalled understanding, and the capacity to think, structure thoughts, and write quickly and independently under pressure. (Some colleagues have pointed out that an examination fulfils its main function of learning and integration as the student walks into the examination room.) Coursework also has the potential to measure the capacity to retrieve and select information from external sources, to deepen understanding and develop problem-solving skills and strategies. On the basis of one's analysis of the different functions of coursework and their order of priority, one has to decide on the appropriate balance of coursework and examinations for a particular programme. There are never ideal solutions: only better ones.

China seems to be the first civilisation to have developed an examination system.

Anybody could enter it, that is, anybody who was male and not the son of torturers, executioners, barbers, brothel keepers, renegade priests and nail cutters. About 1500 years ago the examinations were essentially practical. You had to ride horses, sing songs, fight battles and so on. Gradually, as China developed a bureaucratic structure, the examinations changed from actually riding horses and singing songs and fighting battles to writing about riding horses, singing songs and fighting battles, and then eventually to writing about other people's writing about riding horses, singing songs and battles. To some of you the development will sound rather familiar.

There were about 20 eliminating rounds in the contest over about the same number of years. If at the end of this ordeal you were in the top one per cent of the original entry you could write 'Promoted Man' on your door. This status did not, by any means, guarantee you a job. It did, however, entitle you to apply for the examination for entry into the Chinese Civil Service known quaintly as 'Han Lin', the forest of pencils. If you passed this you went to the Celestial Court and perhaps attained the supreme privilege of becoming one of the chief examiners.

The system had a number of advantages for the Chinese emperors and nobility. It gave the appearance of open free examinations. The very able could get to the top from the bottom of the social ladder. But at the same time the system ensured that these few were so steeped in the Chinese traditions that it was unlikely that they would want to change markedly the social structure. The potential leaders and scholars who might have been radicals or revolutionaries in a different culture instead were absorbed in the social structure.

The examination system, in short, acted as a built-in stabiliser of the Chinese social class system. It helped to maintain the status quo. You might pause for a moment and ask yourself about the similarities between this sketch of education in Imperial China and our system today.

From Brown (1968)

*Figure 2.7* Examinations in Ancient China

## Tutor-led–student-led

Over the past 20 years there has been a shift from assessment tasks being set and assessed by the tutor alone to the introduction of a choice of tasks and in some cases the use of self- and peer-assessment. These forms of assessment may be used to contribute to the course mark and so indirectly to the degree classification. Further information on self- and peer-assessment is provided in Chapters 11 and 12. The advantages of student choice and student-led assessment are that they increase the ownership and commitment of students and they help to develop students' own self-assessment skills and thereby aid their personal and professional development. On the other hand whilst increasing motivation and personal development, they make consistency and fair comparisons across groups more difficult to achieve. Again, one has to take decisions in the light of the primary objectives of assessing the module or course.

## Implicit criteria–explicit criteria

Although many courses in universities provide course objectives, the criteria which are used for assessing the performance of students are often implicit. There are four levels of criteria:

1 The criteria may be implicit to the tutor – 'I know a First when I see one' – and therefore also implicit to the student.
2 The criteria may be known to the tutor but not revealed to the student.
3 The criteria may be revealed to the student but not what counts as evidence of fulfilling those criteria.
4 The criteria and examples of evidence are provided to the student.

In some courses there appears to be a shift towards not only revealing criteria but encouraging students to generate the criteria themselves and to considering what counts as evidence. These criteria and exemplars of evidence are then used by the students and tutors in their marking of essays and other coursework. Whilst such an approach encourages ownership and commitment, it may lead to variations in consistency across groups of students. This conflict, like so many conflicts, can not be resolved, it can only be managed. The key question to ask is 'What is the primary purpose of this assessment task?'

A variation on the use of implicit criteria is found in examples of work-based learning and clinical assessment. A report based on informal observations is written on a student's performance during the work placement. Often the report is confidential, and often the criteria for what counts as good performance are not known to the student. Such an approach can produce undue compliance and uncertainty. It does little to help the student to develop. There is however a shift away from the use of implicit criteria in these settings towards more explicit reporting. Further details are given in Chapter 12.

## Product–process

As well as assessing the product of an assessment task such as a project or group project, some tutors and students are exploring and assessing the processes involved. The assessment of process has usually been formative, although some tutors are now incorporating assessment of processes into summative assessment. The justification for assessing processes is that this helps the students to develop their own assessment of the skills required. The personal or professional skills of time management, working in a team, negotiation and project planning are useful processes to assess and reflect upon in projects. Chapter 8 contains further suggestions.

## Competition–collaboration

Current practice emphasises individual, competitive skills rather than collaborative learning. There is however a move towards using some collaborative learning and assessment in group projects and in group presentations in seminars. The impetus for these approaches springs in part from suggestions by employers and an increase in student numbers. Collaborative learning when used in conjunction with peer- and self-assessment can deepen understanding, develop teamwork skills and draw attention to the processes required for effective group work. Further discussion and suggestions on group work and self- and peer-assessment are given in Chapters 11 and 12 respectively.

## Objectives–outcomes

There are two trends apparently at work here. First, many, but not all, course teams and departments are developing well-defined learning objectives which are used as a guide for assessment tasks. Second, course designers are increasingly using the more fashionable term 'learning outcomes' rather than 'objectives'. This may, in part, be because behavioural objectives have received a bad press. Outcomes are, in fact, learning objectives but they are not necessarily tied to a specific performance variable and they may include exploring what other things have been learnt or achieved, the unintended as well as the intended. The use of outcomes enables one to explore, in a more open fashion, student learning. It also provides opportunities for identifying prior learning and associated learning. Exploratory studies by academics from a wide range of disciplines confirm the usefulness of the approach for clarifying issues in course design and assessment (see Otter, 1992).

## Content–competencies

Associated with the use of outcomes is a shift towards the specification of competencies. In essence, competencies are clusters of skills which students are expected to be able to use in a variety of settings. The approach is derived from the behavioural objectives movement and the workplace. The use of competencies is advocated strongly by the National Council of Vocational Qualifications (Jessup, 1991). Competencies, as defined by Jessup, are the basis of NVQs and GNVQs. Competencies are used widely in BTEC courses and competency-based teacher education. Their effectiveness and efficiency is as yet unproven. Chapter 16 of this book provides a discussion of the competency approach. Leigh (1991) provides a brief, thought-provoking account of the differences between assessing vocational and academic competence and Barnett (1994) provides a strong indictment of their use in higher education. A variation on competencies is capabilities. These too are clusters of what students are expected to learn (Stephenson and Weil, 1992). The distinction between competencies and capabilities is blurred. Indeed the terms might in practice prove interchangeable. But the term 'capabilities' may have a stronger appeal to academics who have a broader view of the purposes of higher education and 'competencies' may be favoured by those who see higher education as primarily concerned with narrow vocational preparation. The emphasis upon competencies and capabilities does provide a framework for identifying outcomes and the transferable skills and subject expertise that students require. However, the distinctions between subject expertise and transferable skills and between knowledge and skills are not as clear-cut as they appear. Subject expertise is probably the core of transferable skills and subject knowledge is rather more than isolated bits of information. Selecting, linking, structuring and coordinating information is both part of subject knowledge and the transferable skill of information handling. Chapter 3 provides a brief discussion of these themes.

### Course assessment–modular assessment

The assessment of modules rather than the assessment of courses is now the norm in most universities although it remains a mystery why so many universities embraced modular structures without thinking through the implications for assessment loads. It is difficult at this stage to discern the precise pattern that is emerging (Jackson, 1995). Modules are usually half-year courses that are assessed independently of other modules. The number of modules per year varies in British universities from six to 16. There are two dangers of modularisation. First, it may lead to excessive use of assessment and a reduction in learning opportunities. Indeed as the number of modules increases so too does the load of assessment and marking. As one student put it 'I don't seem to have had time to learn this before being assessed on it.' The second difficulty with modular degrees is that they can lead to a lack of coherence. Neither of these difficulties is insurmountable but it pays to be aware of them. There is very little evidence that modules are a more effective way of organising and developing deep learning. Indeed American experience suggests the contrary (AAC, 1985). Jenkins and Walker (1994) discuss some of the issues and provide some examples of ways of assessing capabilities in modular courses.

### A levels–APL

The customary route into higher education is through A levels. About 30 per cent of 18- and 19-year-olds enter university through this route. Correlations between A levels and degree class were usually only between 0.2 and 0.4 (Entwistle et al., 1991a). Put another way, between 4 and 16 per cent of the variance in degree results can be attributed to performance in A levels. These figures may seem low but they are higher than the correlations between intelligence or academic aptitude tests and degree results (Entwistle *et al.*, 1991a). However, the dramatic increase in A level candidates, the changes in A level syllabuses and forms of assessment and the drift towards upper seconds becoming the modal class of degree will probably result in lower correlations. This theme is discussed in more detail in Chapter 16.

The term APL (accreditation of prior learning) has two meanings. It is sometimes used to cover assessment of prior certificated learning and prior experiential learning. At other times it is used to cover only the accreditation of certificated learning and APEL is used as an acronym for the accreditation of prior experiential learning. Perhaps the term APAL (accreditation of prior assessed learning) should be introduced to reduce confusion. Both APL and APEL are now being used to enable mature students to enter higher education. Those without qualifications are encouraged to reflect upon their experience, to assess it with the aid of a tutor and thereby gain entry directly (or indirectly through Access courses) into higher education. APEL may be based upon the notion of competencies and skills or upon a more reflective approach. It is as yet relatively untested in terms of reliability and validity but it may be a useful route for those who have not pursued the conventional pathway of O levels (or GCSEs) and A levels. Some recent research by Richardson (1995) indicates that the methods of study, levels of perseverance and degrees obtained by mature students, regardless of whether or not they have been admitted to higher education on the basis of conventional qualifications, are at least as good as those of younger students. However, there may be differences in results across subjects. APL is discussed further in Chapter 12.

## ACTIVITIES

2.1 Re-read Figure 2.2 and tick those items that apply to your department/ school's assessment system and put a cross by those that do not. Compare your checklist with that of a few colleagues. What could be done to minimise the weaknesses of your department/school's assessment system?

2.2 Before reading the section 'What is assessment?', make a few notes on what you regard as the key features of assessment. Then read the section and add to your notes any points that you think are important and any thoughts or comments that were prompted by your reading. If you are working with a group of colleagues, you might like to compare your notes. The notes and comments at the end of the book provide further information on this activity.

2.3 Which of the purposes of assessment given in Figure 2.4 are fulfilled by your assessment procedures? Indicate which purposes are over-emphasised, which neglected but important, and which about right for the students and the course. What are your top three priorities? Are they reflected in the design and assessment of the courses or modules that you teach?

2.4 Draw up a table of pros and cons for written examinations and coursework in relation to the purposes of assessment, the objectives of the course or module and staff and student workloads. Use the table for reconsidering your assessment system.

2.5 Re-read the section on trends in assessment and note your personal views on these trends. Meet with a few colleagues and compare views. You may well find there is a wide spectrum of views within the group so bear in mind the points on giving and receiving feedback which were mentioned in Chapter 1.

# Chapter 3

# Student learning

Before assessing any phenomenon it is necessary to know what it is and what it is for. Hence, in this chapter we describe the nature of student learning and some approaches to the study of learning that are relevant to its assessment. We then explore the nature of skills and propose a simple robust model that may be used to clarify different aspects of learning. The chapter ends with a discussion of various taxonomies that are available for designing courses and assessment tasks. Readers who are interested in an extended discussion of learning are referred to Denicolo *et al* (1992) and Entwistle (1992). Ramsden (1992) provides a discussion of assessment for the purposes of learning and Otter (1992) provides a stimulating discussion of approaches by different subject areas.

## WHAT IS LEARNING?

In essence, learning may be defined as changes in knowledge, understanding, skills and attitudes brought about by experience and reflection upon that experience. The experience may be structured, as in courses and learning packages, or it may be unstructured as in browsing or casual learning from peers. Feedback from others augments the experience and reflection, a form of internal feedback, accelerates learning (Schmidt *et al.*, 1990). As well as being clear what one wants students to learn, one has to provide opportunities for learning, meaningful feedback, opportunities for reflection and further feedback. Figure 3.1 offers various conceptions of learning derived from student interviews (Saljo, 1979).

## HOW DO STUDENTS LEARN?

This deceptively simple question has been the subject of much research. The simple answer is that students learn through reading, thinking, writing, listening to others and note-taking, observing, talking to and with others and doing things. The key processes are various forms of thinking, such as searching for understanding, problem solving, creativity and evaluative thinking, and various

1   Learning as an increase in knowledge. The student will often see learning as something done to them by teachers rather than as something they do for themselves.
*To gain some knowledge is learning . . . We obviously want to learn more. I want to know as much as possible.*

2   Learning is memorising. The student has an active role in memorising, but the information being memorised is not transformed in any way.
*Learning is about getting it into your head. You've just to keep writing it out and eventually it will go in.*

3   Learning is acquiring facts or procedures which are to be used. What you learn is seen to include skills, algorithms, formulae which you will need in order to do things at a later date, but there is still no transformation of what is learnt by the learner.
*Well, it's about learning the thing so you can do it again when you are asked to, like in an exam.*

4   Learning is making sense. The student makes active attempts to abstract meaning in the process of learning. This may only involve academic tasks.
*Learning is about trying to understand things so you can see what is going on. You've got to be able to explain things, not just remember them.*

5   Learning is understanding reality. Learning enables you to perceive the world differently. This has also been termed 'personally meaningful learning'.
*When you have really learnt something you kind of see things you couldn't see before. Everything changes.*

*Figure 3.1* Some students' conceptions of learning

forms of remembering such as rote learning, identifying patterns and learning through understanding. These processes are augmented by using feedback to improve methods of study and the delivery of assessment tasks. Students are more likely to learn effectively if they are motivated to learn. Hence the importance of considering the context in which learning takes place and the deep question: why do students learn?

## METHODS OF STUDYING STUDENT LEARNING

The question of how students learn has been studied by:

• Asking students what they were thinking and feeling when doing a study task such as reading a passage (see Marton *et al.*, 1984).

- Interviewing students about their methods of revision and essay writing (Entwistle and Marton, 1994; Entwistle, 1995).
- Presenting a problem to students and asking questions about their underlying concepts and assumptions (see Prosser and Millar, 1989; Laurillard, 1993; and Ramsden, 1992).
- Identifying stages of development in learning (Perry, 1970).
- Identifying learning styles and orientations through the use of well designed and well tested inventories (see Biggs, 1987; Entwistle, 1987; Kolb, 1984; Myers, 1991, Wankat and Oreovicz, 1993 and Bayne, 1995 for reviews of the Myers–Biggs approach).

These methods spring from different theoretical perspectives although most may be subsumed under the broad headings of cognitive theories and personal growth theories, whereas the roots of competencies and NVQs are in a naive form of behaviourism. Further discussion of theoretical perspectives on learning may be found in Atkins *et al.* (1993) and Brown (1995).

## STUDIES OF STUDENT LEARNING

### Learning in an academic context

Over the past 20 years there has been a steady stream of research on student learning. Most notable has been the work of Entwistle and his associates (Entwistle, 1987, 1992), from which two dominant orientations may be identified:

- knowledge-seeking
- understanding-seeking.

Figure 3.2 sets out the characteristics of the two orientations.

Those who have a knowledge-seeking orientation search for facts and information. Their learning may be mechanical and it may be surface learning rather than deep learning. Their approach to deep learning is through comprehensive knowledge. They are not interested in speculating, playing with ideas or searching for deeper meanings. In contrast, those with an understanding orientation are less interested in facts and more interested in searching for personal meaning in what they are doing. They relate what they learn to their earlier experience, they explore potential connections, linkages and discrepancies. Understanders tend to be holists who prefer to get a global picture before exploring any detail, whereas knowledge-seekers tend to be serialists who prefer to build up their picture of a topic gradually. Understanders tend to be intrinsically motivated rather than responders to a system. Hence they are likely to be deep problem solvers and to be creative and independent.

Both reproducers and understanders may have varying degrees of achievement motivation. When achievement motivation is high there is willingness to

*Knowledge Seeker*

Stores facts, concepts, and so on.
Collects skill, procedures.
Breaks down problems and tasks into separate sub-units.
Makes links within units of knowledge.
Uses memorisation skills.
Works methodically through logical order of task problem.
Analyses.
Uses systematic trial and error.

*Understanding Seeker*

Tries to relate information or task to own experience.
Makes links to other bodies of knowledge.
Restructures for personal meaning.
Synthesises.
Likes to work from 'whole' picture.
Searches for underlying structure, purpose and meaning.
Intuitive use of evidence.
Uses analogies, metaphors.

*Figure 3.2* Orientations to learning

switch to the style of learning demanded by the system of teaching and assessment. There are only a few students who are equally comfortable with both styles of learning. Most students have a predominant style but that style may be influenced by the conditions of learning and assessment. Norms and profiles of styles of student learning may be found in Entwistle (1987). These norms were used in the CNAA funded project on improving student learning together with a shortened version of Entwistle's scales. The project was designed to encourage deeper learning through the use of innovations in teaching and learning as well as in assessment (Gibbs, 1990).

As indicated in Chapter 2, reproductive learning styles are promoted by highly structured forms of teaching and assessment such as lectures and written examinations. Understanders work better in environments that provide some choice of what is studied, flexible approaches to teaching and learning, manageable formal workloads and a variety of forms of assessment. The type of assessment used influences styles of learning. The use of multiple choice questions and other forms of test promotes reproductive styles of learning whereas projects and open-ended assessments promote independence and deeper strategies of understanding.

More recently, Entwistle has turned his attention to the study of forms of understanding that various students report whilst writing essays and revising

(Entwistle and Entwistle 1991; Entwistle and Marton, 1994; Entwistle, 1996). Five forms of understanding during revision were identified and these are shown in Figure 3.3. Entwistle and Marton suggest that some examination questions 'did not seem to require personal understanding, simply the reproduction of the lecturer's understanding' (p. 163). They point out that some students use visualisation and structuring but that understanding goes beyond these processes to perceiving the whole of the domain of knowledge.

The work of Biggs is also concerned with deep processing and levels of understanding. In a recent article (Biggs, 1996) he describes how his taxonomy, SOLO (Structure of the Observed Learning Outcome), may be used for analysing learning tasks and hierarchies of objectives and for assessing students' work. The five levels of Biggs's schema are:

1 *Pre-structural* The task is not attacked appropriately. The student hasn't understood the point.
2 *Unstructural* One or a few aspects of the task picked up or used but understanding is nominal.
3 *Multistructural* Several aspects of the task are learnt but are treated separately.
4 *Relational* The components are integrated into a coherent whole with each part contributing to the overall meaning.
5 *Extended abstract* The integrated whole at the relational level is re-conceptualised at a higher level of abstraction. This enables generalisation to a new topic or area, or it is turned reflexively on oneself (understanding as transfer and as involving meta-cognition).

Pre-structural could be regarded as barely satisfactory and extended abstract as outstanding performance.

How students learn is not determined solely by their method of study or the method of assessment. The style of learning is more likely to be associated

---

A  Absorbing facts and details and procedures related to exams without consideration of structure.
B  Accepting and using only the knowledge and logical structures provided in the lecture notes.
C  Relying mainly on notes to develop summary structures solely to control examination answers.
D  Developing structures from strategic reading to represent personal understanding but also to control exam answers.
E  Developing structures from wide reading which relate personal understanding to the nature of the discipline.

---

From Entwistle and Marton (1994), p. 163.

*Figure 3.3* Forms of understanding developed during revision

with a set of characteristics of a learning environment than with just one characteristic. Hence, to promote a particular style of learning it is necessary to consider the organisational climate of the department or school as well as its use of various approaches to teaching and assessment. Ramsden and Entwistle (1981), Ramsden (1988) and more recently Entwistle and Tait (1990) have related these orientations to students' perceptions of their departments. The findings indicate that departments where good teaching was reported were strongly oriented towards personal meaning. Good teaching included such variables as effective lecturing, help with specific difficulties and perceived freedom to learn. Poor teaching included such variables as ineffective lecturing, heavy workload, inappropriate assessment and lack of freedom to learn. In these departments the orientation towards reproductive learning was strong.

There is a tendency to infer from the studies of student learning that the knowledge seekers produce shallow or superficial learning while the understanding seekers engage in deep processing. The concomitant implication is that the first orientation is inferior to the second. For some subjects and some tasks this may be true but not necessarily for all. The knowledge-seeking domain should not be dismissed out of hand. Knowing what and knowing how are often as important as knowing why. For example, a neurologist needs to know the specific neurological function of the optic nerve before he or she can make a diagnosis of a particular patient. A historian needs to know the terms of the Treaty of Versailles before attempting an analysis of Germany's problems in the 1920s. It seems more helpful therefore to encourage students to develop both a knowledge orientation and an understanding orientation.

Entwistle (1991b) in a most thorough review of research on teaching and learning concludes that:

> Where they have been carefully planned and properly implemented, attempts at encouraging active learning have been uniformly rated favourably by teachers and students. There is also evidence that freedom in learning or student autonomy together with good teaching which encourages students to form their own conceptions, will lead to deep approaches to learning which enhance personal conceptual understanding. Such understanding is a necessary first step in being able to apply knowledge in novel contexts and solve related problems. Adding to conceptual understanding, skills which have been developed through experiential learning (from simulations, projects and work placements) will further strengthen the ability to make these applications. A further step is to use collaborative learning, with its opportunities for developing communication skills and the explicit discussion of the group dynamics involved. These methods seem to foster the social and personal skills so necessary both in working and in everyday life.

Entwistle's summary of research provides a programme of action for those committed to developing learning with their students.

The implications of the research on student learning are profound. Commitment to student learning affects course design, assessment, teaching, staff development and the *modus operandi* of departments and universities, yet paradoxically it is a renewal of long-established goals of universities. Indeed it could be said that unless a university is committed to active deep autonomous learning by its students then it is not providing a higher education.

There are three other points which one needs to consider in relation to student learning. First, and obviously, a knowledge base is necessary for understanding. However, there is evidence that the way that knowledge is acquired can inhibit or enhance understanding. Problem-centred approaches appear to produce more flexible learning networks that are more readily applied to new problems (Norman, 1980). Second, knowledge and understanding are not diametrically opposed. At one extreme of the reproductive style is the learning of isolated facts but at the other is the handling and management of knowledge. This end of reproductive learning merges imperceptibly into understanding. Third, the student's predispositions and early history of the subject draw out different styles of learning. A deep learner in pure mathematics might become a blubbering nervous surface learner in modern poetry – and vice versa. Figure 3.4 sets out the main characteristics of deep and surface learning and Figure 3.5 shows when effective learning is most likely to occur.

## Motivation, personality and learning

One strand of the research on student learning has been directed to the effects of personality and motivation on learning (see Wittrock, 1986 and Berliner, 1996 for reviews). This research shows that the way students perceive themselves and the way they account for their academic successes and failures have a strong bearing on their motivation and their performance.

Fear of failure and anxiety were shown by Entwistle to be associated with surface approaches. Entwistle (1996) and Abouserie (1995) have recently confirmed this finding and shown that low self-esteem also increases the probability of surface approaches. The overall findings suggest that students are likely to initiate learning, sustain it, direct it and actively involve themselves in it when they believe that success or failure is caused by their own effort or lack of it rather than by factors outside their control. Similarly, praise, reward or other positive reinforcements are likely to enhance motivation only if students perceive them to be related to factors over which they have control. Thus building up students' sense of control over their own work, giving them opportunities to exercise responsibility for their own learning, and helping them to develop self-management skills can all help to make them more successful and effective learners.

*Surface approaches* are encouraged by:

- assessment methods emphasising recall or the application of trivial procedural knowledge
- assessment methods that create anxiety
- cynical or conflicting messages about rewards
- an excessive amount of material in the curriculum
- poor or absent feedback on progress
- lack of independence in studying
- lack of interest in and background knowledge of the subject matter
- previous experiences of educational settings that encourage these approaches.

*Deep approaches* are encouraged by:

- teaching and assessment methods that foster active and long-term engagement with learning tasks
- stimulating and considerate teaching, especially teaching which demonstrates the lecturer's personal commitment to the subject matter and stresses its meaning and relevance to students
- clearly stated academic expectations
- opportunities to exercise responsible choice in the method and content of study
- interest in and background knowledge of the subject matter
- previous experiences of educational settings that encourage these approaches.

From Ramsden (1992), p. 81

*Figure 3.4* Characteristics of the context of learning associated with deep and surface approaches

## The development of approaches to learning

Perry, on the basis of his experience of working with students at Harvard, suggested that typically students pass through various stages of learning during a degree programme. A summary of these is given in Figure 3.6.

Perry's view suggests that learning is much more than the accretion of facts, fine-tuning and cognitive restructuring that is advocated by some cognitive psychologists (e.g. Norman, 1980). It also involves the restructuring of one's commitments and priorities, changing one's feelings and attitudes towards others and towards oneself. This view is not limited to learning by young under-graduates. When faced with new contexts or challenges older adults can retreat into stereotyped primitive dualism and associated modes of behaviour. Hence the importance of laying the foundations of effective life-long learning in the undergraduate years. However, the task is not easy. It is likely that students who

- Structure and learning tasks are used that build upon earlier learning.
- The students develop their repertoire of skills from direct teaching, explicit modelling, practice, feedback, reflection on their own approaches.
- The students can take responsibility for their own learning, they have some freedom of choice, they are encouraged and trained in self-assessment and they have opportunities to explore alternative approaches.
- The workload is moderate.
- A variety of assessment methods is used.
- The context of learning is conducive to active engagement in learning.
- The students perceive that effort leads to success and its recognition.

*Figure 3.5* When is effective learning most likely to occur?

**Levels of intellectual and ethical development**
1 Learner seeks and expects right answers for everything.
2 Learner perceives diversity as distraction.
3 Learner accepts diversity as temporary.
4 Diversity accepted but therefore 'everyone has a right to know'.
5 Learner perceives all knowledge as contextual and relative.
6 Learner perceives necessity of making a personal judgement as opposed to simple belief.
7 Learner makes such a judgement and personal commitment.
8 Learner explores implications of commitment.
9 Learner experiences issues of personal identity in undertaking commitment.

Based on Perry (1970)

*Figure 3.6* Perry's stages of development

are fundamentalist in outlook or wedded strongly to extreme ideologies may have difficulty in going beyond Stage 1 in Perry's scheme.

## Learning in professional contexts

The study of how people learn in professional contexts has been influenced by the notion of the reflective practitioner developed by Schon (1983, 1988). Schon argues that professionals must learn how to frame and reframe the complex and ambiguous problems they are facing and then interpret and modify their practice as a result. He distinguishes reflection *in* action, which is akin to immediate decision-taking, and reflection *on* action that provides a longer and perhaps deeper view.

Despite the strong interest in reflective learning there seemed to be no clear-cut definition of its nature. After reviewing the literature, Hatton and Smith (1995) suggested that reflection might be defined as 'deliberate thinking about action with a view to its improvement' (p. 52). They distinguish four kinds of reflection that are manifest in the essays of students writing about their practical experiences. These are:

*Descriptive writing* in which no reflection is evident.
*Descriptive reflection* in which some reasons, based on personal judgements, are provided.
*Dialogic reflection* in which a student explores possible reasons and approaches which may be rooted in their reading of the relevant literature.
*Critical reflection* that involves exploring reasons and approaches and the underlying assumptions and concepts. The exploration is based upon an evaluation of context which takes account of social, personal and historical influences.

Hatton and Smith suggest that discussion with a more experienced person can facilitate dialogue and critical reflection. They warn of the dangers of asking students to reflect too early and too broadly and emphasise the importance of providing students with practice in the skills of reflection.

The experiential theory perhaps most relevant to student learning was developed by Kolb (1976, 1984) from the work of Dewey (1933), Lewin (1951) and Piaget and Inhelder (1969). The approach was initially intended for use with professional groups but it has been used to identify the styles of learning of students. Figure 3.7 outlines the phases of Kolb's learning cycle.

The four phases of the cycle and the corresponding learning styles are Activists, Reflectors, Theorists and Pragmatists.

*Activists* seem to learn best from short 'here and now' activities and least from those that require a passive role.
*Reflectors* do not like to be rushed. They prefer to learn through assimilating information, reflecting upon it and their experience and reaching decisions in their own time.
*Theorists* prefer to integrate observations and experience into a theoretical framework. They dislike situations and tasks which they do not have the opportunity to explore in depth.
*Pragmatists* seem to learn best from activities when they can see the practical value of the subject matter and when they can test ideas and techniques in practice. They dislike learning that seems unrelated to an immediately recognisable benefit or need.

People vary in their predispositions to the different phases of the learning cycle. Very few people are totally locked into one style and very few are good at all four styles or phases of the learning cycle. The questionnaire derived from

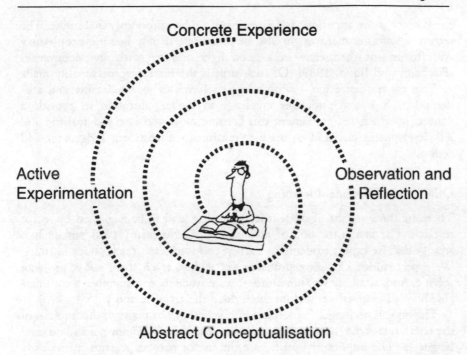

Figure 3.7 The process of learning

Kolb's work was adapted by Honey and Mumford (1983) for use in Britain. Humberside University uses a computerised version of the learning styles questionnaire with all first-year undergraduates. Each student is given his or her own profile and is provided with ideas for developing different types of learning (Hunter and Cook, 1996). Shaw (1992) used Kolb's inventory at Leeds Metropolitan University to explore the changes in learning that are occurring in undergraduate courses based on the principles of Enterprise Learning.

Kolb's avowed concern is the process of learning, not the outcome. But processes and outcomes are not that easily separated in Kolb's theory. An outcome may be an endpoint which becomes a new starting-point. Thus learning is helical rather than cyclical. As a method of learning and teaching, Kolb's theory has much to offer. His questionnaire is also useful for identifying different learning styles. However, there is a danger in assuming that the categories of learning which students use are ones that they may use for the rest of their lives. The questionnaires can be used to help students to reflect upon how they might develop and extend the range of their learning styles. Kolb's theory provides a useful input into the assessment of prior learning, self- and peer-assessment (Falchikov, 1991) and the use of learning profiles (see Brown and Dove, 1991). All of these are valuable components of learning but one also needs a light structural framework of standards in order to help students to match their perceptions against those of others. In particular the notion of self-assessment needs much more attention. Self-assessment can be notoriously inaccurate. The record of self-assessment might also be inaccurate if only because people may wish to present themselves in a good light and to mask any deficiencies (Falchikov and Boud, 1989). Of such stuff is the marketing personality made – 'I am as you desire me' – with all its problems of manipulability and self-deception. It is a considerable challenge in higher education to provide a context in which self-assessment can become more accurate and realistic and self-development can lead to mature, informed, independent judgement and action.

## Other aspects of student learning

There are three aspects of student learning that tend to be neglected by recent research. The first is the skill of memorising. As Norman (1980) put it: 'It is strange that we expect students to learn yet seldom teach them about learning. We expect students to solve problems yet seldom teach them about problem solving. And, similarly we sometimes require students to remember a considerable body of material yet seldom teach them the art of memory.'

The topic is no longer fashionable in psychology but many of the findings of the research are relevant to student learning, particularly in modern and classical languages. The important features are the use of massed practice in the early stages of learning followed by distributed practice, dividing learning tasks into meaningful wholes for the learner, teaching various ways of encoding and organising material, exploring different methods of retrieving information from memory and minimising the effects of interference by ensuring that consecutive tasks are not too similar (see Norman, 1977, 1982 and Thyne, 1966 for further details). Clearly these principles have implications for the design of language classes and language learning tasks.

The second aspect is the notion of holism and serialism developed by Pask (1976). Pask's original work is obscure but his essential point is that some students have a preference for holistic learning and some for serial learning. Holists prefer to obtain the whole picture of a topic and then fill in the detail. Serialists prefer to build up the picture of a topic by assembling the relevant bits – rather like a mosaic. The notion is built into Entwistle's study inventory but it is sufficiently important for highlighting in the context of student learning. It would appear that holistic learning is likely to be favoured as a first strategy in some subjects, such as art, literature and design, and serial learning in other subjects, such as mathematics and physical sciences. However, both are necessary for deep learning. Extreme holists tend to overgeneralise, to leap to unwarranted conclusions and to offer visions that may not be attainable. Extreme serialists can become obsessed with fine detail or with finely detailed plans that never come to fruition. They are often unwilling to take decisions, draw conclusions from evidence or make generalisations. These pathologies of learning are not confined to students.

Finally, there is the obvious distinction that some students prefer to learn and think through visualisation whereas other students prefer to learn and think verbally. Again there are subject differences as well as individual preferences. The usual assumption is that most students are visualisers, but this assumption has not been well tested experimentally. However, if in doubt, it is wise to use diagrams augmented by some words or words augmented by some diagrams.

## LEARNING AND SKILLS

A common definition of skills is 'an organised and co-ordinated pattern of mental and/or physical activity' (ED, 1982). Such a definition sits uncomfortably with many activities in higher education. Indeed many lecturers object to the term 'skills' because of its apparent neglect of discipline content and its associations with industrial work. The definition does less than justice to many personal and intellectual skills and it makes no mention of fitness for purpose. It was perhaps dissatisfaction with the Employment Department's definition of skills that led Tomlinson and Kilner (1991) to define skills as 'purposes realised in context'. Unfortunately their definition requires considerable unpacking. Our own description is based upon approaches common in psychology (see Hargie, 1996).

Skills are constructs used to describe goal-directed sequences of actions that may be learnt and routinised. Once learnt, they have built in feedback which enables us to adjust our actions to the tasks in hand. Riding a bicycle, diagnosing a medical condition or solving problems by a routine method are common examples of skills in action. Skills are patterned sequences of actions in response to cues rather than isolated instances of behaviour. It is only if the sequence is disrupted that one has to stop and think. Skills have perceptual, cognitive, and motor components in varying proportions. Skills, even if defined only as goal-directed sensori-motor activities, are often the prerequisites of learning new methods and theories. For example, keyboard skills are the basis of computing; manipulative skills are the basis of setting up scientific apparatus, performing surgical operations and using survey instruments. When one enlarges the scope of skill to include cognitive skills, such as reading, writing, problem solving, and social skills, such as discussion and negotiation, then skills become not just the basis but the centrepiece of much of the work in higher education. However, it would be wrong to assume that skills are merely one level of activity, for the term may be used to describe a specific activity such as the use of probes and prompts in questioning, questioning as a skill itself, and questioning as a sub-skill of the skill of communicating. Much of the confusion may be reduced by agreeing upon a set of levels for describing skills.

One should be clear that all skills involve *perceptual* and *cognitive* components as well as motor components. The proportions of these components vary across skills. The more complex the skill the greater is its cognitive component. The perceptual and motor components are more important in setting up an intravenous drip or making a denture. Perceptual and cognitive components are more important than motor components when attempting to solve a problem.

All the major skills used in higher education are related to each other in complex ways. A useful way of simplifying the relationships yet preserving the essential features is to present them in the form of a tetrahedron (see Figure 3.8).

The use of skills in different contexts is based upon the cornerstones of knowledge, understanding and attitudes. The essential *cognitive* skills are information handling, evaluating evidence, critical thinking, problem solving,

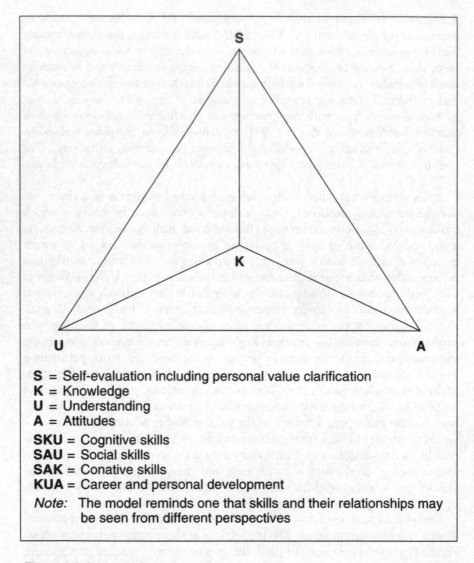

S = Self-evaluation including personal value clarification
K = Knowledge
U = Understanding
A = Attitudes

SKU = Cognitive skills
SAU = Social skills
SAK = Conative skills
KUA = Career and personal development

Note:   The model reminds one that skills and their relationships may be seen from different perspectives

Figure 3.8 A model of learning skills

arguing rationally, creativity and the meta-cognitive skill of learning to learn. The essential *social* skills are working with others in various roles, including as leader, and communicating with others. The essential *cognitive* skills are initiative, independence, risk taking, achieving and willingness to change. All of these contribute to a person's capacity to self-evaluate and to clarify values. Self-evaluation, value clarification and the essential skills provide the structure for understanding working life, career choices and personal development during one's career.

The skills of learning are taught through the medium of academic subjects. Each subject has different emphases and interpretations of these skills. Problem solving in mathematics is not identical with problem solving in social science. Evaluating evidence in histopathology is not identical with evaluating evidence in history. However, there is sufficient commonality to identify a *broad* framework of skills for higher education. Indeed there is a tradition that places some if not all of these high-level skills at the heart of higher education:

> that education which gives a man a clear conscious view of his own opinions and judgements, a truth in developing them, an eloquence in expressing them, and a force in urging them. It teaches him to see things as they are, to go right to the point, to disentangle a skein of thought, to detect what is sophistical, and to disregard what is irrelevant. It prepares him to fill any post with credit, and to master any subject with facility. It shows him how to accommodate himself to others, how to throw himself into their state of mind, how to bring before them his own, how to influence them, how to come to an understanding with them, and how to bear with them.
>
> (J.H. Newman, 1853)

## BUT ARE SKILLS TRANSFERABLE?

Few academics would dispute the importance of the skills adumbrated above. What they might object to is the notion that these skills can be learnt *in vacuo*. Skills are located in content and the content shapes the skills. Despite the claims of the advocates of NVQs and GNVQs (Jessup, 1991), skills are not *identical* across subjects nor do they readily transfer across contexts. The overwhelming weight of evidence indicates that:

* Transfer is most likely to occur when a person understands the underlying principles.
* Knowledge and understanding of different contexts are necessary for transfer.
* Training in transfer, providing a variety of assessment tasks, maximises its probability.

(Annett and Sparrow, 1989; Bruner, 1992; Donald, 1986)

Similar results have been obtained in the research on clinical competence. Fulfilling the requirements of competence on one problem is not a good predictor of performance on another problem or even a different representation of the same problem. (See Chapter 9 in this volume. See also Swanson, 1987; Colliver *et al.*, 1989; Newble, 1992). For example, competence in taking a history of a patient with acute abdominal pain does not correlate with competence in taking a history of a patient with chest pain. Many lecturers will have observed similar characteristics in their students' work. Some students do not recognise a formula if a different notation is used. They may not be able to solve a problem becuse it is in a new context. They commit the same errors of reasoning and presentation from one essay to the next. These characteristics demonstrate the difficulty of transfer of skills and they have important implications for the design of learning opportunities, feedback and assessment.

## TAXONOMIES AND ASSESSING STUDENT LEARNING

Taxonomies of learning provide broad classifications, sometimes hierarchies, of skills or capabilities which are useful for matching assessment tasks against what one wants students to learn in a module or programme. The most common taxonomy was developed by Bloom (1965). A brief description of the cognitive levels is given in Figure 3.9. It provides a quick check on what levels of cognitive skills might be demanded by an assessment task. It should be noted that each succeeding level assumes competence at an earlier level.

A classification by the University of Sydney (Candy *et al.*, 1994) for the skills required of graduates is given in Figure 3.10. This list provides a wide range of capabilities that may be used for matching against a wide variety of methods of assessment tasks. Shaw (1996) has developed a similar range of capabilities that are used by course designers and reviewers at Leeds Metropolitan University. He has also developed a method for examining different levels of skills that might be expected at different years of an undergraduate course (Shaw, 1995; Stoney and Shaw, 1996). Appendix 1 of Atkins *et al.* (1993) also provides a useful classification of possible goals of universities and university courses. The taxonomy developed by Carter (1985) provides a useful, extended framework classifying and developing outcomes of learning in engineering which may be adapted for use in science and medicine. Other useful classifications are Eraut's

| 6 **Evaluation** | Ability to make a judgement of the worth of something. |
| 5 **Synthesis** | Ability to combine separate elements into a whole. |
| 4 **Analysis** | Ability to break a problem into its constituent parts and establish the relationships between each one. |
| 3 **Application** | Ability to apply rephrased knowledge in novel situations. |
| 2 **Manipulation** | Ability to rephrase knowledge. |
| 1 **Knowledge** | That which can be recalled. |

*Figure 3.9* Hierarchy of the cognitive domain

six types of knowledge (Eraut, 1985) which were originally developed from a study of management but are applicable in other settings and Klemp's discussion of three factors of success (Klemp, 1977). Otter's text (1992) describes the approaches used by groups of lecturers in design, environmental science, social science, engineering and English to the development of outcomes that may be used in assessment.

---

### 1 Knowledge skills
*Graduates should*
- (a) have a body of knowledge in the field(s) studied;
- (b) be able to apply theory to practice in familiar and unfamiliar situations;
- (c) be able to identify, access, organise and communicate knowledge in both written and oral English; and
- (d) have an appreciation of the requirements and characteristics of scholarship and research.

### 2 Thinking skills
*Graduates should*
- (a) be able to exercise critical judgement;
- (b) be capable of rigorous and independent thinking;
- (c) be able to account for their decisions;
- (d) be realistic self-evaluators;
- (e) adopt a problem solving approach; and
- (f) be creative and imaginative thinkers.

### 3 Personal skills
*Graduates should have*
- (a) the capacity and desire to continue to learn;
- (b) the ability to plan and achieve goals in both the personal and the professional sphere; and
- (c) the ability to work with others.

### 4 Personal attributes
*Graduates should*
- (a) strive for tolerance and integrity; and
- (b) acknowledge their personal responsibility for (i) their own value judgements; and (ii) ethical behaviour towards others.

### 5 Practical skills (where appropriate)
*Graduates should be able to*
- (a) collect, correlate, display, analyse and report observations;
- (b) apply experimentally obtained results to new situations; and
- (c) test hypotheses experimentally.

---

Based on Candy *et al.* (1994)

*Figure 3.10* Skills expected of graduates

Beneath every taxonomy lurks an epistemology and not everyone will find the taxonomies offered here suitable for their courses. However, a classification of the kinds of skills and capabilities that one wants students to develop is a necessary first step in developing an effective assessment system, so one needs to adapt or develop one's own classification system. Even so, taxonomies provide only a framework, they do not provide fine detail of content. Indeed, if they did, they would clog the decision-making and design process. Just as skills may be expressed at different levels, so too outcomes may be expressed at the level of a class, a module, a year or a degree programme or a university. There is unlikely to be a one-to-one correspondence between outcomes at various levels. None the less one should be able to see how the assessment and outcomes of various levels are linked together. Of these the most important are the links between the assessment, the outcomes of the module and the module programme.

## ACTIVITIES

3.1 Spend a few minutes thinking and jotting down your approaches to learning.

Think of how you tackle learning something new or unfamiliar, e.g. using a new computer program.

Think of how you tackle learning or revising something with which you are familiar, e.g. refreshing your knowledge of stress analysis or of Jane Austen's works.

How do you learn best?
Now think of how and when you learn worst.

Compare your approaches with those of a few colleagues. Draw up a check-list of approaches for 'best' and 'worst' which includes personal approaches to study and the influence of the context.

3.2 Spend a few minutes jotting down what students learn in your subject. Compare your lists with those of a few colleagues. Identify similarities and differences between your lists and answer the following questions.

What guidance and feedback is provided to students on the items on your list?

What items on the list are assessed *explicitly* in assignments and examinations?

Do the students know the criteria?

Compile a master list based upon the group's major items. Use these headings to create your list: Items; Guidance given; Assessed implicitly or explicitly.

3.3 Look again at the brief descriptions of learning styles given in this chapter. What are your predispositions? (If you do this activity as a group discussion it is useful for everyone to express him- or herself in the form of 'Predominantly . . . with some features of.'

3.4 How are you reading this book? Justify your approach.
Compare your approaches with a few colleagues.

3.5 The skills developed in higher education are necessarily grounded in the earlier experiences of students. So the question then arises, what is distinctive about higher education? Spend a few minutes thinking of how learning and its assessment in higher education is different from that in schools and further education. Does your course or module promote deep learning? Compare your views with those of a few colleagues. If you use the pun that 'It's all a matter of degree . . . ', then justify the differences in degree!

3.6 How would you characterise the differences between active and passive learning in your subject? Compare your views with those of a few colleagues in your subject and other subjects.

Chapter 4

# Methods and strategies: an overview

In this chapter we consider the sources and instruments of assessment and describe some of the methods and strategies of assessing student learning. We provide a broad outline of what methods are good for what purposes and explore strategies for easing some of the problems associated with assessing large numbers of students, heavier work loads and reduced budgets.

## SOME RECENT DEVELOPMENTS

Over the past 10 years there has been a renewed interest in different approaches to teaching and assessing students. This interest, in part, arises from the Government's pincer movement of insisting upon 'quality' while at the same time reducing unit costs. Projects and reports of new developments in various subjects have been published: the project on Assessment Strategies in Scottish Higher Education (ASSHE, 1996; Hounsell, 1997) provides a wide range of assessment methods in use in Scottish universities, an inventory and a computerised database of innovative methods of assessment that are being used in different subjects. Project ALTER has produced publications on Records of Achievement (Bull and Otter, 1994), external examining (Partington, Brown and Gordon, 1993), Boards of Examiners (Partington *et al.*, 1995) and the uses of computers in assessment (Bull, 1993). Gibbs *et al.* (1992), in a project funded by the Polytechnic and Colleges Funding Council, provide a series of texts on assessing more students, course design and lectures which are replete with suggestions for use across the subjects. UCoSDA developed a series of modules on effective teaching and learning (Cryer, 1992) which includes assessment (Brown and Pendlebury, 1992). Each module provides an overview, examples of practice and suggestions for workshops. The Effective Engineering Education Project (E-cubed) provides suggestions on making assessment in engineering more effective and efficient (Brown *et al.*, 1994).

Within subject areas there are also useful publications on assessment, teaching and learning. Notable amongst these are three sets of volumes on teaching and assessment in sciences, engineering and medical sciences, compiled by Exley and Moore (1992) and Moore and Exley (1994) and Exley and Dennick

(1996). In the last two, the authors provide a useful cross-index system which enables a reader to identify the problems addressed (e.g. increase in student numbers, different ability levels, financial resources, the transferable skills and competencies developed and the teaching, learning or assessment strategy exemplified). Hart and Smith (1994, 1996) have edited similar texts on computer studies. Booth and Hyland (1995) have published a text on teaching and assessment in history. Jenkins and Ward (1995) provide a text on teaching in geography.

## SOURCES, INSTRUMENTS AND METHODS

At the outset, it may be useful to distinguish between the three terms, 'sources', 'instruments' and 'methods of assessment'. Source refers to the person – the lecturer, student, employer or peer group of students. Instrument refers to the marking scheme, the explicit criteria or implicit criteria. (Strictly speaking, the instrument of assessment is the source in conjunction with the instrument.) Method refers to the approach used to assess learning such as essays, problems, multiple choice tests and so on. Figure 4.1 outlines the range of sources, instruments and methods.

Explicit criteria have four functions. First, they can provide meaningful feedback to students. Second, they can show the links between the assessment task and the outcomes of the course. Third, they ensure that assessors are in broad agreement; and fourth, they can pinpoint areas of disagreement between markers. However, undue specificity is not helpful either to students or assessors. Detailed criteria have been shown to yield low-level learning (Slavin, 1990). Their usefulness is limited to low-level practical tasks and even in low-level tasks, cueing of the key criteria, for the purposes of learning and assessment, is more important than a long list. They are primarily useful for research rather than teaching purposes. Detailed lists are time-consuming for assessors to use and

| Sources | Instruments | Examples of Methods |
|---|---|---|
| Tutor | *Implicit criteria* | Essays |
| Other tutors | Global | Problem sheets |
| Post-grad tutors | *Explicit criteria* | Unseen proses |
| Demonstrators | Criteria reference | Lab reports |
| Student self | Grading | Presentations |
| Student peers | Marking scheme | Projects |
| Employers | Dimensions | Group projects |
| Mentors | Rating schedules | |
| | Checklists | |

*Figure 4.1* Sources, instruments and methods of assessment

lengthy intensive training is required for the use of the instrument to be reliable. The feedback provided from detailed lists of criteria is often difficult to translate into improved practice. In short, mental atomism is not good for assessment.

A question often asked is what is the difference between a marking scheme and criteria. In practice, criteria usually refer to dimensions of an assignment that are assessed such as organisation, style, use of evidence. Similarly, dimensions and rating schedules are usually used to assess qualities that permeate the whole of an assessment task such as fluency of style or the responsiveness of a student interviewer. Marking schemes tend to be linear. They are usually attached to specific operations or procedures such as the correct use of a standard integral, the correct use of the past pluperfect, an accurate translation of a paragraph in a passage of prose. Checklists are also best used to assess sequential tasks and simple design specifications. Global scores can be reliable but the criteria remain hidden. Three or four broad dimensions can be reliable, quick to use and useful for summative purposes. More detailed rating schedules may be useful for formative purposes but variations between markers on individual scales can be high. Checklists when linked to a design specification or sequential task can be reliable but they are time-consuming for assessing complex tasks and, for acceptable levels of reliability, intensive training is required. Detailed checklists are probably the least reliable method and most time-consuming instrument of assessment. Finally, the effectiveness of any instrument is determined by its specific content. For a technical discussion of these issues see Van der Vleuten *et al.* (1991) and Norman *et al.* (1991).

Some of the controversy surrounding new approaches to assessment is due to confusions about sources and instruments. Self-assessment is not a method of assessment but a source which can be used with any method or instrument. Posters are a method that may be used with any source or instrument. The decisions one has to take are whether the combination of source, instrument and method are appropriate for the purpose and whether the costs, in terms of time and other resources, merit the approach. Thus peer- and self-assessment of a group project may be a useful way of encouraging students to reflect upon their teamwork and the product, the project report. Explicit criteria should be used to ensure consistency and fairness. Setting up the system may be time-consuming but the value of the exercise for students may be high. On the other hand, final year marks based solely on self-assessment and implicit criteria would, for most of us, seem a totally inappropriate practice.

## METHODS OF ASSESSMENT

### Varying examinations

Examinations and coursework are the major categories of assessment although the distinction is blurred by various forms of open-book examinations. Some departments allow students to take notes and texts into examinations on the grounds that this reduces stress and rote learning. The procedure could be extended to providing access to databanks via terminals.

These methods assess students' ability to organise, retrieve and handle information when under pressure. Students seem to like open-book examinations, perhaps because their books are a comfort. In a study of open-book examinations in mathematics, able students tended to do better and weaker students tended to do worse (Michaels and Kierans, 1973). More able students know what they are looking for and how to look for it whereas weaker students tend to spend much more time searching for the relevant information. These results probably apply to all subjects. If open-book examinations are to be used then it is important to provide training and, of course, to set questions which require students to think about the knowledge that they are retrieving.

Another attempt to reduce anxiety is the 168-hour examination (Gibbs, Habeshaw and Habeshaw, 1988). The questions are set a week before the examinations. We leave the reader to work out the advantages and disadvantages of this approach.

An alternative to prior-notice questions is the use of prior-notice topics. The specific topics but not the specific questions are provided to students in their revision schedule. This approach focuses revision and it is particularly useful where the syllabus is wide and depth of understanding rather than width of knowledge is being assessed. The questions asked can be challenging but the challenge should be just within the comfort zone of most students. This method may be extended by providing a paper for students to read prior to an examination consisting of questions on it. The method may be used with a scientific paper, a legal or social work case, a business plan or a project report. A variation on the approach is to give the paper out at the beginning of the examination and allow about one and a half hours for reading and note-taking. In the second part of the examination, the specific questions are provided. These methods enable one to assess application of prior expertise, understanding and evaluative skills.

It is often claimed that final examinations are *the* measure of what students have learnt. The notion sits uncomfortably with modularity, free choice and the limited range of capabilities that written examinations can measure. If course designers wish to assess the overall performance of students against the programme's objectives, there is a strong case for a mixture of examination and coursework assessment in the final year that focuses upon skills or capabilities. Hammar *et al.* (1995) have developed this approach in their assessment of medical students at the University of Linkoping. The objectives of the degree programme are, in essence, to develop the clinical and scientific abilities of the students. Four tasks are set in the final phase of assessment:

*Measurement of clinical ability.* Each student is required to spend 30 minutes on examining, taking a history and summarising his or her findings. The consultation is video-recorded and assessed by a clinician for accuracy of diagnosis and management plan and by a psychologist for the student's communication skills.

*Analysis of a scientific paper.* A scientific paper is given to each student and he/she is required to study it carefully before proceeding to a written examination on it.
*Investigation and presentation of a scientific work.* In essence, a project.
*Oral examination.* The students work together in groups of five or six. Their task is to analyse the strengths and weaknesses of each of their projects. They then present a constructive critique of the set of projects, excluding their own.

### Varying coursework

The standard approaches to coursework are essays, problems and writing up practicals. These methods may be extended and new methods introduced. Figure 4.2 sets out some alternatives. In essence, the alternative approaches extend the range of skills that are tested. For example, writing an article for a newspaper requires students to know the essential aspects of a topic and take account of the audience for whom they are writing. Further discussion of these alternatives and others is provided in subsequent chapters.

### Which assessment for which purpose?

Figure 4.3 sets out a range of assessment methods together with a brief comment on their uses, ease of use and reliability. The closer a method is to recall of knowledge and/or well-defined solutions, the more reliable it is, but not necessarily the more valid. One has, as usual, to manage the conflicting demands of validity and reliability, of effectiveness and efficiency. Broadly speaking, essays are better at estimating understanding, synthesis and evaluation than multiple choice questions whereas multiple choice questions are better at sampling a wider range of knowledge. Cases and open problems are better at testing ingenuity than MCQs. However, the effectiveness of the assessment method depends upon the particular assignment set, not merely on the method of assessment. (See also Burgess and Lee (1989) and CNAA (1989) for a discussion of the uses of different assessment methods.)

Although the broad uses of various methods are indicated in Figure 4.3, almost every method can be used to fulfil any purpose of assessment. Lab reports *can* be used to assess practical skills, written essays *can* be used to assess oral communication and projects *may* be used to assess leadership skills. However, there is a danger of sacrificing validity for convenience.

The match between purposes, assessment tasks and outcomes is rather more subtle than it appears. If one wants to rank order rather than pass/fail one needs to design questions that permit answers at different levels. If the primary purpose of an assessment is to provide feedback to students rather than only grade their answers for summative purposes then different criteria and comments may be needed. A further problem is that just as there are different levels of skills so too are there different levels of outcomes: the class level, the module level and the degree programme level. It is unlikely that there is a one-to-one correspondence

Here are a few suggestions to start you thinking of developing some of your existing assessment tasks.

*Existing task: Essay*
*Set:*
Article for a serious newspaper
Article for professional magazine
Article for a popular newspaper
Book review
Paper to a committee
Case for an interest group
Popular book review
Serious book review
Script for a radio programme
Script for a TV programme

*Existing task: Experimental design*
*Set:*
Marketing research bid
Research bid
Design of a survey
Tender for a contract

*Existing task: Lab report*
*Set:*
Instructional guide for beginner
Popular account of experiment and its findings
Brief seminar paper on experiment
Group report of a set of linked experiments

*Existing task: Problem solving*
*Set:*
Real case
Match ideal and possible
Compare precise solution and estimate

*Existing task: Short answer questions*
*Set:*
Set them on a theme which provides more information or complexity as they proceed through the set of questions

*Existing task: Project, dissertation or group project*
*Set:*
For a real client or based in a work setting
Then convert into a brief publication, illustrated presentation or exhibition

*Existing task: Intercalary year project*
*Set:*
Research to be undertaken in their work placement abroad or in this country. The theme of how they have deepened their knowledge and understanding during the intercalary year could be used. They could make records and analyses of their language competence at points throughout the year.

Based on Gibbs, Habeshaw and Habeshaw (1988)

*Figure 4.2* Modifying existing assessments

| | |
|---|---|
| **Essays** | A standard method. Has potential for measuring under-standing, synthesis and evaluative skills. Relatively easy to set. Marking for grading using impressionistic marking is relatively fast. Marking for feedback can be time-consuming. Variations between examiners can be high. |
| **Problems** | A standard method. Has potential for measuring application, analysis and problem solving strategies. Complex problems and their marking schemes can be difficult to design. Marking for grading of easy problems is fast. For complex problems marking can be slow. Marking for feedback can be slow. Variation between markers is usually low. |
| **Reports on practicals** | A standard method. Has potential for measuring knowledge of experimental procedures, analysis and interpretation of results. Measures know-how of practical skills but not the skills themselves. Marking for grading using impressions or simple structured forms is relatively fast. Marking for feedback with simple structured forms is faster than without them. Variations between markers, without structured forms, can be high. Method is often over-used. Different foci for different experiments recommended. |
| **Multiple choice questions (MCQs)** | A standard method. Can sample a wide range of knowledge quickly. Has potential for measuring under-standing, analysis, problem-solving skills and evaluative skills. Measures of knowledge are relatively easy to set. More complex questions require more time to set. Easy to mark and analyse results. Feedback to students is fast. Reliable. Danger of testing only trivial knowledge. |
| **Short answer questions** | A standard method. Has potential for measuring analysis, application of knowledge, problem-solving and evaluative skills. Can be easier to design than complex MCQs but still relatively slow. Marking to model answers is relatively fast compared with problems but not compared with MCQs. Marking for feedback can be relatively fast. |
| **Cases and open problems** | Has potential for measuring application of knowledge, analysis, problem-solving and evaluative skills. Short cases are relatively easy to design and mark. Design of more complex cases and their marking schemes is more challenging. Marking for grading and feedback are about as fast as essay marking. |
| **Mini-practicals** | A series of mini-practicals undertaken under timed conditions. Potential for sampling wide range of practical, analytical and interpretative skills. Initial design |

continued . . .

| | |
|---|---|
| **Mini-practicals (continued)** | is time-consuming. Marking is done on the spot so it is fast. Feedback to students is fast. Reliable but training of assessors is necessary. |
| **Projects, group projects and dissertations** | Good all-round ability testing. Potential for sampling wide range of practical, analytical and interpretative skills. Wider application of knowledge, understanding and skills to real/simulated situations. Provides a measure of project and time management. Group projects can provide a measure of teamwork skills and leadership. Motivation and teamwork can be high. Marking for grading can be time-consuming. Marking for feedback can be reduced through peer- and self-assessment and presentations. Feedback potential. Tests methods as well as end results. Can be variations between markers. Use of criteria reduces variability. |
| **Orals** | Test communication, understanding, capacity to think quickly under pressure and knowledge of procedures. Feedback potential. Marking for grading can be fast but some standardisation of interview procedure is needed. |
| **Presentations** | Test preparation, understanding, knowledge, capacity to structure information oral communication skills. Feedback potential: from tutor, self and peers. Marking for grading based on simple criteria is fast and potentially reliable. |
| **Poster sessions** | Test capacity to present findings and interpretations succinctly and attractively. Danger of focusing unduly on presentation methods can be avoided by the use of simple criteria. Feedback potential: from tutor, self and peers. Marking for grading is fast. Use of criteria reduces variability. |
| **Reflective practice assignments** | Measure capacity to analyse and evaluate experience in the light of theories and research evidence. Relatively easy to set. Feedback potential from peers, self and tutors. Marking for feedback can be slow. Marking for grading is about the same as for essays. Use of criteria reduces variability. |
| **Single essay exams** | Three hours on prepared topic. Relatively easy to set. Attention to criteria needed. Wider range of ability tested including capacity to draw on a wide range of knowledge, to synthesise and identify recurrent themes. Marking for feedback is relatively slow. Marking for grading is relatively fast providing the criteria are simple. |

*Figure 4.3* Which methods of assessment?

between an assessment task and an outcome at the module and programme level. Indeed if there is, there is a high probability of over-assessment. Instead one should design assessment tasks that test a set of overlapping outcomes at the module and programme level. (This suggestion is based on the assumption that permissible module programmes do have some intellectual coherence.) Figure 4.4 is based on a scheme developed in the School of Computing Studies at the University of Hertfordshire. The scheme helps one to identify the match between assessment task and outcome. It also provides an estimate of workloads for students and marking times for staff.

## TIME AT WORK

There appear to be no reliable figures on how long it takes to do various assignments or how long it takes to mark them. Obviously there are variations in time and effort amongst students and staff. In addition, the pressures on both may lead to decisions to match the time available to the task. If you have only four

---

**Part 1 Resources**

Accommodation requirements:
Approx. cost of course materials to each student:
Student hours on each assessment task:
Staff hours allocated to this course:
How many of the staff hours allocated will be spent on:
Contact
Setting work
Marking work
Preparation

**Part 2 Outline of content and learning style**
(based on module or course description)

**Part 3 Outline assessment plan**
(based on objectives specified in module or course document)

3.1  For each in-course assessment to be done in the student's own time, specify objectives being assessed:

3.2  For each in-class test or timed practical work (e.g. 'one-day practical' to be done in class time) specify objectives being assessed:

3.3  For the examination, if any, specify objectives being assessed:

3.4  What does the student need to do in order to pass the course?

---

*Figure 4.4* Course delivery and assessment plan

hours to mark 50 essays then you may aim at marking at the rate of one in less than five minutes. Evidence from a survey at Leeds Metropolitan University (LMU, 1996) provides estimates of time taken by staff for marking as between 15 and 30 minutes for coursework essays and 30 to 45 minutes for an examination script. More important than the estimates of staff and student time provided by academic staff in this survey is the notion that one should estimate and monitor, in one's own department or school, the time involved for doing assignments and for marking them.

## DESIGNING AND MARKING ASSESSMENTS

Seven questions that one might ask when designing a coursework assignment or written paper are:

1 What are the outcomes to be assessed?
2 What are the capabilities/skills (implicit or explicit) in the outcomes?
3 Is the method of assessment chosen consonant with the outcomes and skills?
4 Is the method relatively efficient in terms of student time and staff time?
5 What alternatives are there? What are their advantages and disadvantages?
6 Does the specific assessment task match the outcomes and skills?
7 Are the marking schemes or criteria appropriate?

As indicated above, one has to consider whether the purpose of the assessment is to grade students or merely to pass/fail them. If the former, then one has to design questions that enable responses at different levels of understanding. If the latter, one has to ensure the key knowledge, understanding or skills are being tested at an appropriate level for the student cohort.

The above questions naturally lead into the design of a specific assessment task. Here there are several pitfalls, notably unintentional ambiguities in a question or assignment, under-estimate of time and resources required to do the assignment, or to mark it, and neglect of a suitable set of criteria or a marking scheme.

Strictly speaking the design of an assessment task is not complete until one has designed a marking scheme or a set of criteria. Marking schemes are usually one of two types. Either one assumes a model answer and deducts marks for errors or omissions or one awards marks for correct points or accuracy. The former is sometimes used for marking purposes and problems and the latter is used extensively in science and engineering. The respective strengths and weaknesses of the approaches are left for you to explore with your colleagues.

The principle, 'keep it simple' is apposite for marking schemes. But in order to keep a marking scheme simple one has to design problems that are capable of solution by only a few routes. The exceptional student will sometimes find an elegant solution that is not covered by a general marking scheme, so special cases may need to be considered separately. The exceptions should not prevent one from interlinking the design of the problem and its marking scheme. The use of explicit criteria enables one to match outcomes and assessment tasks but again there is a problem of undue complexity, which increases variability amongst markers and adds to the time required for marking. Our discussions with colleagues in assessment workshops suggests the hypothesis that most people mark globally and then complete the checklist of criteria. In the interests of effectiveness and efficiency, we suggest that the number of criteria used should be less than seven. Seven is probably the maximum number of criteria that one can attend to simultaneously when reading a script.

## Saving time when designing effective assessments

The design of *effective* assessment tasks can be time-consuming. A useful starting-point is to look through and note examination questions and assignments that are set in comparable courses in other institutions. Then look at questions set in other subjects in your own institution. You will almost certainly find questions that are intriguing and surprising and you will also find forms of questions that may be transferred into your own subject. Occasionally, you may find that the content as well as the form of question is relevant to your own subject. Whilst reading and noting the questions, try to work out what the assessor was trying to assess. (The Appendix provides a sample of questions from different subjects. See also Brown and Pendlebury, 1992b.) Return now to the questions in your own subject. Consider what kinds of learning you are trying to develop and assess. Look at the outcomes of your course and think about what kind of things that you want your students to learn and to be able to do.

Alternatively you can develop some new forms of questions and tasks and discuss them with colleagues. Be prepared to provide a rationale for their use. Some people find brainstorming with colleagues a useful way of generating a series of questions on a topic. Others keep a notebook of possible questions, quotes and problems. You could devote a section of your own assessment log to this task. Figures 4.2 and 4.3 offers some approaches that you may not have used.

Choose a few of the questions or tasks that you have developed and try them out with students. It is usually better to include new types of questions in coursework rather than examinations. Be sure that the wording is clear. Eliminate any *unwanted* ambiguities in the questions. Bear in mind that the more open or ambiguous a question is, the harder it is to devise a marking scheme for it, but one can often use broad criteria. Skim-read the answers and assignments and then devise criteria or a marking scheme or adapt an existing approach. Then mark the answers and assignments. If you are giving feedback to each student consider carefully what comments and suggestions will help him or her to improve. Review and summarise the outcomes of your newly developed assessment task:

- What were the strengths and weaknesses of the students' performance?
- How could the students be helped to improve their work? Consider your approaches to teaching as well as their learning opportunities.
- Did the assessment draw out the range of skills, knowledge and understanding that you hoped it would?
- Could the assignment be improved?
- Could its marking be improved?

### Marking efficiently for summative and formative purposes

Marking for grading and marking for feedback are almost different species of marking although the pressure of large numbers tends to conflate the two approaches. Of the two, marking for grading is the faster but potentially less reliable since one has to mark within fierce deadlines. Figure 4.5 offers some suggestions that can alleviate time pressures whilst at the same time reducing marker error.

Marking for feedback is rather more subtle and time-consuming. First one has to decide what the purpose of the feedback is. There are at least three purposes:

1 To relay the grade.
2 To justify the grade.
3 To help a student to improve his or her knowledge-base/problem-solving strategies/understanding/communication skills.

Often the third set of purposes is confused or neglected.

Feedback is probably the best tested principle in psychology. It has been shown to be most effective when it is timely, perceived as relevant, meaningful, encouraging and offers suggestions for improvement that are within a student's grasp. (See, for example, the reviews by Kulik and Kulik (1979) and Turney (1984)). All the practical hints on providing feedback can be deduced from these findings and there are implications for the management of modules and courses, and for one's own time management and approach to marking for feedback, including one's style of writing comments on assignments. Some examples of hints suggested by experienced colleagues are:

> Return assignments promptly. Long, warm, woolly comments or short, sharp, shattering statements are rarely effective. A few succinct, supportive statements that move a student on are preferable. Choose a few points that will produce the greatest improvement and hold back on the rest. Wherever possible state what is good as well as what could be improved so the student knows what does not need attention as well as what does need attention. Simply noting errors is not helpful unless the student knows how to correct them. A balance of encouraging comments and some criticisms is better than a litany of errors.

---

**Preliminaries**: • Design questions that assess key outcomes.
• Have a simple robust marking scheme or set of criteria.
• For grading purposes ensure that the question and scheme will provide a spread of marks.
• Plan the time required for marking well in advance.
• Allocate more time than you think you will need.
• Guard it jealously.
• Allow time for checking, re-marking and slippage.

**Procedures**: • Mark by question not script. Despite having to handle scripts more often, the marking is faster and more reliable.
• Mark intensively until you have the criteria or marking scheme firmly fixed in your head.
• Then you can mark reliably a few questions at a time between other tasks.
• At the beginning of each day, re-mark a few questions and be prepared to re-mark more.
• If you are marking by criterion-reference grading, skim-read the answers and place the scripts in piles of Fail, Pass, 3rds, 2.2s, 2.1s and Firsts. Then read with the criteria in mind and be prepared to change a few scripts at the borderlines.

---

*Figure 4.5* Marking efficiently for summative purposes

## Managing time for feedback

The strategies that are available for managing and saving time, yet providing useful feedback to students, are essentially:

• reducing the assessment load
• streamlining the feedback procedure
• delegating the marking.

You can set fewer or shorter assignments. Ensure the workload is uniform across the set of modules offered by the department. A check on the total amount of coursework required from a student can be revealing. You can also set tests or assignments to be completed and/or marked during class time.

To ease your time management you can set or fix dates for setting and returning marked assignments at the beginning of the module. At the same time, allocate days or parts of days for marking in your diary. Keep to these allocations unless there is a dire emergency. Say 'no' to colleagues and students who wish to encroach on this time.

You can mark some assignments very thoroughly and the rest less thoroughly.

Tell students at the beginning of the module of this intention. Suggest to them that they use the detailed comments when doing subsequent assignments. A most useful strategy for improving learning is to mark and comment on the draft of an assignment. Keep a copy of your comments. Grade the final version and add a brief global comment. This approach is more useful for learning than a thorough marking of the final version of an assignment. It demonstrates to students that they can improve. Once an assignment has been marked, it tends to be archived by the students and there seems to be little transfer of learning to the next assignment.

Use criteria or checklists plus a personal comment. Keep the criteria simple otherwise you will spend more, not less, time fitting your comments to them. Alternatively do a global report based on the students' assignments. The best assignments had these characteristics ... good assignments ... weaker assignments. ... The method can be used for problems, cases and essays and it can form the basis of a large group teaching session or tutorial.

Use peer assessment for one assignment. Provide, or better still, generate criteria with the whole class and provide them with some training in marking based on marking schemes or criteria. Divide the students into groups of four or five and allocate each group some assignments to assess. This task can be built into the timetabled tutorial programme. This approach not only reduces the teaching and marking load, it also teaches students how to evaluate their own work, how to give and receive feedback and how to work in independent groups. The marks and comments are handed in for moderation by you. You might assign a small proportion of marks for the group work on essay marking.

You can delegate some marking to a team of postgraduate tutors or mentors from more senior years. In the Department of Philosophy at Leeds University, the 'tutors' give five-minute feedback sessions to each student as well as written comments (MacDonald-Ross, Parry and Cohen, 1992). Provide the tutors with training, criteria or marking schemes and examples. This approach also provides useful experience for postgraduates in appraising other people's work and in supplying feedback.

## Some other suggestions on formative feedback

There are some other practical issues associated with assessing work for formative purposes which need to be taken into account. These are commonsense but not necessarily common practice.

1 The course design should provide appropriate learning opportunities and familiarisation with the assessment methods to be used. If you are going to assess through poster sessions or presentations, then some practice in these approaches should be provided. Course management should allow time for students to tackle the assignments in a deep, active way. If all the assignments are set at the same time and they have to be handed in at, or about, the same

time, then students may be forced into using quicker, more superficial approaches in order to meet the deadlines.

2 In the early stages of a course it may be tempting to use grades as an incentive. The evidence suggests that neither very tough marking nor over-generosity improves motivation. Students are most motivated when they feel they can achieve more success with a reasonable effort (Harter, 1978). Prompt return of assignments plus consistent standards throughout the module are likely to be more effective than grade-inflation or grade-deprivation. One cannot justify using the best assignments for assessment if the standards change throughout the module or course level.

3 Although learning opportunities are important, most students are reluctant to put their best efforts into work which is not going to count. Rather than deplore the lack of commitment amongst students, one should commend their practical sense and work with it. Four approaches which can be used are offered in Figure 4.6. All of them are likely to encourage students to try out the learning opportunities provided. Each of these approaches has underlying value questions which you may like to consider. For example, if you consider that there is specific knowledge and skills that all students on the course require, then you may need to adopt the second approach. Alternatively, you may have to design a set of assignments that embody the specifics in different forms in each assessment.

---

Provide feedback on all the assignments. Take the best two or three assignments of a larger set to count towards the module or course mark. A few students may do only the number required for submission – that is their choice.

Use for summative assessment one fixed assignment that everyone must do and the two best assignments of each student.

Use the first assignment as feedback which will be marked in detail. This task must be done as a prerequisite to submitting the assignments that will count towards assessment. Comment on this assignment in a way that will help students to improve their subsequent coursework. Again, a student may tackle the first assignment in a desultory way but that is his or her choice.

Students must submit a set of brief assignments before they submit the assignment or written paper that will be assessed. Assign a 'mark' to the brief assignments so students have some idea of its worth. Detailed feedback on the briefer assignments might be given. One can develop a system whereby the briefer assignments feed into the major dissertation or paper that is marked summatively.

---

*Figure 4.6* Some tactics for modular assessment

Dear Dr B——

I would like to take this opportunity to stress a few points about the history course that I feel should be changed. First, tutors' methods and approaches are extremely diverse. I found that to obtain good marks from various tutors I had to 'play the system', i.e. learn what they wanted; this greatly disrupted my development. Some tutors will always be better at communication, teaching, etc., than others, but do the history staff have a set of guidelines? What constitutes a 'tutorial', etc.? From my experience different tutors had very different approaches.

Secondly, I feel that the history department seems largely unaware of the demands of employers. They do value research skills but, for the most part, teamwork is considered much more important. As the graduate marketplace becomes increasingly competitive the history department must come out of its ivory tower and include group projects, field trips and more active seminars as part of the course.

Finally, what is the function of exams? I study a topic for hours, involve myself in research and then have to answer a question on it in 45 minutes or an hour (if you're lucky). I feel that I am not allowed to show what I have learnt; exams place a student under great pressure that for historical study I do not think is appropriate. I hope my answers to your questionnaire will be of help to you.

Yours sincerely,

A final-year history student who obtained a good 2.1.

From Booth and Hyland (1995)

*Figure 4.7* A letter from a student

4 Finally, to be both effective and efficient, apply the principle: *Assess only the important skills, knowledge and understanding of a topic.* This principle is easy to grasp but difficult to apply.

## SOME BROAD STRATEGIES

The rapid expansion of student numbers and modularisation have been achieved at great cost to lecturers and proportionally reduced costs to Government. Further cuts in resources will probably continue during the next few years. Lecturers and universities are faced with the difficult problem of assessing more students. One can either keep using one's existing approaches and overload staff or look for alternative solutions and be prepared to invest some time in implementing them for longer-term savings in time.

Hounsell (1997) has summarised the major strategies and these are shown in Figure 4.8.

---

**1 Reduce assessments (in scale, scope or formal status)**
*e.g.*
- simple reduction in overall volume of assessments
- making some assessments less demanding
- setting fewer but more challenging assignments
- not formally assessing some coursework
- formally assessing some hitherto informal assignments.

**2 Delegate assessment**
*i.e.*
- devolving marking and/or feedback responsibilities to part-time tutors, teaching assistants or demonstrators
- involving students in marking (usually of tests with standard answers) or in giving feedback to one another.

**3 Reschedule demands**
*e.g.*
- spacing assessments out more evenly
- concentrating assessments at fewer points in the course
- sampling only some scripts.

**4 Refocusing effort**
*More attention to e.g.:*
- thorough groundwork (cf. 'front-ending')
- articulating criteria
- providing colleagues with model answers or worked examples
- using proformas for more focused marking and structured feedback
- feedback to groups rather than to individuals
- channelling follow-up guidance to students most in need.

**5 Capitalising on IT and other technologies**
*e.g. using technology (see Chapter 10) to:*
- mechanise assessments (e.g. MCQs)
- make scripts quicker to scan and scrutinise (e.g. via a word-processing requirement)
- or to help process scripts or collate, record and analyse marks.

**6 Reviewing and recasting approaches to assessment**
*i.e.*
- undertaking a more fundamental reappraisal of assessment ends and means in relation to a particular course, module or degree programme.

---

From Hounsell (1997)

*Figure 4.8* Some coping strategies

Some of the strategies have been described earlier in this chapter. In addition to Hounsell's suggestions one might also:

- Do an audit of students and staff's assessment load as a basis for considering ways of changing assessment procedures. Keep the survey simple. Do not expect the figures to be accurate, for it is difficult to estimate accurately time spent on assessment. However, some data will provide a sense of priorities and the act of surveying assessment practices can itself prompt people to think about ways of changing them.

- Look at the degree regulations and procedures to see if they need changing or interpreting differently. For example if part (level) one is essentially a pass/fail procedure does one need to process in detail all the marks? Of course, there has to be a balance between marking for feedback and marking for grading. Can the re-sit procedure be simplified? Often the process is cumbersome and it can be unfair to students who fail a module in the first semester and then are required to re-sit an examination in the following September.

- Finally, we suggest that departments and schools reflect upon their approaches to assessment with a view to easing assessment loads and improving their effectiveness. Achieving the balance of these differing goals is an intellectual and organisational challenge.

## ACTIVITIES

4.1  1  Use Figures 4.2 and 4.3 to indicate the methods of assessment that you currently use, e.g. coursework essays, examination essays, multiple choice questions, problems, etc.
   2  Note how you decide what assessments and examination questions to set (be honest!).
   3  What learning opportunities do you provide that are assessed formatively (for feedback purposes only)?
   4  Ask the students for their views on the assessment procedures on the course.

4.2  Which of the four approaches in Figure 4.6 do you prefer and why? What are the disadvantages and advantages of each of the four approaches for assessment in your subject? Compare your views with those of a few colleagues who are not within the same subject areas as yourself.

4.3  Review the kinds of things that you want your students to learn in your course or module. Match them against the learning opportunities provided, the assignments set, the written examinations used and the objectives of the course.

4.4  Spend a few minutes thinking about the assessment tasks that you have recently set. Then jot down a few suggestions on how they might be modified. What additional skills and capacities will your modified approaches assess? Compare and discuss your suggestions with a few colleagues. Then discuss:

- what criteria one might use
- what criteria you will use.
- whether those criteria should be given to the students.

4.5 Should one assess only the content and skills that have been taught on a course? Discuss this question with a few colleagues.

4.6 What do examinations measure that coursework does not measure? Do examinations measure deep learning?

4.7 Figure 4.7 contains a letter from a student to her tutor which was written after finals. Draft a reply to it. Compare your draft with that of a few colleagues.

4.8 Spend a few minutes jotting down answers to the following questions. If you do not have accurate information make an informed guess.

1 Approximately how many assignments and examinations are students expected to do in Year 1? In Year 2? In Year 3? In Year 4?
2 How much time does a typical student spend on writing an essay or on solving a set of assessed problems?
3 How long does it take you to mark an essay, problem sheet or lab report in which you give feedback to students?
4 How many assignments do you mark in a year?
5 How many examination questions do you mark in a year?

Compare your estimates with those of a few colleagues and then consider the questions: Should the assessment loads be reduced? Could they be reduced satisfactorily?

# Chapter 5

# Assessing essays

In this chapter we argue that essays can be a valuable way of assessing active learning. We identify different types of essays, suggest some approaches to setting and marking essays and explore some of the issues underlying essay marking. We consider the problem of marking large numbers of essays for summative and feedback purposes and suggest some ways of varying the essay method. Colleagues from subjects that use essays will find Hounsell and Murray (1992) and Hounsell (1995) useful sources of advice.

## INTRODUCTION

Essays are the most common form of assessment in the arts and social sciences. A good case could be made for arguing that they are the most useful way of assessing deep learning. For they *can* require a student to integrate knowledge, skills and understanding. An essay writer has to identify the problems beneath the question posed, he or she has to create a structure, display insight and provide a coherent argument. Essays can provide opportunities for students to develop communication skills in different contexts. For example, an essay may be set that requires a student to present arguments that would appeal to different audiences. The method may be extended further by requiring students to write short articles in the style of academic journals, quality newspapers or even popular newspapers.

Essays in science, engineering and medicine are often more akin to factual reports than to essays in the arts and social sciences. But even in the natural sciences, essays, with a mathematical flavour, can be set that require a student to explore the connections between different topics, approaches or methods of analysis. The processes of writing essays in all subjects have features in common. All require planning, selection, structure, coherence and deeper rather than superficial answers to the question posed. For further details on the processes of writing essays Hounsell and Murray (1992), Brown and Atkins (1988), Clanchy and Ballard (1992) or Hounsell (1995). Both Hounsell and Murray and Clanchy and Ballard provide examples of approaches to writing and assessing writing from across a wide range of subjects. Here we are primarily concerned with the assessment of essays but inevitably we touch upon other relevant issues of essay writing.

Essays, as their name suggests, are essentially concerned with trying out ideas and arguments supported by evidence. In Hounsell's seminal study of essay writing (Hounsell, 1984) the undergraduates provided three distinct perceptions of essays:

- an argument well supported by evidence
- a distinctive viewpoint on a problem or issue
- an ordered arrangement of facts and ideas.

These three perceptions are consonant with the styles of learning discussed earlier in this text. The first is akin to the deep active approach of searching for and constructing meaning. The second has elements of deep processing but it is largely concerned with reproducing knowledge. The third is almost wholly concerned with reproducing other people's facts and ideas. A fourth possibility (with which readers will be familiar) is a student's random walk through the literature.

In most examination or coursework essays there are no absolutely right or wrong answers. A student selects and organises material in the way which seems most appropriate to him or her. A choice of questions is often given so comparison of student performance may be difficult. Some questions are harder than others and essay questions may be interpreted in different ways. This is a disadvantage if you are searching for precise information and an advantage if you are looking for fluency, creativity, the ability to organise arguments and the selection of relevant facts. Essays give an estimate of these high-level cognitive skills, they encourage integrated thinking and, of course, they develop writing skills. In a modular degree they can, with a little adjustment of module regulations, be used to integrate knowledge, skills and understanding from different topics, from different modules and different subjects. There is much to commend the use of essays to obtain a student's synoptic view of a major topic. Essays may also be used to develop skills of persuasive writing for different audiences.

Clearly the quality of a student's essay writing is determined by his or her knowledge, perceptions, skills and understanding of the topic. It is also determined by the quality of the question posed. Essay questions are deceptively easy to set and disturbingly hard to mark objectively. At the very least one needs an idea of what counts as a good answer, an indifferent answer and a poor answer. One also needs to know one's values and to be able to distinguish between views that are only different from one's own and those that are both different and wrong.

# DESIGNING ESSAY QUESTIONS

In Chapter 4 we indicated various ways of generating questions for assignments and papers. This section takes the issue further by considering the various types of essay questions and their uses. Each type of essay question demands different emphases and draws on different forms of thinking. So it is sensible to ask oneself:

• What are the purposes in setting this particular question?
• To what outcomes is the question related?

A change of word can alter quite dramatically the meaning of a question. For example, take the two questions:

'Discuss *the* role of a university lecturer.'
'Discuss *a* role of the university lecturer.'

So too can a change of context. The essay title: 'Discuss the effects of starvation on young children' requires a different emphasis in a paper on paediatrics than in a paper on community development.

## Types of essay questions

There is no clear-cut classification of types of essays but there are families of essays that share common characteristics. A linguist, a post-modernist, or a philosopher might enjoy doing a research project on essay questions and their hidden meanings.

### Speculative

'What would have happened to the balance of world power if Krushchev, and not Kennedy, had been assassinated?'
'How would Marx have explained the collapse of Eastern Europe?'
'What would happen to the health of Britain if antibiotics were no longer effective?'

These questions invite the student to construct alternative realities and test his or her ability to provide rationales for alternative views.

### Quote to discuss

'"There is no such thing as social class." Discuss.'

This type of essay stimulates students to examine a perspective or to challenge a view. The source of the quote can alter the meaning of the question: the name M. Thatcher (a past prime minister) or E.P. Thompson (a Marxist historian) after the quote above, would alter the meaning of the question somewhat.

Lengthy or obscure quotes confuse examiners and students. Often such quotes owe more to a lecturer's vanity than to a clear purpose of assessing understanding.

## Assertion

'"Animals should not be used for experiments." Discuss.'
'"Animals should not be used for experiments." Discuss in relation to the use of animals in the Japanese pharmaceutical industry.'

The purpose of these questions is to encourage the student to examine pros and cons. Weaker students focus upon evidence in favour of the assertion rather than evidence for and against it. Sometimes the assertion is buried in the question, such as:

'Discuss the use of animals in the Japanese pharmaceutical industry.'

## Write on

'Write an essay on neuro-transmitters.'
'Write an essay on sex and the epidemiologist.'

Here the students have to select ruthlessly from their knowledge and develop their own framework for the question. Marking may be based upon the framework created by the student and his or her answer within that framework. The issue of interpretative frameworks is considered below. p 66

## Describe or explain

Philosophers argue about the differences between describing and explaining. In essay questions usually the term means 'give an account of and/or rationale for'.

'Explain the use of anova techniques in experimental design.'
'Describe the characteristics of light curing acrylics.'

## Compare and contrast

'Compare and contrast qualitative and quantitative methods of evaluation.'
'What are the major differences between the views of society of Durkheim and Weber?'

Comparison and contrast may be requested directly or indirectly. Although these types of question do not specifically request the student's own views, they are usually required if a student is to obtain a good mark.

It is arguable whether one should specify precisely what is required in a question or whether one should teach students to de-code questions. Those strongly committed to the idea that assessments should always be obvious and transparent might argue for specificity. Those who are concerned to develop analytical and problem-solving skills for use in a wide variety of contexts might argue for teaching de-coding of questions. Ultimately it depends upon your purposes.

## Discuss

'Discuss the role of Bismarck in the formation of the German State.'

This type of question usually has written in invisible ink the word 'critically'. These questions may involve comparison, contrast, analysis, evaluation, description and explanation.

## Evaluate

All essays in practice involve interpretation and evaluation. In these questions the emphasis is focused clearly upon the analysis and assessment of evidence or argument. The student must indicate that the evidence is known but this is not the primary task.

'Evaluate the impact of microcomputers on laboratory work in undergraduate courses in physics.'

Sometimes the evaluation has a wider reach, such as 'What aspects of British culture are worth preserving?'

## Design

'Design an experiment to test the hypothesis that redheads are quick-tempered.'
'Draw up a specification of a recreational centre suitable for use by people in the age range 55–75 years.'

Sometimes this form of question involves working to quite detailed specifications. Usually more than three quarters of an hour is required to answer these questions.

## Problem-based essays

Examples of these are:

'You have been asked to give a talk on the ecological movement to the local Conservative Association. Prepare a draft of your talk and the answers to four questions that might be raised by the audience.'

'What advice would you offer to a small textile company that has the following turnover and characteristics . . . '

'How would you manage a paranoiac schizophrenic who is living in the community?'

## Write a dialogue or script

Examples of these are:

'Write a dialogue between a health services manager and a philosopher on the notion of quality.' (See Loughlin, 1995, for an article that uses this method.)

'Script a discussion between Freud and Eysenck on personality.'

These questions are challenging. They go beyond the recall of information towards deeper understanding of different perspectives.

*Witty questions*

These too can be fun for students but they are probably best set for coursework. Some examples are:
'Was "The Excursion" (by Wordsworth) really necessary?'
'Why did the concept of mind rile so many philosophers in the 1950s?'
'Do you talk as you think or think as you talk?'

The more open the question, the more difficult it is to arrive at specific criteria for its assessment. However, this is a cost one must pay if one is attempting to stimulate creative flair.

## MARKING ESSAYS

(Before reading this section you might like to try Activity 5.1.)

---

**Essay One**
*Assess the economic and social impact of the railways on Victorian Britain*

The first railway was the Stockton–Darlington line opened in 1825. It was quickly followed by the Liverpool and Manchester in 1830, and the success of this line encouraged much further building. The railways transformed the face of Victorian Britain.

By the mid 1840s over 2,000 miles of railway has been built and in 1844 an important Act imposed minimum standards of safety. It also provided for state purchase of the railways in the 1860s, but this was not in fact done.

At first there was considerable opposition to the building of the railways on a wide variety of grounds – there had been severe doubts about slippage between the track and the rail. Gradually however these doubts were overcome and the railways came to be seen as a powerful new force in the country and as a profitable investment. There were several bursts of railway mania with vast sums of money being expended. Much of this was spent on lobbying for the Bills, and other money was wasted by the building of duplicate lines. Much of the engineering was over-elaborate and costly.

Socially the railways had important effects. Newspapers could be delivered on time and ladies' fashions became nationalised. GMT became common. People could now travel considerable distances and see parts of the country not seen before. An increase in illegitimacy followed the building of the railways.

Economically the effects of the railways were tremendous. New avenues of communication were opened up, and goods could be carried faster and cheaper than on the canals which often froze. Jobs were created and new demands arose for steel and other constructional materials.

Thus it can be seen that the impact of the railways on Victorian Britain was very great, although some of the expenditure was wasteful.

Fiona Seaton-Macleod, Year One

continued . . .

---

> **Essay Two**
> *Assess the economic and social impact of the railways on Victorian Britain*
>
> The railway age began in Britain in 1830 with the opening of the Liverpool and Manchester Railway. Within 20 years over 6,000 miles of track had been opened.
>
> The railways succeeded the canals as the major transport link in the country and they extended and improved the services that had been provided by the canals. They were faster, cheaper and more reliable – not being subject to the problems of freeze and drought. This improved transport service lowered costs thus making more products available more widely and thus eliminating local monopolies and encouraging large-scale production. The breweries were greatly affected by this development.
>
> In addition to the better transport services there were other economic effects. Multiplier effects were generated by the employment opportunities that were created and by the greatly increased demands for constructional materials. Technological change was also stimulated.
>
> The railways required much greater sums of money than any previous enterprise and new financial developments were necessary. Not all the money was spent wisely and there was often wasteful competition between lines.
>
> Some towns, such as Crewe, Middlesborough [sic] and Swindon owed their growth and their existence to the railways.
>
> Socially the railways acted as a powerful unifying force. National organisations could now replace regional and local ones and the power of London could be felt more widely. The adoption of GMT is a symbol of this unification.
>
> Overall the effects of the railways were tremendous. Without them the development of the economy would have been both slower and more local and society would have been less uniform. The railways were not sufficient for growth, for they built on the foundations of the canals but they were very necessary.
>
> Harry Greenwood, Year One

Based on a workshop exercise devised by Dr Andrew Wilson, Loughborough University.

*Figure 5.1* Essays on railways in Victorian Britain

There are four key issues in marking essays: reducing variability, using criteria, providing helpful feedback and managing time. Minimising variability is one of the issues of reliability and validity discussed in Chapter 15. It is associated with the use of second markers, anonymity of examination scripts and other factors. Here it is sufficient to note that differences in marks can owe more to variations among examiners than to the performance of students.

## Reducing variability

Some suggestions for reducing one's variability in marking were outlined in Chapter 4 (see particularly Figure 4.5). Some further suggestions are given in Figure 5.2. Awareness of one's prejudices and values is particularly valuable for essay marking. The notion of 'objectivity' dissolves when essays are set on deep issues which are susceptible to the individual response of a lecturer or, perhaps worse, of a department too strongly wedded to a particular ideology. Figure 5.3 offers a couple of extracts from the discussion of this issue by Rowntree (1987). He points out that if the sophisticated cannot agree on what counts as a good answer there is little hope for the candidate. He ends the discussion with a provocative quote from William Cowper: 'and differing judgements serve but to declare that truth lies somewhere, if we knew but where'.

Sometimes a question educes from a student an interpretative framework that an examiner did not expect. This problem is more likely to occur in arts and in newer science subjects where the paradigms of knowledge are not fixed. Should the interpretative framework be rejected? If the framework can legitimately be derived from the question then probably not. The essay should be marked within the student's own framework. To do otherwise is to impose one's own interpretative framework when one should be encouraging students to evaluate and create their own frameworks. There then remains the deeper question, If students use different interpretative frameworks, can answers be compared? The arguments may be infinitely extensible; meanwhile one has to have a policy. The best one is: Use the student's interpretative framework if it is derived logically from the question.

---

1  Know your values and prejudices about style, punctuation, grammar, handwriting and particular ideologies or perspectives.
2  Know when you are likely to feel tired or irritable.
3  Plan and pace your marking.
4  Re-mark the first few essays that you did to check your consistency.
5  Don't be afraid to shift categories after marking.
6  If in doubt, give the furthest mark from the mid-point, but
7  Ask yourself, 'Is this really a fail?'
8  Have a set of criteria. Keep them simple.
9  Consult them regularly.
10  Give the students the criteria.
11  Get a colleague to second mark a sample of your essays.
12  If there is a serious disagreement of more than one grade, get an independent marker to mark using the same criteria.

See also Figure 4.6.

---

*Figure 5.2* Suggestions on marking essays

The school of metaphysical poets sprang up closely after the period of the flowering of drama, following the decline of the theatre of Shakespeare, Marlow [sic] and Johnson. We know that Donne was a great frequenter of plays In his youth: and a drama had a profound effect on his work. This, together with the fact that Donne was a revolutionary, reacting violently against the formal conventionalism which preceded him, shows why the dramatic element is so important in his poetry.

One examiner gave this an 'A' mark and he wrote 'Good opening' in the margin. A second examiner wrote in the margin 'No, irrelevant' and failed the answer.

Husbands (1976) in a discussion of 'ideological bias' has this to say:
  It could be that the free enterprise economist, for example, having read a rather mundane effort that was nonetheless written from his own standpoint, says, 'What a pedestrian attempt. 45, I suppose. But at least he doesn't drop a lot of leftist slogans. OK, 52.' Or the Marxist sociologist may read a strongly pro-functionalist effort and conclude, 'Quite well argued, 62 maybe. But he refuses to get to grips with the real issues. 57.'

From Rowntree (1987)

*Figure 5.3* Fair marking

Should one mark individual answers to the same question and then proceed to answers to the next question? For purposes of reliability the answer is yes. Marking all the answers to a question reduces the halo effect of other answers in the paper. There is a temptation to mark over-generously the last answer on a paper if the rest of the paper is good. For purposes of validity the overall performance in a paper may be a better measure. A weaker student may use the same material for more than one question, a better student may cross-refer in his or her answers and thereby show a much better grasp of the subject. One possibility is that the same tutor marks answers to each question separately and a small proportion of the marks are allocated for overall performance. The papers are then moderated by a second marker. The disadvantage of this approach is that a tutor may not have sufficient expertise in the range of topics or he or she may be a tougher or more generous marker than his or her peers. Again the arguments are extensible. On balance it is better to mark answers to each question rather than answers in each paper.

## Use of criteria

The use of criteria for marking essays is sometimes hotly debated. Certainly, impressionistic marking based on implicit criteria can be fast but there is no way of judging whether it is linked to the outcomes of the course. On the other hand,

| Marks | Notes on the criteria |
|---|---|
| | **Interpretation and introduction** |
| 5 | States clearly the key issues and provides a framework for answering the question |
| 4 | Weaker version of 5. |
| 3 | Introduction is perfunctory or overlong. Framework is present but unclear. |
| 2 | Weaker version of 3. |
| 1 | Little or no attempt at an introduction or description of the framework. |
| | **Quality of argument** |
| 5 | Develops logical argument and marshals clearly the relevant ideas and evidence and their strengths and limitations. |
| 4 | Weaker version of 5. |
| 3 | Some aspects of argument and use of evidence are weak. |
| 2 | Weaker version of 3. |
| 1 | Major weaknesses in argument and use of evidence or no argument is discernible. |
| | **Use of evidence** |
| 5 | Uses and evaluates evidence. Shows connections between evidence and the framework of the question. |
| 4 | Weaker version of 5. |
| 3 | Some inclusion of irrelevant or unlinked material. |
| 2 | Weaker version of 3. |
| 1 | Most of the material is irrelevant or repetitive. |
| | **Presentation** |
| 5 | Correct and effective use of English. Referencing accurate. Legible. |
| 4 | Weaker version of 5. |
| 3 | Some minor errors in grammar, syntax and referencing. Fairly legible. |
| 2 | Weaker version of 3. |
| 1 | Several errors. Illegible. |
| | **Conclusions** |
| 5 | Draws together the strands of the argument. Creates a coherent perspective on the question and indicates tentative links to related deep issues. |
| 4 | Weaker version of 5. |
| 3 | Conclusions are clear and based on the argument and evidence presented. |
| 2 | Weaker version of 3. |
| 1 | Little or no conclusion or not based on the argument and evidence in the essay. |
| | **Comments** |

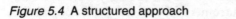

*Figure 5.4* A structured approach

detailed criteria can miss the point and a detailed marking scheme can give high scores to those who provide sets of facts rather than coherent arguments. So one should look for simple criteria which provide feedback to students, are easy to use and allow links to be made to outcomes and to the marking of other examiners. Examples of different approaches are given in figures 5.4, 5.5 and 5.6. Figure 5.4 is a structured approach and Figure 5.5 is semi-structured. Figure 5.6 is an example of criterion-referenced grading. Criterion-referenced grading is usually faster and more reliable than criteria sheets. Other examples of criteria may be found in Gibbs *et al.* (1992), Hounsell and Murray (1992) and Hounsell (1995). Hounsell and Murray also provide suggestions on helping students improve their writing and the use of student self-assessment checklists. An example is given in Figure 5.7. You may wish to add particular criteria for assessing an essay in your own subject. However, be wary of specifying too much detail otherwise you will be giving the 'answers' away and thereby encouraging the students to adopt a surface approach. Whichever system you use, a personal comment and a grade are valued by students. They trust the grade more than the comments.

## Providing feedback

Three broad purposes for providing feedback on essays are:

- Improving written communication.
- Developing thinking.
- Strengthening the knowledge base.

---

Name (or code):
Essay title:
Module:

| Criteria | Comment |
| --- | --- |
| Relevance | |
| Style | |
| Critical skill | |
| Quality of argument | |
| Cohesiveness | |
| Opening | |
| Ending | |
| Score | |
| Global comment | |

---

*Figure 5.5* A semi-structured approach

Each subject has its own emphases. So descriptions offered here should be adapted for use in your subject.

1   Gets to the heart of the matter. Evidence of wide reading, analysed at depth to support arguments. All major points covered. Outstanding organisation and presentation for an undergraduate. Substantial evidence of personal interpretation. No irrelevant material. Correct referencing.

2.1   Wide reading. Issues understood and interpreted intelligently. Major points covered. Well organised and presented. Evidence of personal interpretation and a coherent argument. Material relevant. Correct referencing. Appraises critically each segment of the evidence and links them in a coherent informed argument. Hints at his or her personal interpretation.

2.2   Evidence of reading. Issues understood. Presentation and organisation clear. Most major points covered. Provides the evidence and reports views on it. In so doing provides a fairly coherent answer to the question. Correct referencing.

3   Provides evidence and reports views but does not relate them clearly to the question. A few major points not covered. Some evidence of organisation. Errors in referencing.

Pass   Some major points not covered. Contains much irrelevant material. Little evidence of organisation. The question almost ignored.

Fail   Very little evidence of reading or of understanding of issues. Insufficient or misinterpreted evidence and views. Jumbled. No or little attempt to answer question.

*Figure 5.6* The beginnings of some criteria

These purposes can be used as a framework for comments on a student's essay.

Some of the suggestions in Chapter 4 are relevant here. (See particularly 'Marking efficiently for summative and formative feedback' and 'Some other suggestions on formative feedback'.)

As well as an overview of the essay, one might offer a few detailed points for improving it. Some tutors provide comments in the margins, others use numbers in the margin that relate to comments on separate sheets. For long essays one can use numbers in the margins and a (returnable) audio cassette of comments. There are dangers in providing too many criticisms (an extreme serialist's weakness when marking) or in providing a vague comment that can not be translated into action (an extreme holist's weakness when marking). Figure 5.8 provides examples of tutor's comments which were provided by students in workshops.

**Covering information**
My title/cover page shows clearly:
  My name
  Course title and number
  Tutor's name
  The question I have chosen
  Date assignment handed in

**Introduction**
The introduction:
  Sets the question topic against a wider background
  Clarifies my understanding of the question/topic
  Defines key or problematic terms
  Outlines the approach I will be taking to the question/topic

**Main text**
In the main body of the assignment:
  My key points are clearly presented
  The points I make are systematically backed up by facts/evidence/
  examples/arguments
  Quotations and references to other works are accurately cited
  Any diagrams, figures or tables are labelled properly

**Conclusions**
The conclusion:
  Brings together the main points
  Links back to the question/topic
  States clearly my conclusion(s)

**Style and presentation**
Overall, the assignment:
  Reads clearly throughout
  Makes correct use of spelling, grammar and punctuation
  Accurately lists the background reading I have consulted
  Is within the word limits specified

From Hounsell (1995)

*Figure 5.7* Student checklist

One can build up a bank of selections from essays that illustrate important features such as good and bad openings, well-argued cases and not-so-well-argued cases. One can also use tutorials and some of the larger classes for feedback and opportunities for practice. One can use computer disks or electronic mail to receive essays and comment on them. Further details about using information technology in assessment are given in Chapter 13.

Beneath the practical task of providing feedback are issues of value, such as whether lecturers should try to improve the written communication of

Here are a few comments which were written by tutors on some essays by first-year undergraduates during their first term. The essays were approximately 2,000 words long.

1 C+. C–. Fine
2 Interesting attempt. C+. C–?
3 Opening lousy, main part OK. No conclusion. Give some refs. next time. C–.
4 C–. Good first attempt. Your real opening is on p. 2. Try to give your answer in the concluding paragraph and do provide more refs.
5 Your style of writing is appalling. Didn't you learn anything in school about essay writing? You have no conclusion, a vague rambling opening and insufficient references. This is a university department, not a kindergarten. C–.
6 Clarity of handwriting is no substitute for clarity of argument. You have neither. Need I say more? C–.
7 David. I've made some detailed comments below. The numbers refer to the relevant parts of the essay. The essay had the makings of a good essay but you need to state clearly in your opening the parameters of the essay. Do give your own answer and do provide references. These comments are important to bear in mind before writing other essays. C–.
8 Fine. C

*Figure 5.8* Tutors' comments on first-year essays

their students. Some lecturers regard the improvement of students' writing as someone else's problem, arguing that they have not been trained to do it. However, since almost all academics write, a strong case can be made for at least trying to teach students to write well. One can reflect upon one's own problems in writing and that of one's students; one can read a book such as Hounsell and Murray (1992), Clanchy and Ballard (1992), or Barrass (1978), which provides hints for scientists and engineers, and one can organise, or attend, a workshop on improving students' writing.

## MANAGING TIME: MARKING LARGE NUMBERS OF ESSAYS

As staff–student ratios deteriorate, the pressure of marking increases. Under these circumstances some colleagues use multiple choice questions as an alternative for some essay assignments. Others reduce coursework essays and rely more heavily on traditional written examinations. The more enterprising introduce some self- and group assessment and criteria and checklists for marking essays. Chapters 11 and 12 offer some suggestions on using self- and peer-assessment.

## Marking essays for summative purposes

The fastest and most reliable method of marking essays for purely summative purposes is *structured* impressionistic marking. The broad outlines of this method will be familiar to many readers. The procedure is as follows:

1 Establish a set of brief, precise criteria for each of the grades to be assigned.
2 Do some refresher training on a batch of essays that are closely relevant to the new topic being assessed. Perhaps a sample of a previous year's scripts or coursework could be used. Each essay should be read quickly for overall impression rather than detail. However, particular care must be taken with scripts written in difficult handwriting. (We sometimes wonder why word processors cannot be used in examinations.)
3 Each essay is marked twice *independently*. If grades of the two markers differ by more than one then a third person marks the script. A review and discussion is held at the end of the training session and the criteria adjusted if necessary.
4 The marking of the scripts or coursework is timetabled and it is undertaken in a few days. The first few scripts and the last few scripts of each day are marked again during the following day.

In the study by Mitchell and Anderson (1986) for the Association of American Medical Colleges, 20 markers marked 3,117 scripts in three days! Third marking was only required in just over 5 per cent of the papers. However, rather than following their approach, we suggest that you develop your own team approach, building in time for other activities each day and some time for slippage and review.

An alternative approach is to develop 'model' answers for each of the grades to be assigned. The examiner's task is to read the script quickly and match it to the closest model answer. This approach is more useful for essays in the sciences than in the arts. Creating model answers, particularly for the middle grades in arts subjects, is notoriously difficult. Indeed some would say that such an approach denies the value of creativity and independent thinking.

## Marking essays for feedback purposes

Marking essays for feedback purposes is more time-consuming than marking for grading. So when one has a large number of coursework essays to mark there is a temptation to drift towards marking for grading rather than providing feedback. The suggestions in Chapter 4 are relevant here (see particularly 'Managing time for feedback' and 'Marking efficiently for summative and for formative purposes'). Marking can be speeded up if students are required to word-process their essays. Criteria and checklists can also speed up marking as well as providing feedback. The fastest form of feedback is the global report which identifies the key characteristics (strengths and weaknesses) of different grades of essays. Once written, the report can be modified for use with other cohorts or adapted for use with other questions. Some colleagues are experimenting with automated 'personal' responses. They have a menu of responses which they code using a computer package, such as Filemaker Pro, and a file of the students' names. They select an appropriate set of comments and print them in the form of a letter to each student. The system also enables them to store marks, to keep track of students' progress for tutorials and to provide follow-up work with weaker students. If their system is compatible with the departmental administrator's system, the marks can be transferred electronically during and at the end of each module.

### Regression to the 2.2

When students are required to submit several essays during a course based on modules, there is a tendency for the scores to bunch in the 2.2 class or on the borderline of 2.2 and 2.1. One way of correcting this tendency is to use the conversion table in Figure 5.9. If an essay counts for 10 per cent of the module marks and a student obtains an A the mark is 9. If the student obtains an A and the essay counts for 50 per cent of the module mark then the student receives 39. The table is based on the normal distribution, and was developed by Keith Thomas of the University of Ulster. It enables essay grades to be translated consistently into marks for the purposes of final degree classifications. Other suggestions on converting marks are given in Chapter 15 on examining.

## VARYING ESSAY METHODS

The variations in essay methods extend the range of writing skills as well as providing interest for students and lecturers. Most graduates, one hopes, will be expected to think and communicate ideas, summarise facts, evaluate evidence and offer persuasive solutions to problems. The core of this cluster of skills is essay writing within a discipline. To increase the probability of transfer of writing skills one might include within a degree course at least the first three of the following opportunities:

1 Writing essays on a subject-based topic for an expert, usually a lecturer.
2 Other forms of writing on a subject-based topic for an expert, usually a lecturer.
3 Writing on a subject-based topic for other audiences.
4 Writing on a non-subject-based topic for other audiences.

Figure 4. 2 contains some alternatives to standard essays. Further variations are offered here. Some of the variations may be used as alternatives to other forms of assessment and all may need adapting for use in your own subject.

| Class | Verbal description | Literal Grade | 10 | 12.5 | 15 | Total 16.33 | Mark 20 | Out 25 | Of: 30 | 33.33 | 35 | 40 | 50 |
|---|---|---|---|---|---|---|---|---|---|---|---|---|---|
| 1 | excellent | A+ | 10 | 12.5 | 15 | 16 | 20 | 24 | 28 | 30 | 32 | 38 | 47 |
| | | A | 9 | 11 | 13 | 14 | 17 | 20 | 24 | 26 | 27 | 31 | 39 |
| 2.1 | very good | A− | 8 | 10 | 12 | 13 | 15 | 18 | 21.5 | 24 | 25 | 29 | 36 |
| | | B+ | 7 | 8.5 | 10 | 11 | 13 | 16 | 19 | 21 | 22 | 25 | 32 |
| 2.2 | good | B | 6 | 7.5 | 9 | 10 | 12 | 15 | 18 | 19 | 21 | 23 | 29 |
| | | B− | 5.5 | 7 | 8 | 9 | 11 | 14 | 16.5 | 18 | 19 | 22 | 27 |
| | | C+ | 5 | 6.5 | 7.5 | 8 | 10 | 13 | 15 | 17 | 18 | 20 | 25 |
| 3 | moderate | C | 4.5 | 6 | 7 | 7.5 | 9 | 12 | 14 | 16 | 17 | 19 | 24 |
| | | C− | 4.5 | 5.5 | 6.5 | 7 | 8.5 | 11 | 13 | 15 | 15 | 18 | 22 |
| P | marginal | D+ | 4 | 5 | 6 | 6.5 | 8 | 10 | 12 | 13 | 14 | 17 | 21 |
| | pass | D | 4 | 5 | 6 | 6.5 | 8 | 10 | 12 | 13 | 14 | 16 | 20 |
| | | D− | 4 | 5 | 6 | 6.5 | 8 | 10 | 12 | 13 | 14 | 16 | 20 |
| F | fail | E | 3 | 4 | 4 | 5 | 6 | 8 | 10 | 11 | 12 | 14 | 18 |
| | | E | 2 | 3 | 3 | 3 | 4 | 5 | 6 | 6 | 7 | 8 | 10 |

The higher grades for marks out of small totals are scaled to counteract regression to the mean.

*Figure 5.9* Table for the conversion of literal grades into marks

## Short answer questions

Short answer questions usually require an answer of less than 100 words or 10 lines of problem solving. Often they are set as three linked questions. They are useful for sampling abilities to:

1 select crucial evidence
2 explain succinctly methods, procedures and relationships
3 present arguments briefly
4 describe limitations of data
5 formulate valid conclusions
6 identify assumptions
7 formulate hypotheses
8 formulate action plans.

Good short answers are not easy to set or to establish criteria for. They may be time-consuming to mark but, perhaps as a consequence, their reliability is high. The characteristics of good short answer questions are that they specify precisely the organisation and structure of the response required. The more precise the specification, the greater the reliability. An example of a short answer question is given in Figure 5.10. Multiple choice questions can be used instead of short

---

You accompany some university history students who decide to spend their elective in Barbados diving for sunken treasure; they hire a diving suit and breathing gear and set out for a sunken wreck lying at a depth of 120 feet, a mile offshore. One of them descends and air is pumped to him; he locates the wreck and explores it for two hours before deciding to ascend. Unfortunately his boot gets caught in the wreckage and it takes him another half hour to extract it, during which time he becomes panic-stricken at the approach of a neighbouring shark. He drops his weighted belt and rises rapidly to the surface. On being hauled into the boat he complains of severe pains in his elbows and knees; breathing is painful and he soon complains of headache and double vision.

1  What are the arterial gas pressures when he is at the bottom?
2  What happens to the body gases as he rises?
3  What are the mechanisms involved in the symptoms?
4  Why did central nervous symptoms occur early?
5  What are you going to do?

Note: This problem has been used in the pre-clinical unit on respiration at McMaster Medical School, Ontario. It is used to link pre-clinical stages in a curriculum. It can be used as an aid to learning or for examination purposes. The principles underlying the assessment procedure can be used in many subjects. Why not design such a question? Give it to the students as an assignment or try it out with them in a tutorial or seminar.

---

Figure 5.10 'Sunken Treasure'

answer questions but multiple choice questions are more difficult to write (see Chapter 6). When only a small number of students are involved it is wasteful to prepare MCQs, but beware of setting short answer questions which are too trivial or too complex. Neither trivial or complex questions discriminate between students in the middle range and complex questions can be difficult to mark reliably.

### Modified essay questions

Essentially, this technique consists of a set of linked short answer questions. MEQs may be presented in a booklet, or preferably on a computer screen so that backtracking is not possible. They are used in medicine to assess competence in patient management but they may be used in any subject: history, social work, law for example. Examples are given in figures 5.11 and 5.12. Figure 5.11 is a value question and Figure 5.12 provides an excerpt from an MEQ devised by Dr Jean McPherson of the Facuty of Medicine, University of Newcastle, Australia. Minimum levels of competence can be set for MEQs. For example, the minimum level of competence for the MEQ in Figure 5.11 is that the student is aware of excessive trauma or defect in normal haemostatic regulation, knows that it may be inherited or acquired and explores the family history, including bleeding on other occasions from other sites. An extended example of an MEQ prepared by Dr Elizabeth Wilkinson, Queen's Medical Centre, Nottingham is given on the next few pages. The break lines indicate separate pages:

### Respiratory Diseases in General Practice

1 Do NOT look through this booklet before you start writing.
2 You will have ¼ hour in which to answer 6 questions, after which there will be a discussion. Answers should be brief.
3 Do not alter what you have written. Answers are entered in the spaces provided.

1 Mr T. H., an engineer aged 53, is a large man with a bluff, hearty manner. He consults you, as a general practitioner, saying he has recently arrived in Nottingham and wants to register with you. 'By the way, doc', he says, 'I want some more of my pills – the Cyclospasmol or whatever they're called.'

Some doctors resent patients calling them 'doc'. Why might this be?

2 He has been taking this drug continuously for the past year for 'labrynthitis', by which he means occasional episodes of dizziness and vomiting: from time to time he has attended the ENT out-patient clinic of a teaching hospital in another city.

What considerations guide your information-gathering in the immediate next part of this consultation?

3 Clinical evidence leads you to believe he has a mild bronchitis. In addition to prescribing for him, you give him an 'Insurance Line', excusing him from work for a week. His disability seems relatively mild and you confidently suggest that he should be fit to resume his work on the following Monday without further consultation. However, on the Monday, instead of returning to work he comes to see you. As he enters, you wonder why he should be consulting you at this particular time. Give three possible reasons for this consultation.

i.

ii.

iii.

4 'Your treatment's done no good, doc' he says, a bit huskily. 'I'm no better.'

Clinical examination reveals no new findings: he still has scattered bronchi in both lung fields.

What do you see as an appropriate next step in his management?

5 Having referred him for a chest x-ray at the Mass Miniature Radiography Unit, you receive the following report: 'Right hilum and right paratracheal shadow: refer to chest clinic', and the possibility of lung cancer is raised in your mind.

That afternoon, before you have had time to take action, he puts in a house call. 'My cough is worse', he says aggressively, 'I feel bloody awful – and I've had a letter from the clinic. I've got to go and see them. Why? What is it, doc?'

List three factors governing your response to his question.

i.

ii.

iii.

6 His wife, a rather pretty woman, who looks much younger than her husband, is obviously very worried, but chatters away brightly in an effort

to conceal her anxiety, 'Oh, you'll be all right Tom', she says. Then – turning to you for reassurance – she adds, 'Of course he will, won't he doctor?'

What response do you make to her?

---

**Page 1**

1 Do NOT look through this booklet before you start.
2 Answer briefly each of the four questions in turn, completing each one before moving to the next.
3 Do not go back and add to or alter what you have written.

**Page 2**
It is your night off, and you are relaxing at home. At 22.30 you are startled by the sound of breaking glass and crumpling metal outside your house. You rush out and, in the dark, dimly discern a small shattered sports car on the pavement, wedged between the wall and a lamp-post.
*List but do not elaborate on the main points in your plan of action, putting what you consider to be the most important actions first.*

**Page 3**
The car lights are still lit and in their glow you see a sole occupant trying in vain to get out through the off-side door, which is jammed. Petrol is pouring out from the shattered tank. Already passing cars have stopped and people are running towards the scene of the accident.
*What immediate specific actions do you take, and why?*

**Page 4**
As the driver stumbles out though the near-side door he says, 'It's all right, I'm a doctor.' You recognise him as one of your partner's patients who is working as a pre-registration house physician in the local hospital, half a mile down the road. His breath smells strongly of alcohol and he says in an over-deliberate way – 'Course, I'm under the influence – had six pints – was going too fast – skidded – lost control – bang!' Miraculously, he appears to have escaped without any physical injury, though he is pale and shaken.
*What do you consider you should do next?*

**Page 5**
In fact you run him up to the accident department of the hospital where he works and leave him with the duty surgical registrar. On your return home, half an hour later, you find the scene of the accident swarming with police, firemen and break-down personnel. As you put your car away you wonder if you have discharged completely your responsibilities.
*List but do not elaborate upon the various factors which influence your decisions about your next actions.*

---

Based on a problem devised by Professor J.D.E. Knox, Department of General Practice, University of Dundee

*Figure 5.11* 'Prang'

Mrs Robyn Fields, aged 32, brings her eight-month-old son, Andrew, to you because of bruising, which has been concerning her for several weeks. The infant has large bruises over the limbs and several smaller bruises on the trunk.

Question 1
a) State the possible causes of this problem, basing your answer on the likely mechanisms.

b) For each general cause in a), describe the key features you seek in the history or examination.

Time: 10 minutes.

Cumulative Time: 10 minutes

*Figure 5.12* Extract from an MEQ

As well as assessing likely actions or interpretations, MEQs can also assess processes of thinking and underlying attitudes. This is both a strength and a weakness. A strength in that they provide an aid to diagnosing thought processes and attitudes, a weakness if they are used to penalise attitudes or approaches that are not necessarily wrong but may be different from those of the assessors. To minimise those problems, the draft MEQ should be piloted with experienced judges and a mark scheme devised on the basis of the agreed acceptable and unacceptable answers.

The question is often asked whether MEQs are reliable and valid. The answer, as usual, depends on the particular MEQ and its use. Fabb and Marshall (1983) provided evidence of a high degree of agreement between markers and evidence that experienced doctors are better at MEQs than trainees. Freeman *et al.* (1982) showed that performance in MEQs improved during medical training. Taken together these findings suggest that MEQs are reliable and valid.

MEQs may also be used as a structured learning task in seminars and as a basis for a lecture discussion class and even for assessing the performance of a group. There is much to be said for using MEQs in this way, particularly if MEQs are to form part of the summative assessment of the students.

### Writing for different audiences

One way of encouraging students to extend their range of writing skills is to set and discuss with them tasks of writing for different audiences. In carrying out these tasks students are likely to increase their understanding and their skills of persuasion and negotiation.

For example, instead of setting the question, 'Discuss ultrasonic methods of non-destructive testing with particular reference to oil pipe lines in the middle East', one could set the question, 'You have been invited to give a 20 minute presentation to a group of Chartered engineers on the merits of ultrasonic testing. All the chartered engineers are concerned with ways of simplifying and improving techniques of maintenance of pipelines in Kuwait. Set out your proposed talk in expanded note form using heading and sub-headings. You may use diagrams and sketches. You may include any questions for discussion that you might use with the group of engineers.'

## The presentation and essay

A student presents a seminar paper – not merely reads it aloud. It is discussed by the seminar group and they offer comments and suggestions upon it. The essay is then re-written and submitted for assessment. This approach provides feedback during the process of writing, which is more likely to be used by the student than advice offered after the essay has been marked.

## The paper and essay

A student presents a plan and draft paper on which feedback is given by the tutor. It is then re-submitted in its final form for summative assessment only. Again this method provides feedback at the point of learning.

## Some other alternatives

Other alternatives that are used are:

• The students choose their own essay titles and marks are given for the choice of title as well as the essay.
• The student chooses the topic and the preliminary title with a little advice from the tutor. The student then submits a long essay or dissertation on the theme with its final title. Tutorial advice is given during the writing phase.
• A book review.
• An abstract of an article.
• A brief annotated bibliography.
• A briefing paper for a politician.
• A report for a newspaper based on the student's research.
• A series of questions and answers based on the student's own essay or paper.
• The design of a case study.
• The recommended 'solutions' to a case.
• Case study notes and their implications.

## ACTIVITIES

5.1 Read the brief essays given in Figure 5.1. Assign marks and write a comment that justifies your mark on each essay. You may use your usual system of marking, A, B, C, D, E or A, A–, B+ etc. Compare your marks (and marking system!) and comments with those of a few colleagues. How could the essays be improved within the constraint of 250 words? In the group discussion list the different marks awarded and reasons for the marks. What are the implications of the range of marks awarded for each essay for the processes of assessing student essays and for the awarding of degrees?

5.2 Identify a set of criteria for grading essays. Then write two short essays on a topic in your field. Circulate the essays amongst a group of colleagues and ask them to mark the essays using the procedure described above and the criteria that you have invented. Compare your results and discuss how the procedure might be improved. Record the time taken to mark the essays in this way.

5.3 Read the comments in Figure 5.7 and decide which one would be most likely to help a student to improve his/her essay writing. Which comment did you like and which did you dislike most? Have you ever asked your students what comments they find helpful? What was their reply? Compare your views with those of a few colleagues.

5.4 Is it better to spend your time in thorough preparation of lectures but less thorough marking or vice versa? Compare your views with those of a few colleagues.

5.5 Look through the following sets of short answer questions and comment on the quality of the questions.

1  a) Write a paragraph on stress amongst academics.
   b) Identify three major features of a department which are likely to produce stress in its academic staff.

2  Identify three assumptions underlying this assertion: 'Teachers are born, not made, so we should not waste time on attempting to teach academics how to teach or assess students' work.'

3  Identify two limitations of this approach: 'I only award a First to a student who teaches me something that I did not know.'

4  a) Appraise how research publications are used, in practice, in your university for promotion from Lecturer to Senior Lecturer (or from Senior Lecturer to Principal Lecturer).
   b) Appraise how teaching, in practice, is used for promotion from Lecturer to Senior lecturer (or from Senior Lecturer to Principal Lecturer).
   c) On the basis of a) and b) draw up a grid that shows the similarities and differences in approaches to appraising research and teaching.

5 a) Which heart chamber is liable to become enlarged if there is a narrowing of the tricuspid valve?

   b) What abnormality of the normal heart shadow in a postero-anterior chest X-ray would such an enlarged chamber produce?

5.6 Devise a few MEQs and try them out in tutorials or seminars with students or colleagues or as a coursework assignment. If you are meeting with other colleagues to discuss the activities in this book, then compare your experiences of using the MEQs as a teaching aid and assessment method.

5.7 Which of the essay methods and variations outlined in this chapter do you use? Which do you consider are worth exploring further for use in your courses or modules?

5.8 What counts as a first class essay in your subject? Set out your criteria for a First, 2.1, 2.2, Third, Pass or Fail (six-category system).

5.9 How far should we demand a common standard of knowledge and how far should we allow individual freedom of expression in coursework and examinations?

5.10 How far do you want to develop:

- A student's capacities to understand and communicate your subject to other subject specialists.
- A student's capacity to understand and communicate your subject to other audiences.
- A student's capacity to understand and communicate other topics to other audiences.

What proportions of the assignments and marks in your courses are devoted to these three communication tasks?

5.11 How should a committed post-modernist mark and grade essays?

# Chapter 6

# Multiple choice questions

In this chapter we provide an outline of multiple choice questions (MCQs), and we describe how to construct MCQ items. We offer suggestions on the format of MCQ tests and summarise the technical aspects of MCQ tests. Further information on MCQs may be found in Chapter 13.

## INTRODUCTION

Multiple choice questions are attractive to those looking for faster ways of assessing student learning. But there is a price. First, one has to invest time in the design and preparation of multiple choice questions and second, the design of multiple choice questions is challenging if one wishes to assess deep learning.

Multiple choice questions consist of a question followed by alternative answers from which the student selects the most correct alternative or alternatives. The possibilities may be binary such as True – False or Yes – No. Otherwise, the question may require a choice from a set of three, four or five alternatives or a matching of various assertions and reasons. It used to be thought that four or five alternatives per item were necessary for a standard MCQ. However, recent evidence indicates that three choices are sufficient and, of course, it is easier to prepare two plausible distractors than three or four (Owen and Freeman, 1987).

In the United States, MCQs are used widely for selection purposes in undergraduate courses. They are known as objective tests although they are only as objective as the test constructor makes them. As indicated, MCQs provide faster ways of assessing larger groups of students. MCQs enable one to sample rapidly a student's knowledge of a field and they may be used to measure deep understanding. High quality MCQs are not easy to construct. But the time spent in constructing them can be offset against time taken to mark them. Non-specialists can mark MCQs manually, on a PC or Mac or they may be marked by optical readers attached to a micro-computer or mainframe. The use of computers enables item profiles, group profiles and score analyses to be undertaken. Refinement of the MCQ tests can also be carried out quickly and easily. Further details of the use of computers are given in Chapter 13.

A common criticism of MCQs is that they encourage guessing. However, the effects of guessing can be eliminated if it is thought necessary. More interestingly, guessing can be encouraged and measured, if this is thought to be a useful skill.

MCQs are not only useful for summative purposes. The print-out of results can be given to students together with directions to the relevant literature. The results of MCQs can inform and assist one's course planning and teaching. They may be used in lectures, seminars and tutorials and for revision purposes. Their use in teaching improves test-wiseness as well as learning and thereby increases the reliability of the assessment procedure. Sometimes increasing test-wiseness is thought to be questionable yet if one is going to assess learning in a particular way then one should give students the opportunities to learn and be assessed in that way. As Ebel and Frisbie (1986) put it, 'More error is likely to originate from students who have too little rather than too much skill in test taking.' As an aside, Smith (1982) indicates that the use of MCQs in this way can develop self-confidence as well as test-wiseness.

## CONSTRUCTING STANDARD MCQS

(You may wish to try Activity 6.1 before reading on.)

The essential guidelines for preparing MCQs are given in Figure 6.2. Further details on preparing MCQs and other tests may be found in Gronlund (1988).

## EXTENDING MCQS

The standard form of MCQ provides one set of choices per item. The simplest form is the true/false item, e.g. 'Sex is the same as gender. *True/False.*'

The multiple true/false can be used in sequences and thereby test more sophisticated understanding. The sophisticated examples may be designed for use on

| Stem | initial statement or question |
|---|---|
| Option | the alternatives |
| Key | correct answer(s) |
| Distractors | options other than correct answers |
| Faculty index | number of students giving the correct response to an item |
| Favoured wrong response | the most common wrong response by a group of students |
| Discrimination | measure of difficulty of the item |

*Figure 6.1* Some common terms in MCQs

---

1  Keep a notebook to jot down possible items.
2  Collect items from others.
3  To develop challenging MCQs think of the problems first and translate into MCQs – and check.
4  Avoid 'not' and 'always' in the stem.
5  Use plausible distractors.
6  Put the drafts on one side for a few days.
7  Revise them.
8  Try them on a critical friend.

Next, ask yourself the following:

1  What does the question test?
2  Is the question important enough to be asked?
3  Have all the responses got some plausibility?
4  Is the wording precise enough?
5  Are all the responses about the same length?
6  Are the lettering and numbering consistent?
7  How am I going to use the results of the test?
8  Do the items relate closely to the objectives of the module?

---

*Figure 6.2* Guidelines for preparing MCQs

micro-computers. Alternatively, one can require a student to uncover a particular option which includes instructions for uncovering the next instruction. The problem may be presented as a specially designed paper and pencil test. The results of such problems provide not only a score but a pathway of thinking through the problem. The paths that students take may be used for diagnostic purposes, to identify the thorough but pedestrian student from the efficient problem solver. True/false items are sometimes presented in a more complicated form (the multiple completion) in which the students are given a set of options and then required to identify the sub-set or sub-sets of the options that are correct. This procedure is often unnecessarily complicated, as example 2 below shows.

One can use standard MCQs in sequences of questions about a problem, a case or a case study and as a method of easing the marking of mathematics-based problems. They may be used in conjunction with diagrams, graphs, tables of data and extracts from articles, texts or research findings. They may be used to ask for the best answer rather than the correct answer. MCQs can be a useful form of self-assessment, particularly if the reasons for the answers and suggestions for follow up reading are provided. The system of self-assessment and guidance can be easily computerised.

A wide range of MCQs is provided in volume 2 of Brown and Pendlebury (1996). Gold *et al.* (1991) lists examples in geography which provide useful pointers for other subject specialists, and many instructors' manuals for US textbooks provide MCQs. The examination papers at A level in many subjects use various forms of MCQs which may be adapted for use in first-year courses.

Students should be given opportunities to practise the more complex forms of MCQs before they are used in summative tests; otherwise the results might be due as much to test sophistication as to knowledge and understanding. Some examples of different types are provided below.

## 1 Standard MCQs

The examples are taken from an MCQ devised by MacDonald Ross (1996). Its purpose, which was declared, was to test whether students had read and understood the set text for the introductory course on philosophy. This approach neatly by-passed the issue of whether a viewpoint was true or false. Instead, it focused upon the claims made by an author. The essays tackled in the introductory course tested other student capabilities. A similar approach could be used in many arts subjects.

For each question, strike through the letter (a), (b) or (c) to show what you believe to be the correct answer.

1 The correspondence of a statement with reality is a criterion of the statement's being:
(a) empirical,
(b) true,
(c) valid.

2 A meaningless sentence is:
(a) false,
(b) partly true and partly false,
(c) neither true nor false.

3 'The cat is on the mat' and 'The cat is on the mat' are distinct tokens of the same:
(a) type,
(b) proposition,
(c) cause.

4 'Saturday is in bed' is an example of:
(a) a self-contradiction,
(b) a category mistake,
(c) a proposition.

## 2 True/false based on case-histories

In the following question the examiner is assessing whether the student can apply his/her knowledge to a particular case. The approach may be adapted for use in many subjects.

1 A 45-year-old asthmatic woman who has lived all her life in Glasgow presents with a goitre of 4 years' duration and clinical features suggestive of hypothyroidism. Likely diagnoses include:

(a) iodine deficiency
(b) dyshormonogenesis
(c) drug-induced goitre
(d) thyroid cancer
(e) autoimmune thyroiditis.

*Answer and explanation*

Correct answers: true (c) and (e); false (a), (b) and (d).

The student has to appreciate that in Great Britain iodine deficiency is not likely to be associated with hypothyroidism, that a 45-year-old patient with only a 4-year history is unlikely to have dyshormonogenesis, that asthmatic patients not uncommonly take iodine containing preparations which may result in a goitre, that hypothyroidism is not usually associated with thyroid cancer and that autoimmune thyroiditis typically is found in a middle-aged woman with hypothyroidism.

Example from Harden and Dunn (1981).

Note: Sometimes true/false items are complicated unnecessarily by requiring students to choose the correct set of options. Thus in the above example the instruction might have read:

The question below contains five suggested answers of which at least one is correct. Choose the answer:

1 if a, b, c, d are true and e is false
2 if a, b, c, d are false and e is true
3 if a, b, c, are true and d, e are false
4 if b, c, d are true and a, e are false
5 if b, c, e are true and a, d are false.

## 3 Items based on exceptions

This type is designed to encourage students to pick out the exceptions to a set of principles or findings. The approach could be used in questions in the sciences, law and social work.

All of the following statements about the influence of cardiovascular disease upon sexuality are true, EXCEPT:

(a) some patients have impaired sexual functioning following a myocardial infarction

(b) myocardial infarctions that occur during intercourse are often associated with unusual and stressful circumstances

(c) the most common reason for decreased frequency of intercourse after a myocardial infarction is anginal pain associated with intercourse

(d) there is a higher incidence of return to normal sexual activity by patients who receive exercise training and education than by those who are not involved in such programmes

(e) the spouse of a patient who has had a myocardial infarction needs to be involved in educational programmes as his or her fears can interfere with resumption of sexual activity.

*Answer and explanation*

The answer is (c). The most common reasons for a decreased frequency of sexual intercourse after a myocardial infarction are psychological. Patients who have had a myocardial infarction can have a decreased self-esteem and concerns about impotence. The stress associated with an unusual circumstance (e.g. an atypical sexual activity, inebriation, or a new sexual partner) is often responsible for myocardial infarction during intercourse. Exercise and educational programmes have been effective in helping cardiac patients resume a normal life, but the involvement of the spouse in these programmes is important.

## 4 Best answers

In many subjects answers are not right or wrong so much as poor, good, better or best (at present). MCQs, with a suitable instruction, can be used to discover students' knowledge of the best method, conclusion, etc. The following MCQs are based on a mini-case study. The correct answers require analytical skills, knowledge of relevant theories and judgement. It is important to read carefully the statement on which the questions are based.

*Directions*

Each question below contains five suggested answers. Choose the one *best* response to each question.

A community recognizes a drug problem among its youth and allocates $100,000 from the city's general funds to establish a treatment program. The money is enough to be useful but is insufficient to deal with the problem comprehensively. One approach is to use all of the money for de-toxification and intensive treatment of youthful addicts, a program of little benefit to the larger number of casual and experimental users. The other is to use the money for a combined drug education and surveillance program that will influence drug use among non-users and casual users but will do little to benefit those already addicted.

1  This case presents a conflict that can be analysed in terms of:
   (a)  autonomy versus beneficence
   (b)  beneficence versus nonmaleficence
   (c)  consequentialism versus nonconsequentialism
   (d)  utilarianism versus deontology
   (e)  different theories of justice.

2  Devoting money to the de-toxification of youthful addicts can best be supported by:
   (a)  the Rawlsian notion of devoting resources to benefit the least well-off
   (b)  the Nozickian notion of entitlements
   (c)  a utilitarian calculation of what will yield the greatest net benefit
   (d)  the Catholic doctrine of double effect
   (e)  an argument for compensatory justice.

3  Devoting money to a drug education and surveillance program can best be supported by:
   (a)  the classical idea of distributing social goods equally among all citizens
   (b)  the Nozickian notion of entitlements
   (c)  the principle of beneficence
   (d)  the ethical dictum, 'First, do not harm'
   (e)  the principle of respect for persons.

From Wiener, J.M. (ed.) (1987) *Behavioural Science* New York: John Wiley and Son

*Answers and explanations*

1  The answer is (e). In this case the basic question is how a limited amount of social good should be distributed between the two groups in need. Justice is the issue, and how one weighs alternatives depends on the theory of justice to which one subscribes.

2  The answer is (a). One of the fundamental principles of Rawls's theory of justice is that resources should be committed to benefit those in greatest need regardless of the cost that such an approach might have for those who are less needy. In this situation, the most acute needs are those of the addicts rather than those of experimenting or casual drug users.

3  The answer is (a). The argument to distribute resources among the numerically largest group who will benefit is egalitarian or democratic, an argument with broad appeal in contemporary western society. In this context the argument is not far from an entitlement argument, since in a democratic society, all are generally thought to be equally entitled to the benefits of citizenship.

Another example based on a case history is:

Select the best *initial* diagnosis for the following case(s)
(a) Alcohol abuse
(b) Schizotypal personality disorder
(c) Narcissistic personality disorder
(d) Dysthymic disorder
(e) Sociopathic personality disorder.

A flashily dressed young man is brought to a psychiatrist's consulting rooms by his fiancee who thinks he needs therapy. The couple argue about petty issues in the psychiatrist's presence. After the young woman leaves, the young man demands to see the psychiatrist again that afternoon, even though the psychiatrist explains his appointment list is full.

From Scully, J.H. (ed.) (1985) *Psychiatry* New York: John Wiley and Son

*Answer and explanation*

The answer is (c). The young man may be characterised by attention-seeking, demanding, shallow relationships and little empathy. Although sociopathy is possible there is no direct evidence in the case history. The young man demonstrates narcissistic personality traits which include an inflated sense of importance coupled with little concern for other people.

## 5 Matching items

Here the task is to match a statement and an item.

*Directions*

The groups of questions below consist of lettered choices followed by several numbered items. For each numbered item select the one lettered choice with which it is most closely associated. Each lettered choice may be used once, more than once, or not at all.

Match each statement below with the type of medication that it describes.
(a) benzodiazepines
(b) anti-histamines
(c) barbiturates
(d) neuroleptics
(e) tricyclic and tetracyclic antidepressant drugs.

1 These drugs may cause tardive dyskinesia if taken chronically.
2 There is low incidence of toxicity, but these drugs are not always effective.
3 Addiction rarely occurs with these drugs.
4 These drugs are indicated for endogenous anxiety and phobias.
5 There is high danger of tolerance, abstinence syndromes, and addiction.

*Answers and explanations*

The answers are: 1 – (d), 2 – (b), 3 – (a), 4 – (e), 5 – (c). Recent evidence indicates that few medical patients become addicted to benzodiazepines when the drugs are prescribed appropriately. Barbiturates, on the other hand, tend to cause intolerance, abstinence syndromes, and addiction. Anti-histamines can be particularly useful as anti-anxiety drugs or hypnotics in the elderly, but they are not as predictably effective as other medications and may cause anti-cholinergic side effects. In low doses, non-sedating neuroleptics (anti-psychotic drugs) may help to relieve anxiety in patients who fear sedation, but the danger of tardive dyskinesia must not be ignored. Anti-depressants may be very effective in the treatment of endogenous anxiety and phobias.

## 6 Assertion–reason

These questions provide an assertion and a reason. The student has to decide whether the assertion and reason are true and whether the reason is a 'correct' explanation of the assertion. Some examples from different subjects are given below. Typical instructions are:

Each question below consists of an assertion and a reason. Indicate your answer from the alternatives below by scoring out the appropriate letter. Your answer should be based upon the evidence considered in this module and not upon unfounded personal opinion.

|   | *Assertion* | *Reason* | |
|---|-------------|----------|---|
| A | True | True | Reason is a correct explanation |
| B | True | True | Reason is NOT a correct explanation |
| C | True | False | |
| D | False | True | |
| E | False | False | |

| *Assertion* | | *Reason* |
|-------------|---------|----------|
| The blood sugar level falls rapidly after hepatectomy. | BECAUSE | the glycogen of the liver is the principal source of blood sugar. |
| Increased government spending increases inflation under all conditions. | BECAUSE | government spending is not offset by any form of production. |
| Chloroform has a dipole moment. | BECAUSE | The chloroform molecule is tetrahedral. |

Based on Matthews (1981)

## How much time is needed to prepare MCQs?

The answer depends on how well you know your course materials, the objectives of the course and the students. Andreson *et al.* (1993) suggest that it would take 3 years to recoup staff time if MCQs were used with a class of 50 students. Their suggestion is not supported by the research literature. For example, Stalenhoef-Halling *et al.* (1990) compared the cost of developing and marking a true–false test and an open-ended test based on the same content and to achieve comparable reliability. 224 hours of tutors' time was required for the essay test and 159 hours for the true–false test. Our experience is that a 40-item test on material we are familiar with can be prepared in half a day, less if we have collected together examples of relevant MCQs. More complex MCQs take longer to set but, as one becomes more familiar with the format, one speeds up.

## SOME TECHNICAL ASPECTS OF MCQS

### Should guessing corrections be used?

Whatever the system of scoring it should be given to the students, for the strategies adopted by students will vary according to the rules of the game. If incorrect responses score minus 1 but no response scores nought, then some students will not guess and some will take a chance. Guesses may be intelligent, they may be based on partial information, mis-information or sheer ignorance. The formulae to correct these forms of guessing make many assumptions. The standard formula assumes all wrong responses are of the same value. It over-corrects for guessing by weak candidates and under-corrects when the distractors are obvious. Guessing corrections do not usually change the rank order or distribution of marks. If you must use the standard formula, it is:

$$CR = R - W/(K-1)$$

CR  =  responses corrected for guessing
R  =  number of right responses
W  =  number of wrong responses
K  =  number of alternatives per item.

We are sometimes puzzled by the obsession with using guessing corrections in objective tests but the lack of concern about improving the reliability of other forms of assessment. We also think that intelligent guessing may well be a skill that one wishes to encourage.

### Items and alternatives

The formula above indicates that as the number of alternatives increases so the effect of guessing decreases. However, in deciding on the number of alternatives per item there are other considerations, such as the time available for testing, the proportion of items requiring thought, the course specification being tested and last but not least whether one can think of sufficient meaningful distractors. For questions requiring thought we recommend three alternatives. Owen and Freeman (1987) in a well-designed experiment compared three and four alternative choices. The only significant differences were that three-choice items were preferred by students and they took less time over them.

MCQs are fatiguing, so, as a rule of thumb, the test time should never exceed 90 minutes. Allow a maximum of 40 items per hour for standard MCQs if higher levels of thinking are being assessed and fewer items if more complex MCQs are being used. If in doubt, pilot the items in lectures, or preferably, seminars.

### Arrangement of items and responses

It is better to arrange the items according to some acceptable classification of subject matter or teaching method than in order of item difficulty. If different types of MCQ are being used in a test it is better to group by type and within each type group according to subject matter or teaching method. One should also check the total number of keys and the pattern. For example, in a four-alternative test of 40 items one would expect each key to occur between 8 and 12 times and there to be no prolonged run of any one key.

### Pre-tests, post-tests and analyses

Pre-tests of new items are desirable but not always possible. None the less it is important to check for ambiguity and other faults in the design and instructions to students. Post-tests can, of course, be the pre-tests of the next use of the items. Three common item analyses that are useful are facility, discrimination and wrong answer analyses. Most computer-based programs provide these analyses but one should check which formulae they are based on. The following simple formulae can be used manually or with a spreadsheet program.

*Facility* refers to the ease or difficulty of an item. The formula is:

$F = R/N$

F equals facility
R equals the number of candidates who gave the correct response to the item
N equals the total number of candidates

$$1 - \frac{R}{N}$$

gives the difficulty of the item.

*Discrimination* is a measure of the degree to which an item discriminates between better and weaker candidates. The easiest formula for describing this is

$D = (H - L)/N.$

D = the discrimination of the item
H = the number of correct responses to this item by the top third of test scorers
L = the number of correct responses to this item by the bottom third of test scorers
N = the number of students in the sub-group.

For example, 90 candidates took a test. In the top 30, 20 got the item correct. In the bottom 30, 10 got the item correct so

$$D = \frac{20 - 10}{30}$$
$$D = 0.33$$

One can use the top and bottom quarter of test scorers if these are easier to calculate. However, be consistent in your choice of group sizes so that the discrimination indices are comparable.

D scores range from −1 to +1. Positive D scores are essential. So if an item yields a negative or near zero D then discard it.

An easy way of identifying *wrong responses* is to draw up a matrix for each item based on the alternatives and the responses of the top third, middle third and bottom third of candidates. You might like to try interpreting the matrices given in Figure 6.3, which is based upon Matthews (1981).

## Pooling MCQs?

Given the challenge of writing high-quality MCQs, it seems curious that with the exception of the medical colleges, few British learned societies or professional organisations have concerned themselves with designing and pooling MCQ items. Much would be gained from such an activity in terms of increasing expertise in curriculum development, teaching and learning as well as in assessment procedures. If you are interested in developing MCQs in your subject then you might consider forming a consortium of colleagues across universities. Another useful suggestion was provided by the EHE network of geographers. They organised a conference on MCQs. The registration fee was a set of MCQs on a topic. At the end of the one-day conference each participant was provided with a complete set of the participants' MCQs. It is worth exploring texts and instructor's manuals published in the United States and Australia. They often provide banks of items that may be adapted for use in one's courses. A level boards often set multiple choice questions and many of these might be adapted for first-year courses.

## MCQs or essays?

Should one use MCQs or essays? The answer depends on the time available for marking, costs and what one wants to measure. If one has large classes then

This shows which distractors (incorrect responses) attracted the greatest proportion of the students. It is often best set out in the form of a simple matrix showing how many students chose each response. (* indicates the correct response.)

|  | A | B* | C | D | Total |
|---|---|---|---|---|---|
| Top third | 2 | 27 | 1 | 0 | 30 |
| Middle third | 6 | 21 | 3 | 0 | 30 |
| Bottom third | 10 | 15 | 5 | 0 | 30 |
| Total | 18 | 63 | 9 | 0 | 90 |

F = 0.70, D = 0.40

|  | A | B* | C | D | Total |
|---|---|---|---|---|---|
| Top third | 20 | 8 | 0 | 2 | 30 |
| Middle third | 15 | 12 | 0 | 3 | 30 |
| Bottom third | 10 | 16 | 0 | 4 | 30 |
| Total | 45 | 36 | 0 | 9 | 90 |

F = 0.40, D = -0.27

*Figure 6.3* Favoured wrong responses

MCQs are worth considering for *some* of the assignments or examinations. The correlation between MCQs and essays is usually above 0.9 if corrections for reliability are made. (See Norman *et al.*, 1991.) However, high positive correlations do not imply that MCQs and essays are assessing the same range of capabilities. There is a highly positive correlation between height and weight in the general population but clearly they are different. One can use height to predict weight and the predictions are, for two thirds of the population, within plus or minus 5 per cent. Similarly one can use MCQs to predict essay scores on the same content or vice versa. However, to be fair to students, and to be perceived as being fair, it is better to use a mixture of essays and MCQs within and across modules.

## ACTIVITIES

6.1 Identify and discuss the weaknesses in the following MCQs.

   1 The Battle of Hastings took place in:
   a) Sussex
   b) 1066

   c) Hastings
   d) Early May
   e) Good weather.

2 The capital of Great Britain is:
   a) Brussels
   b) Washington D.C.
   c) London
   d) Brighouse.

3 It is not true that MCQ's cannot measure high-level cognitive ability:
   a) True
   b) False.

4 Styles in women's clothing in 1990 differed from those in 1909 in that:
   a) They were more beautiful
   b) They were shorter
   c) They showed more variety
   d) They were easier to live, work, move and play in and were generally less restrictive.

5 There are more grandfathers in the world than fathers.  True? False?

6 The essential characteristic of an item in an MCQ test is:
   a) It is based upon specific learning outcomes
   b) No subjective judgement is required in its marking
   c) It is based upon a verifiable fact or principle
   d) It consists of a statement or question with a set of items
   e) Subject matter and the alternatives are unambiguous.

6.2 Select a small topic from one of your courses and construct up to 10 MCQs based on stems of three- or four-choice alternatives. Vary the difficulty of the MCQs by including some items that require only simple recall, some that require more subtle distinctions and some that require application of knowledge to solve a new problem or issue. Discuss the items with a group of colleagues and students. (Note: three-choice questions are easier to invent for MCQs requiring thought.)

6.3 Meet with a few colleagues and select one or two of the more complex MCQs. Work independently on the production of a few examples of the types chosen and compare your results. Try the examples with a few students. Do provide clear instructions, particularly if the type of MCQ is unfamiliar to the students.

6.4 Read Figure 6.3 and compare the two matrices. Which is the better question and why?

# Chapter 7

# Assessing practical work

In this chapter we focus upon the assessment of practical work in laboratories although many of the suggestions that we offer may be applied to field work. The chapter begins with a brief review of research on practical work and an outline of how to conduct an audit of a laboratory course. An audit will provide you with a benchmark of the range of learning and assessment tasks of a course. To assist you to extend your approaches to assessment we offer some guidelines on assessing laboratory reports and notebooks and we provide some alternative approaches to the assessment of the outcomes of laboratory work and the way that students work in laboratories.

Practical work has a time-honoured place in the education of engineers, clinicians and scientists. Yet it is the most expensive and time-consuming part of any course (Elton, 1983). So at a time when departmental grants are being cut and demonstrators' time reduced, it is particularly important to ensure that practical work and its assessment are effective. Furthermore, practical work and its writing up occupies a substantial part of the work of students yet its importance is not always reflected in course marks.

The main principle underlying the laboratory and other practical work is that students learn more effectively when engaged actively in practical tasks. However, this principle has limitations. First, the task has to be perceived as meaningful and relevant by the students – otherwise involvement is minimal. Second, students need constructive guidance and feedback on their performance – otherwise learning is minimal. The goals of practical work are to:

- Improve technical skills relevant to the subject
- Improve understanding of methods of scientific enquiry
- Reinforce theory with practice
- Develop problem-solving skills
- Nurture professional attitudes.

If any proof is needed that laboratory teaching can improve technical skills it may be found in the carefully designed experiments of Yager, Engen and Snider (1969). They demonstrated that technical skills require practice but intellectual skills may be learnt as well in discussion settings as in the laboratory. Other studies show that the acquisition of technical skills requires practice and feedback over long periods but, once acquired, is well retained. Laboratory teaching fares less well in the development of understanding and methods of enquiry. The results from a comprehensive survey by Garratt and Roberts (1982) were equivocal. Hegarty (1982) concluded from her review that if the development of scientific enquiry is a major goal of laboratory teaching then there are three prescriptions:

1 Students cannot conduct meaningful enquiries in areas in which they have no background. Course planners should design activities that provide for prior learning of the basic concepts and laboratory skills that will be required.
2 If students are to conceptualise the processes of scientific enquiry as conducted by scientists (and engineers) there must be explicit teaching about what scientists do and the nature of scientific enquiry as well as any implicit teaching that may be embedded in enquiry/discovery oriented laboratory exercises.
3 If students are to experience the processes of scientific enquiry, course planners must design special learning activities. Laboratory cookbooks are not effective.

The use of the structures concerned with enquiry rather than recipe are also shown to be related to students' interests in laboratory work (Bliss and Ogborn, 1977; Bliss, 1990). Almost all the 'good' stories that they report are concerned with enquiry-based projects and almost all the 'bad' stories are concerned with laboratory disorganisation and cookbook approaches. When a course stresses verification and illustration it seems to promote reproductive learning. Indeed there is a risk that students in such laboratory courses will resort to superficial rote learning and store the knowledge gained as an isolated unit. Their beliefs and preconceptions are not modified by practical work that is based upon recipes (Tisher and White, 1986; Hegarty-Hazel, 1990). However, there is some evidence that the use of self-assessment procedures leads students to having a better grasp of what they do and why – even within the structure of verification and illustration (Daines, 1986).

It is perhaps those disquieting findings that have led to the development of alternative and augmented methods of laboratory teaching. These methods are, in essence, extensions of enquiry approaches which are used together to develop the full range of capabilities in laboratory work.

Observational studies of laboratory work show that talk is largely centred upon laboratory procedures and low-level discussion. Higher-level enquiry processes such as data interpretation or the formulation of conclusions were detected but uncommon. Even rarer were extended-thought questions and discussions of the nature of scientific enquiry (Hegarty, 1979; Hegarty-Hazel, 1990 and Shymansky, Kyle and Pennick, 1980). One study has explored styles of learning of students as manifested in experimental design in physical chemistry. Three styles of learning were identified:

*empiricists* whose methods of scientific enquiry were systematic,
*borderliners* who got to the heart of the problem but by random methods and
*dead-reckoners* who could only work to recipes

(Pickering and Crabtree, 1979)

These styles have affinities with deep and surface learning and they are almost certainly products of earlier learning strategies. It is likely that well-thought-out structures and course designs can shift students towards an empirical approach.

## AUDITING LABORATORY WORK

As a first step towards improving the assessment of laboratory work one can begin with an analysis of one's laboratory course. A useful starting-point is to cross-reference objectives, content and assessment of laboratory classes. A simple chart is given in Figure 7.1. The resulting analysis may reveal obvious features such as too frequent assessment of lab reports and less obvious features such as an absence of objective 7 and little evidence that objective 1, to instil confidence, is being fulfilled. The chart can form the basis for appraising the links between the aims of the module or course, the objectives and content of the laboratory classes and the objectives and methods of assessment. Each experiment need not be assessed and each objective need not be assessed by each experiment. If every objective is being used and assessed in every experiment then the course is probably over-loaded.

On the basis of the table you can decide which assessments may be omitted or modified, which assessments will be used for feedback purposes only and which assessments will be used for course assessment. You might decide to require only brief write-ups during laboratory classes plus one or two more detailed reports. You could use some experiments to develop self- and peer-group assessment work.

If you are interested in developing understanding, you might classify the range of experiments in your course using the category system given in in Figure 7.2. The key to the terms is given in Figure 7.3. Level 1 is demonstration without any practical work. It can be useful for exemplifying theory and developing understanding. Level 4 provides the best opportunities for developing deep, independent learning. Structured enquiry, level 2, is probably the most effective way of getting students to think within set parameters and safe procedures.

We have found only one published report of audits of laboratory classes (Meester and Maskill, 1993). They surveyed first-year laboratory classes in chemistry. You may wish to match the summary of their findings against your own laboratory classes.

1   One of 22 university departments provided introductory or summary talks on the laboratory.
2   Three of 22 allowed open access to labs if a demonstrator was available.

| Objectives of labs | Content and assessment for each lab class |
| --- | --- |
| | A   B   C   D, etc. |

1  To instil confidence
2  To learn basic practical skills
3  To familiarise with important standard apparatus and measuring techniques
4  To illustrate material taught in lectures
5  To train in observation
6  To train in making deductions from measurements and interpretations of experimental data
7  To use experimental data to solve specific problems
8  To learn some theoretical material not taught in lectures
9  To foster a critical awareness (e.g. extraction of all information from the data; the avoidance of systematic errors)
10  To help bridge the gap between theory and practical
11  To improve report writing
12  To stimulate and maintain interest in scientific methods

*Figure 7.1* Objectives, content and assessment

|  | Level | Aim | Materials | Method | Answer |
| --- | --- | --- | --- | --- | --- |
| Demonstration | 0 | Given | Given | Given | Given |
| Exercise | 1 | Given | Given | Given | Open |
| Structured enquiry | 2 | Given | Given part or whole | Open or part given | Open |
| Open enquiry | 3 | Given | Open | Open | Open |
| Project | 4 | Open ? | Open | Open | Open |

Based on Herron (1971)

*Figure 7.2* Levels of experiment I

3 Time scheduled for lab work in first-year courses varied from 70 to 330 hours. The mean was 160 hours.

4 Completing the practical work took from 100 to 380 hours. The mean was 195 hours.

5 Pre-lab preparation by students took 0–2 hours/lab class.

6 Post-lab preparation by students took 0–4.5 hours/lab class.

7 The number of skills and techniques taught was not related to the length of the course. Some shorter courses taught and assessed more skills than the longer courses.

8 The student–demonstrator ratio varied from 10:12–25:1. The mean was 15:1.

9 17 of 22 universities use one or more of: video-tapes, CAL, computer simulations, film loops, interactive video and specially prepared spreadsheets to augment laboratory work.

10 All universities relied heavily on written work for the assessment of practical work. About half include questions about the implications of the experiment. None assessed practical work directly. Some used oral reports as an adjunct to written reports.

11 Only two manuals provided a marking scheme for students. Five universities stated that detailed marking schemes for demonstrators were available.

12 Only two universities used structured worksheets rather than lab reports for students to complete. Sometimes the manuals provided very detailed guidelines but no examples of poor reports or common errors. In six of 22 manuals there was no guidance on how to write reports, even though students were required to write them. Their practical work was assessed on the basis of those reports.

13 Error analysis tended to be neglected.

14 About half the manuals did not contain a description of the course aims and objectives. Only six of 22 made explicit the aims and objectives of the individual experiments. Usually aims and objectives of an experiment were either buried in the introduction or not stated.

15 90 per cent of the experiments were at levels 0 and 1.

## ASSESSING LABORATORY REPORTS AND NOTEBOOKS

The customary method of assessing laboratory practical work is to mark the student's lab report after each experiment or at the end of the semester. Such an approach assumes that practical skills may be inferred reliably from written reports and that students should use exactly the same format for each experimental report. Unfortunately the marking of laboratory notebooks can be unreliable. For example Wilson (1969) in a study of laboratory assessment discovered a 25 per cent variation between sets of demonstrators who marked the same laboratory notebooks. However, rather than throw out the laboratory notebook it would be better to reduce such variability by using explicit criteria, double marking of samples of work and training demonstrators to be more effective assessors of laboratory learning.

You can save time and increase reliability by using a standard laboratory report marking sheet for each experiment (see figures 7.4 and 7.5). The guidelines may be adapted for particular experiments or they may be used for the whole set of experiments. Either way it is better to give the report sheets to the students before the practicals and to return them with their laboratory reports. When you have established the essential points that you wish to assess in each experiment, you can provide the students with an explicit directive:

> In this experiment, we want you to focus particularly upon the discussion and interpretation of your results, so do not describe in detail the procedure or data analysis. Instead, analyse the results and discuss their implications in the light of your knowledge of the topic. You may want to include a brief note on the limitations of the experimental methods.

You can vary the emphasis for each experiment. For example, you might ask students to focus primarily upon data collection or at other times ask them to describe calibration procedures. You can also provide students with a pro-forma that structures, directs and limits their report.

## STRUCTURED MINI-PRACTICALS

Mini-practicals provide a simple, effective method of assessing quickly a wide range of skills. They may be used in laboratory-based subjects or in person-based subjects such as social work, social psychology or law practice. The impetus for their use comes from the assessment of clinical competence in medicine although some assessment centres in industrial organisations also use them.

### Objective Structured Clinical Examinations

Objective Structured Clinical Examinations (OSCE) were developed by Harden and Gleeson (1979) and subsequently reported by Harden and Cairncross (1980). They are now widely used in medicine, dentistry, nursing and other health professions. A set of assessment stations is designed on the basis of the objectives of a course or module. In a typical OSCE, each station has a five-minute task. Examples of tasks are: taking readings from an EEG, interpreting a radiograph, identifying a malfunctioning heart from an audio-recording of heartbeats, taking a history of a patient, interpreting biochemical test results, diagnosing a patient's problem, selecting treatment, setting up a drip, identifying tissues.

The student is assessed at each station by a trained observer, trained interviewer, simulated patient, short answer question or mutiple choice questions. At the end of each five-minute interval, the student moves to the next station. Usually about 20 stations are used so in two hours 20 students can be assessed

**Demonstration** Usually done to demonstrate theoretical principles. The demonstrator is usually a lecturer or postgraduate student.

**Exercise** Tightly structured experiments designed to yield well-known results. Students learn to follow precise instructions and in so doing learn specific techniques of observation and manipulation. Careful reading of instruction can often reveal the answers required.

**Structured enquiry** Lightly structured experiments which require students to select materials and to develop procedures. Students develop problem-solving and interpretative skills as well as manual and observation skills.

**Open-ended enquiry** Students identify a problem, formulate the problem clearly, choose and design experimental procedures, interpret results and consider their implications. The constraints on the student may be time and the range of equipment and materials available. Open-ended enquiries use in miniaturised form the skills of the research scientist. They can be useful as a preliminary for project work.

**Projects** Based on long experiments or a series of experiments or field studies. The project may be selected by a student or offered by a supervisor or by local industry or the community. The end products may be a dissertation, design plan, model, computer program or simulation. They enable students to explore a field deeply, they develop initiative and resourcefulness, they may stimulate a student's intellectual curiosity and they also develop project- and time-management skills. Guidelines for project work are essential (see Chapter 8).

*Figure 7.3* Levels of experiment II

on 20 different tasks and have four rest periods. The 20 tasks can be interleaved so that two or more measures of the same set of skills can be taken. One can select tasks that are not easily assessed in other parts of a course or one can select key tasks.

OSCEs may be used for summative purposes or they may be used to provide feedback to students. The initial planning and organising of the first OSCE is time-consuming but once established, they may be used over and over again. The assessment tasks may be changed at each station for each group of students doing the OSCE. If the OSCE is primarily for feedback purposes, there may be no need to change substantially the content of the tasks.

### Performance Evaluation Guides

Performance Evaluation Guides were developed in Britain by Brown and Pendlebury (1996) to assess practical work in dentistry. The approach is also the

| Course Experiment title | | | | |
|---|---|---|---|---|
| Report sections | Guidelines* | Max mark | Your mark | Comments |
| Introduction | | | | |
| Method | | | | |
| Results | | | | |
| Discussion | | | | |
| Conclusion | | | | |
| General criteria | | | | |
| Accuracy | | | | |
| Presentation | | | | |
| Total | | 100 | | |
| Overall comments | | | | |
| Your notes and suggestions | | | | |

* This column is intended for emphasis of a key feature.

*Figure 7.4* Laboratory report sheet

basis of the Self-Assessment Manual of Standards in dentistry (SAMS) (ABGDP, 1992). A PEG consists of a set of explicit criteria that is usually pitched at four levels of competence. A PEG may be developed for any product, including designs, models and artefacts. The procedure for designing a PEG is given in Figure 7.6 and an example of a PEG in Figure 7.7. Both OSCEs and PEGs can be used to identify strengths, weaknesses and errors of a student or group of students. So they can be used for summative, formative or diagnostic purposes.

## OTHER METHODS OF ASSESSMENT

(We are indebted to Chris Butcher, Staff and Departmental Development Unit, University of Leeds, for many of the suggestions in this section.)

| Section | Briefing | Max Mark | Your Mark | Feedback |
|---|---|---|---|---|
| Introduction | | | | |
| Background | | | | |
| Methodology | | | | |
| Use of equipment | | | | |
| Results | | | | |
| Data analysis | | | | |
| Discussion | | | | |
| Conclusions | | | | |

*Figure 7.5* Laboratory report sheet

| Define the task | What should be achieved? How does it relate to the objectives of the course? What skills are required? |
|---|---|
| Analyse the procedures | Which aspects of the procedure are needed to achieve the most important desired outcome? |
| Define four levels of competence for the task for the target group of students (beginners/ final year students) | Unsatisfactory level Minimum level of competence Good level of competence High level of competence |

*Figure 7.6* Designing a PEG

|  | Descriptions | Aesthetics | Structural and biological integrity |
|---|---|---|---|
| Grade D | Unacceptable outcomes as a result of treatment or lack of treatment which has already caused irreversible damage to the patient's oral environment, or will cause severe damage in the future. | Restoration looks obviously false. No characteristics of natural morphology. Width, length and position of restoration incorrect. Shade is many units wrong and does not blend with the surrounding dentition. | Restoration made on a tooth with undiagnosed non-vitality. Restoration made on a tooth with inadequate root filling which would be easy to correct. Restored tooth has active apical pathology. |
| Grade C | Outcomes as a result of treatment or lack of treatment which have the potential for damage, or where reversible damage has already occurred. | Shade is incorrect by one unit. The core shows through body and neck zones. Black/green restoration margins. | Restoration made on a vital tooth with inadequate pulpal protection if the cavity is deep. Restoration made on a tooth with an inadequate root filling that would be difficult to correct. Restored tooth has non-active apical pathology which has not been treated. |
| Grade B | Outcomes which achieve the minimum acceptable standard below which there is a potential for damage to the patient. | Restoration can be seen by the professional observer but not by the patient or his or her friends. The patient is satisfied with the result. | Restoration made on a tooth with healthy pulp. Restoration made on tooth with healing apical area. |
| Grade A | Outcomes achieved by a standard of excellence where there are no clinical limitations imposed by affordability, time, or the patient's wishes. | The presence of the restoration cannot be detected by any observer 3 feet from the patient. The patient is extremely pleased with the result. | Restoration made on a tooth with healthy pulp. Restoration made on a tooth with technically proven root filling. Restoration is stable at try-in without cement. |

Based on ABGDP (1992)

*Figure 7.7* An example of a PEG

## Students as teachers

In addition, or as an alternative to the traditional laboratory report, one can ask the students to provide ideas and assistance for the next student group.

- Two things to watch out for during this experiment . . .
- Problems I encountered during this experiment and what I did to overcome the difficulties
- Mistakes that I wish I had avoided . . .
- Two things that are worth doing before the lab session are . . .
- Safe and acceptable short-cuts are . . .

Not only are these pointers useful to the students, but they can also give good ideas when you revise the experimental details.

## Students as diarists

The above ideas can be extended by asking students to keep a learning diary or log of their thoughts and reflections on doing the practicals and writing up. Often it is not so much the practical work as the reflection upon practical work that helps a student to develop.

## Design a follow-up experiment

Similarly, the students can be asked to design a follow-on experiment that improves or extends the work completed.

## Drafts

Some people refer to the lab sheets as recipes. In the same way the reports that students write are often recipe-like. Frequently, the reports lack evidence of thinking and originality. In addition to providing clear assessment guidelines, it is useful to promote the idea of passing draft reports to other students for feedback. This feedback can be used to improve the report prior to submission.

## Feedback and review

A means of reinforcing the learning from laboratories and practical sessions is to stage a review session. At this session, the students are required to look at their work and note down learning points. In addition, the lecturer can summarise the main points of the laboratory course and show the links between the various laboratory sessions in order to give the students a coherent picture. Assignments or examination questions can be set that are based on the methods of enquiry and findings and likely errors in the laboratory classes.

## Audience

The reports that students produce about the practical sessions are usually written with the lecturer in mind. In order that the students think more carefully about their audience, it may be appropriate to ask for a report for

- a consumer group
- a popular engineering/science/medical/ journal or a local newspaper
- a student lab book or lab sheet.

## Seminars

Instead of requiring a report for every practical, one can ask students to do an individual or team presentation at a seminar of an experiment or set of experiments. If laboratory space is scarce one can form seminar groups of, say, 12. Each trio does an experiment and reports findings, pitfalls and implications so that each seminar group has three 'vicarious' experiences of experiments and one 'real' experence. The seminars can be structured to develop understanding of methods of enquiry and interpretation of findings. Peer- and self-assessment can be used in addition to tutor assessment. (See Chapter 10 on assessing oral communication.)

## Poster sessions

A poster session based on the experiments carried out during a semester can be used as a group task. It may be combined with a presentation or it may be a stand in an 'exhibition' of posters. The posters can be peer- and/or tutor-assessed. This approach is used widely in many laboratory- and field-based subjects. Examples of checklists and procedures are provided in Chapter 8 on assessing projects.

## DIFFERENT LEARNING TASKS

As well as changing the assessment of conventional laboratory work, one can change the nature of laboratory work itself. This is not the place to discuss all the alternatives to laboratory work. Ogborn (1977) contains many observations on laboratory work from the standpoints of students, demonstrators, technicians and lecturers, and the work of Brewer (1985) contains valuable insights into developing deep active learning within the framework of laboratory work. Brown and Atkins (1988) has a chapter on laboratory work. Texts by Boud, Dunne and Hegarty-Hazel (1986), Hegarty-Hazel (1990), Exley and Moore (1992), Horobin and Williams (1992b), Moore and Exley (1994), Exley and Dennick (1996) provide examples of alternative approaches.

## Task rather than topic

Traditionally laboratory and workshop sessions are organised around topics. This is often convenient in that they can mirror the theoretical sessions and so allow the students to draw links. Alternatively, the content and/or concept could be presented as a problem to be solved:

• design of a procedure/protocol
• design of equipment
• equipment that is not functioning correctly
• a 'case study', i.e. a real-world problem from industry.

## Research labs

Include in each module an aspect of work requiring the students to carry out individual research. This could be as simple as finding out the accepted procedure from the literature, through to a mini-project that demands original thought. The emphasis here is to train the students in the necessary skills. They will require some support and guidance during the research lab.

## Designing experiments

Based upon the theory and the practised skills and procedures, the students could be asked to design an experiment to demonstrate x, test y, elucidate z, for another group of students with similar backgrounds to themselves.

## Method menus

Often we give students a range of practical tasks to do, and for each one write the procedure/method. This process has merit in that the students learn specific skills and protocols in each case. However, they may perform these instructions without thinking. In order to generate a more thinking approach, it may be possible to offer a series of sub-routines that have application across a number of problems. The students are then required to select appropriate sub-routines that assemble into the methods needed to solve the problems that are set.

Example for a kinetics laboratory in chemistry:

*Routines*

| | |
|---|---|
| using a water-bath; | measuring enthalpy changes; |
| using a conductivity meter; | using a pH meter; |
| using a colorimeter; | measuring optical properties. |

*Problem 1*

The inversion of sucrose (an optically active molecule) by dilute acid is temperature sensitive – true or false?

*Problem 2*

The conductivity of a strong acid, as it is neutralised by a weak alkali, decreases in a linear fashion with respect to added alkali – true or false?

Both of these problems will require the students to select appropriate routines and then rehearse the skills.

## Mosaic

Each practical session contributes to a larger problem that has been set. For example, geology students may be given a map of an island. Each experiment in the course is designed to elucidate one aspect of the geology of that island. Over time the students gain the information to answer a 'bigger' question that integrates a number of the different aspects that have been covered in the practical sessions.

## Alternative media

Rather than the standard laboratory sheets, consider alternative media for introducing work, providing data, scene-setting, etc. Tapes, slides, videos, photographs, books and articles have all been used to effect. For example, Chris Butcher of the University of Leeds designed a video that provided instruction in the use of a complicated piece of equipment that modelled an industrial process. The students had to use the equipment, but more importantly, the idea was to see the outcomes of changing variables and conditions. The video ran for the two-hour lab sessions, with instructions to pause or turn off at appropriate times in order that the equipment could be used. The video also acted as a timer for the experiment as it was essential to maintain a fairly brisk pace.

In another instance, a series of enlarged photographs of the views through the eye-piece of a polarimeter were used to instruct students in the correct use of the equipment. Rather than trying to describe what to look for, or what it ought to look like, the photographs were used: 'At balance, it should look like this (photo 1), . . . but if it looks like this (photo 2) then it means that . . . or if this is what you see (photo 3) then it needs adjusting/there is an air bubble in the specimen tube . . . '.

Further uses of multi-media are provided in Chapter 13.

## Theory–practice

### *Chicken or egg?*

Use the laboratory work to drive the theory. Ideas and concepts that are introduced in the practical sessions could be discussed in lectures and small group sessions. Alternatively, the practical work might direct guided reading or independent research.

*Interface or divide*

For ease of organisation and timetabling, theory and practice are often separated. Overcome the divide by

- designing lab tasks during lectures
- demonstrating an experiment to illustrate the theory
- holding theory seminars as part of the lab sessions
- using lab time to finish reports, answer quizzes based on lectures, hold question and answer sessions.

Additional examples that may be used for learning and assessment are given in Figure 7.8.

---

1 Paper and pencil activities which require a student to solve an experimental problem or create an experimental design.
2 Provide the experimental data such as the output of a mass spectrometer, and ask groups of students to interpret it.
3 Present a video-recording of an experiment which shows readings on various instruments. Ask the students to note, calculate and interpret the results.
4 Set up a spreadsheet so that students can enter the results and obtain immediate graphic displays or calculations of data.
5 Set up the apparatus for the students so all they have to do is take readings.
6 Side-step part of the experiment. Ask students to perform the parts of an experiment which can be done quickly and provide pre-prepared materials for the slow part of the experiment (as is done in some Open University courses).
7 Ask the students to carry out a set of brief, simple experiments which exemplify some fundamental principles.
8 Design an MCQ to test understanding and knowledge of specific laboratory procedures. Go through the results with students so they are aware of their strengths and weaknesses.

Note: Each of these requires detailed planning.

---

*Figure 7.8* Alternative approaches to laboratory work

## OBSERVING STUDENTS AT WORK

Assessment of outcomes of laboratory work, however, may not be enough in certain circumstances. The way a student or group of students carry out the procedures may be at least as important as the product of that procedure. One can study the processes of learning in two ways:

- By watching and noting.
- By using checklists.

The live event may be observed or the event video-recorded and analysed. Although the observations may be done by the lecturers, there is much benefit for the students themselves to conduct the observations, discuss them and decide what changes in their work pattern and task allocation are necessary. A structured approach is probably best for inexperienced observers. Such an approach has the merit of providing specific criteria and of pinpointing areas of disagreement between observers. An example of a checklist is given in Figure 7.9.

## PROVIDING GUIDANCE AND FEEDBACK

Guidance, feedback and reinforcement provide the basis for developing laboratory skills and instilling confidence in students. To be effective in these areas one needs to be able to:

- Do the experiment, analyse the findings and interpret them.
- Analyse the experimental task.
- Provide clear instructions.
- Develop a set of hints, prompts, cues and questions that guide the students without telling them what to do.
- Give accurate, meaningful oral feeedback when requested.
- Provide encouragement and occasionally reproof that leads to improvement.
- Mark lab reports and other assessment tasks fairly and consistently.

These tasks are commonplace to most laboratory superintendents and lecturers but not to demonstrators. Common errors we have observed are information overload to undergraduates, providing unintelligible hints, not specifying clearly the goal of an operation, not monitoring students at work and inconsistent marking. Some training for demonstrators, particularly on feedback and assessment, is recommended. Figure 7.10 lists some important skills of demonstrators that could provide the basis of an induction course and Allison (1995) provides some useful suggestions.

Finally, it is worh re-visiting one's laboratory sheets and manuals to ensure that they are sufficiently clear and accessible to students. Diagrams, flow charts and pictures can provide more precise guidance than mere words. The manual may be supplemented by tapes or slides, video loops, multi-media and simple wall charts.

## PRACTICAL WORK OR WRITTEN TESTS?

Should one reduce or abolish the assessment of practical work in undergraduate courses? The answer depends on what you value, the objectives of the degree

This checklist may be used for observing groups of students who are setting up apparatus. Tick each activity the first time it occurs in each of the minute segments. A similar procedure may be used for observing the conduct of an experiment.

| Time in minute intervals | 1 | 2 | 3 | 4 | 5 | 6 | 7 | 8 | 9 | 10 |
|---|---|---|---|---|---|---|---|---|---|---|
| Reads instructions | | | | | | | | | | |
| Looks at apparatus | | | | | | | | | | |
| Handles apparatus but does not set it up | | | | | | | | | | |
| Ask each other questions | | | | | | | | | | |
| Checks layout of apparatus | | | | | | | | | | |
| Checks instructions in relation to apparatus | | | | | | | | | | |
| Seeks advice of another group | | | | | | | | | | |
| Seeks advice of demonstrator | | | | | | | | | | |
| Attempts to set up apparatus | | | | | | | | | | |
| Checks apparatus in relation to instructions | | | | | | | | | | |
| Checks apparatus is working properly | | | | | | | | | | |

Estimate the proportion of time spent on each activity. If the group you are observing is small then use initials of each member of the group.

Figure 7.9 Checklist for setting up apparatus

- observe students at work
- anticipate major difficulties of understanding
- recognise major difficulties of understanding
- give brief, clear explanations of processes and procedures
- give directions
- ask questions that clarify difficulties of understanding
- ask questions that guide students
- answer questions in a simple, direct and non-critical way
- offer supportive and encouraging remarks
- know when to help and not help a student
- know how to mark fairly and consistently

*Figure 7.10* Demonstrator skills

programme, the allocation of resources and the opportunity costs (what else you want to do). Written tests correlate positively with assessment of practical work. Typical correlations are in the range of +0.3 to +0.5 but these correlations are not high and they do not take account of differences in the content of the written and practical tasks. Some of the objectives of practical work such as analysing and interpreting data might be assessed by other methods some of the time. But reduction or abolition of practical work or its assessment will have unfortunate side effects. If one downgrades practical work then students will attend to other aspects of their work. The immediate saving may be a short-term gain for a department or university but a long-term loss to science and the community.

## TIME TO DEVELOP SCIENTIFIC EXPERTISE?

Enough has been said in this chapter to indicate that laboratory courses do not always fulfil their promise. If you wish to develop students' understanding of procedures, methods of enquiry and key concepts you may need to reappraise and redevelop your laboratory module. If the module is the practical component of a set of modules, then you may have to redevelop the level of the programme. Broadly speaking, the sets of experiments and assessment tasks should move the students from level 0 to level 4 (see Figure 7.2) and, within each year of the programme, provide opportunities at level 4 to work on mini-projects. If students have an inadequate (or wrong) grasp of key concepts or their practical skills are limited, it is worth developing a first-year module that consists of simple exploratory practical tasks and associated deep questions. These might be followed by lecture/discussion classes and assignments in which students are required to apply the knowledge gained from the practical tasks and follow-up. This approach is known as the 'scientific learning cycle' or the discovery–invention–application cycle. There is considerable evidence in college and high school courses in the United States that the scientific learning cycle is more effective in teaching science than standard methods (see Lawson *et al.*, 1989 and Hegarty-Hazel, 1990).

The above tasks are daunting so it is tempting to keep the status quo or merely tinker with it. But given the cutback in resources, the increase in student numbers and official concern for quality of educational provision, this may be the time to rethink and redesign one's laboratory courses so that time and resources in teaching, learning and assessment are well spent. Boud, Dunne and Hegarty-Hazel (1989) provide guidelines for redeveloping a laboratory course and monitoring laboratory work, and some examples of instructions for enquiry-based approaches and assessment sheets.

## ACTIVITIES

7.1    Use Figure 7.1 or your own approach to identify the links between the aims, objectives and assessment methods of your laboratory course.

7.2    Identify the range of assessment methods used in your laboratory course. How well do they match with the methods outlined in this chapter? What methods in the chapter could you adapt for use in your laboratory course?

7.3    Use the grids in figures 7.2 and 7.3 to classify the experiments in your course or module. It is better to do this in conjunction with a colleague. You might like to work together on each other's courses. Be prepared for prolonged discussion and disagreement about some of the experiments!

7.4    Draw up a checklist of the correct procedure for making a pot of tea, given a kettle, water, teabags, milk, sugar and teapot. Identify the likely sources of error by a novice tea maker.
How do you assess the quality of a good cup of tea?
Identify up to four criteria that you would use for assessing a good cup of tea.
Compare your criteria with those of a few colleagues. Provide a marking scheme for each criteria. You may use 3 or 4 levels for each criterion (unsatisfactory, minimum level of competence, good, very good).
Discuss and compile a list of implications of the above tasks for writing laboratory instructions and designing assessment tasks.
What are the implications of your discussions of the above activities for the assessment of laboratory and project work in your subject?

7.5    Invite a group of students to draw up a checklist for setting up an apparatus or test rig, to use it and provide a report of their findings.

7.6    Invite a group of students to draw up a checklist for observing how they work on an experiment, to use it and provide a report of their findings.

7.7    Watch and note what students do in your laboratory class for about one hour. Time a few activities, watch for points where time is wasted through queuing for an apparatus or confusion over the task. Observe which students do what in what order. For example, some students always read the instructions whilst others listen. Some students always do the experiment whilst others watch. Some students read only part of the instructions and then seek help from a demonstrator. Other students persist even though it is obvious to everyone else that they are on the wrong track. Write a brief report of your observations and present it, tactfully, to the laboratory class.

Invite a group of students to draw up a rating schedule for assessing their views on how the teams of students work together, then how to use it and provide a report of their findings.

7.9   Draw up a set of criteria for marking laboratory notebooks or reports for use with colleagues and demonstrators. Ask the team of markers to use the criteria to assess the same experimental report. Discuss the differences in marking and how they might be minimised.

7.10  What proportion of the marks of a degree are devoted to assessment of practical work?
How long does it take students to complete the assessed work?
How long does it take to mark the work?
How consistent is the marking across demonstrators in a course?
How consistent is marking across different courses?
*Note:* Check that the marks assigned do reflect the amount of work required of students and staff.

7.11  The following case study may be adapted for a half-day or day course:

You have been asked to write the course document and assessment procedures for a first-year module (12-week course). Your colleagues are, at this stage, supportive. They have agreed that the module may be re-designed as well as the assessment procedures but they are worried about overload of marking on staff and workload for students. The number of students taking the module has increased from 60 to 100 in the past 3 years but there has been no increase in academic staff.

The existing course consists of:

24 lectures – two per week
12 practicals – three hours per week
12 tutorials in groups of 5 – one hour per week
10 examples classes in groups of 50 – one hour per week.

Demonstrators assist in the labs and examples classes but do not mark the students' work.
Two lecturers share the lectures and labs. (You are one of them.)

Half the tutorials are taken by staff who have no other input to the course. All marking is done by the two lecturers.

There are only enough spaces for 30 students (at most 35) in the labs so an extra lab class has had to be run each week on Saturday mornings. This has not been popular.

There is a budget of £1000 which may be used for payments to demonstrators or for developing materials.

The assessment consists of:

Laboratory notebook of the 12 practicals (12 per cent)
Two problem sheets (18 per cent)
One three-hour written paper (70 per cent).

The students have never been informed officially of the proportion of marks but most know that the written paper is the most important.

Attendance at examples classes is low. Non-attenders tend to be either very successful or the least successful. Attendance at lab classes is variable. It is lower prior to assessment deadlines in other modules.

Students have complained about the tutorials and the heavy load of writing up practicals.

Staff are finding the load of tutorials and other work burdensome.

The two lecturers who mark students' work find the task onerous.

The external examiner had, prior to modularisation, pointed to the high failure rate, the lack of understanding of experimental methods and the inability of the students to write clearly.

Employers and past students have often suggested that students should be encouraged to do some independent work and to develop presentation and discussion skills.

Under the new university regulations, a total of 80 hours for contact, learning and assessment time is available for the module.

The course is intended to provide an introduction to:

basic laboratory skills
elementary problem-solving
essential theory and experimental findings.

The existing course document is essentially a list of topics taught and the timetable.

How will you set about designing the new module and its assessment procedure? (You may draw on experience of laboratory work in your own subject.)

Spend about 15 minutes thinking about the tasks involved.

Discuss and develop, in groups of three or four, an outline of a course design and assessment procedure.

Provide estimates of the time required for the development of the course, contact time for staff and students, time for students to complete assessment tasks and for staff to set and mark the assessments.

Allow up to two hours for this discussion. Then set out the course outline, assessment procedures and times involved on three flip chart sheets. One member of each group should be prepared to outline briefly the proposed solution at the plenary session.

After each presentation, have a brief plenary. When all the presentations and discussions are completed, each participant might spend 10 minutes deciding which approach or combination of approaches he or she prefers. A discussion and straw poll should follow.

7.11  Design a set of 5 mini-tasks and the assessment criteria that are suitable for an OSCE. Match them to the objectives of the module. Pilot them. Ask colleagues who are teaching the same module to do the same. Brief the students. Run the OSCE for feedback purposes. Provide feedback to the students. Then amend and adapt the OSCEs for use with another group of students.

# Chapter 8

# Assessing projects

In this chapter we consider some of the advantages and disadvantages of project work and outline some relevant research. We offer some suggestions on guidance and feedback to students and we describe various methods of assessing projects and group projects. The chapter ends with a brief discussion on ways of saving time in assessing and providing feedback on project work.

Projects may be laboratory-based, library-based, studio-based, work-based or community-based. The outcome may be a project report, a dissertation, a design, a working model, a computer program, an interactive learning programme or a portfolio of artwork. Projects may be undertaken by individuals or in groups. Usually, projects are carried out in the final year of the course although a good case may be made for using a small-scale project in the first year of the course to encourage students to become active, independent learners. Many direct-entry students have experience of project work at A level so it would be a pity if their experience was neglected, and many mature students enjoy project work. Whether projects are used early or late in a course, the time devoted to projects should be timetabled for staff and students. Too often projects are treated as an unrecognised extra for tutors rather than as a central part of their work.

The primary purpose of projects is to develop enquiry-based skills. These skills are generally held to be transferable to other contexts and to be useful in most work situations. The advantages claimed for projects are that they:

enable a student to explore deeply a field or topic
develop initiative and resourcefulness
enhance time- and project-management skills
provide personal ownership of learning
foster independence and creative problem-solving.

The disadvantages of projects are that they may be time-consuming to set up, monitor and provide feedback on and difficult to assess fairly. Variations in the help sought by students are a further disadvantage, as is fear of plagiarism.

None of these disadvantages is insurmountable and the technical difficulties of assessing projects are no more than those involved in assessing coursework essays or written papers.

## GUIDES ON PROJECT WORK

There is plenty of guidance on project work available for scientists and engineers but little published advice on project work or dissertations in the arts and social sciences. When projects first became popular, Adderly *et al.* (1975) and Dowdeswell and Harris (1979) provided suggestions on the assessments of project work and group projects which are still worth using. Horobin and Williams (1992) provide some suggestions on project work and Owers-Bradley and Exley (1993) describe a course in physics in which undergraduates work in pairs on graded projects. Hindle (1993) discusses the advantages and disadvantages of projects in geography and describes a large-scale project at Salford University that involves groups of students. Mellor (1991) describes an integrated project in soil science. Arnold *et al.* (1994) describe group projects in which students work as apprentices to members of staff in psychology, and McGuiness (1984) describes group projects in psychology that develop transferable skills. The texts edited by Exley and Moore (1992), Moore and Exley (1994) and Exley and Dennick (1996) provide examples of different approaches to projects in science, engineering and medicine. In the arts and social sciences, Watson (1989) provides useful suggestions for writing a dissertation in the arts, Bell (1994) provides a guide for students in the social sciences and education and Herbert's text (1990) provides advice for students in the helping professions. Nicholls (1992) describes the use of projects in history in which students work with local employers. FitzGerald *et al.* (1994) set out clearly a successful approach to small group project work in English that could readily be adapted for use in other arts subjects.

## RESEARCH ON PROJECT WORK

The increasing popularity of project work has not as yet led to substantial research on project work or its assessment. Henry (1994) describes methods of teaching through projects that are based on a survey of Open University students and a review of the literature. Evidence from studies of research supervision provides some clues on effective project supervision. Studies of research supervision by Welsh (1981) and Rudd (1985) indicate that many students: 'Experience problems such as methodological difficulties, time management, writing up, isolation and inadequate or negligent supervision.'

Wright and Lodwick's (1989) survey of first-year research students show that they value these functions of a supervisor: Gives critical feedback. Checks on progress. Provides academic guidance. Provides support and encouragement. Allows student to work independently on own initiative some of the time.

In an international comparison of the supervision of science research students, Brown *et al.* (1993) showed that over a quarter of the sample of students across four countries wanted more help in planning, analysing and interpreting results, drafting theoretical models, writing up and publication.

Wright (1991) indicates that successful supervisors, as measured by completion rates, have 'Regular and frequent schedule meetings with their students, they set tasks, review progress regularly, comment on drafts and teach their students time-management skills.'

In a study by Gabb (1981) the students reported that their efforts were directed towards getting a good mark rather than using the project as a learning experience. The rules which they seemed to work by were:

1  *Supervisor.* A topic must be chosen on the basis of who is supervising it rather than for any intrinsic interest. Important criteria for choosing a supervisor are helpfulness, approachability and friendliness.

2  *Assessment Procedure.* Discover as much information as possible on the assessment procedure. It is supposed to be secret but friendly staff members will reveal it if encouraged.

3  *Results.* Most assessors are more interested in results than any other aspect of the project. Results make the projects easy to mark. Advise your supervisor of any results obtained. If no results are forthcoming, don't tell your supervisor until it is absolutely necessary.

4  *Length.* The report should be approximately 30 pages in length. Padding may be necessary to obtain sufficient words but do not exceed the 30-page limit as you will be marked down for waffle.

5  *References.* A long list of references. These can be obtained from abstracting journals, which provide enough information for a decision to be made.

What seems to be missing in this field is research that demonstrates the efficacy of project work, compared with other methods, for developing understanding and transferable skills. Morgan (1983) has demonstrated the links between project work and various theories of learning and motivation, and a persuasive argument for project work could be derived from the constructivists' viewpoint that students learn better when they perceive a learning task as 'real' (see Ramsden, 1992; Laurillard, 1993; Steffe and Gale, 1995 and Marton and Booth, 1996). But empirical testing has yet to be done. However, absence of research evidence on project work is not evidence against project work. There is sufficient experiential evidence and favourable evaluations to suggest that projects are a valuable approach to learning and its assessment.

## OBJECTIVES AND ASSESSMENT

The specific objectives of projects or dissertations in a department provide a guide for their assessment. Some typical objectives are given in Figure 8.1. If the objectives specify that students should write a review of the relevant literature then the assessment should reflect this objective. If teamwork and presentations are objectives then some estimate of these objectives should be undertaken. A quick check of the alignment between objectives and assessment can be made by comparing the stated objectives of projects and the method of marking them.

By the end of the module, it is expected that students will be better able to:

1 Select and use appropriate qualitative and quantitative methods of research in clinical education.
2 Read and evaluate research papers in clinical education.
3 Design investigations in clinical education.
4 Analyse data collected in investigations in clinical education.
5 Interpret data collected in investigations in clinical education.
6 Write a focused evaluative review of research literature in clinical education.
7 Present a well-constructed dissertation in clinical education.

*Figure 8.1* Examples of objectives

Alternatively one can look at the assessment criteria and infer from them the 'real' objectives of the project. If there are no specified objectives for the project and no clear criteria, start thinking.

## GUIDANCE AND FEEDBACK

Time and needless frustration can be saved by giving students, before they embark upon a project, guidelines on project management, the objectives and the precise criteria on which projects will be assessed. However, the written word may not be enough so it should be supplemented by a workshop or interactive lecture.

During most projects, guidance and feedback are provided – unless the department regard projects merely as summative exercises. A useful approach is to ask students to provide a protocol of what they intend to do in the project and to indicate the time-phases of the project. This plan can be used as a basis for tutorials and for monitoring progress. However, be wary of overloading the instructions for the protocol lest the main points of the project are lost in a sea of paper.

The tutorial is the key source of guidance for students and, given the pressure on staff time, a well-defined structure is advisable. Shaw (1987) developed such a structure which may be adapted for use in most projects (see Figure 8.2). The key questions to ask in tutorials are:

• What are you trying to do?
• What have you been doing?
• What problems are you having?
• What are you going to do next?

The tutorial is more likely to be effective if the student has to provide a brief written report that can feed into the project report and if the tutor provides

| | |
|---|---|
| **Opening** | Rapport established |
| **Review** | Current context established |
| **Definition** | Scope and purpose of present meeting |
| **Exploration** | Problems, interpretations, issues, results and so on |
| **Clarification** | Decisions needed |
| **Goal-setting** | Decisions taken, next task identified and date of next meeting |
| **Conclusion** | Evaluation, summary, farewells |
| **Recording** | Notes on supervision recorded and filed |

*Figure 8.2* Stages in a project tutorial

focused, constructive feedback and encouragement. Too often students leave all the writing up until the final stages of a project. Consequently the tutor may have no indication of the quality of the student's writing until it is too late and the student may be unaware of his or her strengths and weaknesses in report writing and presentation. Similar remarks apply to PhD theses in the sciences.

## Project and time management

Time and project management are assessed indirectly and summatively by whether the project was handed in on time and by the quality of the design, implementation and delivery of the project report or dissertation. Such summative assessment may be too late for learning unless one requires students to write a section or a chapter in their reports that considers how they might have tackled the project better within the time constraints. Even this approach is not as effective as asking the students to monitor their time- and project-management during the project itself. One can help students to do this by asking them to complete a weekly log along the lines indicated in Figure 8.3. Students can complete and discuss the log with other students or in a tutorial. They can analyse what went wrong and why and they can try to correct their estimates of time for tasks. After the project has been marked the students might be asked to review their project- and time-management skills in a discussion or as a brief assignment. It is important to separate assessment of the quality of time-management from the quality of the report so that contamination is minimised. Further suggestions on time-management may be found in Kemp and Race (1992) and in Hopson and Scally (1992).

## STRUCTURED APPROACHES TO PROJECTS

An approach that can assist students to produce good projects and dissertations is to split the project into a set of assessed tasks such as development of a

On the left-hand side make brief notes of what you will try to do in each week of the project.
On the right-hand side make notes at the end of each week of what you did.
(Use a separate sheet for rescheduling your tasks and use this sheet as a summary.)

|  | *Plan* | *What achieved* |
|---|---|---|
| Week 1 | | |
| Week 2 | | |
| Week 3 | | |
| Week 4 | | |
| Week 5 | | |
| Week 6 | | |
| Week 7 | | |
| Week 8 | | |

*Figure 8.3* Timetabling a project

protocol (design plan), report of the experiments or data collection, data analysis, and review of the relevant literature. These tasks are marked during the project and feedback is provided. Note that the review is submitted *after* the data has been collected and analysed. This approach is used to ensure the review is focused sharply on the topic of the project. The total marks available for the project are divided between these tasks and the final project report or dissertation.

A variation of this method has been used successfully by one of the authors in a two-module-based project. In the first module, the relevant theories and findings were taught through lectures, seminars and practicals. The second module was independent study in which groups of students held fortnightly meetings. In addition, each student had three brief tutorials during the module. The assessment tasks provided to students in the first module were:

1 Identify a problem or hypothesis that you wish to explore and say why. Provide a summary of not more than two pages of the problem and your likely approach. Be prepared to outline the problem in five minutes in a seminar. 10 per cent.
2 Prepare a draft review of the literature which seems relevant to the problem that you propose to investigate and write a report on it in not more than 3,000 words. 20 per cent.
3 Design an experiment or protocol to enable you to test or explore the hypotheses that emerged from your review and initial thinking. Include in your proposal your estimates of time for different sections of the project. 20 per cent.

The previously marked assignments 1 and 2 were handed in with assignment 3 and returned before the written examination. The written paper included one compulsory question on the students' approach to a research problem.

In the second module the project was carried out. The students met to plan further their approaches and to discuss progress. Further clarification, reading, data collection and interpretation were undertaken. Tutors met with the students at the beginning, in the middle and towards the end of their project. The students were advised to write up their project throughout the whole of the semester rather than leaving it to the end. Guidelines on writing the project and criteria were provided. The project had to be no more than 20,000 words. (100 per cent)

The more effort that students put into the first module, the better and easier their task was in the second module. A variation on this approach is used in the humanities degree at Bradford University. Students are required to submit their coursework for feedback and marking on a pass/fail basis. If they pass, they can then complete and submit their dissertations. The total mark for the module is based upon the dissertation. The far-sighted students use the feedback from coursework to produce a better dissertation.

# ASSESSING PROJECTS

The major methods of assessing projects are:

- Assessing artefacts
- Assessing the report or dissertation
- Vivas
- Poster sessions/exhibitions
- Presentations
- Log books
- Written papers.

Each of these methods may involve tutor-based, peer-based or self-based assessment, although written papers are almost always assessed by tutors.

## Assessing artefacts

Artefacts include such products as a computer program, a design, a working model, a video, an interactive learning programme or a portfolio of artwork. It is not proposed to outline examples of approaches for each type of artefact but there are two principles that apply to assessing all artefacts:

- Derive criteria that are linked closely to the objectives of the project.
- Provide the students with the criteria or, alternatively, develop the critieria with the students and in the light of the objectives of the project.

The choice of instruments depends upon the purposes of the assessment and type of artefact. (See Figure 4.1 and the discussion in Chapter 4.)

## Assessing projects and dissertations

Three common difficulties in the assessment of projects are variations between assessors, variations in the difficulty of projects and the variations in students' and supervisors' contribution to the project report.

One way of reducing variability of assessors is to use an agreed set of criteria. Figures 8.4 and 8.5 provide examples for a science-based project and an arts-based dissertation. The schedules may be adapted for use in one's own subject.

Whatever method of assessment is adopted, it is important to discuss the criteria with the students. One can explore the criteria with them at a group tutorial or even develop the criteria with their help. One can convert criteria into a checklist and assign maximum marks for each section. An interesting exercise is to develop one's own criteria, checklist and allocation of marks and then compare them with those of colleagues and students. In this way you get an indirect measure of what different people value in projects. By using checklists and guidelines in this way one can help students to be more focused in the planning and execution of their projects. If the same checklist is used for all

| Guidelines | Max. mark | Your mark | Comment |
| --- | --- | --- | --- |

**Introduction**
Sets out clearly the content and structure of the project. Identifies clearly the problem to be examined.

**Review**
Well structured. Relates closely to the problem/hypotheses of the dissertation. Is critical and probing of the literature. Shows an awareness of different types of evidence.

**Design**
Describes clearly so that the experiment could be replicated by a fellow student.

**Results**
Methods of data collected and analysis indicated clearly.

**Results**
Presented clearly. Some brief discussion of the results.

**Results summarised**
Interpretation and discussion. Results put into context of the literature. The limitations of the experimental study and data analysis indicated.

**Conclusions drawn**
and related to hypotheses. Possible next steps of research and other implications indicated.

**Layout, referencing, bibliography**
Clear and accurate.

**Global view of project and project management skills**

**Responses to comments and advice offered.**

Supervisor's mark
Second marker's mark
External examiner's mark

**Mark awarded**

Note: A small percentage, say 5 per cent, could be reserved for overall impressions of the dissertation since the overall quality of a project may be greater than the sum of its parts. A modified checklist may be necessary for a project based on a series of linked experiments.

*Figure 8.4* Assessing an experimental project

| Criteria | Maximum mark | Your mark | Comment |
|---|---|---|---|
| **1 Information gathering**<br>Range of reading<br>Use of primary and secondary<br>sources | 20 | | |
| **2 Structure and organisation**<br>Sequence of chapters<br>Links between chapters<br>Sequence and links within chapters<br>Use of themes | 10 | | |
| **3 Use of evidence**<br>Distinguishes and evaluates<br>different types of evidence and<br>links them to various interpretations<br>Distinguishes generally agreed facts<br>from speculations and opinions | 10 | | |
| **4 Historical analysis and argument**<br>Displays a conceptual grasp of<br>problem tackled<br>Analyses critically a range of<br>evidence for and against various<br>interpretations. Provides a clear line of<br>argument. Provides own interpretation<br>and links to other interpretations<br>Indicates limits and reservations<br>about own interpretation<br>Shows awareness and understanding<br>of an underlying assumption and<br>rationale of various approaches to the<br>problem, including own. | 40 | | |
| **5 Presentation**<br>Grammar and syntax<br>The language is relatively free of<br>obscurities<br>Bibliographic references and footnotes<br>are in agreed format<br>Style is within the conventions of<br>historical writing<br>Headings and summaries are used | 10 | | |
| **6 Overall impression of the dissertation** | 10 | | |

*Figure 8.5* Assessing a dissertation

students then it is seen to be fairer – and is fairer. Where there are disagreements between project supervisors and internal examiners or second markers then these disagreements are easily pinpointed. If a disagreement is more than 10 per cent overall then an independent examiner's view may need to be sought.

Assessing the difficulty of a project is cumbersome. One can use weightings for the difficulty of a project but there are problems in doing so. The use of weightings might prove more unfair than a global approach. A project may appear to be simple and prove to be complex; the approach that a student takes might convert a simple problem into a deep problem or vice versa. Weighting at the beginning of a project might deter students; weighting when the project is completed might be perceived as unfair. Alternatively, one can allow for 'difficulty' in a small proportion of marks awarded or trust the professional expertise and integrity of the assessors. Interestingly, the concern for equal difficulty of projects is not usually matched by concern for equal difficulty in questions on an examination paper.

There are similar issues with regard to a supervisor's and student's contribution to a project. The supervisor can make an assessment of the relative contribution of supervisor and student or a joint assessment score can be provided. Black (1975) offered a suggestion for minimising the problem. He based his assessment of projects on:

| | |
|---|---|
| Carrying out stage | 30 per cent |
| Log book | 5 per cent |
| Draft report | 50 per cent |
| Final report | 15 per cent. |

The draft report stage is largely the student's own work. The carrying-out stage is known only by the supervisor and student and some would argue it is open to abuse. So it is. It is also open to the use of criteria grade referencing and the professional judgement of the supervisor.

### Reading a project report or dissertation

When reading a project report or dissertation one should of course keep in mind the criteria that have been established. It is also helpful to have your own set of tactics for reading projects and dissertations and for preparing for vivas. Once again the suggestions offered will need to be adapted for your own purposes. If vivas are part of the assessment process then you should consider the questions you wish to raise in the viva as you are reading the project. The advice and suggestions offered here are based upon an approach developed for reading dissertations by Brown and Atkins (1988).

#### 1 Get a global impression

Start by reading the full title and the abstract in order to get hold of the central idea, or question, or topic that is being researched. Then turn to the final chapter(s) to see how far the student seems to have got in developing the idea, solving the problem, and so on. Make a note of any methodological weaknesses raised. A scan of the contents page and appendices (if any) should indicate whether there is likely to be sufficient appropriate evidence to support the conclusions reached. Return to the introduction and re-read for a closer definition of the problem in its context.

## 2 Reflect and formulate questions

Stop reading and reflect on the overall impression obtained. Formulate a number of questions which, on the basis of what has been read so far, you would hope to see discussed or answered, for example questions on congruency of methods and problem, on likely sources of bias.

## 3 Read systematically with questions in mind

Read each chapter in turn. Make notes on points to be raised in the viva. Figure 8.6 provides some guidelines.

## 4 Reflect

Put the report or dissertation down and look through the notes. Return to the original questions posed in stage 2 and see whether they have been satisfactorily answered. Consider also at this stage the more fundamental questions:

- Is the standard of literary presentation adequate?
- Is the dissertation (substantially) the candidate's own work?
- Does the candidate have a general understanding of the relevant field and how this dissertation relates to it?
- Has the candidate thought through the implications of the findings?
- Is there evidence of originality?
- Does the study add to existing knowledge of the subject?
- Is there evidence that the candidate has developed skills in research at this level?
- Is it worth publishing, albeit in modified form?

Where you find yourself in disagreement with the candidate's methods, interpretations or views, it is worth asking whether the disagreement is the result of differences in ideology (or values) between yourself and the candidate or whether it is due to something else.

## Vivas

Vivas are often used for assessing borderline cases although a strong case could be made for a brief oral examination of each student. A good viva like a good

**Review of the literature**
To what extent is the review relevant to the research study?
Has the candidate slipped into 'here is all I know about x'?
Is there evidence of critical appraisal of other work, or is the review just descriptive?
How well has the candidate mastered the technical or theoretical literature?
Does the candidate make the links between the review and his or her design of the study explicit?
Is there a summary of the essential features of other work as it relates to this study?
**Design of the study**
What precautions were taken against likely sources of bias?
What are the limitations in the design? Is the candidate aware of them?
Is the methodology for data collection appropriate?
Are the techniques used for analysis appropriate?
In the circumstances, has the best design been chosen?
Has the candidate given an adequate justification for the design used?
**Presentation of results**
Does the design/apparatus appear to have worked satisfactorily?
Have the hypotheses in fact been tested?
Do the solutions obtained relate to the questions posed?
Is the level and form of analysis appropriate for the data?
Could the presentation of the results have been made clearer?
Are patterns and trends in the results accurately identified and summarised?
Is a picture built up?
**Discussion and conclusions**
Is the candidate aware of possible limits to confidence/reliability/validity in the study?
Have the main points to emerge from the results been picked up for discussion?
Are links made to the literature?
Is there evidence of attempts at theory-building or re-conceptualisation of problems?
Are there speculations? Are they well grounded in the results?

*Figure 8.6* Reading a report or dissertation

tutorial has structure and purpose. Here again an agreed procedure across the department or school is preferable – in the interests of perceived fairness and reliability. So you may want to devise a set of guidelines and a brief rating schedule for vivas in your department. Again, you might like to provide an abbreviated form of the guidelines to students. The guideline might include the following:

- Establishing rapport with candidates so they are sufficiently relaxed to be able to provide their best performance. After all it is the quality of the work and the students' thinking that one is assessing and not the capacity to withstand intensive interrogation.
- Key questions on the research design, data collection, interpretations.
- Reflective questions – questions which determine whether the candidate has thought about the ideas and assumptions underlying the research and how that research might be improved. For example: 'If you were going to do the project again what would you do differently?' 'What are the strengths and weaknesses of the approach that you used?' 'What have you learnt from the research?'

You might want to consider if, when and how you should tell a student that he or she has failed and you might also like to consider what particular approaches to adopt for handling very nervous or over-confident students.

### Poster sessions and exhibitions

Poster sessions and exhibitions are increasingly common in the sciences and engineering. They provide a quick way of assessing group work in projects, laboratories and design classes. They can be used by peers as well as tutors and one can quickly assess the layout and content of the posters or displays. The issues for a tutor or school to consider are given in Figure 8.7; figures 8.8 and 8.9 provide examples of criteria from a workshop by Kate Exley.

---

1 Who should assess (tutors, audience, peers and self)?

2 Is the poster the sole means of assessment?
- One sheet of A4 as a back-up?
- Oral explanation as a back-up?

3 Normal use is for assessing a *group* product.

4 Presentation and content
- Be clear about criteria for presentation and content
- Assign some marks for design and visual presentation.

5 Efficiency and resources
- Limited space for presentation e.g. one flip-chart sheet
- Reduced marking time
- Suitable for peer assessment e.g. by ranking
- Large display area needed (especially for peer assessment purposes)
- Need to provide production materials.

---

*Figure 8.7* Some issues when considering poster sessions

**Visual impact**
Immediate, striking impact, attractive         Ugly, messy, poor visual impact
                          5        4      3      2         1

**Clarity of design**
Clear, self-explanatory                        Confusing: needs explanation
                          5        4      3      2         1

**Creativity of presentation**
Novel, surprising, different                             Dull, obvious
                          5        4      3      2         1

**Rationality of argument**
Clear, rational argument                       Lacks justification or rationale
                          5        4      3      2         1

**Practicality**
Workable, realistic                                Unworkable, unrealistic
                          5        4      3      2         1

**Overall evaluation of poster**
Excellent content                                          Poor content
                          5        4      3      2             1
Excellent presentation                                 Poor presentation
                          5        4      3      2             1

Date:                                                      **Total score**
                                                               **/35**

*Figure 8.8* Example of poster assessment sheet

### Presentations and logbooks

Presentations are discussed in Chapter 10 and logbooks in Chapter 13. One has to be careful how one assesses logbooks in a project. It is patently unfair to assess the *private* thoughts and reactions of students and, if they are to be assessed, then sensible students will amend them for their supervisors. So why assess them? We suggest that logbooks should be a private record and that students should be asked to provide only a sample of their logbooks from the beginning, middle and end of the project.

### Written examinations?

Some faculty boards and professional bodies still require a written examination on project work, particularly those involving group work. At a time when staff and students are overloaded with assessment, it is wise to ask:

• What is the purpose of the written paper?

- Will such a paper distort the purposes and processes of the project?
- Will it add substantially to our knowledge of the student's capabilities?

Often it is claimed that such an examination provides an indication of whether the student did the project. Such a claim under-estimates the capacity of students to consult, rote learn and regurgitate. If you must use a written paper in this context then link it to broader understanding of methods of enquiry. Better still, have a section in the project report or dissertation, or a separate assignment on ways in which the project could have been improved.

---

**B. Eng. Mechanical Engineering Year Two**

**Name of assessing student:**
**Name of assessed student:**
**Poster display assessment**

Please include a mark and comment for each of the criteria indicated below:

| Criteria | Comment | Mark 1–4 1 = weak 4 = good |
| --- | --- | --- |

**Impact**
Was the display:
Visually interesting and attractive?
Effective in its use of colour?
Balanced in its use of a variety of images
and text?

**Content**
Did it:
Convey a clear message?
Interest the reader/viewers?
Contain accurate technical information?

**Structure**
Did it:
Have a clear and logical structure?
Show evidence of planning and preparation?

**Further comments**

Total mark

---

*Figure 8.9* Poster assessment

## ASSESSING GROUP PROJECTS

Group projects may be based upon an academic task such as a review, a laboratory investigation or a field study. They may be a simulation or a search for a practical solution. They might be based upon a problem that a local employer is interested in; they could be used to help the local community or they might be related to the future careers of the students. Whether they are pure, applied or a mixture, they can encourage students to work together, to study, to think, to present their findings and to reflect upon them. Figure 8.10 provides a set of possible objectives for group projects.

Assessment of the processes of group project work such as working together and team building is discussed briefly in Chapter 12. Here we are concerned with assessment of the project report of a group. The nub of the problem is fairness. If a group has done the project, should all the group receive the same mark or should one allocate marks on the basis of each person's contribution? If so, how? Because there are no easy answers to these questions, some people are reluctant to use group projects even though they can be easier to organise and

| Your objectives? | Students know | Objective assessed? |
|---|---|---|
| Explore more deeply a topic | | |
| Apply knowledge to a problem | | |
| Provide training in research | | |
| Develop initiative | | |
| Foster independent learning | | |
| Enhance time-management skills | | |
| Develop project management skills | | |
| Improve written communication of findings | | |
| Improve oral presentations of findings | | |
| Develop teamwork | | |
| Develop leadership skills | | |
| Others (please specify) | | |

*Figure 8.10* Some objectives of group projects

mark than individual projects and they do provide a set of valuable learning experiences for students. A few suggestions are given in Figure 8.11. The theme is also discussed under the heading 'Using peer assessment' in Chapter 11.

## TIME FOR ASSESSING PROJECTS

The time required to mark a project obviously depends on its length, complexity and quality. Less obviously, it depends on the time you have available to mark it. The data collected at LMU (1996) indicate that tutors expect to spend one to two hours on marking each project. The time for providing feedback and guidance is more difficult to estimate since it merges into teaching time and 'informal' tutorials. As in most assessment methods, there is a conflict between providing effective guidance and feedback and efficient use of a tutor's time.

Some tutor time can be saved by using workshops, student-led seminars and group tutorials. Briefing on the project and its requirements and useful hints can

---

1 Everybody gets the same mark.
2 The group decides the marks of individuals at the end of the project. (Group project 62: 5 students x 62 = 310 marks to be allocated.)
3 Group decides criteria at beginning of project and allocates marks at end of project.
4 Group allocates roles at beginning of project and criteria for each role. It allocates marks at end of project.
5 Group agrees that everybody will contribute equally to each task of the project. At the end of the project those that did little get marks below the mean, those that did more get marks above the mean. The decisions are taken by the group.
6 Tutor plus group use any one of 2–5. (For convenience in a discussion you might want to label these 6.1, 6.2, 6.3, 6.4, 6.5.)
7 Tutor only does any one of 2–5 (7.1, 7.2, 7.3, 7.4, 7.5.)
8 Individual viva.
9 Individual project exam mark plus group project mark.
10 Yellow card and Red card. Group gets the same mark. If group reports a malingerer, he/she gets a Yellow card and his/her mark reduced by 10 per cent. If no improvement, Red card issued at the end of project and student gets zero.
11 Everybody gets the same mark for the project but additional marks are given for contributions to the project. (See 'Uses of peer assessment' in Chapter 11.)

Variations on the above approaches are possible.

---

*Figure 8.11* Suggestions for marking group projects

---

1  How do we assess projects at the moment? Are there any additional steps that we can take to ensure that the assessment of projects is fair and assesses the skills that we want to assess?

2  Should we ask ex-students for their views on the value, organisation and marking of projects?

3  Could we try a pilot including some self-assessment of some aspects of project work?
   Should it based upon the students' comments in the final chapter of the project report? Should it be based upon a separate report?

4  Are there any other aspects of project work such as project presentation and teamwork that we wish to assess? Could peer-assessment be used? How? Would it be helpful?

5  What can we do about students' marks if negligent project supervision occurs?

6  What can we do about a student's marks if his or her work is part of a larger research project which is foundering?

7  What can we do about a student's marks if the apparatus, test rig or library resources promised were not available?

8  What can we do to minimise the likelihood of plagiarism? Is it a problem?

---

*Figure 8.12* Some issues for discussion in a department

be provided at workshops. In the preparatory phase, students can meet in groups to share, discuss and formulate problems and procedures and to develop their protocols. The tutor need not be present at all of these sessions. The protocols could then be presented and discussed in seminars and the tutor provide written or oral feedback on the spot. In the investigative and report phases, groups of students could hold one or two meetings to share ideas and approaches although the increasing competition between students may deter them. One can use some group tutorials rather than individual tutorials and one can require that individual tutorials are based on brief notes provided before the tutorial.

## ACTIVITIES

8.1  What are the objectives of the project in your course? How are each of them assessed?

8.2  Re-read the section on 'Research on project work' concerned with supervision and the views of students. Discuss your reactions and your views with a few colleagues.

8.3  Try the following activity with students (or colleagues) as an introduction to self-assessment of time-management of a project:

Imagine that you have to submit a project, dissertation or long essay (20,000 words or 60 pages) in three months' time as part of your degree. If you are a scientist or engineer you may have to do experimental work as part of the project; if you are a social scientist you may have to conduct a survey or do a series of interviews; if you are an arts student you may have to read texts or original documents. The project (dissertation) has to be typed, bound and submitted in 13 weeks' time. (For the purpose of this exercise assume today is 1 October.)

Think about all the tasks that you will have to carry out and jot them down. Then on a separate sheet of paper produce a 'time line' of the schedule of work required. You have 15 minutes for this task.

Compare your time line with that of a few colleagues.

(For this activity with students you could use a modified version of Figure 8.3.)

8.4 Use the suggestions for a checklist from figures 8.4 and 8.5 to design your own approach. Do this activity independently or with a group of colleagues. Allocate marks for each section of your checklist and compare these with those of your colleagues.

8.5 Choose a project report from a past student. Ask a few colleagues to read the project using the devised checklist. Compare the range of percentages awarded for the report and for the sections of the report.

8.6 How do you read a project or dissertation? Note, in your learning log, how you do it. Compare your views with those of a few colleagues and note also their views if they seem appropriate. If you decide to try a different strategy, note it and try it on a couple of last year's projects.

8.7 Devise a brief guideline and checklist for use in vivas. Discuss it with colleagues and, if appropriate, the external examiner. Try it with this year's candidates and evaluate its usefulness.

8.8 Use Figure 8.7 as a basis for discussing and developing the use of a poster session as part of the assessment of group projects.

8.9 Use Figure 8.10 as a starting-point for a discussion on introducing group projects or on improving the assessment of group projects.

8.10 You have recently introduced group projects into your course. You were so busy planning, and organising contacts, that you forgot to think out carefully how you will assess the projects – that problem seemed light years away. Now it is upon you.

How are you going to assess group projects?

Figure 8.11 provides a few ideas to start you thinking how you will do it. Consider the advantages and disadvantages of each. Remember that there are no ideal solutions – but some are better than others. You may assume it is still early enough to implement your approach.

8.11 Read the issues presented in Figure 8.12. Use a lunchtime meeting to discuss some or all of these issues in the assessment of project work.

8.12 A student asked if projects were marked down if they did not yield significant results. He was assured that if an experiment was well designed but it did not yield significant results then the student would not be penalised. He checked the dissertations of the previous 2 years. Of the students who had obtained non-significant results only one had obtained a 2.1. The remainder had obtained 2.2 or below on their projects. Would this finding apply to your assessment procedures of projects? How well do project marks correlate with other marks in the final year?

# Chapter 9

# Assessing problem-solving

In this chapter we do not attempt to tackle the whole field of problem-solving. Instead we focus upon problems in which methods and solutions are known to the tutors. The chapter provides an outline of relevant research and its implications for teaching and assessing problem-solving. It offers some hints, suggestions and activities on designing and marking problems for summative purposes, giving feedback on problem-solving and developing problem-solving. It suggests a few alternatives to the standard approaches for the assessment of problem-solving.

This chapter is concerned primarily with the assessment of problem-solving in the sciences and engineering. Problems in these contexts are usually based on methods and acceptable solutions known to tutors although in more advanced work the methods may have to be developed and the solution may not be known. The chapter is not concerned with problem-based learning as used in an increasing number of medical schools. Such approaches have been shown to be effective (Vernon and Blake, 1994) but the range of assessment methods used in problem-based learning is virtually all-encompassing, including methods described in this chapter. Nor is the chapter concerned with creative problem-solving in art and design. Assessment in these areas requires broad but clear objectives and corresponding dimensions or rating scales for assessing the students' work.

The term problem-solving is itself problematic. In its widest sense it is any response to a question that requires thought and/or planned action. It may refer to problems when the methods and solutions are known, the methods are known but not the solutions or neither methods nor solutions are known. Problems may have unique solutions, more than one solution, best solutions or open-ended solutions. As one moves across the continuum from closed to open problems, the assessment process itself needs to become more flexible. Tight procedural marking schemes are appropriate for problems with unique solutions but they are not appropriate for creative design. To complicate matters further, there may be arguments about the validity of certain methods or there may be a range of better solutions rather than a unique solution or a best solution. As the complexity of the problem increases so too does the difficulty of assessing problem-solving.

Values are more likely to obtrude in complex problem-solving than in simpler situations, but values are always implicit in any assessment decision.

Problem-solving involves the whole spectrum of thinking from logical thinking to creative thinking. Even dreams can provide the tentative solutions to problems. Kekule dreamt the structure of the benzene ring in the form of snakes swallowing their tails. Many scientists working on a problem wake up with a solution. It should be noted that there are elements of creativity in the use of logic in problem-solving and elements of logic in the production of a creative solution. Studies of creative processes in problem-solving indicate that typically there are four phases: *preparation and immersion, incubation, illumination* and *verification*. (See Hudson, 1966.) It follows that as well as time for practice, students need time for deep study and consolidation. Such time is not available in many modular courses.

Readers interested in problem-solving processes are referred to Brown and Atkins (1988), the many publications of De Bono (e.g. 1968, 1973), Wickelgren (1974), Polya (1957, 1962), and Schoenfeld (1985). Starfield *et al.* (1990) discuss suggestions for using computers to solve problems. Kemp and Race (1992) provide some hints on solving open problems. Hubbard (1991) provides useful suggestions on teaching and assessing problem-solving. Both Ramsden (1992) and Laurillard (1993) discuss methods of studying the problem-solving processes of students.

## STUDIES OF PROBLEM-SOLVING AND THEIR IMPLICATIONS

The roots of research in problem-solving are in Gestalt psychology and information processing. The Gestalt psychologists stressed the importance of *percepts*, of seeing the connections and making intuitive leaps (see Wertheimer, 1957). Information processing is more concerned with *precepts*, the methods of problem-solving (see Johnson-Laird, 1988). Both are important. The hidden link is how a student represents the problem to him- or herself. Unless the problem is represented meaningfully then efforts to solve it are likely to be ineffective.

Early work on problem-solving suggested that one could teach directly general problem-solving skills but it is now clear that problem-solving needs to be embedded in a subject context and it does not readily transfer (Mayer, 1992). For transfer to occur the problem solver has to be able to abstract the principles and apply them in a new context. The process involves:

• Knowledge and practice in one context:
• Reflection and abstraction:
• Knowledge and practice in the new context.

It follows that reflective learning needs to be built into teaching and assessment for transfer to occur. The task is not easy for students. Less able students stumble at the first hurdle. They fail to see that a formula expressed in one notation may be identical to a formula expressed in another notation. Often they cannot link the mathematics to the representations of reality. Nor is the task easy for tutors. It is much easier to provide elegant solutions than it is to teach others to solve problems.

In fact, the studies of expert and novice problem solvers suggest that they use quite different strategies (Mayer, 1992). For example, Woods (1987) in his studies of problem-solving identifies six steps.

0 I can – the motivation step.
1 Define – draw a figure, list knowns and unknowns, etc.
2 Explore – think about it, is it a routine problem, is it a problem in a problem, etc.
3 Plan – set up the steps or flow chart, use formal/mathematical logic or procedural steps.
4 Do it – put in the values.
5 Check – for errors in reasoning and number crunching, check against external criteria.
6 Reflect and generalise – how did I do it, how could it be done more effectively, what can be ignored, etc.

Novices falter at step 1, rush step 2, ignore step 3, tend to ignore step 5 and rarely do step 6, unless specifically asked to do so. They often try to start with 3 and 4 combined and then get stuck. The more expert a problem solver is, the less likely he or she is, initially, to understand the difficulties of novices.

Recent research on misconceptions of fundamental laws and principles suggests that students retain primitive concepts which obtrude in their thinking and problem-solving. Both Ramsden (1992) and Laurillard (1993) describe studies in which different levels of understanding of Newtonian physics were manifest in the students' answers. Prosser and Millar (1989) looked at changes in first year-students' conceptions of Newtonian mechanics. At the end of the year students who had adopted a surface approach to problem-solving still retained Aristotelian notions of force and motion. Those who had used deep approaches did change their conceptions. Bowden et al. (1992) in their related study of first-year physicists showed that many students could not use Newton's Third Law to explain why a box falls to the ground. These findings and other research – such as the studies of clinical diagnosis by Whelan (1988), Balla et al.'s (1996) study of learning elementary statistics and behavioural science based on the SOLO taxonomy and Saljo's (1979) study of 'how much does a bun cost?' – suggest that the analysis of errors and misunderstandings can provide valuable information for teaching. Feedback that merely tackles surface errors may not be sufficient. One may need to probe the deeper misconceptions to change the nature of understanding. In a study of younger children's errors in subtraction, Brown and van Lehn (1980) identified 89 common errors. Subsequently Resnick and Omanson (1987) showed that these were largely due to two common misconceptions. Obviously it is better to spend time on two misconceptions than on 89 types of errors. Similar remarks apply to students' misconceptions in problem-solving. This is an area that needs further research and the dissemination and application of existing research findings.

## A TAXONOMY OF PROBLEM-SOLVING

A taxonomy for problem-solving is shown below. The taxonomy was originally developed for use in engineering by Plants *et al.* (1980) but it may be adapted for use in other subjects. The description given here is adapted from Wankat and Oreovicz (1993).

1 *Routines.* Routines are operations or algorithms which can be done without making any decisions. Many mathematical operations such as solution of a quadratic equation, evaluation of an integral, analysis of variance, and long division are routines. In Bloom's taxonomy these would be considered application-level problems. Students consider these 'shove and-chug' problems. You shove in the values and chug along.

2 *Diagnosis.* Diagnosis is selection of the correct routine or the correct way to use a routine. For example, many formulae can be used to determine the stress on a beam, and diagnosis is selection of the correct procedure. For complex integrations, integration by parts can be done in several different ways. Selecting the appropriate way to do the integration by parts involves diagnosis. This level obviously overlaps with the application and analysis levels in Bloom's taxonomy.

3 *Strategy.* Strategy is the choice of routines and the order in which to apply them when a variety of routines can be used correctly to solve problems. Strategy is part of the analysis and evaluation levels of Bloom's taxonomy.

4 *Interpretation.* Interpretation is real-world problem-solving. It involves reducing a real-world problem to a representation of one so that it can be solved. This may involve assumptions and interpretations to obtain data in a useful form. Interpretation is also concerned with use of the problem solution in the real world.

5 *Generation.* Generation is the development of routines which are new to the user. This may involve merely stringing together known routines into a new pattern. It may also involve creativity in that the new routine is not obvious from the known information.

The taxonomy should be matched to the experience of the students. What may be a routine problem for you (level 1) may be a real-world problem (level 4) for first-year students. The taxonomy may be applied to the problems set in coursework and examinations. As a course progresses one would expect to find a greater incidence of questions pitched at levels 3 and above which are appropriate for the experience of students.

## DESIGNING AND MARKING PROBLEMS

A 'good' problem fits the objectives of the course and the abilities of the students. If only minimal levels of competence (criterion referenced) are required then set the problems accordingly. If you are interested in deepening understanding, rather than testing it, then set sequences of problems that move the student through the taxonomy. Set some questions that require students to reflect upon and abstract the methods and principles that they are using and set some deep problems that require the students to explain their conceptions. If a rank order of students is required then set problems that enable students of varying abilities to display their prowess. In some mathematics papers full marks can be obtained for answering five questions fully. Very able students may answer six or seven questions and obtain 120 per cent, much to the amazement of colleagues in arts subjects.

A problem has not been fully designed until it has an appropriate marking scheme. If there is only one correct method of solution then the design is relatively simple, but even simple problems require a scheme to ensure consistency between and within markers. For example, in various workshops on assessment we have asked colleagues to assign a mark out of 10 to the following long multiplication.

$$
\begin{array}{r}
1234 \times \\
\underline{34} \\
4936 \\
\underline{37120} \\
\underline{42056}
\end{array}
$$

Marks awarded ranged from 0 to 9. The most common mark was 6 or 7. More complicated problems require even more specific criteria for assessing errors and a willingness to accept solutions that are unconventional, yet economical and elegant. Clearly, values and opinions are involved in all of these matters.

When there is more than one known pathway through a problem then one has to develop a set of marking schemes. If there are more than three legitimate pathways then the problem will be time-consuming to mark. If you have large numbers of problems to mark it is better to invest time in design so as to save time in marking. Eventually one develops a repertoire of marking schemes that one can draw on. Some markers award marks for correct procedures (positive marking) and others deduct marks for wrong procedures (negative marking). Other markers award method marks and accuracy marks. Two (sometimes three) errors in accuracy result in the loss of all subsequent marks. This method of marking can result in very low scores for some students.

Three common types of errors are lapses, knowledge errors and rule errors. Knowledge errors may be separated into choice of the wrong method or lack of knowledge of the context. Rule errors may be due to the application of a correct but inappropriate rule, or the application of a rule that is wrong. (For a deep discussion of human errors see Reason, 1990.) The distinctions are not always clear-cut but one should consider what weighting one gives to different types of errors. Error-free solutions are easy to mark but when an error occurs early in the solution one should, strictly speaking, track the error through. Tracking is time-consuming, hence the use of method/accuracy schemes mentioned above. If you know the common errors you will probably save time by working out the solutions based on errors before commencing marking. You can also save time by using problems in which you change the values and the verbal description rather than the core problem.

Well-presented solutions are easier to mark so it is worth training students to set out work clearly. Marks awarded for presentation of coursework can motivate students. So too can the knowledge that marks will be awarded for presentation in examinations.

For summative purposes when no feedback on solutions is given, one can use a structured form of impressionistic marking. Most solutions can be divided into major sections. Use a four-point scale for each section. Award a mark for each 'correct' section, one of the middle two points for answers that are partially correct and no marks for a fundamental error. When used with second marking this system is reliable but, of course, the markers must understand the marking scheme. For formative purposes in which you wish to give meaningful feedback then more detailed marking schemes are required. The marking schemes could be provided to students so they can mark their own or each other's work. Abbreviated model solutions are sometimes provided to students for feedback purposes. Such models are not always helpful. The hidden steps in the solution are often where the students' confusions lie. 'How did you know to do *that*?' is not an uncommon question.

If demonstrators or teaching assistants mark students' work then it is in their and your interest to provide them with some training in marking for feedback, in recognising misconceptions, in explaining clearly and in asking probing questions. Further suggestions on marking are given in Figure 9.1.

Finally, be wary of highly detailed marking schemes. They are time-consuming, difficult to use, often unhelpful to students, and, without intensive training, unreliable.

## HELPING STUDENTS TO DEVELOP PROBLEM-SOLVING STRATEGIES

Clearly feedback is essential for helping students to develop their problem-solving tactics and strategies. Feedback that is precise and gets at the heart of a student's difficulties is more useful than a mark or a mere indication that the step or part solution is wrong. The absence of feedback was the major cause of failure in the first year of an engineering course (Entwistle *et al.*, 1989). But one can go beyond feedback to encouraging students to reflect upon and extend their approaches to problem-solving. This approach will help them, in a structured

1  Everyone who is marking the problem-solving sheets should have done the problems.
2  Before giving the problem-solving sheets to undergraduates, there should be a briefing discussion between the lecturers and demonstrators who are supervising the problem-solving classes.
3  Ask the undergraduates to leave a three inch margin for comments on written work or set a three inch margin for work on the micro computer. ·
4  Be specific in your comments. Don't just say wrong, say why. 'You forgot to transform the boundary conditions' is better than 'Error'.
5  Identify the loops in thinking and long-winded solutions. Suggest briefer alternatives in the form of either statements or questions.
6  Set problems of increasing difficulty (but see below*).
7  Identify the key questions that one should ask oneself when solving the problems or problem. State these in the opening stages of the problem-solving class, perhaps after students have tackled the first problems.
8  Identify the common errors and report them in a meaningful written form to the class of students. Pay particular attention to the loops in thinking (e.g. proving $0 = 0$) and long-winded solutions.
9  Set further problems which enable the students to identify and eliminate common errors.
10  Discuss with students how they tackle the problems and why they tackle them in that way.
11  Be sure that the problems set in examinations match the problems used in problem-solving classes. It is unfair to provide training in one set of tasks which is not directly relevant to the set of tasks used for assessment purposes only.
12  Marking for feedback should be concerned with misconceptions as well as errors and elegance.

* Whilst this is a useful guideline, it should occasionally be ignored in tutorials. Instead set a deep or difficult problem for teams or small groups of students to tackle and to present their attempted strategies and solutions. This approach can be used to explore misunderstandings and/or to provide a  stimulating challenge to students.

*Figure 9.1* Some suggestions on marking

way, to become more independent learners and it may reduce the pressure of marking problem-solving sheets.

You might try the following:

• Set a tutorial task or assignment which asks students to analyse the types of problems within a topic. As a starting-point you might indicate that some of the problems set in science and engineering courses follow a pattern consisting of:

1  Repetition of basic knowledge.
2  A problem that may be solved by applying that knowledge.
3  A final part which requires a more subtle application of knowledge to solve the problem.

Other problems require transformation of variables, an unusual application of a theorem, a variation of a standard equation, a hidden variable or assumption. Take these ideas further and encourage the students to provide labels for the types of problems that they have tackled.

• Show the students different approaches to marking solutions and their underlying rationale. In A levels the marks to be assigned to different parts of a question are often specified and this is a valuable aid to the student and a method which could well be used more frequently in the earlier undergraduate years.

• Show students the differences between marking to estimate the quality of a solution and marking to help someone to improve.

• Ask students to mark and discuss each other's solutions in a tutorial or problem-solving class. Where there are any remaining difficulties or disagreements then you or a demonstrator should help.

• Have a problem-solving swap shop in which students invent problems and their solutions, swap problems and compare solutions and methods of approach.

• Invent a couple of complex – but not necessarily deep – problems that can be split into components. Give the first problem to a group of students. Their task is to analyse the problem, allocate individual tasks, share their solutions, plan and present the solution of the whole problem to you or another group of students. After the presentation you might discuss with the students how the solution and activities involved should be assessed. Then set and assess the second problem in the way agreed.

• Meet with a few interested colleagues and devise a set of intriguing problems for students which will help them to develop their problem-solving skills. Try the problems in a tutorial or with groups in a problem-solving class. Outline *and* discuss with the students the links between the problems and problem-solving strategies and the usual problems that they have to tackle. Some suggestions are given in the next section.

## DEVELOPING STRATEGIES

Rather than tell students about different approaches to problem-solving it is better first to ask them to describe how they do it and then to summarise various approaches that they and you use. A common approach is the five-pronged attack:

1 Have I met a similar problem before?
2 What is the nub of the problem?
3 What approaches can I use?
4 What should I do when I get stuck?
5 How should I check the solution?

Each of these questions needs unpacking further and the approach may be non-linear. One can work backwards from a solution or estimated solution, one can start in the middle and work outwards, one can change or simplify variables or hold a variable constant or one can try to invent a simpler version of the problem and tackle that as a preliminary. All of these strategies and many more will be familiar to you. But they are not necessarily familiar to your students or demonstrators.

One can devise problem-solving tutorials or classes in which students outline and discuss their approaches to problem-solving when tackling a particular set of problems such as integration by parts. After the initial discussion, they might be asked to record their approaches to problem-solving, to solve some problems and then compare their stated approach with what they actually did. They can then be invited to refine and note their strategies. Alternatively, the tutor 'thinks aloud' whilst solving a few problems. The students try a few problems and then discuss how they tackled them. The tutor then summarises and adds further suggestions and the students try further problems. A similar procedure can be used to match tutor and student conceptions of core principles. This approach can lead to discussion of common misconceptions and how these result in errors.

The purpose of these exercises is to encourage students to assess and develop their approaches to problem-solving so that they are better equipped to solve other kinds of problems in their academic subjects and eventually in their working lives. This may seem a grandiose aim, but out of acorns do oak trees grow. Some further suggestions for activities on developing and assessing problem-solving are given in the activities at the end of the chapter.

## ALTERNATIVE FORMS OF ASSESSMENT?

The written examination appears to be the preferred mode of assessment in mathematics, science and engineering. Underlying this preference is often a concern that students might copy from each other in coursework assignments. A few might do so, but straight copying is as easy to detect in mathematics as it is in English literature. Furthermore, those who look at other students' solutions to create their own are likely to be learning. Their actions are not far removed from the use by lecturers and research students of other people's solutions to create their own. Under what conditions is it appropriate to learn from someone else? Under what conditions is it dishonest?

Leaving aside these deeper questions, a combination of coursework and written papers will provide a better sample of a student's capabilities than either one alone. Serious discrepancies between a student's results in coursework and written papers can be explored. One should not assume *a priori* that such discrepancies attributable to copying in coursework.

As well as standard approaches to assessing problem-solving one can adapt many of the alternative approaches described in chapters 5, 6, 7 and 8 of this text. Further suggestions may also be found in Hubbard (1991). Here a few examples:

### Open-book examination

Set an open-book examination as part of coursework assessment in which students know the topic but not the questions. They may be allowed to bring to the examination approved lists of formulae and notes.

### Write not solve

Set coursework assignments that require students to articulate their approaches to problems or to explain the use of fundamental laws and core principles to account for various physical phenomena. The questions posed can be apparently simple, such as 'Use Newton's laws to explain why an apple falls to the ground.' The 'essays' can provide both you and the students with information that can be used to correct misconceptions and develop thinking.

### Use concept maps

Invite students to prepare and justify a concept map of a topic. In particular, they should explain the connections between the various sections of their concept map. The method is useful for identifying linkages and for developing understanding. It is useful as a coursework assignment and for group work.

### MCQs

Use multiple choice questions in coursework and written papers that test the grasp of underlying concepts as well as the capacity to identify correct solutions and arguments. One can use MCQs for assessing problem-solving but there are limitations. When the pathway through a solution is clear, one can ask students to choose the value closest to the one that they arrived at and use this chosen value in the next stage of the solution. The procedure reduces marking time for summative purposes but it does not allow for the award of method marks and it does not provide useful feedback to students.

### MEQs

These were described in Chapter 4. In science and engineering a long problem or case study can be designed and divided into parts that require calculation and decision-making. At the end of each section of the problem the student is informed what the 'expert' actually did and the next part of the problem is presented. The procedure continues until a solution is arrived at. The method can also be used as a teaching tool in design classes. It is relatively easy to set up these problems on a PC or Apple Mac.

### Incomplete solutions

Provide problems and part solutions or solutions containing common errors that students have to complete or correct.

### Self-marked assignments

Provide problems, alternative solutions and marking schemes to groups of students. As part of the coursework each student has to mark two other students' solutions and submit the marking as well as his or her solutions to two other problems.

### Computer-marked assignments

Similar to self-marked assignments but there are problems of different notations and of keying in solutions. None the less, the method is worth exploring, particularly when one wishes to use different data sets.

### Projects

Set or invite a student or groups of students to select a deep or a practical problem and to investigate, write a report on their findings and suggestions, and give a presentation to their peers and tutors.

### Learning logs

Design a learning log for students to keep. The log could be based on how they solved sets of problems, what false starts they made, what loops in their reasoning occurred and what approaches they found helpful. The students could, as part of an assignment, be asked to submit a re-drafted part of the log for assessment.

## ACTIVITIES

9.1   How do your students solve problems?
      Ask them to discuss and prepare a set of guidelines for 'less experienced problem solvers than themselves'.

9.2   Repeat Activity 9.1 with demonstrators.

9.3    Use some of the ideas in this chapter as the basis of tutorials or problem-solving classes on the assessment of problem-solving.

9.4    Give a short training course to the demonstrators on the assessment of problem-solving.

9.5    How will you monitor the work of demonstrators in problem-solving classes and tutorials?

9.6    Ask colleagues to assign a mark out of 10 for the long multiplication given in the section on designing and marking problems in this chapter. If they ask for the level of student or the context say you will come to that later. In the meantime ask them to give a 'gut' reaction mark. Discuss the marks awarded and the implications of the exercise for marking schemes.

9.7    Set a problem and ask colleagues or students to draw up a marking scheme for the problem. Discuss what counts as a good problem and marking scheme.

9.8    Use the taxonomy given in the chapter to identify the range of problems set in your module(s).

The following problems can be used in tutorials to stimulate discussion of problem-solving and its assessment. You might also like to collect or invent problems of your own that are relevant to your subject.

9.9    The vicar said to the verger, 'How old are your three children?' The verger replied, 'If you add their ages together you get the number on my door. If you multiply their ages together you get 36.'
The vicar went away for a while but then came back and said he could not solve the problem. The verger said, 'Your son is older than any of my children.'
Then the vicar told the verger the ages of the verger's children.
Use the above information to find the ages of the verger's children.

9.10   Thirty-two teams enter a knock-out competition. Assuming there are no replays how many games will it require to obtain the winning finalist? How many games if the initial entry was 2,048?

9.11   How can you tell if a hard-boiled egg is indeed hard-boiled without breaking the shell?

9.12   A factory is making oven doors for cookers. When the doors have been cast they have to be given a protective coating. This coating has to be bonded on to the doors by being heated at high temperature. There are two furnaces available for doing this. However, there is a problem. In order to bond the coating to the thick central section of the door, the door has to be left in the furnace for 20 minutes. Unfortunately, by this time, the coating on the thin edges of the door has got too hot, has 'run', and formed ridges. The ridges make it difficult to fit the door on to the oven properly, and there are a lot of rejects.

How could the problem be solved?

9.13 How would you set about making an approximate estimate of how much it cost to build the Tyne Bridge in 1928? (You may assume that you cannot obtain the exact figure from existing records.)

# Chapter 10

# Assessing oral communication

This brief chapter outlines ways of assessing oral communication. It focuses on assessing presentations, discussions and oral proficiency, and on the uses of vivas and assessing consultations. Oral communication is often taught via videoed practical exercises so the chapter also includes some suggestions for teaching oral communication and providing feedback to students. Peer- and self-feedback are often used in teaching oral communication so these methods are discussed briefly. Indeed, oral communication is a useful way of introducing students to self- and peer-assessment.

## PRESENTATIONS AND THEIR ASSESSMENT

Oral presentations in seminars and tutorials provide a sound base for explaining and presenting information in a variety of settings. As usual students (and lecturers) do better at these tasks if they are provided with learning opportunities, guidance and feedback.

Research on explaining and common sense concurs that the key variables in presentations are clarity and interest. The difficulties arise when one attempts to help someone to be clearer and more interesting. The guidelines in figures 10.1 and 10.2 are based upon the research on explaining (Brown and Atkins, 1996). An evaluation of a training programme based upon research on explaining indicated that lecturers improved in clarity and interest during a two-day course (Brown, 1982). There is plenty of anecdotal evidence from courses in engineering, medicine, dentistry, pharmacy, nursing, social sciences and science that short training courses improve the presentation skills of students.

The most effective methods of improving oral communication are based on video feedback. However, video feedback *per se* is not sufficient. The students need some guidance on the analysis of presentations and an opportunity to develop their own self-assessment skills of presentations. One method which has been used frequently by the authors is to provide two half-day sessions on oral presentations. The students are divided into groups of six. Each person is required to give a four- to five-minute presentation on a topic of his or her choice. They also take turns at acting as time keeper, camera operator and

Know what you intend to explain.
Produce a structured summary before the talk.
Use the structuring tactics of:

- **Signposts** – statements which indicate the content, e.g.:
  *'I want to deal briefly with lactation. First I want to outline the composition of milk; second, its synthesis; third, the normal lactation curves.'*

  *'Most of you have heard the old wives' tale that eating carrots helps you to see in the dark. Is it true? Let's have a look at the basic biochemical processes involved.'*

- **Frames** – statements which indicate the beginning and ending of sub-topics, e.g.:
  *'So that ends my discussion of adrenaline. Let's now look at the role of glycogen.'*

- **Foci** – statements (and gestures) which highlight the important points of the talk, e.g.:
  *'So the main point is . . . '*

  *'Now this is very important . . . '*

  *'But be careful. This interaction with penicillin occurs only whilst the cell walls are growing.'*

- **Links\*** – statements which link the different parts of the talk together and the talk to the listeners' experience and knowledge, e.g.:
  *'So you can see that reduction in blood sugar levels is detected indirectly in the adrenaline gland and directly in the pancreas. This leads to the release of two different hormones . . . '*

Use aids if appropriate.
Summarise during the presentation and at the end.

*Links are often conspicuous in their absence. Often an explainer misses out a chunk of an explanation because he/she assumes the listeners are familiar with the missing section. The more knowledgeable one is about a topic the more likely one is to commit this error. One way of avoiding it to look at the topic from the standpoint of the explainees. This will help you to pitch the explanation at the appropriate level.

*Figure 10.1* Making explanations clear

'student'. Then follows a brief workshop on aspects of explaining which includes some brief discussion tasks and presentations by the tutor. The video recordings are then viewed, discussed and analysed by the group. The theme of this discussion session is 'how could one improve this presentation?' The first person to comment on the presentation is the presenter. His or her task is to indicate the strengths and weaknesses of the presentation. This approach is a form of

- Show your own interest in and commitment to the topic.
- Think of and use examples, analogies, metaphors and models that are apt for the audience and the topic.
- If the material is unfamiliar, begin with several examples.
- Use a mixture of modes of explaining but particularly the narrative mode (informal, personal and story-telling).
- Play on the intellectual curiosity of the audience through the use of puzzles, problems and questions.

*Figure 10.2* Making explanations interesting

self-feedback and assessment. Often the presenters are unduly negative about their performance so the task of the tutor is to provide support, to ask questions and comment occasionally. After the presenter has commented upon his/her performance, the time keeper comments on the use of audio visual aids (if any), the camera operator on the body language and the 'students' on the structure and interest of the presentation. This phase is a form of peer feedback and assessment. The tutor summarises the main points at the end of each discussion of a presentation and adds his or her own comments and suggestions, if necessary. This last phase is a form of tutor feedback. When all the presentations have been viewed and discussed, the students are asked to discuss what they have learnt from watching each other's presentations and to make a note of what things they need to improve for the following week's presentation. Between the two half-day sessions the students are asked to prepare a brief explanation on a different topic. The second workshop provides further discussion activities, inputs from the tutor and a recapitulation of the first session. In the viewing and analysis section of the workshop the presenter indicates before the viewing of the presentation what he or she was trying to improve. The ensuing discussion follows the same pattern as on the first half-day. The second session of training is crucial for helping to build students' confidence and to give them an opportunity to learn from the feedback that they have received in the first session. At the end of the training course the students are asked to write a brief report on their experiences and, in particular, to highlight what points they need to develop in their presentations in the future. Clearly, such a course is a useful introduction to providing feedback, to self- and peer-assessment as well as to the skills of oral presentation.

Criteria for the presentations may be generated by the whole group of students with a little help from the tutor. Lecturers in arts subjects may be interested in integrating presentations with the study of rhetoric. A thematic approach to feedback and assessment of presentations could be based on Aristotelian notions. In particular upon:

*Logos* – the persuasive use of argument
*Pathos* – emotional engagement with the audience

*Ethos* – perceived personality of the presenter and the stance adopted to the topic and audience.

Cockroft and Cockcroft (1992) demonstrate how these concepts can be applied to the study of speeches and writings.

Studies of effective teaching provide another possible set of criteria. The most well known and well tried are:

Systematic, businesslike *versus* unsystematic, slipshod
Enthusiastic, interesting *versus* boring, dull
Warm, friendly *versus* cold, hostile.

From Ryans, 1960

These can be set out as four- or six-point scales with a space for comments.

A simple four- or six-point rating schedule based on items derived from research on explaining could be used. This might include:

Structure of presentation
Clarity of presentation
Enthusiasm of presenter
Interest of presentation.

Alternatively a checklist, such as the one given in Figure 10.3, may be used. Whatever approach is used for feedback and assessment, it should be provided to students before the short course for it provides objectives for preparing the presentation as well as for observing and evaluating the outcomes. One can use points on rating scales or sum the yes's on the checklist, but more important than the grading is the quality of feedback provided by students to each other and by the tutor. We do not award marks for presentations in the training course nor do we ask students to provide marks. Instead we focus upon giving and receiving feedback so that students feel secure enough to take risks. Attendance at the presentation is a prerequisite for the presentation of projects which are marked. Marks for the project itself, its oral presentation and, sometimes, the management of discussion are allocated. Further suggestions on oral presentations may be adapted from Brown (1978), Brown and Atkins (1988), Mandel (1988) and Kemp and Race (1992). Many of the Enterprise in Higher Education HE units developed useful materials on presentation skills for students. (For example, the universities of Sheffield, Nottingham Trent and Teesside.)

## ASSESSING THE MANAGEMENT OF DISCUSSION

Presenting information or giving an explanation without interruption is, after the initial nervousness, relatively easy for most students. Equally important and more challenging is the ability to listen, to respond to questions and, where appropriate, to deflect them.

We have provided training in these skills in three ways. First, by inviting the presenters to identify the questions that are likely to be asked. Second, one

---

*Opening*
1  Does your opening gain the group's attention?          Yes/No
2  Does it establish rapport with the group?              Yes/No
3  Does it indicate what you intend to explain?           Yes/No

*The Key Points*
1  Are your key points clearly expressed?                 Yes/No
2  Are your examples apt and interesting?                 Yes/No
3  Are your qualifications of the key points clearly stated?   Yes/No
4  Is each key point summarised?                          Yes/No
5  Are the summaries clear?                               Yes/No
6  Are the beginnings and ends of the key points clearly
   indicated?                                             Yes/No

*The Summary*
1  Does your summary bring together the main points?      Yes/No
2  Are your conclusions clearly stated?                   Yes/No
3  Do you come to an effective stop?                      Yes/No

*Presentation*
1  Can the group hear and see you?                        Yes/No
2  Do you use eye contact to involve but not to threaten?  Yes/No
3  Do you use audio-visual techniques effectively?        Yes/No
4  Are you fluent verbally?                               Yes/No
5  Is your vocabulary appropriate to the group?           Yes/No
6  Do you make use of pauses and silences?                Yes/No
7  Do you vary your intonation?                           Yes/No
8  Is the organisation of your material clear?            Yes/No
9  Do you avoid vagueness and ambiguities?                Yes/No
10 Is the presentation as interesting as you can make it?  Yes/No

Any 'No' answer indicates that your explanations are not as explanatory as
they might be. (But everybody gives quite a lot of 'No' answers if he or she
is honest.)

This checklist may be adapted for self, peer or tutor feedback.

---

*Figure 10.3* Explanations evaluated

group of students present the project and another group of students identify
the key questions and ask questions after the presentation. Third, by planting
questioners in the audience. All of these methods have been supplemented
by an outline of common questions, types of questioners and the tactics to
handle the questions and questioners. The training in handling communications
from others is sometimes incorporated in the course described in the previous
section. Figure 10.4 may be used to assess presentation and management of
discussion in a seminar. It is important that one asks students what is good about

Twenty per cent of marks are awarded for your presentation at the seminar. The criteria are as follows:

| Criteria | Marks | Comments |
|---|---|---|
| **Content**<br>Opening, clarity of argument<br>or explanation, summary<br>and conclusion. | 0  1  2  3  4  5 | |
| **Evidence**<br>Experimental design,<br>literature review,<br>interpretation. | 0  1  2  3  4  5 | |
| **Presentation**<br>Fluency, use of audio-visual aids,<br>handouts, body language. | 0  1  2  3  4  5 | |
| **Discussion skills**<br>Listening, responding to questions,<br>engaging others in the discussion,<br>managing the group and individuals. | 0  1  2  3  4  5 | |

**Total mark**  _____

**What's good?**

**What needs improving?**

**Tutor/student** . . . . . . . . . . . . . . . . . . . . . . . . . . . . . . . . . . . . . . . . . . . . . . . . . . . .
**Date**

*Notes*
1  The form may be used for peer, self or tutor feedback or assessment.
2  Whatever method you use, do give the students the criteria before they prepare the presentation.
3  Some tutors remind their students that the tutor has the right of arbitration.
4  The form may be adapted for use for individual or group presentations.

*Figure 10.4* Seminar presentation and discussion

a presentation and its ensuing discussion – otherwise, in correcting their weaknesses, they may neglect the good features of their presentations and their management of discussion.

If you are assessing presentations and the management of discussion for summative purposes then peer assessment based on agreed criteria is likely to be more reliable than a single tutor's assessment. The criteria should be brief and simple, some training in the use of the criteria should be provided, preferably using video-recordings, and the marks awarded should be moderated by the tutor. For reliability and validity purposes, at least two presentations should be assessed summatively, but this may not be possible. Total scores derived from a brief checklist are sufficient for peer marking.

## ASSESSING THE QUALITY OF DISCUSSION

Rigorous assessment of the quality of discussion is a research task that is beyond the scope of most assessment procedures but one can use a few simple devices that provide feedback. The purpose of the analysis should be to improve the quality of discussion rather than to assign marks for individual contributions. Marking for the quality of discussion is likely to distort it rather than enhance it.

Given that the success of small-group-discussion is dependent upon the students as well as the tutor, it is useful to conduct a joint assessment of a discussion class. A powerful method of assessing the quality of discussion is to analyse extracts from a video recording of the seminar or discussion class. Ensure that the sound quality is good otherwise the exercise is fruitless. As a start, one can invite students to discuss 'what counts as a good seminar or tutorial?' Videoed examples of small-group discussions can be used as prompts. (The packs by Griffiths and Partington (1992) and Mack *et al.* (1996) contain videos of small-group teaching in different subjects.) The discussion should lead to the identification of key themes to observe or to the development of a checklist. During or after the discussion it may be helpful to draw students' attention to the common weaknesses observed in small-group teaching. These are:

- goals unclear to students
- tutor talks too much
- questions rarely rise above the level of recall
- discussion unfocused
- level of discussion is predominantly descriptive rather than analytical.

Based on Brown, 1994

A video recording of a seminar or tutorial can then be made and assessed using the themes or checklists that have been previously developed. You might discuss the purposes of the exercise with the students. In so doing you might also point out that raising the quality of discussion raises the quality of thinking and, indirectly, of writing.

For those who prefer a more structured approach, the guides in figures 10.5, 10.6 and 10.7 may be useful. They are not intended as rigorous instruments so much as prompts for analysis of discussions. All have been used extensively by one of the authors for analysing small-group discussion. Figure 10.5 is a simple category system which yields patterns and proportions of talk. It is best used for a sample of the seminar and it can be used in conjunction with other methods. Although the data collected is crude it does provide a useful basis for discussion.

The system can be extended in various ways. For example, if the tutorial group is five or less, one can assign a number or initial to each student and explore the pattern and frequency of interaction. Instead of recording which student contributed, one can record the type of contribution such as 'e' for explaining, 'q' for question, 'r' for response. Interestingly, in lively discussions, the questions are 'silent': the students move from response to response.

Figure 10.6 focuses upon the types of questions asked. In using the system you have to decide what counts as a recall or thought question for a particular group of students and whether 'observation' is a category that you wish to use. The encouraging/threatening dimension may be related to the tone of voice or to the phrasing of the question. It is useful to sample a series of questions to explore whether there is a movement from recall to thought questions or from closed to open questions. One can introduce 'p' for probing questions into the framework. A probing question may demand more recalled evidence or more thought. Figure 10.7 provides a crude indicator of level of discourse. Again it is better to use it on a sample of the video rather than the whole recording. Each segment of one or two minutes is observed and categorised using the system given in Figure 10.7. Social episodes are necessary for task effectiveness, particularly in the early stages of a seminar. They also occur when concentration lapses or there is a tension in the group. Descriptive or procedural discussions are very common. They are arguably at the same level of discourse and analogous to surface learning. But they may be necessary in the early stages of a discussion. Interpretative and explanatory discussion often requires the use of probing or reflective questions by the tutor or students.

Compare your classifications and provide a justification for them.

If the discussion group is 15 or more one can divide it into threes and invite each trio to view a few segments of the discussion and make notes on their contributions to it. A set of simple questions such as those given below might be used.

• Note whether each contribution was a direct response to a question from the tutor or whether it was an unsolicited comment or question.
• Did the contribution move the discussion on track or divert it?
• Did the contribution link to what anyone else had said in the discussion?
• Did the contribution change the level of discussion?

The checklist given in Figure 11.3 in Chapter 11 might also be used by a group to explore their own group processes.

## ASSESSING ORAL PROFICIENCY

Orals are used in most modern language courses as part of the assessment of linguistic proficiency, that is proficiency in speaking, listening, reading and writing. Boscolo (1996) is developing criterion-referenced grading scales for assessing language proficiency that are based on her earlier work for the Oxford

This system may be used to analyse interactions in a tutorial or seminar. Code who is speaking every *fifth* second by placing a tick in the appropriate box. Use only one column for each five seconds. At the end of the sample of the tutorial, explore the patterns and percentages of tutor talk, student talk and silence. After a little practice start using, in the boxes, e for explaining, q for questioning, r for responding.

Total

| Lecturer | | | | | | | | | | | | | |
|---|---|---|---|---|---|---|---|---|---|---|---|---|---|
| Student | | | | | | | | | | | | | |
| Silence | | | | | | | | | | | | | |

Total

| Lecturer | | | | | | | | | | | | | |
|---|---|---|---|---|---|---|---|---|---|---|---|---|---|
| Student | | | | | | | | | | | | | |
| Silence | | | | | | | | | | | | | |

Total

| Lecturer | | | | | | | | | | | | | |
|---|---|---|---|---|---|---|---|---|---|---|---|---|---|
| Student | | | | | | | | | | | | | |
| Silence | | | | | | | | | | | | | |

Total

| Lecturer | | | | | | | | | | | | | |
|---|---|---|---|---|---|---|---|---|---|---|---|---|---|
| Student | | | | | | | | | | | | | |
| Silence | | | | | | | | | | | | | |

Total

| Lecturer | | | | | | | | | | | | | |
|---|---|---|---|---|---|---|---|---|---|---|---|---|---|
| Student | | | | | | | | | | | | | |
| Silence | | | | | | | | | | | | | |

*Figure 10.5* BIAS: an interaction system

This system of analysis is designed to help you to classify the questions asked in seminars and tutorials.
Please note down a sample of the questions asked. Immediately after taking the sample classify each question on each dimension and examine the pattern of questions asked.

| QUESTIONS | DIMENSIONS | | | | | | | | |
|---|---|---|---|---|---|---|---|---|---|
| | 1 | | | 2 | | 3 | | 4 | |
| | Recall | Observ | Thought | Broad | Narrow | Confused | Clear | Encour | Threatng |
| | | | | | | | | | |
| | | | | | | | | | |
| | | | | | | | | | |
| | | | | | | | | | |
| | | | | | | | | | |
| | | | | | | | | | |
| | | | | | | | | | |
| | | | | | | | | | |
| | | | | | | | | | |
| | | | | | | | | | |
| | | | | | | | | | |
| | | | | | | | | | |
| | | | | | | | | | |
| | | | | | | | | | |
| | | | | | | | | | |
| | | | | | | | | | |
| | | | | | | | | | |
| | | | | | | | | | |
| | | | | | | | | | |
| | | | | | | | | | |
| | | | | | | | | | |
| | | | | | | | | | |
| | | | | | | | | | |

*Figure 10.6* ASKIT: analysing questions

Classify the predominant type of discussion in each one- (or two-) minute segment.

| Type | Description |
| --- | --- |
| 5 Explanatory | Searching for connections, causes, reasons, underlying assumptions and perspectives. |
| 4 Interpretative | Exploring meanings, providing different interpretations of the evidence, formalising definitions of terms. |
| 3 Procedural | Outlining what was done in a task or situation rather than why. Listing what an author said rather than what the author was driving at. |
| 2 Descriptive | Relating and exchanging experiences or opinions and assertions without supporting evidence. |
| 1 Social | Friendly conversations of a personal kind that are marginal to the task. |
| 0 Social | Unfriendly conversations of a personal kind that are marginal to the task. |

*Figure 10.7* Levels of discussion

A level board. The scales for speaking include pronunciation and intonation, spontaneity and fluency, range of structures and vocabulary, accuracy, development of ideas and relevant opinions, and fulfilment of task. The scales for writing might also be of interest to colleagues in arts subjects. These are vocabulary, range of expression, syntax, grammatical accuracy, structure and development of ideas, relevance to essay title or topic set. The scales provide a useful starting-point for tutors interested in developing their approaches to oral assessment. As usual, some practice in their use is necessary. The scales may be adapted for use in peer feedback and assessment and as a guide for students. An example of one of Boscolo's scales is given in Figure 10.8. The term 'native speaker' refers to a well-educated native speaker.

## THE USE OF VIVAS

*Viva voces* are used in the examination of British PhDs, in the assessment of undergraduate projects and for deciding degree classifications in borderline cases. Brown and Atkins (1988) offer suggestions on preparing for and giving vivas for PhD candidates. Here we are concerned with vivas in undergraduate courses.

A good viva, like a good research tutorial, has purpose and structure, so even if the assessors are presenting independent reports on a project or dissertation they should at least agree in advance the form that the viva will take and some

| 80+ | Outstanding | As close to native use of structures, idioms and vocabulary for the purposes of discussion as can be detected. (Stating, describing, reasoning, persuading, reacting.) |
| --- | --- | --- |
| 70–79 | Excellent | Confident and appropriate use of a wide range of structures, idioms and vocabulary for the purposes of discussion. |
| 60–69 | Very good or good | Some appropriate use of more complex structures and idioms. Good range of vocabulary for purposes of discussion. |
| 50–59 | Satisfactory | Some attempt at complex structures and idioms with some success. Suitable vocabulary for purposes of discussion. |
| 45–49 | Weak | Inconsistent. Some attempt at a wider range of structures. Beginning to use vocabulary for the purposes of discussion. |
| 40–44 | Barely adequate | Simple sentence structure. Little vocabulary beyond the basics. |
| 39- | Inadequate (fail) | Struggles to create sentences or use authentic words. |

Adapted from Boscolo (1996)

*Figure 10.8* Assessing structures and vocabularies

of the questions that will be asked. The checklists given for assessing projects and dissertations in Chapter 8 (figures 8.4 and 8.5) provide a basis for a structured approach to vivas.

The first stage in a viva is usually to establish rapport and make the candidate feel comfortable and relaxed so that he or she can present and defend the work to the best advantage. The capacity to withstand stress should not be part of an assessment of a dissertation or project. So a friendly but detached stance is most useful here. The purposes of the viva should be made clear to the student. Thereafter, the assessors may wish to address major questions and engage the students in discussion of them. Where the viva is being used to determine the degree classification, it is important to design a set of questions which cover the same core areas for each candidate. A set of guidelines and prior practice by tutors, preferably with video, improves consistency and fairness to students. Some departments do 'mock' vivas for their PhD students. This approach might also be used with undergraduates, particularly if the viva makes a substantial contribution to the mark for the dissertation or project.

It would be wrong to leave this discussion of vivas without pointing out that unstructured interviews are notoriously unreliable methods of selection and classification. There is a naive belief that a face-to-face discussion is sufficient to make an accurate assessment of an interviewee's performance or, even worse, an accurate prediction of his or her potential. Our view is that if one is using vivas to assess students then one should also assess the vivas that one is using.

## ASSESSING CONSULTATIONS

Consultations are conversations with a purpose that usually take place between a professional and a client. Consultations are part of the everyday life of most health professionals, lawyers and social workers. They are important in business, management, architecture and design engineering. Their prevalence in the professions has led to the use of consultations as a learning task in undergraduate courses.

The bulk of research has been upon the consultation between doctor and patient. The overall findings are that doctors who are perceived as competent, trustworthy and friendly are perceived favourably. Such doctors have a clearly structured consultation and they allow their patients to tell their own story. These characteristics are correlated highly with patient recall, understanding and satisfaction and positively but less highly with willingness to follow treatment plans and improved health status (Brown and Atkins, 1996). These results are probably generalisable to consultations between all health professionals and their clients and they provide pointers for consultations in other fields. The common errors in medical consultations are given in Figure 10.9. These too can be used as a basis for discussion of professional–client consultations in other fields.

As with other forms of oral communication, the consultation is best learnt about and assessed through video recordings. For learning purposes, students can take the roles of 'professional' and 'client'. The client should be provided with a suitable case history and role description. Students gain insights from playing the role of client/patient and their insights can be used in discussions

---

 1  Use of jargon.
 2  Lack of precision.
 3  Avoidance of personal issues.
 4  Failure to pick up verbal leads.
 5  Undue repetition of questions.
 6  Inappropriate questions.
 7  Lack of clarification.
 8  Lack of control.
 9  Non-facilitation.
10  Assumption there is only one problem.
11  Time management of consultation.

---

Based on Maguire *et al.* (1986)

*Figure 10.9* Common errors made by young doctors in consultations

4 = Very good  3 = Good  2 = Satisfactory  1 = Inadequate
0 = Not present

Note: Very good does not mean perfect

**OPENING**

Welcoming into the surgery.
Mutual introduction.

**4  3  2  1  0**

**RAPPORT**

Forming a social link between patient and dentist, enabling
fruitful communication.

**4  3  2  1  0**

**DIAGNOSIS**

Questioning, listening, watching and leading the patient where
necessary to disclose the patient's real problem or worry,
medical and dental including the unstated ones (hidden
agenda).

**4  3  2  1  0**

**EXPLANATION**

Discussing the problem and implications with the patient, using
a suitable vocabulary that is understood by the patient.

**4  3  2  1  0**

**RESPONSIVENESS**

The recognition and follow-up of verbal and non-verbal clues
given by the patient when proposing, negotiating and carrying
out treatment.

**4  3  2  1  0**

**EDUCATION**

Inserting into the consultation a preventive and dental health
message with encouragement of self care.

**4  3  2  1  0**

**DISMISSAL**

A clear and mutually acceptable termination to the consultation
containing a definite indication of continuing care.

**4  3  2  1  0**

**GLOBAL IMPRESSION**

**4  3  2  1  0**                                    **Total Score  /32**

Overall impression is more than the sum of the parts!

*Figure 10.10* The well-ordered consultation

and analyses of the role plays. For summative purposes, 'simulated clients' can be used. Sometimes these roles are taken by trained actors but others who are capable of a high degree of consistency may be used. For summative purposes at least three assessed consultations are necessary to ensure the results are generalisable.

Two common methods of viewing and discussing videotaped consultations are the 'stop and view' and the 'global view'. In the 'stop and view' approach, either the tutor or the student who took the role of the professional stops the tape and discusses what was going on at that point in the consultation. This form of stimulated recall can lead into a discussion of decision-making and thinking. The 'global view' allows the student 'professional' to appraise his/her overall performance. It is less threatening for the student 'professional' if he/she speaks first, the student 'client' should speak next, the tutor asks probing reflective questions, other members of the group offer views and the tutor summarises.

The primary purpose of the discussion and feedback is to help students improve their skills of consultation. These might include examination and diagnosis for health professionals. The criteria for what counts as a good consultation will vary according to its purposes. Different subjects will have different emphases. The criteria can be generated by the students with a little help from the tutors or they can be developed or adapted from existing guidelines. Figure 10.10 is an example of a guide developed initially for dentistry and adapted for use in nursing, pharmacy and general practice. The items are used for feedback and the rating scales are only used if a mark is required.

## ACTIVITIES

10.1 Use the suggestions on presentations in this chapter as a basis for a staff development activity. The presentation by each person should consist of an explanation that takes about five minutes. Examples of topics that have been used in this exercise are:

1 How local anaesthetics work.
2 How penicillin kills bacteria.
3 The basic principles of occupational therapy.
4 Why rotate crops?
5 What are the basic principles of speech therapy?
6 What is job evaluation?
7 The basic concepts of linguistics.
8 What is microeconomics?
9 What is entropy?
10 How do we see?
11 What is cholesterol?

12  Why is DNA important?

13  What is tragedy?

14  What are the main elements of physiotherapy?

15  Why was Dr Johnson so prejudiced against Jonathan Swift?

If there are six people in the group, the exercise takes about two hours including a 20-minute presentation by the course leader.

10.2  Use 10.1 as a basis for developing a six-hour course for students in which they give a presentation and then manage a discussion. The course should include hints and suggestions that are, preferably, based on research on explaining.

10.3  Discuss with students what counts as a good tutorial or seminar. Video-record a tutorial or seminar. Analyse the discussion in the seminar or tutorial with the students who participated in it.

10.4  Meet with a group of tutors and use the criterion-referenced grading given in Figure 10.8 (or one of your own) to assess a few video-recorded orals. Repeat the exercise with a group of students. Modify the scales in the light of the discussions.

10.5  What differences would you expect between the oral proficiency of first- and final-year students? Compile a list of probable differences.

10.6  What is the 'viva' for in your course? Devise a simple guide for assessing student performance in the viva that is based on the purposes of the viva. Try the guide, with a few colleagues, on a few video-recorded mock vivas. Modify it in the light of your discussions.

10.7  Discuss with students what counts as a good consultation. Invent some simple cases for the students to role play. Video-record them and review them with the students in the light of their criteria. Discuss what changes the students would now make to their criteria.

# Chapter 11

# Peer- and self-assessment

Earlier chapters have focused upon the tutors and examiners as sources of assessment. In this chapter the focus is primarily upon the students as assessors – with a little help from tutors. The chapter considers peer and self-assessment, their advantages and limitations and the role of self-assessment in learning to learn. We offer some suggestions for introducing and using self-assessment and peer-assessment in courses. The next chapter considers some of the approaches often used in conjunction with self-assessment.

Peer- and self-assessment are increasingly used in higher education. Brew (1995a, 1995b) in her review chapters cites examples of self-assessment from several subjects and shows how the processes of self-assessment are linked to knowledge, skills understanding and competence. Falchikov (1995a, 1996a) reviews empirical research on peer- and self-assessment and reports a wide range of self- and peer-assessment studies from across the undergraduate curriculum. The texts edited by Exley and Moore (1992), Moore and Exley (1994) and Exley and Dennick (1996) provide practical examples of peer-assessment in science, engineering and medicine. Brown and Dove (1991) provide further case studies and discussions of peer- and self-assessment and Lewis (1984) provides guidelines for preparing self-assessment tasks and checklists. All of the examples of peer- and self-assessment are, in varying degrees, forms of collaborative assessment between tutors and students or groups of students. Despite the increasing use of peer- and self-assessment, they are not always well understood. In Chapter 2 it was indicated that peer- and self-assessment are not methods of assessment but *sources* of assessment that may be used with different methods and instruments of assessment. In this chapter we seek to provide you with a clearer understanding of the notions of peer- and self-assessment, to explore some of the issues involved and to describe some of the uses and approaches to peer- and self-assessment. At the outset we stress that we regard peer- and self-assessment as primarily tools for learning rather than tools of summative assessment.

## PEER-ASSESSMENT

Strictly speaking, peer-assessment is assessment of the work of others by people of equal status and power. There is usually an element of mutuality in peer-assessment. The term is also used to describe approaches to accountability carried out on behalf of government agencies. It is a moot point whether such accountability exercises are best described as peer-based or power-based forms of assessment. Peer-assessment in the context of student learning may be divided into the giving and receiving of feedback and making formal estimates of worth of other students' work.

Giving and receiving feedback were discussed in Chapter 1. Here we wish to add that if students are engaged in giving and receiving feedback then one should encourage them to reflect upon these processes and on the use of different forms of evidence to support their views. Beneath the processes of giving and receiving feedback are implicit criteria of what counts as 'good' for different purposes in different contexts. The students' notions of 'good' can be drawn out in tutorial discussions and large group classes and so provide a basis for reflective learning and more formal peer-assessment. This approach is described by Mowl and Pain (1995) in their study of peer- and self-assessment for marking essays in geography. The approach is readily transferable to other subject areas.

Making estimates of other students' work is sometimes described as *peer marking*. In the pure version all peers mark each other's work. The approach requires careful planning and, preferably, the use of spreadsheets for analysing marks. Feedback sessions based on the results of the peer-assessment exercise make the process more useful for students. 'Peer marking' is also used to describe one student marking another student's work (strictly speaking this is not peer-assessment). This approach has been used in schools for generations. It may be used in classes to save assessment time by getting students to mark each other's work (MCQs, simple problems or questions) in class. Answers to MCQs and simple questions can be displayed on an overhead transparency. The approach may also be used for more challenging tasks such as marking prose translations, essays or solutions to problems.

*Peer feedback marking* involves students in deriving criteria, developing a peer-assessment form, providing anonymous feedback and assigning a global mark. The method was developed by Falchikov (1994, 1995a, 1996b) initially for oral presentations and subsequently for marking essays. Anonymity of feedback is preserved by removing the students' names from the feedback forms before passing them to the individual student. Falchikov's findings indicate that the approach was viewed favourably by the students; it reduced the dislike of marking the work of friends; there was a slight tendency for students to award higher marks than the tutor but the variation was no greater than that between external and internal examiners (see Newstead and Dennis, 1994 for a recent study of variations between examiners). Peer feedback marking may be used as a preliminary to summative assessment of a task, as part of summative assessment or for the whole of summative assessment of a task. It is probably less threatening and more useful as a form of feedback than as the method of summative assessment.

When using peer-feedback methods it is advisable to provide students with some training in the use of feedback and marking criteria. The approach not only may save time, it can provide a rich source of support and constructive feedback and it can deepen understanding of the topic and of the processes of assessment. Figure 11.1 provides some examples of the uses of peer feedback and marking.

Resistance to informal peer feedback is rare, resistance to formal peer-assessment is relatively more frequent. Informal feedback, that is giving and receiving feedback, is the core of small-group teaching and of many training exercises in leadership and oral presentations. Resistance by students to formal peer-assessment for summative purposes is based on dislike of judging peers in ways that 'count', a distrust of the process and of the time involved. Some do not want to accept the responsibility of assessing others' work or their own work.

---

**Peer feedback marking**

| Assessment task | Examples of subject areas |
|---|---|
| Case solutions | Business, health sciences, law, medicine, social work |
| Essays | Virtually all subjects |
| Lab reports | Virtually all science-based subjects |
| Problems | Virtually all science- or social-science based subjects |
| Proses | Modern and classical languages |

**Peer-assessment**

| Assessment task | Examples of subject areas |
|---|---|
| Consultations/interviews | Business, health sciences, law, medicine, social work |
| Exhibitions | Art, design, architecture |
| Group projects (presentations) | Most subjects |
| Poster sessions | Most science-based subjects but other subjects could use them |
| Presentations | Most subjects |
| Teamwork | Subjects doing group projects |

*Note:*
In peer feedback marking, one student provides feedback and possibly marks on another student's work.
In peer-assessment all students within a group assess each other's work and perhaps provide marks on it.

---

*Figure 11.1* Some uses of peer feedback and assessment

Many would prefer to trust the judgement of the 'expert', the lecturer, and many are sensitive to the conflicts of loyalty to the peer group and the process of making balanced objective assessments of their peers' achievements. *In extremis*, peer-assessment can destroy a group's morale and working relationships. Staff question the reliability, fairness and time involved in the process. Beneath the concerns of students and staff lie their expectations of the lecturer's role. Students expect staff to be expert judges and want that expert judgement. For lecturers, peer- and self-assessment involves giving up some of their power. The more one is committed to assessment as judgement, the less willing one may be to help students to develop their own skills of assessment. Yet, if one considers carefully the purposes of higher education, it becomes clear that peer- and self-assessment are part of the preparation for life that a university education should give. Providing and giving feedback is central to managerial tasks in any organisation and self-assessment provides the basis for reflective learning and career planning. However, one should not confuse goals and methods. The goal may be to develop independent active reflective learners; the path to that goal requires some guidance by lecturers and safe opportunities to develop assessment skills. Hence our view that peer- and self-assessment are primarily tools of learning. But to demonstrate that these tools are valuable it is necessary to incorporate some peer- and self-assessment into the system of summative assessment otherwise most students will use them indifferently.

## RESEARCH ON PEER-ASSESSMENT

The research evidence on peer-assessment indicates that it can promote critical thinking, the skills of task management, increases in self confidence, responsibility and awareness of group dynamics. These findings are subject to the provisos that:

- Adequate training in small-group work is given.
- Adequate training in self- and peer-assessment are given.
- The learning task is clearly defined.
- There is a learning contract or agreement between the members of the group and between the group and the tutor.
- The assessment procedure is clear and known to the students.
- The assessment marks reflect the time and effort invested by students.

The overwhelming weight of evidence indicates that peer-assessment is useful, reliable and valid but in some circumstances student overmarking occurs. The latter can be minimised by moderating peer marks. However, there are the usual difficulties of comparing small-scale studies in which a wide variety of designs and measuring instruments have been used. Although students express some reservations about peer-assessment, particularly concerning conflicts of loyalty, their views are broadly that the experience is beneficial (Falchikov, 1994, 1995a, 1995b, 1996a, 1996b).

Peer-assessment which involves all students in a group marking each other's work is potentially more reliable than single or double marking because it involves repeated measures of the same tasks. Peer marking, in the sense of individuals exchanging papers to mark, has been shown to be as reliable as tutor marking when structured marking schemes are used (Montgomery, 1986; Boud, 1987). However, one should treat these results cautiously: they are dependent upon the marking scheme used and the training provided to students. One should analyse the overall results of a peer-assessment to check that biasing factors are not at work. Students can penalise themselves by marking other students' work generously. Scapegoating can occur and cartels can operate. These factors can be identified by examining the matrix of scores or, for very large groups, the matrix of correlations. Goldfinch (1994) offers further suggestions for minimising such difficulties and easing the administrative burdens of peer-assessment.

There appears to be little work on the time involved in peer- and self-assessment. Obviously planning the first try of peer- and self-assessment is likely to be time-consuming and the use of unduly complex procedures can put a burden on students and staff. Miller (1992) in her use of self- and peer-assessment of practicals based on poster sessions estimated that the assessment of 89 students took 14 person-hours (that is, two members of staff present at two two-and-a-half-hour sessions) and the calculations of ranks and grades a further four hours. Individual marking of this number of projects would, she estimated, have taken 40 to 45 person-hours.

## USING PEER-ASSESSMENT

The main uses of peer-assessment are to help students to:

- develop their skills of assessment
- deepen their understanding of the processes of assessment
- deepen their understanding of a topic or method
- develop their skills of group work and task management
- facilitate the development of self-assessment and reflective learning.

Peer assessment may be used for assessing educational *products* such as essays, solutions to problems, poster sessions, and design artefacts. It may be used for assessing *performances* such as oral presentations and doctor–patient interviews, and it may also be used for assessing *processes* such as leadership, group and project management and how well a group works together. Indeed, peer-assessment may be the only satisfactory way of assessing how students work together in a group project. Many of the rating schedules and checklists given in other chapters of this book may be adapted for use in self- and peer-assessment.

The criteria for peer marking may be developed by the groups of students involved. This approach develops understanding and a sense of ownership of the criteria. Alternatively, preliminary training in the use of criteria may be given, perhaps using examples from the work of a previous year. An intermediate strategy is to provide the criteria and ask the students to assign weightings to them. This method is used by Hedges (1993) in a civil engineering group project on water resources. Figure 11.2 gives the criteria that he used. Criteria may be used in semi-structured questions, rating schedules or checklists. A global mark may be awarded or a mark for each dimension or rating scale. Global marks are faster and probably sufficient for most purposes. The less structured approaches are unwieldy in large-group exercises. The usual advice of 'keep them simple' applies. The purpose of the peer-assessment should be kept in mind. If it is to obtain a mark then less detail is needed than if it is to provide feedback to each student. Figure 11.3 provides an example of a global approach.

There are two approaches that one can use with peer-assessment instruments. One can ask students to assign a mark around the group mark awarded. A major contributor to the project is given an extra few marks above the group project mark and a lesser contributor is given a mark below the group project mark. The net effect is to balance all the marks around the group mean. In other words, the sum of the deviations of the individuals' scores from the group mark is zero. In effect, the method is a form of norm referencing. It requires students to rank order each of their peers on each of the dimensions. Not surprisingly the process is time-consuming and it does not always find favour with students. The second approach is to ask each student to give a mark to his/her peers out of a fixed total. The mark may be a global score or a mark for each dimension. The criteria are developed by the students or provided by the tutor. This is a form of criterion-referenced grading in which students are asked to rate, not rank order, their peers' competence against a set of criteria. In effect the method separates out the mark for the product from the mark for the process. The method is simpler and less threatening.

The peer-assessment of group processes may be handled by use of Figure 11.4. The schedule is a reflective tool that may be used in various ways. Each individual can complete the schedule and the results can be collated by the tutor

| Skill | Criteria for self/peer-assessment | Weighting |
|---|---|---|
| *Ability to work in a group* | 1 Ability to arrive at consensus/ overcome difficulties | |
| | 2 Giving and accepting support/ facilitating group effort | |
| *Contribution to group initiative* | 3 Attendance and time-keeping | |
| | 4 Application; taking fair share of work | |
| | 5 Ability to generate good ideas/solve problems | |
| | 6 Gathering/researching additional/new information | |

*Figure 11.2* Criteria for self- and peer-assessment of group processes

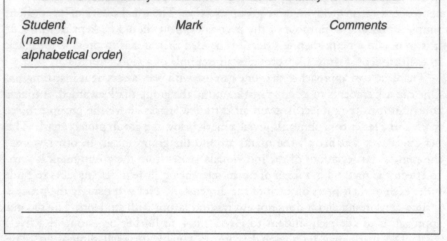

**Confidential**
Please complete your assessment of everyone's contribution to the project, including your own. Provide a mark out of 10.

    10–9 = Outstanding contribution   8–7 = Very good contribution
    6–5 = Good contribution   4–3 = Fairly satisfactory contribution
    2–1 = Unsatisfactory contribution   0 = No or virtually no contribution

| Student (names in alphabetical order) | Mark | Comments |
| --- | --- | --- |

*Figure 11.3* Peer-group assessment: a global approach

or a member of the group. The results are then discussed in a tutorial. The group can discuss each item and arrive at a group decision on each rating and then report their ratings and reasons in a tutorial. If there is more than one group involved, then each group can complete its own assessment and, in a seminar or large class, the results of the 'self' assessment can be discussed. This approach is particularly useful for developing awareness of group skills.

Finally we want to touch upon a consequence of using peer- and self-assessment: the role of the lecturer changes towards that of an external examiner and moderator. The new role of the lecturer in self- and peer-assessment is to monitor the processes, protect students from unfair marking and guard standards. And, as in the case of the external examiner, the lecturer is the final arbiter of the marks awarded.

## SELF-ASSESSMENT

Self-assessment is an intriguing concept with a long history. In everyday language it involves one part of the self assessing another part of the self's actions and outcomes. Step back from this description and you will see it raises some deep questions about the nature of self, self-awareness and self-monitoring. These questions are barely visible in the literature on self-assessment and they

| Most of our meetings were confused | 1  2  3  4  5 | Most of our meetings were well organised. |
|---|---|---|
| We often got side-tracked. | 1  2  3  4  5 | We stuck to the task most of the time. |
| We didn't listen to each other. | 1  2  3  4  5 | We did listen to each other. |
| Some talked too much and some did not talk enough. | 1  2  3  4  5 | We all contributed to the discussion. |
| We did not think through our ideas sufficiently. | 1  2  3  4  5 | We thought through our ideas well. |
| Some got aggressive and some got upset. | 1  2  3  4  5 | We were able to argue and discuss without rancour. |
| Most of us seemed to be bored by the discussion. | 1  2  3  4  5 | Most of us seemed to enjoy the discussion. |
| Most of us did not improve our discussion skills. | 1  2  3  4  5 | Most of us did improve our discussion skills. |
| Most of us did not learn much. | 1  2  3  4  5 | Most of us did learn through our group work. |

*Note*: the discussion is more important than the rating.

How could the group have worked better?


Name _____        Group _____


Thank you for your views.
There will be an opportunity to discuss the overall reactions of the group at our next meeting.

Based on Gibbs (1992)

*Figure 11.4* How our group worked

are unfashionable in late twentieth-century psychology. It is at least arguable that advocates of self-assessment should examine their own perspectives on self-assessment.

In western culture the I–Me approach to self-assessment appears in various guises. In Christianity it is part of meditation, examination of conscience and public and private confession. In Freudian psychology the ego assesses and controls the impulses of the id, the residual guilt of the super ego and the ego's own cognitive processes. In mid-twentieth-century social psychology, self-assessment emerges through the concept of self and looking-glass self and, in cognitive psychology, in the form of meta-cognition, the processes of thinking about one's own thinking and learning about one's own learning. In a speculative paper, Brown (1992) suggests that an economical explanation of self-assessment can be developed from the notion of long-term memory (information storage and retrieval) and intrinsic feedback loops. Put rather simply, as one gains in experience one is more able to assess more accurately and more deeply. The accumulation of accessible information provides us with prospective and retrospective feedback. We develop a 'sixth' sense of intuition that informs us when we are about to commit an error or have just made an error. We can sense when previous actions, outcomes and diagnoses are faulty although we may not be able to articulate immediately the reasons or causes. Examples of these incidents occur in situations where we are using sensori-motor, social or intellectual skills. We may 'know' when we are about to miss a golf ball, make a wrong incision, commit a social gaffe, or go wrong in an explanation or a solution to a problem.

The interesting question from the standpoint of learning and assessment is how one can accelerate the development of self-assessment. The answer is apparently simple: practise.

## USES AND USAGE OF SELF-ASSESSMENT

Self-assessment is central to effective life-long learning and the development of professional competence. Many students self-assess their work, they learn and check their learning, they revise drafts of essays and problems and they revise and check that they know what they have learnt. Most of us assess our own work, whether it is writing, doing research, conducting surgical operations, carrying out consultations or teaching. If one wishes to lay the foundations of effective life-long learning then self-assessment is a *sine qua non* of course design and delivery. This point has long been recognised by the Open University which builds several self-assessment tasks into its courses.

The long-term uses of self-assessment are summarised by Boud *et al.* (1995) as:

• For individual self-monitoring: students monitor their own work for their own purposes. They may be introduced to ways of doing this but are left to their own devices.

- To promote good learning practices and learning to learn.
- For diagnosis and remediation.
- As a learning activity to improve professional or academic practice.
- To consolidate learning over a range of contexts: this use is of increasing importance for integrating learning from different modules. Guidance and support from tutors is required.
- To review achievements as a prelude to recognition of prior learning.
- To promote self-knowledge and understanding. Here the predominant interests are self reports, analysis and reflection that move beyond the present task towards long-term development.
- As a substitute for other forms of assessment. Here the predominant interest is the generation of marks to be used in formal assessments.

Boud (1995) suggests that there are two parts to self-assessment: the development of criteria and their application to a particular task. He suggests that the development of criteria is the more important and the more neglected feature. Certainly it is relatively easy to mark one's own work if one has the answers, a marking scheme or clear criteria. Much of the self-assessed work that is computer-based uses this approach. The development of one's own criteria requires opportunities for practice and discussion, hence the link with peer discussion and assessment. Criteria may be taught directly but a more effective approach is to use 'good' and 'bad' examples on which the students work. The criteria then emerge through attempts at judgement and the students can then apply the criteria to their own work.

Self-assessment, like other forms of assessment, may be used for judgmental or developmental purposes. In other words, one can look back to make an estimate of how well one is doing or one can look back with a view to developing what one is doing. Self-assessment may be used to reflect upon the content of what one has learnt, upon one's actions or upon the processes of learning itself. The last is intimately related to learning to learn. This is a theme of a later section in this chapter.

Self-assessment tasks are usually built into projects and dissertations in the form of critical appraisals of methods and findings, although the marks for self-assessment are not usually separated out. They may be used as adjuncts to other assignments such as essay writing or problem-solving or in separate exercises such as the compilation of portfolios and learning logs. The separate exercises are discussed in the next chapter.

Self-assessment, like its sister, peer-assessment, may be used to assess products, performances and processes. The instruments used may be open-ended self-reports, semi-structured reports, ratings or checklists. Many of the checklists and rating schedules given in other chapters may be adapted for use in self-assessment. The purposes may be primarily to improve learning or primarily to generate marks, and, as for peer-assessment, we would argue that self-assessment is more useful as a learning tool than as a tool of summative assessment.

## RESEARCH ON SELF-ASSESSMENT

Research on the development of self-assessment across the age span indicates that self-assessment grows out of assessment by one's peers and significant adults. It is carried out by primary school children: 'I am cleverer than Siobhan but I am not so good at drawing.' Usually their assessments in relation to their immediate peers are accurate. At this stage, high achievers tend to over-estimate what they can do and low achievers tend to under-estimate what they can do (Wittrock, 1986). In higher education, high achievers tend to under-estimate and low achievers tend to over-estimate (Falchikov and Boud, 1989). The reasons for this shift are probably associated with the development of self and self-presentation. We learn to distinguish between assessing oneself for oneself and assessing oneself for others.

Most research on self-assessment has been concerned with comparisons of tutor, self and peer marks. Falchikov and Boud (1989) in their review point to the methodological weaknesses of these studies but they also point out that self-assessment can be as reliable as other forms of assessment. It is more accurate in the science subjects than in arts. This may be because the criteria and values are clearer in science. Self-assessment is more accurate in the later stages than in the earlier stages of a course, thereby indicating that students do learn to self-assess even when not provided with training in self-assessment. Self-assessment is more accurate when training is provided. Evidence on gender differences in self-assessment is conflicting.

The evidence suggests that it is possible to develop accurate, reliable self-assessment. The difficulties arise if these procedures are used for judgmental purposes by those in authority. Prudent students are unlikely to reveal evidence that may be held against them, particularly in highly competitive, low-trust situations.

The reviews and research on reflective learning conducted by Hatton and Smith (1995) suggests that there may be a hierarchy of self-assessment tasks (see also Chapter 3). At the lowest level, decision-making is about immediate behaviours and skills. This could be likened to self-assessment for survival. The next three levels are concerned with reflection-on-action. The lowest of these levels is labelled 'technical' description of what one has done. The next level they describe as 'dialogic' reflection. At this level competing claims are weighed and alternative solutions explored. The uppermost level of reflection-on-action is 'critical' reflection where one evaluates existing goals, practices and criteria and considers the effects of changing social circumstances. Hatton and Smith argue that the highest level of their hierarchy is reflection-in-action in which an experienced professional is able to draw on any of the previous four levels to make informed professional judgements on the spot. We suspect that reflection-on-action is a different type of reflection from reflection-in-action and that it facilitates reflection-in-action. The implication of the work of Hatton and Smith is that one should develop learning opportunities that move a student through the hierarchy. A corollary of their views is that one should not set general reflective tasks too early in a course. Finally, the work on experts and novices indicates that reflective learning can accelerate the acquisition of expertise (Boshuizer, Norman and Schmidt, 1990).

## META-COGNITION: LEARNING TO LEARN

A central purpose of self-assessment is to develop one's cognitive processes so that one's learning is developed. Nisbet and Shouksmith (1984) describe this capability as the seventh sense, meta-cognition. It builds upon intuition, the sixth sense. Like Hatton and Smith, they argue that as a first step specific skills learnt in the context of a topic or subject need to be put together as strategies of planning, monitoring, checking and self-testing. These strategies should lead the learner to analyse what is required in a new task, what strategies he or she has available, how best the two can be matched together and what new strategies need to be developed.

For learners to develop the capability of transferring learning strategies from one context to another, they need to:

- Be able to articulate their strategies.
- Have opportunities to practise them in different contexts.
- Have opportunities to assess their strategies and outcomes.
- Receive feedback on their efforts to assess.

A lecturer can facilitate a student's capacity to learn to learn in seven ways:

- As a direct teacher of skills and strategies.
- As a model who makes explicit the processes going on in his or her own mind as a problem or task is tackled.
- As a provider and assessor of learning tasks.
- As a guide during learning tasks.
- As a provider and facilitator of peer-group assessment.
- As a provider of opportunities for self-assessment.
- As an assessor of self-assessment tasks.

## INTRODUCING SELF- AND PEER-ASSESSMENT

Clearly, it is not enough to introduce self- and peer-assessment by *diktat*. One has to provide opportunities for students to develop and check their skills against their criteria and other people's criteria. One also has to encourage them to explore the nature of appropriate evidence to match the criteria. Here, peer- as well as tutor assessment are valuable adjuncts to self-assessment. Brown and Dove (1991) offer the advice given in Figure 11.5. We would add that it is important to develop self- and peer-assessment in the very early stages of the course when students may be more open to new approaches. Like all

| | |
|---|---|
| **Start:** | Don't prevaricate, give it a try. |
| **Start small:** | Don't be over-ambitious at first, *festina lente*. |
| **Convince:** | Ensure the students know that what they are doing is useful. |
| **Clarify:** | Let students know what is expected of them and be aware that criteria can be problematic. |
| **Be relevant:** | Make sure that what you are doing relates to course aims and philosophy. |
| **Be flexible:** | There are no hard and fast rules, adapt as you go along. |
| **Reflect:** | Think the processes through carefully so that you are aware of the implications of what you are doing. |
| **Innovate:** | Treat each event as new but recycle the useful elements. |
| **Rehearse:** | Let students have an opportunity to try things out before the assessment that counts. |
| **Liaise:** | Share good practices with friends and colleagues and support each other, don't try to invent the wheel, persist, don't let failure discourage you. |

Based on Brown and Dove (1991)

*Figure 11.5* Getting started with self- and peer-assessment

innovations, the introduction of peer- and self-assessment techniques requires careful planning, discussion with the groups involved and sensitivity to the issues raised.

## DESIGNING SELF-ASSESSMENT TASKS AND CRITERIA

The core questions to ask when engaged in self-assessment are:

What have I been doing?
How have I been doing it?
What do I think of what I have been doing?
How could I improve my approach?

These questions can form the basis for designing self-assessment tasks and criteria although it is less threatening to begin with what counts as good or bad in other people's work.

The usual precepts of design apply to self-assessment. The task and instruments used should fit the purpose of the self-assessment task and the objectives of the course. If the primary purpose is the development of reflective learning then use open-ended or, preferably, semi-structured reports. If you do use check-lists, rating schedules or marks for this purpose then invite students to justify their marks. Awarding oneself 7 out of 10 for an essay is neither meaningful nor useful without a justification of the mark. The tasks and the instruments should be discussed with students so they are perceived as useful in themselves and for subsequent assessment tasks. Otherwise they will be regarded as yet more meaningless, time-consuming exercises. The tasks should be concrete rather than abstract. It is better to ask students to reflect upon their approach or competence in relation to a particular task than to ask for a self-assessment of a broad range of skills. 'What were your major strengths and weaknesses in the presentation you gave in the seminar?' is better than 'Discuss your communicative competence'. The criteria should be brief and to the point. If rating schedules or criterion-graded referencing are used then ensure the categories for each point on the scale or each grade are well defined and intelligible. Similar remarks apply to marking schemes. The task is not easy.

|  | Yes | No |
|---|---|---|
| 1  Do you almost always turn up to give your lectures or seminars? |  |  |
| 2  Do you like most of your students? |  |  |
| 3  Do you enjoy teaching your subject? |  |  |
| 4  Do you keep up to date in the aspects of your subject that you are teaching? |  |  |
| 5  Are you patient with those who don't seem to understand? |  |  |
| 6  Are you usually on time? |  |  |
| 7  Do you make the objectives of your assessment clear? |  |  |
| 8  Are your lectures and seminars well structured? |  |  |
| 9  Do you explain complicated ideas clearly? |  |  |
| 10  Do you provide useful feedback to students on their coursework? |  |  |
| 11  Do you return coursework quickly? |  |  |
| 12  Are you expecting students to do more than regurgitate facts? |  |  |
| 13  Do your coursework and examination questions demonstrate your answer to 12? |  |  |
| 14  Do you comment on first drafts of dissertations or projects? |  |  |

Figure 11.6 Lecturer: know thyself

If you want students to develop their own criteria, you can use two basic approaches or variations on these approaches. The first is group discussion in which the task is to identify what counts as 'good' and 'bad' and then develop an assessment instrument. Concrete examples provide a focus. If the task is complex, provide extremes of good and bad and then some examples which have elements of both good and bad. Alternatively provide 'bad' examples. These can be treated light-heartedly. Then provide good and mixed examples. The group – or, if it is a large class, the groups – then decide on the important criteria. Members of each group should be invited to give concrete instances to exemplify their criteria. You might then discuss whether these should be used in criterion-referenced instruments, in a rating schedule or as a checklist. The second approach is to ask students to develop their criteria independently. If you ask them to do this as private study then you should expect, and perhaps encourage, joint efforts. The instructions follow the same path as those for group discussion. Our experience suggests that most students prefer to work together on the development of criteria. Criterion-referenced grading is preferred by students for essays and reports, rating schedules and comments for performance in seminars or role plays, and checklists for setting up equipment and taking measurements.

## ACTIVITIES

11.1 Since this chapter is about self-assessment, you might like to complete the self-assessment schedule in Figure 11.6. Compare your results with those of a few colleagues. You might also like to develop, with a few colleagues, your own self-assessment schedule on teaching.

11.2 What do your friends think of your teaching and approach to research?

11.3 Devise a simple checklist with students for either marking an essay, checking solutions to problems or assessing oral presentations. Ask them to use it and report back on its usefulness at the next tutorial.

11.4 Write down your thoughts on self- and peer-assessment. Use them as a basis for discussion with colleagues.

11.5 Spend a few minutes thinking and jotting down your approaches to learning. For example: Think of how you tackle learning something new or unfamiliar. Think of how you tackle learning or revising something with which you are familiar. Think of how you tackle learning ways of working with people.
Now think of how and when you learn worst.
Compare your approaches with those of a few colleagues. Compile a list of approaches for 'best' and 'worst' and consider their implications for teaching and assessment.

# Chapter 12

# Self-assessment: some related approaches

In this chapter we explore the uses of self-assessment in learning logs, records of achievement and related approaches, and the assessment of prior learning. We consider various forms of work-based learning and how these might involve self-assessment and we offer some guidelines for developing and assessing work-based learning.

Self-assessment permeates the use of a wide range of new approaches to learning. The most common are learning logs, diaries, journals, portfolios, records of achievement and profiles, and the accreditation of prior experiential learning. These terms are used differently by different authors. Strictly speaking these approaches are not methods of assessment but methods of recording materials for feedback and assessment purposes. In short, they can become the content of assessment. Because the methods are not widespread there has been no substantial empirical research, as yet, that compares the effects of these methods upon reflective learning, deep learning or changes in practical skills. Amongst the difficulties of such research are that the purposes of the approaches may differ, the methods can be used differently, some people prefer to keep their private thoughts to themselves and some may resist attempts to change their learning style.

There appear to be two quite distinctive emphases in the use of these approaches. One springs from the competency movement. It stresses detailed objectives or learning outcomes and structures, and it emphasises instrumentality. It uses the approaches as a preparation for employment. Job appraisal and the development of detailed curriculum vitae appear to be its hidden concerns. At a deeper level, it encourages the internalisation of accountability and it may be linked to notions of surveillance and social control. Self-assessment then moves closer to self-accountability. It may be likened to the recent use of the term 'self-assessment' by the Inland Revenue. The second approach emphasises personal development through reflection and joint exploration with tutors. Its concern is to help a person to develop new forms of understanding. At a deeper level it may be linked to humanism and the notion of constructivism: that knowledge and understanding are created by individuals from their experience.

Self-assessment in this approach moves closer to reflective learning and meta-cognition. It may be likened to an inner journey of discovery. These two emphases produce tensions and confusions both in the literature and in the practice of these approaches in different disciplines.

All of the approaches raise the question of feedback and assessment, of trust between tutors and students, of self-assessing for oneself and self-assessing for others, and of workloads for students and staff. The competency approach is useful for demonstrating particular skills and competencies so it has a place in technical subjects (see Chapter 15 for a discussion of its limitations), some aspects of modern languages and the social sciences, although not necessarily in the rigid framework advocated by the National Council of Vocational Qualifications (NCVQ). Challis (1993) offers guidelines on using competency approaches in accrediting prior experiential learning and Evans (1992) provides a guide on developmental approaches. The development approach has an intuitive appeal to many academics. It values the development of understanding and knowledge and it encourages personal and professional growth through reflection. It is based on the persuasive argument that writing aids reflection and improves learning. Writing for oneself helps to clarify one's thoughts and feelings and it is a useful preliminary to planning and to communicating a sample of one's thoughts. Walker (1995) and November (1993) discuss the uses of writing and provide examples of its uses to aid various forms of reflection.

## LEARNING DIARIES, LOGS AND JOURNALS

These approaches are essentially the same. They are based on the assumption that students will benefit from self-assessment and reflecting upon their own learning. No comparisons appear to have been made of students who use learning journals and those who do not, nor whether the use of learning journals changes the style of learning towards Kolb's reflective learning style. The use of learning journals has been reported, *inter alia*, in sociology (Wagenaar, 1984), in medicine (Ashbury *et al.*, 1993) in nursing (Landeen *et al.*, 1992) and in dentistry (Wetherall and Mullins, 1996). All the reports indicate that students and staff benefit from the approach and all point to the contentious issue of feedback versus formal assessment.

The purposes of learning journals are to provide students with opportunities to:

• record their learning experiences
• reflect upon the progress and problems of learning
• integrate theories and practice and different aspects of a subject
• express feelings and mood states about their learning.

These purposes provide the basis for feedback and encouragement to students and they provide feedback to lecturers on the course, methods of teaching assessment and how students see them. Clearly there are problems and issues about the use of journals – who will see them and for what purposes. We are not convinced that all entries in journals should be seen by staff or that the whole of a journal should be submitted for formal assessment. Open journals require high-trust, low-risk situations, perhaps built on long-term relationships, if they are to be used in summative assessment. The style of writing private notes is not the style of writing public documents and self-assessment for others is different from self-assessment for oneself. If journals become part of the formal assessment procedures then students, rightly in our view, will sanitise their reports. We suggest that students should be invited to provide an edited sample of their journals for feedback purposes and assessment. In return, lecturers should provide useful feedback on the issues and problems raised by the students. Some students will probably not complete the journals except for the assessment exercises. On balance, the approach suggested above is better than coercion.

Explicit guidelines on journal writing should be developed for students and staff and, preferably, both groups should be involved in the development and modifications of the guidelines. The guidelines should include notes on content and style, the structure and topics of the journal, how much to write, how long to spend on each journal task, the issue of confidentiality and examples of different types of reflective writing. The writing should be focused on specific tasks, such as learning in a particular experiment rather than on diffuse tasks ('What have I learnt about practical skills in the last semester?'). Writing reflective notes can be a difficult task so do provide students with practice and discussion in safe situations.

## PORTFOLIO-BASED LEARNING

Portfolio-based learning is essentially a collection of evidence that learning has taken place. The term comes from fine art and graphic design where students collect together examples of their work or photographs of their work. Nowadays most art courses require students to include commentaries that explain and justify their approaches. In other subject areas, the portfolio is not quite as portable. It might include assignments, reviews of key articles, project reports, audio or video clips, reports on critical or significant incidents and reflective notes in the form of a diary. Checklists and structured self-assessment schedules might be provided by the course team. An extract from a portfolio is shown in Figure 12.1. Needless to say, portfolios can be very time-consuming for students to compile and staff to mark. One must therefore think out carefully the purposes of the portfolio, how it fits the objectives of the course and how useful the exercise is to students. Important features of implementing portfolio-based learning are careful planning of the contents required, the guidelines for students and staff, realistic estimates of student and staff time, the stated usefulness of the portfolio to students and the kind of feedback that will be provided to students – and when. Again we suggest that only sections of the personal notes should be submitted for formal assessment purposes.

By the end of Year 1 you should have achieved the relevant objectives outlined in Section 1 of the workbook and your portfolio should show evidence of this. The table below gives an outline of what we expect, but we want you to have your *own* ideas.

| | Examples of what you should have done – outcomes | Possible evidence in portfolio |
|---|---|---|
| **to introduce you to the course, the school, the university and the Sheffield area** | – have found your way around the university and the local colleges where teaching on the course takes place<br>– have a working knowledge of relevant procedures and organisation for your course, the school and the university | – maps, lists of places visited, visit reports<br>– examples of problems you have sorted out and how (e.g. grant, accommodation, examinations queries) |
| **to develop effective study and learning skills** | – taken accurate and usable notes from a range of lectures<br>– gathered information from a range of sources<br>– produced a work schedule and reviewed its effectiveness<br>– identified and used effective revision and exam techniques<br>– contributed and worked effectively in groups | – examples of your notes<br>– answer sheet for Group Exercise, list of sources consulted for assignment<br>– e.g. of weekly plan and your comments on it<br>– revision plan reviewed and related to examination performance<br>– self and peer reviews of group exercises and assignments; evidence of involvement in clubs/societies/teams |
| **to develop interpersonal and communication skills** | – given a short presentation to a group<br>– produced well presented reports/assignments<br>– demonstrated word processing skills | – your notes and feedback you received<br>– your best one<br>– word processed assignment |
| **to develop self-assessment and self-development skills** | – reviewed your expectations and goals for the course and HE<br>– produced a personal profile outlining current strategies and areas for development<br>– made and used personal action plans<br>– reviewed your career and made tentative plans | – initial list of these, dated and reviewed<br>– Entry Profile (4.6) or a summary<br>– completed Review Sheets and your comments on the process<br>– sheets showing areas considered, information gathered, views and plans |
| **problem-solving** | – solved routine and more difficult problems and reviewed how | – e.g. of problems encountered and accounts of your ways of dealing with them |

*Source:* From Sheffield Hallam University; Personal and Professional Portfolio

*Figure 12.1* Example from a portfolio

## RECORDS OF ACHIEVEMENT AND PROFILES

Records of Achievement (RoAs) were developed in schools and led to the development of the National Record of Achievement which all secondary school pupils are expected to keep. The official RoA was developed by the Department of Employment and the original forms implied that they should become a life record. It was intended that the RoA should be a comprehensive record of action plans, subsequent actions and achievements, records of extra-curricular and curricular activities and self-assessments. Whoever developed it appears to have had little grasp of employers' likely reactions to a massive portfolio of documents or the realities of most pupils' lives. RoAs provide many pupils with yet another opportunity for failure.

The use of school RoAs for admission into higher education was surveyed by Gretton (1992). The main conclusions are that RoAs are potentially useful but admission tutors are reluctant to use them. Bull and Otter (1994) suggest the potential benefits of RoAs in higher education are:

- improvement of the quality of information available during selection
- they provide a method of recording development that may be an alternative or supplement to existing personal tutorial systems
- they provide a more detailed record of student achievements than degree classifications.

Many universities, particularly newer universities, are developing their own form of RoAs. These usually involve action plans, self-assessment, reflective learning tasks and attempts to record the development of transferable skills in academic or work settings. RoAs are, nowadays, usually divided into private, personal records of the student, a personal record for the tutor to see and return with comments and a compilation summary for use in job and higher degree applications (Butcher and Ball 1995; Assiter and Shaw, 1993). The usual suggestions, concerning objectives, planning, time estimates and involving students, apply. Assiter and Shaw provide examples and discussion of their uses.

Profiles are a variation of RoAs. Like other approaches cited above, they can provide a framework for formative and summative assessment. Profiles tend to be structured, list sets of objectives and provide detailed (perhaps too much so) instructions. They may include a summary of the record of achievement. They may take the form of a commentary under various headings or a grid of skills which have been learnt and assessed or they may be a transcript of the scores achieved in assignments. Occasionally the term 'profile' is also used to describe statistically derived typologies – although this use of the term is no longer as prevalent. Assiter, Fenwick and Nixon (1992) distinguish learning outcomes profiles, negotiated outcome profiles (learning contracts) and personal development profiles. They provide guidelines and examples of their use in higher education. The guidelines stress the importance of clarity of purpose, involvement of the parties concerned and opportunities for training in their use.

Recently there has been discussion whether profiles should be used to replace the degree since degree classifications reduce the achievements of undergraduates to one of five categories (of these, two are used rarely). Occasionally the argument is advanced that a form of profile should replace the honours classification, as is the case in the United States. Expressed in this form the argument is fallacious. Because A does X it does not follow that B should necessarily do X. Indeed the claim that this approach has replaced the use of honours degrees in North America is less strong than is supposed by some advocates. Grade-point averages in the United States, which are comparable to our degree classifications, are the basis for entry into advanced courses and better-paid employment.

## ASSESSING PRIOR LEARNING: APL AND APEL

Approaches based on the assessment of prior learning are intended to replace traditional approaches of giving access and exemption to non-traditional students. The traditional approach for non-qualified entrants to higher education in Britain was based upon a written examination and interview or by invoking the clause in degree regulations that permits entry to academic subjects, subject to the approval of the Faculty Board and possibly a Board of Undergraduate Studies. Such an approach worked well when the numbers of such entrants were small. APEL is a more radical approach that matches the student's capabilities and competencies with the capabilities and competencies required in the initial stages of the course. For this process to occur one has to have a clear idea of the capabilities and competencies demanded by the course and a satisfactory way of assessing prior experiential learning. The approach has implications for the identification of learning outcomes, course design, and the organisation of Access courses with local FE colleges.

The assessment of prior learning is sometimes divided into APL, or credits for academic work which have already been received, and APEL, the assessment of prior experiential learning. Other terms in use are APA, the accreditation of prior achievements, and APLA, the accreditation of prior learning achievements. We prefer the term APAL, the accreditation of prior assessed learning for the use of academic qualifications for entry to or exemption from courses. Here we are particularly concerned with APEL although it overlaps to some extent with other forms of accreditation. Its main function is to gain access to higher education courses or exemption from the first year of a course by obtaining credits for prior experience.

Evans and Turner (1993) report the first attempts to introduce APEL in universities. Their project involved four universities and outlines the achievements and difficulties encountered. The findings indicate the difficulties of implementing APEL procedures, especially in the older universities. They claim that the experience of demonstrating prior learning for academic credit is motivating for students and it does help people to recognise that they know more than they realise. They recommended that clear admissions procedures and guidelines be developed and tutorial support is necessary to help students prepare proposals for assessment. Some of the difficulties of implementation included: initial lack of understanding of procedures; biased lecturers' views of the students involved in APEL; the time-consuming nature of APEL and the overriding problem of developing clear understanding among staff, students and employers about the nature of APEL. They conclude that APEL is an important method of linking education and employment, and it *can* save time and money for participants.

Developing a clear understanding of the term APEL is not easy if only because APEL is a fuzzy concept. Experiential learning and learning from experience are at its core. These popular terms, when analysed, become virtually meaningless. All learning is based on experience but that experience may take various forms and structures. Experience may be acquired in academic and non-academic settings, by formal means or informal means. It may be vicarious or 'real', it may be predominantly physical, cognitive or affective. In APEL, experience from outside of academic settings is transformed into a record of 'acceptable' knowledge, assessed and accredited. The process of transformation involves self-assessment, reflection and some knowledge of academic contexts. There is general agreement that the process works best as collaborative assessment in which the tutor plays the role of counsellor, critical friend, supervisor, editor and possibly audience. The task is time-consuming. It can be reduced by giving students the opportunity to apply but not providing them with support. Such an approach wipes out the component of supported reflective learning and it disadvantages those very students that the system claims it is seeking to assist.

Butterworth (1992) suggests there are two approaches to APEL, the credit exchange version and the developmental version. These are related to the competency and developmental approaches described earlier in this section. The credit exchange system relies heavily on a national credit framework. Robertson (1994) in his comprehensive review of credit systems, concludes that such a framework has potential benefits for universities and students but universities, particularly older universities, are reluctant to participate in it. The credit exchange approach is exemplified by the work of Simosko (1991) and the developmental approach in the earlier work of Evans (1988). Trowler (1996) provides a stimulating discussion of the two approaches in which he argues that credit exchange and developmental approaches are the poles of a continuum and that the developmental approach is the most appropriate for higher education. He concludes that APEL is not likely to become a main route into higher education.

However, if you are interested in developing APEL, you will find Evans (1988) and Simosko (1991) provide useful suggestions on how to help students assess their experiential learning. Many of the suggestions would also be helpful to all undergraduates. They both identify four stages in the assessment of prior experiential learning:

- Systematic reflection on past experience to identify what individuals know and can do.
- Identification of significant relevant learning and achievements which can be equated with specific standards or qualification requirements.
- Assembly and assessment of evidence that the learning claimed has really been acquired.
- Crediting and recommending the appropriate award of academic credit.

The first three stages require some assistance from tutors or others to ensure the evidence presented for assessment is appropriate and the fourth stage is the responsibility of the course team.

Bloor and Butterworth (1990) suggest that a typical portfolio for APEL might contain:

- an abstract summarising the claim
- a list of the learning outcomes
- extended reflective writing that describes and analyses the experience and demonstrates how the experiences produce the learning claimed and meet the criteria of the programme
- provenance. Evidence such as working papers to support the claim.

Other approaches are based on very detailed checklists supported by documented evidence. For a more detailed exploration of the research on the value of experience in a learning context see Usher and Bryant (1989), Simon (1988) and Collins (1991).

## THE SPECIAL CASE OF WORK-BASED LEARNING

Work-based learning is a special form of experiential learning in which students can develop, as part of their course, a range of social skills, academic and technical knowledge and expertise in a workplace. It gives them the opportunity to develop and explore ideas, attitudes and opinions and to challenge assumptions. Work-based learning was customarily the province of vocational subjects although there is a long tradition in modern languages of the use of an intercalary year and some students on business and engineering courses are now spending one or two semesters in work experience in other European countries. It is claimed work-based learning helps students to learn to transfer and apply skills to work situations and the expertise acquired during work experience deepens their understanding and increases their self-confidence, commitment and awareness. Assessment of work-based learning has traditonally been the task of visiting tutors and work supervisors or mentors but increasingly self-assessment and project work are being used as part of the assessment. Work-based learning can be divided into four broad categories:

1 *Specific vocational training*: this involves students focusing on specific skills and methodologies, such as those used in medicine, nursing and engineering.

2 *Structured work experience*: this provides students with a systematic experience of a range of tasks which may not be related to specific technical expertise.
3 *Semi-structured work experience*: this involves students in developing skills and abilities through less structured tasks and opportunities in a more informal learning experience.
4 *Random work experience*: this involves no clear definition of what is expected of either the student or the employer. This may be a deliberate or opportunistic approach but it is often a default mode of one of the previous categories.

These methods of work experience can be used for varying time periods, and more than one method may be combined. Specific vocational training usually takes place as a sandwich placement or as a three-monthly work placement. Highly structured approaches may not allow the flexibility to learn related skills or take advantage of unexpected opportunities. At the other extreme, students who are able to benefit from random work experience are probably highly motivated and capable.

Ashworth and Saxton (1992) suggest that the main purposes of work-based learning are to develop maturity; enable the exploration of the theory–practice links; encourage the development of critical but pragmatic thinking; and facilitate systems thinking. They offer a set of dimensions on which maturity might be assessed. These include dependence to autonomy, subjectivity to taking other people into account, focus on particulars to focus on principles. We are not convinced that maturity *per se* can or should be assessed by the use of dimensions. The theory–practice links are not merely about applying theory to practice but interrelating them so that each informs the other. This notion of theory–practice has implications for the role of supervisors, tutors and students. Critical but pragmatic thinking is essentially evaluative thinking that leads to action or recommendations for action. Systems thinking, in the sense used by Ashworth and Saxton, is concerned with how groups and teams work together within an organisation.

### Studies of work-based learning

Most research on work-based learning has focused on a variety of aspects of sandwich placements and their relationships to vocational courses. These include: the purpose and role of placements (Rankin, 1972; Dorsman, 1984; Duckenfield and Stirner, 1992); the role of students (Ashworth and Morisson, 1989); the supervision of students on work experience (Cohen, 1971; Saxton and Ashworth, 1990; Fuller and Saunders, 1990). Initial findings about the assessment of work-based learning (Rankin, 1972; Topping, 1975; Smithers, 1976) led to the RISE Report (1985), which highlighted the unsystematic approach towards the assessment of placements, and its lack of contribution towards the final degree awarded.

The difficulties surrounding the assessment of work-based learning are not unlike those surrounding the assessment of projects and dissertations. The placement, its opportunities and the mode of work supervision that students experience are not identical, hence it is difficult to compare the achievements of students. The use of profiling and learning contracts to assess work-based learning allows a shift towards criterion-referenced assessment but it necessitates the drawing up of specific learning outcomes.

The work-based learning initiative entitled 'Working for Degrees' involved 20 projects between 1992 and 1994 (ED, 1992). The projects focused on: assessment; credit frameworks and learning outcomes; and guidance and learning autonomy. Some of the projects explored in depth the use of self- and peer-assessment procedures in work-based learning and concluded that they are useful (Saunders, 1995). Further studies have been carried out through various initiatives such as the Partnership Project which aimed to credit students for work-based learning combined with academic study (Lyons, 1994) and the Learning from Experience Trust who have supervised various projects concerned with work-based learning and the assessment of prior experiential learning (Evans and Turner, 1993).

Findings from a study to investigate the assessment of supervised work experience by Lee *et al.* (1991) and a further related study of self-assessment (Lee and Tuck, 1992) at Huddersfield University indicate that self-assessment is a useful approach but students, tutors and supervisors do require training in the use of these methods. Students, as a group, tended to over-estimate their performance as estimated by others, but only a minority differed significantly from the assessment of tutors and supervisors. Moderation procedures could be used to minimise this problem just as they do for tutor marking. Further work by Lee (1995), reinforces the need for staff development if the self-assessment of work-based learning is to be successful and of benefit to students.

Overall, the evidence suggests that students do change their approaches to study and deepen their understanding of the world of work, and that they are more willing to take responsibility for their own learning (Smithers, 1976; Davies, 1991). The studies also show some student dissatisfaction at the organisation of work placements and of its links to their continuing academic study. CNAA and Employment Department studies revealed that the purposes and assessment procedures of work-based learning are not always clear to employers, students or tutors (ED, 1990; Davies 1991). Work-based learning *can* provide useful learning opportunities for students. This is, however, dependent on careful planning, briefing and organisation of work-based learning, its integration into the course and its assessment. The use of self-assessment can also contribute positively to the experience of work-based learning if it is accompanied by effective staff and student development.

Despite the claims of some parties (ED, 1992), work-based learning is probably an inadequate replacement for deep active learning in an academic context. Experience gained in specific workplaces may not *per se* provide broad prospectives. In the longer view of the growth of civilisations, knowledge and understanding grew out of the need to analyse and record particular experiences and to systematise those analyses and experiences.

Reliance on translating experience gained in workplaces into propositional knowledge implies that the 'translator' already has expertise in propositional knowledge. Undue reliance on translating experience is a denial of the collective wisdom of earlier generations. Re-inventing wheels is a useful, but limited, learning strategy. However, work-based learning is potentially a useful adjunct to more traditional forms of learning. At root, the value one places on work-based learning is determined by what one considers are the purposes of higher education and of a degree.

### Assessing work-based learning

Some of the possibilities for assessing work-based learning are given below.

#### 1 Unstructured reports

These may be completed by tutors, mentors (work supervisors) or students. They may be insightful but they may also be biased or uninformative. The tutor's reports are inevitably based upon a small sample of observation. So too may be the mentor's report if the mentor is not working closely with the student.

#### 2 Highly structured reports

These again may be used by mentors, tutors or students. They may be based upon detailed checklists and ratings. There is a danger that such an approach emphasises trivialities and the immediately observable. Halo effects may occur. Some of the items may not be relevant to a particular work experience and some features of a particular workplace may be overlooked in such a report.

#### 3 Semi-structured reports

These may be a mixture of checklist items and some open questions which provide an overview of the work experience. The headings provide some guidance on the objectives of work experience and its assessment. This mixture can be insightful and illuminating and it can provide additional information upon the particular workplace and work experience.

#### 4 Learning contract assessment

A contract of learning objectives is drawn up by the tutor, mentor and student. The student assesses his/her achievements in the light of these objectives but includes other and unanticipated learning outcomes. The contract may be used to prepare a personal report by the student or a joint report.

## 5 Learning logs/diaries

Students write a personal record of their experience which they can use to provide a self-report of their work-based learning. A semi-structured approach is recommended so that students can complete their records easily and usefully. Time to complete the learning logs needs to be built into the work pattern. Students need not, perhaps should not, submit the full learning log for assessment purposes.

## 6 Personal report

This approach addresses the question, 'What have I learnt from this work experience?' Guidance on what points to cover is recommended. Obviously this guidance will be determined by the nature of the work experience and its specific purposes. The personal report may be assessed by a tutor and its marks contribute to the overall assessment or award.

## 7 Joint report

This may be a variation of 6 above in which the mentor and student have an appraisal discussion based upon the personal report and self-assessment by the student. The discussion is summarised and agreed by the mentor and student. It is then sent to the tutor and may be used in the assessment of the student's work experience.

## 8 Project report

The student may be required to write a technical report on some of the methods and technical skills that he/she has developed during the work placement. Normally this report should integrate the practical experiences gained with a knowledge of the relevant literature. It could be assessed and contribute to the overall degree assessment. The proportion of marks allocated to this task should reflect the work involved.

## 9 Professional report

A variation of 8 above in which the students are required to explore the relationships between what and how they learn in their academic subject and in their work placement. They might be encouraged to analyse other characteristics of the culture of their work placement and academic setting so that they develop a deeper understanding of academic and other forms of work and work settings.

## 10 Poster sessions

These may be used for assessment instead of or in addition to the written report.

Tutors, mentors and peers could assess the poster sessions according to a set of agreed criteria. These tasks and the criteria should be known to the students before they embark upon a work placement. Pre-placement students could be invited to the poster sessions so that they can learn from the experience of those who have recently completed a work placement.

## 11 Oral presentations

Students prepare and give presentations in a seminar which is based upon their written report. Alternatively, the written report can be based upon their presentation and the ensuing discussion. The presentations may be given to other placement students, mentors and pre-placement students. The approach may be used to develop and assess the skills of presentation and discussion management. If a group of students have worked together on a placement, they could provide a group presentation. The assessment of the presentation may be done by the tutors, mentors, peers or some combination of these. Sufficient time for preparing the presentations should be built into the programme. The criteria for the presentations should be given to the students well before the presentation seminars and the marks allocated for the tasks should again be consonant with the effort involved.

## Problems of assessing work-based learning

The problems of assessing work-based learning are sometimes used as a justification for not incorporating any work experience into a course. It has been suggested that the assessment of work-based learning should be more reliable and transparent than traditional assessment (Tolley, 1985). It could equally be argued that virtually all assessment could benefit from being more rigorous. Whilst some suggest elaborate and complex assessment procedures for work-based learning (Dunster, 1982), others promote oral presentations (Rankin, 1972) or a combination of methods (Thompson, 1973). The common problems are:

- different work settings offer different learning opportunities
- variations between assessors
- halo effects
- validity of the assessment procedures.

All of the problems may be minimised by training students, mentors and tutors in the modes of assessment, by the use of explicit guidelines and criteria and by moderating the assessment procedures.

## Guidelines for establishing work-based learning

Work-based learning and assessment is an interaction between students, tutors, mentors and the tasks involved in the work experience. All of these occur within the framework of an undergraduate course and its objectives. It must be said that in some courses, work experience appears to be a fashionable extra rather than a genuine attempt to provide opportunities to transfer skills and gain a deeper understanding of work and its relationship to academic study. The suggestions that follow are based on the studies of work-based learning already cited and our own observations of work-based learning.

## Curriculum planning

Careful planning by the course team is necessary to ensure that work experience is prepared for and also feeds into subsequent sections of the course.

## Partnerships

It goes without saying that the building of close co-operative partnerships with the employers, including managers and mentors, is necessary. The providers of work experience may include voluntary and community organisations as well as public authorities and employers. It is useful to include members of these organisations in the initial planning and organisation of the work placements.

## Matching students and placements

This can be a time-consuming and demanding challenge. In some departments this is the responsibility of one member of staff but it may be done by placement tutors, placement mentors or the students themselves. Often it is not possible to match students and placements closely, but if there are guidelines on what particular placements have to offer and what particular students have to offer then the task is made somewhat easier.

## Briefing

Students, tutors and mentors do require briefing. The tasks and roles of each need clarification and mutual exploration. In particular, the importance of giving and receiving constructive feedback by mentors and tutors is stressed in many reports.

## Assessment of student performance

Clearly the methods of assessment should be related to the purposes of the work placement and the wider purposes of the course. Students should be informed of the methods of assessment before the placement commences. Procedures for monitoring and moderating the assessments should be built into the system.

*Monitoring and evaluation of work-based learning*

A review of the placements should be undertaken annually. The role and value of work-based learning and its assessment procedures in use should also be reviewed regularly and certainly it should form part of the normal curriculum review and accreditation process. It is particularly important to have a detailed review of work-based learning at the end of the first year of its implementation.

## Some guidelines for assessing work-based learning

If work-based learning is being used as a component of a course then clearly it should be assessed, otherwise it will not be taken seriously, by students, employers or academics. Coates and Wright (1991) offer practical suggestions for developing and assessing work-based learning and the appendices of the text by Ashworth and Saxton (1992) provide examples of guidance for students, mentors and tutors. Some guidelines for effective assessment of work-based learning are given in Figure 12.2.

---

- Agree the objectives of a placement before it commences.
- Agree the measures to be used to assess the placement.
- The assessor, student and tutor should discuss formative assessments (feedback) at several stages throughout the placement.
- Establish mutual agreement on the standards of performance.
- Provide examples of different levels of performance, preferably from earlier work placements.
- Provide training for all assessors, including students, so that they understand the purpose, process and standards of assessment.
- Ensure everyone knows their responsibilities for the assessment.
- Encourage students to take responsibility for self-assessment.
- Keep the administration as simple as possible.
- Design a scheme for moderation of the assessments and ensure that this is understood and used.

---

*Figure 12.2* Guidelines for effective assessment

## ACTIVITIES

12.1    How could you use the notions underlying APEL to develop students' capacity to reflect upon their learning?

12.2    How could portfolios or profiles be used by students in your department so that they gain the maximum benefit from them without the task of putting them together being unduly onerous?

12.3    Look through your own learning log. How could you improve it? How could you improve your approaches to assessment and developing students' capacities to self-assess?

12.4    Some questions to discuss:

1 Should learning portfolios contribute to the degree result, or should they merely complement it?
2 Should the national record of achievement be used for selection into higher education?
3 Should learning profiles be used to replace the existing honours degree system?

12.5    Jot down your thoughts on the similarities and differences between academic work undertaken by students and work undertaken by students on work placement. Compare your views with those of a few colleagues.

12.6    Compare the problems of assessing work-based learning with the problems of assessing projects and written examinations. What are the relative merits of work-based learning, projects based on academic work and written examinations as learning tasks?

12.7    What kinds of skills and capabilities would you like students to develop on your courses and extend during work placements? How would these skills and capabilities be assessed? What proportion of marks would you allocate to the assessment of work experience in your courses?

12.8    Your department is debating whether the first semester (or term) of the final year of the course should be devoted to a work placement. List the arguments for and against this proposal.

12.9

EITHER

Your department has decided to give students the choice of a library-based dissertation or a work placement for one semester (or term). The time to be devoted to the placement is 40 days and the remainder of the time is for the writing of reports and any other assessment tasks. What methods of assessment would you advocate for these options?

OR

Your department has decided to give students the choice of an experimental project or a work placement for one semester (or term). The time to be devoted to the placement is 40 days and the remainder of the time is for the writing of reports and any other assessment tasks. What methods of assessment would you advocate for these options?

12.10 What aspects of work-based learning could be integrated into your courses so that they develop the students' academic expertise and competence in your subject?

# Chapter 13

# Using computers in assessment

In this chapter we outline the uses of computers in assessment. We remind readers that computers can assist in the design and development of assessment tasks and feedback as well as in the processes and recording of assessment. We discuss the use of technology to aid and assess student learning and the issues of implementation and evaluation.

There are three areas in which computers can assist the assessment process: the design and development of assessment tasks; the assessment itself either via a computer or on a computer; and the recording, transmission and analyses of grades awarded. Although the literature focuses upon the second of these uses, considerable savings in time are possible through quite simple uses of PCs, networking and the mainframe computer.

## USING COMPUTERS FOR DESIGNING AND DEVELOPING ASSESSMENT TASKS

Most academics use PCs or Apple Macs and many will have discovered various ways of saving time in the design and development of assessment tasks. For those who have not done so we offer the following suggestions.

After the initial thinking, word-processing packages can be used to amend guidelines, sets of criteria and assessment tasks. Spell-checking, storing and updating bibliographical references for guidelines is easy. 'Shells' for rating schedules, checklists and feedback forms can be created and the appropriate criteria inserted. Summary reports on a class's performance on an essay or other task can be created and updated. Such reports save time in providing feedback to students (see Chapter 5: 'Marking for formative purposes' and 'Managing time: marking large numbers of essays'). Some lecturers have developed a menu of feedback comments that they retrieve and print in a personalised comment on each student's work. Finally, word-processing packages can be used to analyse elementary aspects of textual analysis such as frequencies of particular words or phrases, lengths of sentences and complexity of word structure. These methods can be applied by students to examples of texts supplied to them and to their own essays.

Spreadsheets may be used to develop relatively simple problems and their marking schemes. One can change the variables or vary the conditions and the spreadsheet provides the new solution and marking scheme. One can also set, more easily, 'what if' problems. Students can be encouraged to explore the effects of changing parameters and so get a feel for the magnitudes of parameters and, perhaps, what effects can be ignored. Graphics can easily be incorporated into the problems and their solutions. However, spreadsheets can be cumbersome for complex problems. For large systems of equations and numerical methods, equation-solving software is preferable. With an equation-solver program, the user lists equations and the program generates the variables, the user gives values for the known variables and asks for a solution which may be outputted in numerical or graphical form. Graphics packages can be used to draw diagrams or sketches on which questions can be based. Maps, anatomical drawings and flow charts are obvious examples but one can also use them for questions on design, diagnosis and error analysis.

All of the above can, of course, be used by students. Word-processed essays are easier to mark and, arguably, easier to write. Students can spell-check, develop their own bibliographies and check their referencing. Graphics packages enable students to present more clearly diagrams, graphs and pictures in their written work, poster sessions and oral presentations. Problems, including discovery problems and design questions, can be set that require students to use a spreadsheet or equation-solver. However, one should be aware of the dangers of the black-box syndrome. As an approach becomes more complex, students may not understand what the computer is doing, they may not be able to detect errors, and they may not care – providing it gives them an answer. Doing some calculations by hand is often a useful preliminary to solving problems with the aid of a computer.

Networked computers enable one to receive essays or, less easily, problems by electronic mail. Feedback can be transmitted electronically and one can create bulletin boards on assessment for students. One can communicate easily with colleagues in other universities and 'discuss' approaches to assessment. Finally, the personal computer can give you access to the Internet where you will probably find examples of assessment questions and other information. Surfing is enjoyable but it may not save you time.

## USING COMPUTERS FOR ASSESSMENT

Computers are a mode of processing but not a method of assessment. If the computer, or other medium, does not have an advantage over traditional methods then the computer-based component will not survive after the innovator has moved on. A computer's uses are limited to matching students' responses to those stored in its memory and to performing sophisticated analyses on the sets of matched and unmatched responses. Computers cannot yet cope with creative essays, short answer questions that are capable of a wide range of interpretations, or problems that have several potential pathways. They can cope with a wide range of multiple choice questions, highly structured short answer questions and 'what if' questions involving the manipulation of well-defined variables. These methods of assessment can be applied to a wide spectrum of subjects, including the humanities, a wide range of learning situations, including projects, practicals and computer-based learning, and for a variety of sources including self- and peer-assessment.

Computer-assisted assessment (CAA) is a common term for the use of computers in the assessment of student learning. Various other terms are used, such as computer-aided assessment, computerised assessment, computer-based assessment and computer-based testing. CAA encompasses the use of computers to:

- deliver, mark and analyse assignments or examinations
- collate and analyse data gathered from optical mark readers (OMRs)
- record, analyse and report on achievement
- collate, analyse and transfer assessment information through networks.

In this section of the chapter we are particularly concerned with the first three of these uses. The next section considers the fourth use.

Within the framework of computer-assisted assessment one should distinguish the use of computers to assess students' work, in which the computer is programmed to take the assessment decisions, and the use of computers to aid assessment through the use of spreadsheets to collate and analyse the results of assessment (Bull, 1993). A further distinction is between the uses of a computer to mark input from students' responses on paper, which may be entered manually or via an optical mark reader, and to mark the direct input of student responses to the computer. Computer-assisted assessment may involve the use of hypertext, simulations, microworlds and so-called intelligent tutoring systems. It may be augmented by the use of video or interactive videodisc. These aspects are touched upon later in this chapter.

### Finding out more about CAL and CAA

Those who are new to the field may find the various publications of the Teaching Learning and Technology Programme useful. These are available from the HEFCE at Northavon House, Bristol BS16 1QD. If you have access to the world-wide web you might try the Beginner's Guide Web Site at http::www.icbl.ac.uk/begin/. The site will provide details and contacts for the major projects.

Reports on new approaches and applications of CAL are plentiful. The whole of *Psychology Teaching*, Vol. 4, part 2, is devoted to the use of computers in teaching psychology. The approaches are relevant to teaching in other areas. Most of the studies of computing have been reports of innovations (e.g. Hart and Smith, 1994, 1996) or of general usage (e.g. Derby and Gardner, 1991).

Bull (1993) provides an accessible description of the uses and problems of computer-based approaches and case studies drawn from arts and sciences in UK universities which exemplify a variety of methods of computer-assisted assessment. Lloyd *et al.* (1996) describe their computer testing system in engineering but in general, assessment of a formal nature has been relatively neglected: an afterthought, as in teaching generally. More recently, a cross-educational survey reports that a range of computer-assisted assessment techniques including computer-based testing, codes of practice, computerised adaptive placement tests, paperless exams and integrated learning systems are being used in primary, secondary and tertiary education and commercial training (Glover, 1994). A recent issue of *Active Learning* (No. 1, 1995), focused on computer-assisted assessment in which the majority of articles were based on the use of MCQs, sometimes known as 'objective tests', and optical mark readers. The survey by Stephens (1995) identifies almost 400 academics using either computerised objective tests or optical mark readers. Whilst this survey does focus on those already known to be active in the area it provides an indication of growing interest and development. It indicates that 37 per cent of computerised assessments are used summatively, and 29 per cent formatively. The majority of testing takes place at foundation and first-year undergraduate level, although over a third of tests identified were used for second- and final-year assessments. In short, the bulk of computer-assisted assessment in higher education is computerised multiple choice questions including self-assessment courseware. Its potential has not yet been fully exploited.

Some of the resistance to the use of MCQs is because many potential users of computer-assisted assessment have a primitive notion of MCQs. They assume they are limited to true/false dichotomies or three- or four-choice items that test only recall. As Chapter 6 demonstrates, there are many different types of MCQ and MCQs can be used to ask challenging questions. Most of the different types of MCQ may be used in software packages such as the recent version of Question Mark. If you or your potential users do not like the term 'MCQs' then use the term 'objective tests' – but remember the tests are only as objective as you make them.

## Studies of CAL and CAA

There has been plenty of research on computer-assisted learning. Kulik and Kulik (1991) meta-analysed 254 carefully controlled evaluation studies and concluded that it is effective and sometimes more efficient than traditional methods of learning. Most of the studies were concerned with knowledge acquisition rather than the development of understanding. Atkins (1993) goes beyond meta-analyses to consider the links between multi-media and theories of learning. Her review indicates that approaches based upon behavioural psychology are effective in inculcating knowledge but not as yet in developing understanding. Approaches based upon cognitive psychology appear to be less effective in knowledge acquisition, but with more able students they do develop and deepen understanding. It would seem that a pre-requisite of cognitive-based programs is that the learners already have the meta-cognitive strategies of learning to learn. Atkins also points out that high levels of interactivity with a computer or reports of enjoyment are not guarantees of learning. In a subsequent article, Atkins and O'Halloran (1995) show that multi-media applications can speed up the development of expertise but the relationship between propositional knowledge and experiential knowledge in expert performance is poorly understood. They also argue, from the evidence available, that we need many more stringent studies of transfer from computer simulations to live situations before we can be confident of the efficacy of simulations as a training tool. Finally, Hartley (1991) contains studies of writing that suggest that electronic processing does influence thinking, preparation for writing and the writing process itself. If this is the case, students who are required to word-process their coursework but use pen and ink in their examinations are likely to experience cognitive conflict. Training on one system and testing on another may not be a fair approach.

The above findings parallel those described in Chapter 2 on the effects of assessment and context on student learning. They suggest that one should look more critically at the use of computer-based learning. The general method of CAL may be good but its success is dependent upon the particular design and its purpose. CAL works but only if the students use the programs. It is the quality of the learning program, not the use of a computer, that is important. If the program looks no better or worse than a book, then most students will probably choose a book for its portability and accessibility.

### Computer-assisted assessment and teaching

Figure 13.1 sets out a simple but illuminating table of the approaches to computer-assisted assessment and teaching. The frequency of use in higher education is given in descending order. By far the most common approach remains tutor taught and marked. The next most common use is tutor taught and computer marked. The main method used is multiple choice questions. The third approach is where the computer 'teaches' and perhaps provides some feedback but the summative assessment is tutor marked. The least-used approach is where the computer teaches and assesses the student's work for both formative and summative purposes.

### Levels of computer-based teaching

As you can see from Figure 13.1 the least-used approaches to assessment appear to be those that are taught by computer. The terms used for such teaching include computer-based learning (CBL), computer-based teaching (CBT), computer-aided instruction (CAI), computer-assisted instruction (CAI) and computer-assisted learning (CAL). Given the relative neglect of these approaches,

| | Tutor taught | Computer taught |
|---|---|---|
| Tutor marked | 1 Most common | 3 Third most common |
| Computer marked | 2 Next most common | 4 Least common |

*Figure 13.1* Computer-assisted assessment and teaching

it is worth considering their characteristics. Figure 13.2 sets out an approximate hierarchy of different forms of what we prefer to call CAL. For a more detailed analysis of the characteristics of CAL, see Laurillard (1993).

*Drill and practice*

Drill and practice can be useful for hammering home detailed facts, definitions and grammatical structures. These are only part of academic learning and so, one hopes, assessment practice for summative purposes will go beyond these details. Drill and practice programs were originally based upon the principles of linear programmed learning of the 1960s. Such an approach assumes the way to learn is though the acquisition of tiny bits of information. This form of mental atomism is only satisfying to extreme serialists, a minority in the student population. The bold claims of the efficacy of drill and practice were often based on narrowly defined objectives. The narrow objectives were achieved, *ergo* the programs were claimed to be effective. This circular argument did little to convince sceptics of the value of CAL in higher education. However, newer programs are more modest in their claims and they have a role in introductory courses. A good example of a sophisticated drill and practice program, which has elements of other levels of CAL, is CALM, Computer Aided Learning Mathematics, which was devised at Heriot Watt University, Edinburgh.

*Hypertext and hypermedia*

The linear approach may be supplemented by a few branches in the program or one can move to the use of hypertext and hypermedia. Hypertext works on a series of 'buttons' which enable a user to track interconnected key words or phrases. A word may be highlighted in a document. This reveals a menu of other documents. Words highlighted in these documents reveal further documents. The process is rather like a detailed literature search except that the documents can include pictures, diagrams, sound bites and animation. Hypermedia is based on the same principle and in conjunction with a video disc can provide even more information such as copies of manuscripts or paintings, detailed concordances and thesauri, and so on. Some modern hypertext programs allow

| Type of programme | Characteristics |
|---|---|
| **6 Tutorial programmes and systems** | Interactive and responsive. Provides guidance and explicit feedback. Can develop fuller understanding. Student has control and choice. |
| **5 Modelling** | Interactive and responsive. Provides feedback and more explicit (but not full) understanding. More choice and control by student. |
| **4 Microworlds** | Interactive and responsive. Provides some feedback on one's actions and opportunities to develop intuitive understanding through the creation of commands and their effects. More choice and control by student. |
| **3 Simulations** | Responsive. Provides opportunities to see effects of one's actions. Provides some feedback and may develop some intuitive understanding. Some choice and control by student. |
| **2 Hypertext and hypermedia** | An interconnected library of information. Potentially useful for study purposes but, as yet, rarely contains assessment questions. Is not interactive or responsive. Provides no feedback. |
| **1 Drill and practice** | Usually focuses on rote learning or, at best, surface learning. No control or choice by student. Response of computer limited to right and wrong. Information and feedback divided into tiny chunks. Does not develop understanding except in the most trivial sense. |

*Figure 13.2* Levels of CAL and assessment

the student to create his or her own links between the material. It is possible to build in feedback and assessment questions but, at present, it offers a wider range of knowledge rather than a deeper understanding. It has little to offer, as yet, for formative or summative assessment purposes. As Laurillard (1993, p. 2) observes, 'on the one hand it is nothing more than a small but beautifully connected library, on the other hand, by its very nature it undermines the structure of the "texts" and it reduces knowledge to fragments of information'. Her view is reminiscent of that of T.S. Eliot, who, writing in a different age and context, asked,

Where is the wisdom we have lost in knowledge?
Where is the knowledge we have lost in information?
The cycles of heaven in twenty centuries
Bring us farther from GOD and nearer to the Dust
(from 'Choruses from "The Rock"',
Eliot, 1958, p. 157)

## Simulations, microworlds and modelling

Simulations model a process and allow the users to make inputs, run the model and obtain the outcome of their actions. In some simulations, in order to turn the outcome into feedback on their actions, the users have to remember what they did. The outcome statement may be 'You have just killed 1500 patients.' The simulation might not tell you how you did this. More sophisticated programs do offer some suggestions, such as 'Try lowering the drug dosage of patients weighing less than 70 kg.' These simulations are moving towards tutoring. Given suitable instructions, simulations can develop interpretative skills (see Moyse, 1992) but they do not allow exploration of the processes going on in the simulation. Microworlds go one step further. They enable students to create their own program of commands, see the outcomes and reflect upon the relationship between their commands and outcome. The most well-known microworld is Papert's Logo, which has been used to teach geometry and elementary mechanics (Papert, 1980). The approach has also been used in music (Holland, 1987) and physics (Sellman, 1991). Microworlds develop intuitive understanding on which rational understanding can be based. In modelling, students create and refine their own models of how a system works within the broad constraints provided by the modelling program. They therefore have greater opportunities to control and explore, to receive feedback and develop their understanding of the relationships within the model and, possibly, its links with the real world. The distinctions between simulations, microworlds and modelling depend upon the degree of explicitness of the rules in the system and their susceptibility to change by the user.

## Tutorial programs and systems

Tutorial programs are often based upon what experts can do on the grounds that the best way for a novice to learn is to act like an expert. The assumption is questionable since the paths that students may take to expertise depend in part on their styles of learning. Tutorial systems, unlike approaches lower down the hierarchy, do have the capability to adapt to the student's responses and to offer guidance and explicit feedback. The program collects, stores and analyses sets of a student's responses and decides what tasks to set and how much practice to offer. The 'tutor' responds to the student's responses with feedback and guidance. This form of CAL comes closest to high-quality face-to-face teaching.

Indeed it may be better than some tutorials experienced by students. In more flexible tutorial programs the student can override the computer's requests, skip problems and try them in a different order. Tutorial systems provide a more generalised form of tutoring that can be adapted to different subject areas.

All of the above can be valuable approaches to learning and all but hypertext, in its present form, could be adapted for more formal assessment procedures. We await developments. In the meantime the single most common form of assessment that is done by computer is objective testing: the use of multiple choice questions. These are built into some learning programs but for the most part they are used as separate measures of performance.

## Marking via computer

The design and uses of MCQs for assessment were discussed in Chapter 6. The added dimension of computer technology enables one to assess rapidly large numbers of students and to give immediate feedback, if required. Banks of questions can be stored on computer and software used to generate and print tests. The level of difficulty and discrimination of each item can be calculated, stored and updated. Individual and class profiles can be calculated and used for the analysis of student learning and the quality of the test, and for course evaluation. The analysis and feedback can be provided to each student together with guidance including specific references to texts. The students' responses to the test may be fed manually into the computer or they may be read by an optical mark reader. The OMR reads the marks on specially designed cards – providing the students' marks on the cards are clear. (The questions may be on a separate sheet.) The computer then processes the responses. The cards constrain the type of MCQ that may be used. Before purchasing an OMR, it is advisable to check the flexibility of card design, analysis and compatibility of software, speed of scanning, type of questions allowed, marking schemes; and, of course, price. After purchase, some training of secretarial, administrative and academic staff is desirable. OMRs may be used for any question that has fixed choices of response. Consequently, they are also used for evaluating courses and teaching. Some departments add a few such items to the end of a summative MCQ test and thereby ensure a very high response rate. Others use separate course-evaluation forms. In a university of 8,000 undergraduates that operates a 12-module system, a 100 per cent response on the evaluation of courses and individual teaching requires over 250,000 questionnaires and cards. It is worth reflecting upon the value and costs of such an exercise. OMRs might be better deployed assessing student learning.

## Marking on the computer

MCQs can be presented to students on a computer screen (strictly speaking, the screen is not part of the computer). The linked software records and marks their answers, collates, analyses and prints the results. Such tests can be used for all types of assessment: formative, self-, diagnostic and summative. Computerised tests provide several options which may not be available on a test marked by OMR. Multiple response, reason-assertion, text match, exceptions, brief explanations, questions based on graphical hotspots and mathematical-based problems can be used. The use of computers for MCQs is limited by the skills of the question designer rather than by the software available. Figure 13.3 indicates some of the advantages of marking on computer.

In medicine and allied disciplines banks of MCQs are available to students at computer terminals for self-assessment purposes. These allow students to check their progress regularly in their own time. Similar approaches could be developed in other subjects. The question bank of the medical school at the University of Limburg contains 16,000 questions on all aspects of medicine and preclinical sciences that a medical graduate should have mastered. A stratified random sample of 250 questions is drawn from the bank four times a year. All students in each year of the programme take the test and are provided with their results, norms for their year group and other year groups and some guidance. Recently the test has been used to compare performance across six medical

---

1 Questions can include animated images, click and drag, video disc links and recorded sounds.
2 Adaptive testing, to allow for students of differing ability.
3 Allow the students more than one attempt at each question.
4 Can feed distractors to students as they progress through a question.
5 Can give clues to students, and mark accordingly.
6 Allow students the choice to discover the answer to a question.
7 Provide instant and detailed feedback.
8 Continuous, formative assessment available, on student demand if necessary.
9 Monitoring and early identification of students with academic problems.
10 Monitor use of a particular test, when used for self-assessment.
11 Provide students with the opportunity to take the test until they have achieved a particular score.
12 Detailed records of when the test was taken, how long it took and scores achieved.
13 Can prevent plagiarism through randomisation of questions.
14 More time for student contact?
15 Accurate marking.
16 No marking for academic staff, no double marking necessary.
17 Statistical analysis of results – facility and discrimination.

---

*Figure 13.3* Advantages of computerised MCQs

schools in Europe. There were no significant differences between the graduates of four of the schools but comparisons of year groups across the six medical schools revealed differences in rates of progression that appeared dependent upon whether the course was traditional or problem-based (Albano *et al.*, 1996). Many computer-aided and computer-based learning packages include elements of self-assessment, either embedded in the courseware or as stand-alone tests relating to particular topics. Computerised self-assessment can give students instant, tailored feedback and a level of evaluation and support which tutors rarely have the time to provide. The feedback can be as brief or detailed as the tutor requires. It may be used to point students to alternative resources and references for further study. However, this form of self-assessment does not usually contribute to the skills of reflectiveness and critical appraisal (see Chapter 12 for a discussion of self-assessment). Figure 13.4 outlines some practical issues to be tackled when introducing a computerised self-assessment system.

### Software

There are several software packages currently available which provide shells for the design of MCQs for use on paper or on computer screen.

---

1 Do all the students know it exists?
2 Do they really know where it is located?
3 Do they know how to access the system, or even turn the computer on?
4 Is there help if they have problems?
5 Does the system provide meaningful, formative feedback?
6 Can the students choose from a variety of topics and levels?
7 Is there a logical progression through the topics?
8 Does the system refer them to resources and references for further information?
9 Can they obtain a print-out of results, or store their results on disk?
10 Do you have a method of checking which questions are answered correctly and incorrectly most often?
11 Is it possible to obtain information about when the system is used most and by whom?
12 Is there the opportunity for students to give you feedback about particular questions, topics or the system as a whole?
13 Can you easily update the questions and topics?
14 Is there provision for students with special needs?

---

Adapted from Bull (1993), p. 11

*Figure 13.4* Checklist for the implementation of computerised self-assessment systems

*Question Mark*

Question Mark software appears to be the most common computerised testing package in higher education. Versions are available for Windows, DOS and Macintosh, and consist of four components.

The *Designer* allows the writing of questions compiled as either tests or libraries. The question types available vary slightly between the different platforms. The Windows version includes: multiple-choice, multiple response, text match, explanation, numerical and graphical hotspot. Macintosh and DOS versions also allow matching and ranking questions, fill-in blanks and free-format text. The next version of Designer for Windows will also include fill-in blanks and logical questions allowing matching and ranking. Creators of questions can use varying fonts and colour graphics, and create multimedia links. Test files and libraries are encrypted, and it is possible to build up banks of questions in libraries and extract randomised tests from these. Adaptive tests can be developed that allow the user to be moved to different parts of the test according to the cumulative test score or the response to particular questions.

*Presenter* is the part of the software which displays the tests created to students, either on stand-alone computers, over a network or on floppy disk. A range of options can be used when designing the test to customise individual tests in terms of: feedback; timing of the test; user identification; test caption; freedom of movement through the test and so on.

*Reporter* is the component which generates and records assessment information. It can record details such as test name, user name, date and time the test was started. Reports of analyses of responses can be requested, including a detailed analysis of the answers to each question.

The final component is *Printer*, which allows you to print tests, either with or without the correct answers showing.

The Designer for Windows version has a foreign language edition, a snapshotter which allows the importing of graphics from other applications into questions, and the ability to create adaptive tests which direct students to different questions according to their responses to previous questions. Question Mark Computing have recently released an add-on program to Question Mark Designer for Windows: Network Guardian. This is a security device for network users. It locks test files and it creates a 'key' file which controls access to the tests by a specified list of users within specified time-periods. For more detailed information about the use of Question Mark software see Neill (1993), Proctor and Donoghue (1994) and Lucas (1994).

The following case study illustrates the use of Question Mark Designer for Windows in a university-wide computerised assessment system.

Case study one: University of Luton, computerised assessment system

The University of Luton has a university-wide networked computerised assessment system based on Question Mark Designer for Windows. It was used initially to assess a first-year course in comparative psychology in 1994. The pilot group was approximately 150 students. This size of group presented the logistical and practical problems which could be expected should the system be used in future years. The pilot study is reported in more detail in Pritchett and Zakrzeswki (1996).

The pilot study involved three sittings of the examination, and pre- and post-evaluation of student experiences were carried out using the Speilberger State Trait Anxiety Inventory. This is based upon a set of positive and negative descriptors such as practical, easy, interesting, fun and controlling, stressful, irritating, unfriendly. The results of the evaluation indicate that a major benefit of the computerised examination was the quality of the students' experience. The software and network also operated successfully. The investment of time prior to the examination in the design of the questions was 8–10 hours plus four hours for checking, entering the test into software and amending. Some of the time involved was 'learning time'. These figures do not include the time involved in convincing senior mangement of the value of the system or the time required to set up the university system of computer-assisted assessment.

Computerised objective testing has now been adopted on a university-wide basis. A central unit responsible for providing support and development to staff who wish to design questions for computerised examinations has been established. Advice is given to academics about good practice in question design. The unit is responsible for entering tests on to the system once academics have designed the questions. It organises, in conjunction with computing services staff and the Modular Office, the practical arrangements for each examination. Back-up procedures, technological invigilation, monitoring forms, the organisation of successive examinations and the compilation and analysis of results are dealt with by the central unit. Academics invigilate, as they would for traditional examinations. Results are compiled within an hour of the examination and given to academic staff on paper and on disk, in order that they may carry out their own statistical analyses using Question Mark software. Students are introduced to the assessment method and software prior to the examination and have the opportunity to take sample tests, on a voluntary self-assessment basis. They also have continual access to a guided tour of Question Mark software, on the computer network.

Currently, evaluation of student experiences of both the software and the method of assessment are being carried out. The system was used recently to test almost 2,000 students in formal end-of-semester examinations in a range of subjects including: psychology, systems, networks, programming, politics, business and economics.

*Examine*

Examine is a multiple choice authoring and delivery system for interactive self-assessment in either a Windows or Macintosh environment. The software was developed under the Information Training Technology Initiative (Alexander, 1995) and is written in Authorware Professional. It is currently distributed as a software package with a few sample questions or as 'Begg Examine', a customised version to support the book *Economics*, by Begg *et al.* (1991), including a bank of economics questions.

The software package consists of two programs, Examine and Quizmaker. *Examine* delivers tests to students and *Quizmaker* provides tutors with the facility to design questions in tests or banks (libraries) from which defined or random tests can be selected. The data of Examine is stored as ASCII text files, which allows easy modification, but does not provide security against students who wish to look at question or answer files. Several question types are supported in Examine including: comments; multiple choice; multiple response; true/false; multiple true/false; and numeric. Graphics and sound can be used within questions. Students are provided with test caption information and, if required, the opportunity to print out questions from the test. Examine also has support for the Microcosm hypermedia system developed by the University of Southampton, and is compatible with network use. For more information on Microcosm, see Davis *et al.* (1993).

*EQL interactive assessor*

This software package enables the design and delivery of objective tests on computer, and was developed initially for use in accounting and finance. The software uses a Windows interface, and it can be run over a Novell network. The software allows the design of different question types, freedom of movement through tests, help facilities and a calculator. Questions are designed in the Question Editor and presented in a separate program to students. The results are compiled and displayed through a reporter program, which also allows export to spreadsheets for detailed analysis. Some universities use Interactive Assessor, often in conjunction with computer-based learning packages. For further details see Alexander (1995).

*Authoring individual systems*

Some departments and institutions have developed their own system using programming or authoring software. Software in use includes: Authorware; Toolbook; Hypercard; and Guide. A brief report of the use at the University of Derby of an interactive assessment system, written in Authorware Professional, is given in the next section.

Case study two: University of Derby, computer aided assessment

The Division of Earth Sciences at the University of Derby has been routinely using computer-aided assessment since 1989. Early assessments were produced using a first-generation, DOS-based authoring system but by 1991 assessment requirements became more sophisticated with respect to graphics and network capabilities. The best solution was provided by Authorware Professional which has been used to develop the current University of Derby Interactive Assessment Delivery System (DIADS), a toolkit for Authorware users.

**The DIADS System** The DIADS system is now used to annually deliver across the university network one formal examination and 10 summative coursework assessments in the fields of geology, geography, biology, resource development and environmental sciences. The system could however be used for assessing a wide range of subjects. Each question is contained within a standard shell of code and can be saved as a separate file that can be pasted into the Question Sequencer as desired. Screen dumps are catalogued so that the tutor can easily select questions for new tests once created. Results files are outputted in spread-sheet- and word-processor-compatible format or may be saved encrypted for later translation.

Most assessments are produced by a central unit, thus relieving academic staff of the burden of software production; one software author has been adequate to cover the needs of four disciplines. Guidance concerning question styles is given to tutors before the development of their first assessment. A variety of question templates are now being developed so that assessments may be compiled by tutors with limited authoring experience.

**Question Types** Many question styles are available, including the following types:

- *Multiple choice*: Text selections, text + graphics, text + data, rectangular and polygonal 'hot spot' graphic selection, clickable object, matrix (>20 choices), scrolling multiple choice, text or graphics (under development).
- *Move object*: Move text and/or graphics to position, position a slider, label a diagram, fill a table, sequencing graphics or text.
- *Text input*: Single or multiple text input.
- *Plot point*: Plot a graph, plot location – test position.
- *Plot line*: Draw best fit etc. – test slope and intercept.
- *Supplementary*: Any of the types listed above as a supplementary question that may or may not be asked according to the response given by the user to the primary question. Primary and secondary questions are scored together as a single question.
- *Combination and simulation*: Combinations of any number of the types listed above into single question or simulation.

A standard feedback template is available for formative assessments, and facilities for full tutorial feedback are also built into the system. The degree of authoring skill required by the tutor varies from virtually nil for text-based multiple-choice-type questions to high level for some simulations.

The DIADS system has been tailored over the last four years to provide maximum flexibility for the tutor and has the facilities of a powerful, multi-media, authoring package at its disposal. Many of these facilities are not available on commercial dedicated assessment systems and some of the features of DIADS have been developed in response to requests from both tutors and students, rapid changes that are not generally possible when using a commercial system.

**Tutor and student response to DIADS assessments** In both cases, response has been favourable. Students have found little difficulty in adapting to such assessments and even find them enjoyable in some cases!

Academic staff have seen benefits in both quality and efficiency of assessment, although many have seen marginally lower pass-rates when compared to traditional essay-type assessments because of the higher standard deviation associated with objective tests (typically 15 per cent with a mean of 50 per cent).

Computer-based assessments are not applicable to all areas of assessment and it is envisaged that traditional methods will remain important in the future. Indeed, an overbalance towards computer-based assessment could lead to a diminution of communication skills in students. However, computer-based assessments are invaluable in testing the knowledge base of students, an aspect that is often overlooked in the dash to student-centred learning.

*With thanks to Don M. Mackenzie, University of Derby, who supplied this summary of DIADS.*

Finally, it is worth observing that software provides only the technology for the shells of questions and the analysis of responses. The real technology is in the heads of the question designers.

## Recent developments

Not surprisingly, computers are used to assess computer programming skills. Halstead (1994) describes the use of computerised evaluation of programming skills, specifically for the checking of consistency and accuracy between various stages of program design and implementation. Benford, Burke and Foxley (1992) outline the use of the CEILIDH (Computer Environment for Interactive Learning in Diverse Habitats) system. This provides an on-line submission and automatic marking facility for coursework and a course management system that includes general course information, specific coursework assessment information, outline programs, model solutions and a help facility. McCabe (1994) describes the use of practical examinations where students rotate between three labs. The examinations involved the use of several software packages, including: Turbo-Pascal; QuickBasic; Quattro Pro; Paradox; and Word for Windows. Question Mark software was also used for about a quarter of the examination, and students were examined on programming, use of spreadsheets and macros, databases and word processing. Bull (1993) also gives details of the use of practical examinations for the assessment of spreadsheet and word-processing skills, database management, statistics and management science for a cohort of 1800 students. Some of the marking is done instantly by computer software and the remainder by tutors who collect the students' disks at the end of the examination.

Testing software such as Question Mark is used to assess vocabulary and grammar in many languages. LUISA, a software program for the teaching and assessment of Italian grammatical forms, has been developed by the University of Leeds, and Wida Software Ltd and Eurocentres provide assessment software such as Gapmaster which allows the testing of function gaps in European languages. Other developments include the assessment of laboratory practicals, problem-solving and the self-assessment of project work (see Bull, 1993; Hart and Smith, 1994, 1996).

## RECORDING AND TRANSMITTING MARKS

Computer networks *can* save time in recording and transmitting modular marks throughout the academic year and at the peak times at the end of each semester. The marks can be collated using spreadsheets, analyses of modular marks can be undertaken and marks converted into prescribed categories. The major obstacle appears to be lack of compatibility of the central management information system and local networks. It is not unusual to find universities in which a department prints out its results, a secretary takes them to the Registry where they are keyed into the central system and the print-out is returned to the department for checking. In some universities, downloading of results in the format required by examination boards is not possible. Improvement of the links between departments and the central system could reduce frustration and the likelihood of errors, as well as saving time.

Academic tutorial systems can benefit from the use of networks to record and store marks. In the Department of Engineering at the University of Leicester, students, with their academic tutors, develop action plans based on the marks and comments that are stored on their computer. The action plans are also keyed in and used in subsequent tutorials as the basis for progress reports. This system has replaced the weekly tutorial system.

## INTRODUCING AND EVALUATING COMPUTER-ASSISTED ASSESSMENT

The problems involved in changing assessment procedures are considered in the next chapter. Here we are concerned particularly with the implementation and evaluation of computer-assisted assessment. Fear of the unknown and loss of the familiar are the major barriers to implementation. Computer-assisted assessment is not an exception. Fear of technological failure, perceived lack of time, inadequate technical support and lack of expertise are commonly cited as

---

1 Student, academic and administrative staff questionnaires on perceived strengths and weaknesses of the system.
2 Structured or semi-structured interviews with students, academic and administrative staff.
3 Structured or semi-structured group interviews with students, academic and administrative staff.
4 Comparison of student results before and after implementation.
5 Comparison of quality of feedback to students before and after implementation.
6 Comparison of speed of feedback to students before and after implementation.
7 Comparison of number of appeals within a paper-based and computerised system.
8 Comparison of student time spent on assessment tasks, before and after implementation.
9 Comparison of costs of development, implementation and maintenance of computer-assisted and traditional systems.
10 Usage rate, where the testing is for self-assessment.
11 Accuracy of marking, reduction of clerical errors.
12 Academic and administrative staff time saved.
13 Evaluation of the visual presentation on computer screens.
14 Ease of use of the assessment.
15 Flexibility of the system to incorporate change.
16 Level of technical support needed to maintain the system.
17 Level of hard- and software needed to support the system.

---

From Bull (1994)

*Figure 13.5* Evaluation of computer-assisted assessment

major obstacles in computer-assisted learning and assessment. The 'not invented here' syndrome appears to be less important (Laurillard, Swift and Darby, 1993). Lack of confidence in software, networks and technical support are claimed to be greater barriers than lack of expertise in assessment or learning (Stephens, 1995). But lack of confidence in technology may be a cloak for lack of expertise in assessment and for the reluctance to give up familiar approaches. Investing more time in design and less time in marking is, for many, a profound change in working practice. Some tutors miss the bitter-sweet experience of reading their students' examination scripts and some feel a loss of control when a computer takes over the marking.

Most of these obstacles are surmountable. Back-up procedures can be developed to minimise the risk of technological failure. Seminars and training programmes can be established for all staff and students involved in CAA so that they are able to explore the issues and thereby reduce their anxiety. Some seminars for staff can be devoted to designing assessment tasks and MCQs.

Briefings on invigilation and the use of terminals can be provided for staff and students.

Innovations are more likely to be embedded when they are evaluated sensitively and the evaluations are seen to be acted upon. Wills and McNaught (1996) point out that a full evaluation of computer-based approaches encompasses the context in which staff and students work as well as their views of the particular innovation. Bull (1994) summarises some approaches to the evaluation of computer-assisted assessment (see Figure 13.5). Qualitative methods may be more important than quantitative methods for the purposes of adopting a new approach. She points out that the evaluation of a CAA system is different from the evaluation of the assessment task. The system provides the mode of delivery, the task provides the method of assessment.

Finally, we turn to the question of so-called efficiency gains of CAA. In the short term, CAA is unlikely to save time and resources (Stephens, 1994; King, 1994). All innovations require detailed planning and organisation. The 2/3 rule applies. An innovation can be cheap, fast and of high quality. At best, it can only have two of these three characteristics. If it is cheap and fast, it will not be of high quality. If it is fast and high quality, it will not be cheap. Make your choice.

## ACTIVITIES

13.1 How do you use your PC or Apple Mac to design assessment tasks and to provide feedback to students and to collate marks? Compare your approaches with those of a few colleagues. How could you extend your existing approaches?

13.2 You have a class of 400 students, you are short of time and you have to assess what they have learnt from the last six weeks of your course. You have an OHP and blank transparencies. How will you do it?
As well as an OHP and transparencies you now have access to an optical mark reader (OMR) and a mainframe computer. How would this change your approach?
What other uses would you make of the mainframe computer for improving the assessment of student learning?

13.3 Two colleagues share the marking of 450 2,000-word assignments and 450 examination scripts. The total time involved is about 250 hours excluding examiners' meetings. Develop a plan that eases their burden of marking. Include CAA and other approaches in the plan. Make an estimate of the time involved in developing and using the new approach.

13.4 Meet in groups of four or five for about one hour.
Each person should spend five minutes thinking and noting ways in which IT could be used to assess, mark, record and manage assessment.

The group should then spend the remainder of the hour on a discussion and compilation of the various suggestions.

13.5 Meet with a few colleagues and compile a list of strengths, weaknesses, opportunities and threats of CAA. Use the compilation as a basis for developing an approach to CAA.

13.6 How are marks recorded and transmitted within your department and school and between your department/school and the Registry? How could the system be improved?

# Chapter 14

# Changing assessment procedures

This brief chapter provides a perspective on change and resistance to change together with some suggestions for anyone who wishes to change, or persuade others to change, their approaches to assessment in a department, school or university. It is based upon studies of innovation and the authors' experience of introducing innovations in teaching and assessment.

Change *per se* is not necessarily good. If you have a stable, fair system that assesses a wide range of academic and other transferable skills then don't change it – although you might wish to fine-tune it. On the other hand, if you are concerned about overload of assessment on students and staff or you consider that the assessment procedures are too narrowly focused then you may wish to change your system. But be warned: changing assessment procedures is often more difficult than the process of assessment itself.

## PERSPECTIVE ON CHANGE

Resistance to change is normal. Fear of the unknown and the loss of the familiar were mentioned in the previous chapter. When the change is imposed and linked to punitive accountability procedures then it may induce superficial compliance but not necessarily commitment. When it is also frequent it may lead to alienation and, perhaps, despair. Given the battering that higher education has received in the past decade it is not surprising that many of us are even more suspicious of change. Relatively few academics will have read Halsey's analysis of the proletarianisation of academics (Halsey, 1992) but most of us are well aware of changes in working conditions, remuneration and management styles. All of these factors influence our attitudes to change – even if that change may be beneficial. Hence the importance of understanding the processes of change, particularly if one wishes to change the approach of others, to assessment.

Changing assessment procedures is a political process and political processes are not wholly rational. They involve considerations of key players, opinion leaders, stakeholders, external forces and equilibria. All of these were brought together in a model developed by Lewin (1951) over 40 years ago. That model has been extended and modified but never displaced. In essence, Lewin's model is based upon forces within a field. External forces such as, in the 1990s, the establishment of the Higher Education Funding Councils (HEFCs), the drive towards mass higher education whilst reducing unit costs and the ideology of the quality assurance movement are producing a disequilibrium in higher education that Lewin would have labelled as 'unfreezing'. This unfreezing creates the possibility of change or 'moving' as the forces re-align themselves around a new centre of equilibrium. This new balance he called 're-freezing' and it becomes the new orthodoxy until it is challenged again. This simple but robust model may be used to understand and illuminate changes in attitudes of an individual, of the development of a university and of a higher education system. Berg and Ostergren (1977) based their analysis of innovation in higher education upon Lewin's model. They argued that most aspects of innovation in higher education may be accounted for by the four concepts of power, leadership, ownership and gain/loss (needs and interests) together with the looser notions of the degree of conflict within organisations, the visibility of the innovation, changes in personnel, linkages within the organisation and correlations of internal changes and external changes. Lueddeke in his review of change and innovation in higher education argues that key factors are involvement, timing, authenticity of the need to change, the role of the change agent and adequate resourcing (Lueddeke, 1995). In addition one might consider the processes of creative problem-solving based upon genuine participation. This theme is considered briefly in the section of this chapter concerned with changing a university's approach to assessment.

These views provide the key strategies to adopt when wishing to introduce or avoid change. Figure 14.1 provides some of the standard arguments against change which you should know and be able to counteract with either concession, apparent concession or attack. By way of pleasure, you might also read Cornford's witty observations on how to resist and promote change in academe (Cornford, [1908] 1993). Figure 14.2 suggests some ways of reducing resistance to change. Resistance to any change is often more of an obstacle than the change itself. These suggestions may be augmented by persuasive argument for change. Figure 14.3 provides some guidelines that are based on the reviews of attitude change by Zimbardo et al. (1977).

## CHANGING ONE'S OWN APPROACH

We asked colleagues who have introduced different methods of assessment into their courses what advice they would give to someone wanting to try out a new assessment procedure. Their advice was easy to understand but perhaps difficult to put into practice:

1 We're already doing it.
2 We've already tried it and it didn't work.
3 We've never tried anything like it before.
4 The reduction in our funding prevents it.
5 Have we really got the time for this?
6 Of course if we had the right staff . . .
7 We'd like to but the Dean/Director/Vice Chancellor/ED would never let us.
8 This sort of thing has been turned down before.
9 What a good idea – let's set up a working party.
10 There's a working party/government committee looking at just this area.
11 Isn't there a report coming out on this soon?
12 Isn't this something really for HEFCE to look at?
13 The idea is very good in principle but it wouldn't work in this department/faculty.
14 Our research will suffer.
15 It's a good idea but the timetable won't allow it.
16 Ah – this is something to put to the Academic Audit Unit.
17 Have you looked at the cost-effectiveness factor?
18 That's just not possible. There are other factors which I am not at liberty to disclose.
19 Well it might work in the States but I don't think . . .
20 It's not necessary in this department/school/faculty/university/college.
21 You should read the comment on this in the minutes of the Faculty Board of 1968.
22 Our Heads of Departments are far too busy for this sort of thing.
23 Look, we're just about to re-organise the curriculum review and assessment structure.
24 Look, we've just re-organised the curriculum review structure.
25 I don't think the Examinations Unit would cope with that.
26 Our staff are overstretched as it is.
27 Bring it up at the next meeting.
28 Why don't we talk about it when I get back from South America?
29 And who did you say came up with this idea?
30 It will lower academic standards.

*Figure 14.1* Thirty ways of avoiding change

- Think, plan, try it, modify it and *then* tell others about it.
- If others are involved, involve them earlier rather than later.
- If others are involved, don't spend too long on talking about the difficulties and too little on action.

This advice may be expanded into a series of guidelines which you may wish to adapt for persuading others to change their assessment procedures.

**Who brings a change?**
*Resistance is less:*
If those involved feel it is their own project.
If it has whole-hearted and visible support of the leaders and the leaders continue to support the project after the initial stages and into the 're-freezing' stage.

**What kinds of change?**
*Resistance is less:*
If the change appeals to values which have long been acknowledged but perhaps neglected.
If the change is seen as reducing rather than increasing present burdens.
If the programme offers the kinds of new experiences which interest participants.
If participants feel that their autonomy and security are not threatened.
If visible efforts are made to maximise gains and minimise losses.

**What procedures?**
*Resistance will be less:*
If participants have shared in the evaluation and development and they agree that the problems identified are important.
If the project is adopted by group consensus.
If proponents empathise with opponents, recognise and accept valid objections and suggestions and allay unnecessary fears.
If it is recognised that innovations are often misinterpreted and misunderstood – so patient, clear and perhaps frequent explaining is required. So too are opportunities for feedback and further clarification.
If the project is kept open to revision and re-evaluation.
If the experience of the participants indicates that changes are desirable.
If participants support, trust and have confidence in their relations with one another.

Based on Berg and Ostergren (1977)

*Figure 14.2* Reducing resistance to change

## CHANGING THE DEPARTMENT'S APPROACH

The first step is to check that what the department or school claims to be doing is what it is doing. The usual questions to address are:

- What kinds of things do we want our students to learn?
- What opportunities are provided?
- What assessment tasks are set?
- What methods of assessment are used?
- Are they worthwhile?

- How much time is spent by students on assessment tasks?
- How much time is spent on setting, marking and managing assessment?

You might conduct a review of students' views on assessment by questionnaire or discussion. The results can be helpful and sometimes surprising. In a survey of a cohort of fourth-year dental students and their tutors the three most common views of students and staff were the improvement of consistency, more discussion of reasons for grades and the introduction of explicit criteria (Manogue and Brown, 1995). The findings from the survey provided a basis for changing the assessment procedures. Some items that you might use in a questionnaire are given in Figure 14.4. Group discussions can also be illuminating. Figure 14.5 provides a few of the many comments made by students at workshops on assessment. You might also look at the comments of students and staff collected by Miller and Parlett (1974) in their study of the assessment game. Their

---

1 Know your participants and think of what kinds of arguments may be appealing to them.

2 People are more likely to listen to you and accept your suggestions if you are already perceived as credible, trustworthy and having expertise.

3 When there are arguments in favour of and against a procedure, it is usually better to present both sides.

4 If you have to stress risks in a procedure, don't overdo the arousal of fear.

5 Say what experts or expert groups do when faced with the problem you are discussing.

6 If the problem is complex for the group, you should draw the conclusions or at least give them time for discussion. If it is not too complex let the group members draw their own conclusions.

7 If the suggestions you are making are likely to be challenged by others, describe their views in anticipation and show how they may be wrong.

8 If the task you are asking a group to do is complex, acknowledge that there is a risk of failure and the need for revision and reconsideration. Never say a new task is easy, rather say it may not be easy at first.

9 If a task is threatening admit it is and consider ways of reducing that threat.

10 Do not deride cherished traditions. Rather show how the approach links to those traditions or indicate that people used to hold that view but that it is no longer appropriate.

11 Do not deride people for their views. Instead state that their views may once have been correct but that changes in the context and in knowledge suggest a new approach is required.

---

*Figure 14.3* Some pointers to persuasion

comments have a contemporary ring and they may provide you with clues of what to ask and how. As well as conducting a review of what students think of the existing assessment procedures and how they might be improved you might also discuss with them the new approaches that you are proposing. Involve the students in some of the processes of assessment, for they too may fear and resist change.

---

*Here are a few suggestions for questions you might include in a student questionnaire.*

We are interested in your views on our present assessment procedures. Please spend a few minutes completing this form. The information provided will help us in our review of the assessment procedures.

**Coursework**
Are assignments for the modules set at the beginning of the module?
Are the deadlines set at the beginning of the module?
Is the coursework returned promptly?
Are the comments and feedback on the coursework useful for helping you to do the next piece of coursework?
Are they useful for preparing for examinations?
Are there opportunities to receive feedback without being assessed for your degree?
Are there opportunities to discuss the coursework with your tutor?
Are the coursework tasks relevant to the lectures and seminars?

**Compared with other modules**
The coursework load is about the same.
The marking is fair.
The assessment tasks are relevant.
The comments and feedback are useful.

**Examinations**
Is there sufficient guidance on the content of the examinations?
Is there sufficient guidance on the format and procedure of examinations?
Is the proportion of marks for the examinations compared with the proportion of marks for coursework about right?

**Organisation of course assessment and examinations**
Please write a few comments on the coursework and written examinations in this module and other modules.

*Thank you for your help*

---

*Figure 14.4* Your assessment of our assessment

Here are a few comments from students on assessment procedures.

'You didn't have time to learn the stuff before you were assessed on it.'
'They say be creative and take risks but you daren't if it counts towards your degree.'
'I'm just a full-time essay writer.'
'They are obsessed with assessing us all the time.'
'I had no coursework for two months then bang! All the lecturers set us essays to be handed in by the end of term.'
'I like the coursework. It gives you a chance to think and express your own ideas.'
'Written examinations are a con. You just have to cram and hope the right questions come up.'
'Exams make me work and then I begin to get interested.'

*Figure 14.5* Student comments

More radical changes in assessment procedures may require an examination of the degree or departmental regulations to see what is permissible and what regulations may need changing. Often a re-interpretation of the regulations can liberate new approaches to assessment so do not be trapped by a taken-for-granted assumption. Of course one may have to win colleagues over to new approaches to assessment. (See figures 14.1, 14.2, 14.3.)

If you wish to change the regulations or procedures, outline and discuss your approaches with sympathetic colleagues, listen to their views and their analyses of other people's views. Then outline and discuss informally your suggestions with the chair of the curriculum review committee and other senior members of the committee. Regrettably not all chairpersons are as well informed as they should be about new approaches to assessment. Perhaps your institution should run seminars on new approaches to assessment for all chairpersons of review committees? Some colleagues have suggested that attendance at such seminars should be a condition of appointment to the chairs of review committees.

Outline and discuss your proposed approach to assessment with external examiners and leading members of professional bodies. They too may not be as well informed as they should be about new approaches. If you are appointing a new external examiner, ensure that he or she is sympathetic to the approaches that you are introducing.

Within the new regulations (or interpretation of existing regulations) you might explore ways of modifying existing assessment tasks that fit more closely the objectives of the module. Alternatively, change the objectives of the module. Extend the range of your assessment tasks. The test of what you value in student learning is revealed in what and how you assess. If you want students to develop the capacity to reflect on their approaches to learning, then set tasks that require them to do this and provide feedback on their performance. If your primary aim is the development of understanding then set learning tasks that encourage thinking and assessment tasks that provide estimates of understanding. Use some learning and assessment tasks that develop self-critical and reflective approaches to learning, for these lay the foundations of effective life-long learning. Use some tasks that require students to apply their expertise to problems in different contexts and to communicate to different audiences. These approaches increase the probability of transfer of learning. Many of the ideas in this book may be used for these purposes.

It is unlikely that you will have anticipated all the problems before you introduce a new form of assessment. However, there are some common errors that you might avoid. These are:

- Excessive detail in the assessment procedure.
- Under-estimating the time required by students to complete the assessment tasks.
- Lack of preparation of students and staff for the new forms of assessment.
- Not planning the evaluation of the new assessment procedures at the start of the programme.

At the end of the first year or semester one should review and modify the procedures – slightly. Radical changes are not recommended on the basis of one trial – unless that trial is a serious disaster. There is much to be said for trying any new approach at least twice. The first time is for all staff to get used to it, the second, for all students to get used to it too.

## CHANGING THE UNIVERSITY'S APPROACH?

Assessment is locked into the organisation of teaching and learning in universities so an assessment strategy for a university cannot be divorced from its teaching–learning strategy nor can these strategies ignore diminishing resources and increases in student numbers. A realistic assessment strategy in the 1990s and beyond (see Chapter 1) needs to balance:

*efficiency* – saving staff and, perhaps, student time
*effectiveness* – the assessment fits the objectives of the module or course
*enablement* – develops the understanding and expertise of students.

Experience suggests that the 2/3 law applies: you can only have any two of the three at one time. If you opt for enablement and effectiveness then you will not save time. If you opt for efficiency and effectiveness then you will probably neglect enablement. If you opt for effectiveness and enablement then you will have less control over effectiveness as measured by the fit of assessment to objectives. The solution here may be to change the objectives of the module or course although this change will have effects upon teaching and learning.

The implications of the above discussion are that a university, or department, has to develop an optimal strategy that is sensitive to the nature of different subjects, to the wider range of students entering universities and to the external environment. It may be that the existing strategy can be adapted but, more likely, it may require a radical change in course organisation, teaching and learning and other demands upon academic staff. Inevitably this leads to the issues of the balance between research, administration and teaching, to the purposes of higher education for staff as well as for students and to the likely changes in the higher education system. The problem is profound.

The development of the optimal strategy for a university is well beyond the scope of this book. However, it is worth spending a little time on some of the key questions to ask when solving problems of change, for these may provide pointers to solutions. The questions that might be addressed are:

• Is a change really necessary?
• If the answer is yes, what are the primary purposes of the change?
• Which of these are the most important?
• Is the problem presented the real problem?
• What are the alternative solutions?
• What are the effects of the solutions on other aspects of the system?
• How will the problem and alternative solutions be explored?
• How will staff participate in the definition of the problem and the development of a viable solution?

To illustrate the use of some of these questions in action, consider the problem of increases in student numbers and its effect upon staff workloads. The problem is often presented wrongly: 'How can we cut back on contact time with students?' Any solution to the presented problem does not address the underlying problem. The main load produced by increases in students is on assessment, not on teaching, so one needs to develop a realistic assessment strategy. But this solution is, at best, partial. The underlying problem of increases in student numbers may be staff time. Once this is established, one can look for alternative approaches such as reducing the internal quality demands imposed upon academic staff. In industry, the National Health Service and universities, some of the time that is being devoted to internal quality demands could be devoted to customers, patients or students. Considerable savings might be made by reducing the number of reports and meetings concerned with quality assurance. The costs of a component of a quality assurance system should always be less than the probable costs of failure of that component in the system.

Now consider the question of modularity, an approach to course organisation much favoured by some senior managers. What are the purposes of modularity? Ostensibly, modularity is to increase student choice and to ease transfer and access. What proportion of students in your university do choose modules outside their programmes? What proportion transfer across programmes or to other universities? What proportion of final-year students transfer to other programmes or universities? Would reducing the number of modules per semester to three reduce the workload of staff? At first sight the answer to the last question may appear to be no. Certainly it would be an upheaval but one could easily reduce the assessment load on students and staff in such a system and it would increase the probability of developing deeper understanding and expertise. The other consequential effects would be a reduction in student choice and a weakening of linkages between assessment and specific objectives. The former may be a small price; the latter can be safeguarded against. Indeed there may be advantages in loosening connections between detailed objectives and assessment. The development of understanding needs a framework, not a straitjacket. Very few students transfer out of the final year of a course and achievements at earlier levels are either ignored or given a lower weighting than the final year. So, could the final year be assessed differently so as to reduce assessment and teaching load and provide a measure of the students' expertise matched against the aims of the degree programme?

These are just a few of the possibilities that can emerge from the use of questions on change. We have not tackled the question of who should address them and how. In large-scale organisations one has to balance efficiency and participation. Some managers prefer coercion: it appears so much easier. In the longer term the principles enunciated by Berg and Ostergren (see Figure 14. 2) are more likely to strengthen commitment.

Finally, the forthcoming Deering report on higher education will offer *a* solution for the system of higher education based on increasing specialisation and vocationalisation and, in so doing, provide problems rather than solutions for universities.

## ACTIVITIES

14.1 Meet with a group of colleagues who are interested in introducing self-assessment (or some other approach) into a course. Identify the likely arguments against the introduction of self-assessment (or some other approach) and how you would counteract them.

14.2 Meet with a group of students and invite them to discuss assessment procedures within the department (or within a module). Ask them to design a draft questionnaire – keep it brief and simple, as a rule of thumb no more than two sides with space for comments. Show them some of the items from Figure 14.4 after they have begun drafting their own approach.

14.3 What is the rationale underlying the approach in 14.2?

14.4 Repeat Activity 14.2, this time with colleagues.

14.5 Read through Figure 14.1 again and add any other tactics used to avoid change.

14.6 Consider the suggestions in figures 14.2 and 14.3 in relation to your own department, school, faculty or institution. Do the suggestions provide a useful framework?

14.7 Use the suggestions in figures 14.2 and 14.3 to draw up a strategy for introducing changes in your own assessment procedures.

14.8 A few participants should be invited to prepare a 10-minute persuasive presentation on the values of project work or some other form of assessment or learning task. The presenters may use the suggestions in Figure 14.3 as a guide to preparing the presentation. They should identify arguments against the proposal and dispose of them as well as identifying arguments for it. After the presentation the group should discuss the relative merits of the proposed form of assessment and how it might be improved.

14.9 What advice would you give to a colleague in another department who wants to introduce changes to existing assessment procedures? Compare your views with those of a few colleagues. You may if you wish choose a particular procedure such as peer marking or the use of MCQs.

# Chapter 15

# Reliability, validity and examining

This chapter describes approaches to reliability and validity and their links to common practices of assessment in higher education. It considers ways of improving consistency, the special case of competency and the role of the external examiner. It does not delve into statistical techniques of estimating reliability and validity nor does it provide guidelines on how to approach external examining. Useful references on the former are Ebel and Frisbie (1986) and Gronlund (1988). Partington, Brown and Gordon (1993) provide useful information on the latter.

In this chapter we examine the nature of reliability and validity and their implications for assessing student learning. We do not describe the statistical techniques that can be used. All such techniques are based essentially on measures of agreements and differences and range in complexity from correlations and analyses of variance to factor analyses, multi-variate analysis and beyond. Useful texts on these matters are Ebel and Frisbie (1986) and Gronlund (1988). Instead we focus upon the underlying concepts since it is the concepts that are crucial to a fair and effective assessment system.

The standard approaches to reliability and validity are derived from psychometrics, a subject which is particularly concerned with the development of personality and intelligence tests. The psychometric approach is based upon the notion of an ideal which can be achieved if only one can reduce the errors. In practice there is such a range of values involved at the higher levels of knowledge and understanding that it would be dangerous to assume that there is only one ideal. Despite this reservation, discussions of reliability and validity do help to clarify the purposes of assessment and one's evaluation of assessment procedures. However, assessment in education requires a slightly different approach from psychometrics. Knowledge and understanding are significant features of assessment in education. The specific content of assignments and examinations and their purposes differ from the content and purposes of psychological tests. Consequently, non-statistical approaches such as the use of judgement in the identification of appropriate tasks and content, the use of blueprints of learning objectives (outcomes) and assessment tasks and the translation of task performance into marks are required, as well as the approaches provided by statistical analysis.

The underlying concepts of reliability and validity in psychology and education are both based on the notions of precision and accuracy. A useful analogy is telling the time from a watch. The mechanism of a watch may be precise (reliable), it may measure the minutes and hours consistently, but the time shown may be wrong. The time shown by a watch on a particular occasion may be correct (valid) but the watch may have stopped or its variable rate of loss or gain rather than its consistency may have provided the result. There is a further variable involved in telling the time from a watch: the observer. He or she has to be able to read and interpret the watch dial correctly. The same remarks apply to interpreting the results of an examination, test or coursework assignment. Even if checklists, guidelines or rating schedules are provided, ultimately the assessment instrument is the person in conjunction with the particular checklist or procedure.

## RELIABILITY

The two main measures of reliability in assessment are measures of agreement between assessors and within assessors. There is plenty of evidence on the disagreement between assessors, even when using marking schemes. The earliest report we have come across was by Edgeworth (1890), who obtained marks of 28 qualified assessors of a Latin prose. They were requested to mark the prose as if it were by candidates for the Indian Civil Service. The range of marks was from 45 to 100. The modal (most common) mark was 75. Leaving aside the question of using Latin proses to select civil servants to work in India, the lack of consistency between the assessors was remarkable. Similar results have been obtained by Hartog and Rhodes (1935, 1936) in school certificate history, English and chemistry. The same candidates when marked by different examiners were failed, passed or awarded a credit. Diederich (1957) asked 53 experts to mark 300 short essays by first-year college students. 34 per cent of the essays obtained all the grades and no essay received less than five grades of the nine possible. Similar results have been reported by Bell (1980) and Newstead and Dennis (1994). In an earlier study, Pieron (1963) concluded that 'assessment by different examiners produces marks with considerable variability, such that in the determination of these marks the part played by the examiner can be greater than that of the performance of the examinee'.

Obviously, the broader the assessment grade used the more likely are two assessors to agree on marks – but not necessarily on reasons. Specific, but manageable, criteria or marking schemes increase reliability. Double blind marking based on criteria *may* yield a slightly more reliable result (Murphy, 1979; Newton, 1996) but doubles the marking load. Second marking is a useful form of moderating all scripts but, again, it is unnecessarily time-consuming. Moderating a sample of scripts from each class division followed, if necessary, by re-marking the set is probably the most efficient way of reducing inter-assessor disagreement. When two internal markers disagree, it is customary for a third person to mark the scripts. The third marker may be the module coordinator, programme coordinator or external examiner. Often the third marker is tempted to compromise rather than refer to the explicit criteria for the assignment or paper.

The major threat to reliability is the lack of consistency of an individual marker. In other words, the consistency of a marker is more important than whether he or she disagrees with another marker. Hence, again, criteria or marking schemes are important. So too is training to reduce capricious variability. All markers should check the consistency of their marking. The advice given in Chapter 5 (Figure 5.2) is relevant. The moderator's task is to check the internal *consistency* of the marker. This is more important than whether moderators and first markers are in close agreement. If the marking of an assessor is consistent then it is possible to adjust fairly the range of marks awarded.

Anonymous marking is increasingly fashionable on the grounds that it minimises the effects of previous knowledge of the student's performance. It reduces the effects of stereotyping, halo effects and prejudice and thereby increases reliability. In some universities anonymous marking is used for written papers and in others for all formally assessed written work. At the University of Edinburgh all assignments and scripts are identified by bar codes that are known only to the student and the Registry. These approaches probably increase the correlations between the marks awarded for coursework and examinations. They may reduce some of the biases attributable to the assessor's perception of a student but they will not reduce biases that are due to differences in values. Anonymity is difficult in small departments. It may distance tutors and students and it may weaken the effects of assessment on improving student learning.

Higher levels of reliability are more readily attainable when using low-level tests. Such tests may not be a valid measure of a module but they may have a place in a range of assessment tasks of a module. The more complex or open the assessment task, the more difficult it is to attain high measures of agreement between observers or to maintain consistency. This well-known finding is cold comfort to assessors and external examiners but one can minimise the major sources of error by careful attention to criteria, training and the use of moderators. Increasing the sample of coursework and written papers also increases reliability and, possibly, validity. However, there are costs involved of over-burdening students and tutors and of stultifying learning.

A third measure of reliability is the internal consistency of the assessment task itself. This method is used to refine MCQs and other forms of test. Reliability is measured usually by correlating the scores on items to other items and the total test score. This form of reliability virtually eliminates the role of assessor as interpreter and marker. Interpretation and correctness are the province of a test constructor who may not be the assessor and whose objectives may not be the same as those of the assessor who is applying the MCQ or test. Arguments about the degree of choice that students should have in examinations, coursework and projects are often, at root, a concern for this form of reliability. One has to sacrifice some degree of consistency in the interests of motivating students and enabling them to provide their best performance.

To complicate matters further, there is another variable at work: the students themselves. The variation between a student's performance from one task to another is described, curiously, as 'content specificity' (see Van der Vleuten *et al.*, 1991). Students may have good days and bad days, they may try an approach to the assignment which was bold and innovative but a failure. They may perform better in some contexts than in others and they may change during their undergraduate years. Increasing the range of assessments may offset some of the failures of an assessment system. The costs are, again, staff and student time and its consequences for student learning. Increasing the range will reduce the risk of errors in one sample marking, of errors by examiners or of errors in the design of a particular examination or test. However, it may also increase the risk of including performances that are no longer extant or relevant. Some universities separate the assessment of each year (level) of a programme so as to minimise the risk of including performances that are not relevant. Their degrees awarded are based solely on performance in the final year.

## IMPROVING CONSISTENCY

Consistency across modules or degree programmes is more concerned with equality of treatment than reliability. But such consistency is dependent upon the internal consistency (reliability) of the individual markers. Put another way, the methods described in this section will reduce variability across modules but they will not eliminate errors.

The first, and more important, set of methods is based on the use of grids so that marks are reported consistently. An example of such a grid was given in Figure 5.9. It may be used to report marks of examinations and assignments that have different weightings in different modules. A more comprehensive approach has been devised by Millican (1994) for use across faculties at the University of Leeds. Figure 15.1 summarises the system. Assessors can use literal grades or numerical marks. They then translate them into the standard form. In effect, the approach stretches the range of marks customarily awarded in arts and reduces the range of marks awarded in sciences and thereby ensures greater comparability. The system also cuts through the difficulties caused by some faculties using a preponderance rule and others basing degree classes on total marks awarded.

Another simple but effective way of improving consistency within a university is to use the same principles for the awarding of degrees. Differences of weighting across faculties can produce anomalies. For example, three students at the same university compared notes on how their degree results were calculated. For one student, the mean score based on all six modules is carried over into the third year

| Alphabetical grade | Literal grade | Numerical grade | Class | Alphabetical grade | Literal grade | Numerical grade | Class |
|---|---|---|---|---|---|---|---|
| AA+ | Exceptional | 85 | 1 | D+ | High | 48 | 3 |
| AA | Excellent | 82 | 1 | D | Middle | 46 | 3 |
|  | Unclassified | 78 | 1 | D– | Low | 44 | 3 |
| A+ | High | 76 | 1 | DE | Marginal | 42 | 3 |
| A | Middle | 74 | 1 |  | Unclassified | 39–41 |  |
| A– | Low | 72 | 1 | E | Ordinary | 38 | Pass |
| AB | Marginal |  |  | FE | Unclassified | 37 | Pass |
|  | Unclassified |  |  | FE | Adjustable fail | 36 | Fail |
| B+ | High | 68 | 2.1 | FE | Unclassified | 35 | Fail |
| B | Middle | 66 | 2.1 | F | Moderate | 34 | Fail |
| B– | Low | 64 | 2.1 | F– | Bad | 32 | Fail |
| BC | Marginal | 62 | 2.1 | FF | Very bad | 30 | Fail |
|  | Unclassified |  |  | FF– | Disastrous | 28 | Fail |
| C+ | High | 58 | 2.2 | G | Irretrievable | 25 | Fail |
| C | Middle | 56 | 2.2 |  |  |  |  |
| C– | Low | 54 | 2.2 |  |  |  |  |
| CD | Marginal | 52 | 2.2 |  |  |  |  |
|  | Unclassified |  |  |  |  |  |  |

From Millican (1994)

*Figure 15.1* A grade score scale

and contributes 25 per cent of the degree awarded. Another student carries over the best two module scores and these count towards the final degree classification, and the third student is judged on the best six of the 12 modules taken in the last two years of the degree. Such differences can obviously affect the degree awarded. More important, the differences in procedures are perceived by students, parents and possibly employers as unequal treatment of students and inconsistencies of standards. The removal of these anomalies is probably more important and easier to effect than trying to impose a national standard upon all universities.

The second set are *post factum* methods of adjusting marks. All of these have the disadvantage that any marks reported to students before the Board of Examiners meet may be changed, perhaps quite dramatically, by the method used.

The simplest method is to add or subtract an agreed number of marks from each student's score in a module. Its effect is to change the mean score but not the rank order of students. The approach reduces the effect of 'hard' and 'soft' marking or 'hard' and 'soft' papers. A more rigorous approach is to standardise marks by using the same mean and standard deviation for all modules. The approach is used by GCSE and A level boards when large numbers of candidates are involved. As a rule of thumb, the approach should only be used when 500 students or more are taking the same set of modules. This approach does change the rank order of students.

Figure 15.2 shows the effects on the total marks awarded when one assessor uses a narrow range of marks and another uses a wide range. The point is not merely theoretical. If a student takes a module that has a different range of marks from other modules then his or her degree class can be affected. The problem usually occurs when an optional module is taken outside of the main programme.

Figure 15.3 shows the results of a hypothetical set of candidates. They are extremes designed to highlight the effect of standardising scores and of using rank orders. They are used in the handbook for external examiners (Partington, Brown and Gordon, 1993) and the video learning package on improving examiners meetings (UCosDA, 1996). They serve as a warning against undue reliance on *post factum* statistical methods.

The most common *post factum* method is to adjust marks at the meeting of the Board of Examiners. These boards in some universities are now two-tiered. One tier considers modules and the second tier considers programmes and degree awards. Discussion of the personal qualities of a candidate and his or her papers and assignments that have been seen by the external examiner lead to recommendations that the candidate be moved up or down the class list. Strong advocacy rather than reasons based upon well-defined criteria often wins the case. The consequences for other students of comparable marks are not often considered, so inconsistency is introduced rather than reduced. The implications are clear: the procedures for Boards of Examiners need to be explicit, consistent and scrupulous.

| Candidate | Course A | Course B | Course C | TOTAL | RANK |
|-----------|----------|----------|----------|-------|------|
| 1 | 58 | 62 | 40 | 160 | 1 |
| 2 | 68 | 42 | 45 | 155 | 2 |
| 3 | 60 | 40 | 50 | 150 | 3 |
| 4 | 31 | 59 | 55 | 145 | 4 |
| 5 | 48 | 32 | 60 | 140 | 5 |

In Course C the examiner has awarded marks ranging from 40 to 60. Now see what happens if the examiner had used a mark range from 20 to 80:

| Candidate | Course A | Course B | Course C | TOTAL | RANK |
|-----------|----------|----------|----------|-------|------|
| 1 | 58 | 62 | 20 | 140 | 5 |
| 2 | 68 | 42 | 35 | 145 | 4 |
| 3 | 60 | 40 | 50 | 150 | 3 |
| 4 | 31 | 59 | 65 | 155 | 2 |
| 5 | 48 | 32 | 80 | 160 | 1 |

From Heywood (1977)

*Figure 15.2* Effects of a wide range of marks in one module

## VALIDITY

Validity is a form of truth-seeking. It is often described as the match between what is intended to be measured and what is measured. The closer the match between objectives and assessment tasks, the greater the intrinsic validity of the assessment procedures. The notion is not dissimilar from that of fitness of purpose. This form of validity may also be labelled 'appropriateness'. There are other forms of validity and these may be in conflict with validity as determined by appropriateness. Five common approaches are given below. All of them raise more questions than they answer. Judgement is essential for all forms of validity and statistical measurement can aid judgement of some forms of validity. There is a form of validity known as *face validity*. This is the surface impression or plausibility of a test, examination or assignment. Face validity is not a measure of validity but if a test, examination or assignment does not have some face validity then it is unlikely to draw out the best performances from students. Hence the importance of ensuring face validity by explaining clearly the purposes of an assessment. There is also a form of validity known as *consequential validity*. This form is concerned with the consequences of the nature and load of assessment upon teaching and student learning and other aspects of a system such as administration and research. Strictly speaking, this is not a form of truth-seeking but it provides some truths about an assessment system.

### Raw Marks
#### Subject

| Name | A | B | C | D | E | F | G | H | Total | Class |
|------|----|----|----|----|----|----|----|----|-------|-------|
| Condon, B.W. | 74 | 68 | 43 | 99 | 48 | 45 | 39 | 32 | 448 | 1 |
| Kennett, A. | 62 | 58 | 66 | 89 | 44 | 63 | 19 | 40 | 441 | 1 |
| Franks, B.F. | 47 | 52 | 76 | 60 | 41 | 77 | 40 | 38 | 431 | 2.1 |
| Goldsworthy, M. | 92 | 67 | 31 | 62 | 52 | 62 | 29 | 34 | 429 | 2.1 |
| Hill, P.J.C. | 84 | 37 | 37 | 55 | 42 | 64 | 44 | 57 | 420 | 2.2 |
| Burgess, V.C. | 66 | 42 | 16 | 79 | 50 | 53 | 64 | 47 | 417 | 2.2 |
| Ing, O.L. | 57 | 77 | 56 | 22 | 46 | 47 | 59 | 49 | 413 | 2.2 |
| Listerdale, N. | 72 | 17 | 61 | 37 | 53 | 75 | 55 | 37 | 407 | 2.2 |
| Eggar, K.C. | 42 | 48 | 26 | 84 | 61 | 70 | 28 | 42 | 401 | 2.2 |
| Arnold, B.D. | 12 | 32 | 71 | 71 | 51 | 81 | 25 | 56 | 399 | 2.2 |
| Dursley, L.J. | 40 | 57 | 6 | 47 | 56 | 51 | 69 | 59 | 385 | 3 |
| Jolley, D. | 26 | 27 | 54 | 9 | 60 | 85 | 34 | 62 | 357 | 3 |

### Scaled Marks
#### Subject

| Name | A | B | C | D | E | F | G | H | Total | Class |
|------|----|----|----|----|----|----|----|----|-------|-------|
| Jolley, D. | 18 | 17 | 69 | 0 | 95 | 100 | 30 | 100 | 429 | 1 |
| Dursley, L.J. | 35 | 67 | 0 | 42 | 75 | 15 | 100 | 90 | 424 | 1 |
| Arnold, B.D. | 0 | 25 | 93 | 69 | 50 | 90 | 12 | 80 | 419 | 2.1 |
| Eggar, K.C. | 38 | 52 | 29 | 83 | 100 | 63 | 18 | 33 | 416 | 2.1 |
| Listerdale, N. | 75 | 0 | 79 | 31 | 60 | 75 | 72 | 17 | 409 | 2.2 |
| Ing, O.L. | 56 | 100 | 71 | 14 | 25 | 5 | 80 | 57 | 408 | 2.2 |
| Burgess, V.C. | 68 | 42 | 14 | 78 | 45 | 20 | 90 | 50 | 407 | 2.2 |
| Hill, P.J.C. | 90 | 33 | 44 | 51 | 5 | 48 | 50 | 83 | 404 | 2.2 |
| Goldsworthy, M. | 100 | 83 | 36 | 59 | 55 | 43 | 20 | 7 | 403 | 2.2 |
| Franks, B.F. | 44 | 58 | 100 | 57 | 0 | 80 | 42 | 20 | 401 | 2.2 |
| Kennett, A. | 63 | 68 | 86 | 89 | 15 | 45 | 0 | 27 | 393 | 3 |
| Condon, B.W. | 78 | 85 | 53 | 100 | 35 | 0 | 40 | 0 | 391 | 3 |

### Ranks
#### Subject

| Name | A | B | C | D | E | F | G | H | Total | Class |
|------|----|----|----|----|----|----|----|----|-------|-------|
| Arnold, B.D. | 12 | 10 | 2 | 5 | 6 | 2 | 11 | 4 | 52 | 2.2 |
| Burgess, V.C. | 5 | 8 | 11 | 4 | 7 | 9 | 2 | 6 | 52 | 2.2 |
| Condon, B.W. | 3 | 2 | 7 | 1 | 8 | 12 | 7 | 12 | 52 | 2.2 |
| Dursley, L.J. | 10 | 5 | 12 | 9 | 3 | 10 | 1 | 2 | 52 | 2.2 |
| Eggar, K.C. | 9 | 7 | 10 | 3 | 1 | 5 | 10 | 7 | 52 | 2.2 |
| Franks, B.F. | 8 | 6 | 1 | 7 | 12 | 3 | 6 | 9 | 52 | 2.2 |
| Goldsworthy, M. | 1 | 3 | 9 | 6 | 5 | 8 | 9 | 11 | 52 | 2.2 |
| Hill, P.J.C. | 2 | 9 | 8 | 8 | 11 | 6 | 5 | 3 | 52 | 2.2 |
| Ing, O.L. | 7 | 1 | 5 | 11 | 9 | 11 | 3 | 5 | 52 | 2.2 |
| Jolley, D. | 11 | 11 | 6 | 12 | 2 | 1 | 8 | 1 | 52 | 2.2 |
| Kennett, A. | 6 | 4 | 3 | 2 | 10 | 7 | 12 | 8 | 52 | 2.2 |
| Listerdale, N. | 4 | 12 | 4 | 10 | 4 | 4 | 4 | 10 | 52 | 2.2 |

*Figure 15.3* Effects of scaling and rank ordering

## Intrinsic validity

Do the assessment tasks measure the learning objectives of the course?

Intrinsic validity assumes that objectives are clearly expressed and are measurable. But it is arguable whether all objectives may be expressed in measurable terms unless one takes the circular route that if it cannot be measured then it is not an objective. In practice, most assessments are based on judgement which is translated into a literal grade or numerical score. Judgement rather than measurement is also required for this form of validity. The judgement may be supplied by the course team, perhaps in conjunction with external examiners. There is the familiar risk in this form of validity of undue specificity. Specificity produces long lists of learning outcomes and this may reduce reliability of marking and validity. Tutor fatigue and halo effects are likely to be salient features of unduly specific assessment procedures. The more complex a topic is and the more able the students are, the greater the difficulty of using long lists of objectives and the greater the risk of not allowing for valuable unintended outcomes. If appropriateness is limited to one-to-one correspondence between long lists of objectives and assessment scores then creative thinking might be excluded. None the less a useful, and often salutary, exercise in intrinsic validity is to analyse the content of students' assignments or written papers and match them to the learning objectives of the course and the expected level of performance of the students.

## Construct validity

Do the assessment tasks measure the underlying theory or factors on which the assessment is based?

Construct validity is the measure of the underlying theory or construct of a particular test or examination. It is an intrinsic form of validity which is used to confirm the underlying constructs or, more frequently, discover what the underlying constructs are. Statistical methods assume that the features of the examination can be translated into numerical scores. For many examinations and assessments, informed judgement rather than statistical analyses is more feasible. Construct validity is used to determine to what extent two examinations are measuring the same factors or to what extent the items in an examination are measuring the same factors. However, in practice it is what the two examinations or assignments do not have in common which may be more important. If two examinations or assignments are actually measuring the same characteristics then one might dispense with one or the other. However, one has to be wary of the consequences. For example, abolishing coursework on the grounds that examinations measure essentially the same characteristics might weaken student learning and, in turn, the validity of the examination.

## Concurrency

Does performance on the assessment tasks match that obtained by other assessments of the same group of students taken at roughly the same time?

Concurrence within a course is rarely possible in practice. At best one can compare coursework and written papers. The correlations between coursework and written examinations are usually positive but not perfect. Coursework marks tend on the whole to be higher than examination marks. There are several possible reasons for these results. The examiners may be using the same standards in marking that they use for written examinations. So the quality of the student's coursework is higher on those standards. Tutors may be using coursework marks to encourage and praise students and consequently they may be more generous in their marking of coursework. Some tutors may be reluctant to negotiate and explain a relatively low range of marks so they award marks higher than perhaps they would if marking in a written examination.

## Predictability

Do the assessment tasks predict future performance accurately?

Predictive validity relates performance in one set of assessments to performance in subsequent assessments. Predictive validity is useful for specific purposes such as testing a set of well-defined skills which are used in a profession. The assessment task need not be identical to the real task. Low-fidelity tasks such as paper and pencil tests may provide good predictions of the ability to choose an appropriate method of patient care. High-fidelity tasks such as simulated patients may be required for high levels of predictive validity of patient consultation skills.

As one moves into more general or long-term predictions then validity drops. Success at A level predicts degree class as well as any other criteria but the correlations are only between 0.2 and 0.4. They tend to be higher in the sciences than in arts, perhaps because of the similarity of approaches at A level and university in the sciences. Correlations within a course between Part I and Part II tend to be between 0.4 and 0.6. This may be because examiners share a common perception of the course and students. Correlations between performance in undergraduate and postgraduate courses tend to be at the same level. Correlations between degree class and performance in research has not, as far as we know, been studied. Indeed, the selection of only those with Firsts and II.1s and the use of pass/fail at PhD level precludes sensitive field studies. The use of pass/fail degrees would reduce the opportunities for predictive validity and selection based on degrees.

More general predictions such as performance beyond graduation are even less useful. Performance in careers, as measured by income, is easily predicted by degree class. But such predictions may have little validity. Better students tend to come from better backgrounds and go to better universities (what 'better' means here is worthy of exploration). Incomes of good honours graduates and non-honours graduates do suggest that those with good honours degrees earn more than other graduates, but these results may not be attributable simply to the degree classification. The predictive validity of a degree may owe as much to the socio-economic system as it does to the system of higher education and its degree classification.

## Criterion validity

Are the results of the assessment tasks comparable with those obtained on other assessments of known standard by similar groups of students?

Criterion validity is concerned with matching performances on assessment tasks with those obtained on other assessments of known standard by similar groups of students. The flaws are obvious. The measures of 'similar' may not be appropriate and the phrase 'known standard' begs questions. This form of validity has the dangers of infinite or circular regress. Assessment A is valid because it correlates well with Assessment B. Assessment B is valid because it correlates well with Assessment C, and so on. The issue of criterion validity takes one into the realms of standards of degrees. Such issues as 'what counts as a first class honours degree' or 'what is a graduate' are at root questions of criterion validity. Clearly there are conflicts between intrinsic validity, as measured by goodness or fit of objectives and assessment, and validity as measured by comparable standards. This theme is addressed in the section below and again in Chapter 16 in the discussion of standards.

A measure of criterion validity that is sometimes used is the ability of a test to discriminate between those who have been trained and those who have not. This is a crude form of criterion validity but it is one that is at the root of the popular notion of 'value added'. When extended to education the problems of judging accurately (or measuring) criterion validity become formidable.

## Some deeper issues

There are other issues related to the validity of an assessment procedure. First, there is a distinction between the intrinsic validity of a procedure and its extrinsic validity. A set of criteria may match the objectives of a course but the course itself may not be appropriate for its broader purposes. Put another way, the assessment may be appropriate for the course but the course may not be appropriate for its task. Nor does it follow that if the criteria are explicit that they are necessarily valid. Explicitness aids validity, it does not *per se* provide validity. Second, validity is determined not by the method *per se* but by the content of the method. Face validity (surface impression) of a method is no guarantee of its efficacy. Third, high measures of validity for one purpose do not guarantee high validity for another purpose. A diagnostic examination might fulfil its purpose of improving student learning but be a poor measure of construct or predictive validity. Fourth, users of an assessment system tend to become believers in that system – particularly if they themselves are successful products of that system. As a consequence, they are more likely to question the validity of systems that are new to them than to examine critically the assumptions of the system that they are using. Clearly questions of validity are, at root, questions of value, not questions of statistical analysis. As we move towards a system of mass higher education the issues of validity will emerge more strongly.

## THE SPECIAL CASE OF COMPETENCE

Approaches to competency are based upon criterion-referenced assessment. In the more common approaches the criteria are based upon observable performance or readily inferred performance. This method fits well with the assessment of a single low-level task, although even on a single task people do not neatly separate themselves into the competent and incompetent. When one tries to measure competence on a set of low-level tasks the question of pass/fail becomes more complicated. When one tries to measure competence on high-level tasks that demand greater understanding and knowledge the question of pass/fail becomes complex. The issues then become: what are the standards, who should decide and how? Problems of reliability and validity become more salient as intellectual complexity increases and values obtrude.

Standards are, of course, a matter of judgement. In a profound sense they are arbitrary and dependent on the values of those who have the power. Judgement is necessary for establishing the criteria and for matching the evidence against the criteria. For specific tasks such as deciding who should pass or fail in a vocational course methods such as Ebel's may be used (Ebel and Frisbie, 1986). His method requires a set of judges who are expert in the subject and in what can reasonably be expected of students at different levels. The task of the judges is to classify each item in the assessment in terms of item relevance (essential, important, acceptable, questionable) and in terms of level of difficulty (easy, medium, hard). Initial estimates are made by each judge of how many items in each of the 12 categories one would expect a borderline student to get correct. Similar methods can be developed for use in most subjects but they are time-consuming.

Another approach is provided by the architect of National Vocational Qualifications: pretend the problem does not exist. Jessup (1991, p. 182) argues that the use of a competency approach disposes of the need for measures of reliability. He states that validity is measured by checking whether the assessment 'conforms to the requirements in the elements of competence and their performance criteria . . . If two assessments are both valid, *they will naturally be comparable and thus reliable* . . . I therefore suggest we drop the concept of reliability in the NVQ model of assessment' (our italics).

The issues of reliability and validity are not so easily disposed of as advocates

Once upon a time, as the crow flies, the king of Dentonia decided to have his teeth cleaned.
'It is an event that will bring attention and fame – not to mention tourists', he beamed. 'Bring the Royal Odontologist.'
'But Sire,' lamented his adviser, 'there isn't one. No-one has had oral prophylaxis for a hundred years.'
'Halitosis and Damnation' exploded the king. 'No wonder we're so shunned. Sally ye forth, therefore, and find me the best in all the lands.'
Which she did. And when at last the most famous odontologist was found, he was sent to the Royal Three Committees for the Royal Testing.
'Tell us about the history of odontology', asked the first committee.
And he did.
'Tell us about the importance of odontology,' asked the second committee.
And he did.
'Tell us what instruments you would use to perform odontological procedures', asked the third committee.
And he did.
Whereupon they draped his neck with their Medallion of Approval and led him before the king. Wasting no time, the odontologist prepared his tools and spread his cloth. But when he picked up his finest sharpest hoe with a swirling flourish, he accidentally sliced a piece off the king's tongue.
'Gadzooks!' cried the king, lispingly. 'You've cut off the royal tongue!'
'Ooops', chorused the nine voices of the Royal Three Committees.
'Oops?' spluttered the king. 'I ask for skill and you give me oops?'
'We're very sorry', apologised the Royal Three Committees. 'We must have lost our heads.'
'A capital idea', rejoiced the king, and sprang himself forth to make it permanently so.

And ever since and forever more,
There hang nine heads on the Royal Door.
For this was the fate of the Committees Three
May it never befall such as me . . . or thee.

Based on a view of assessment of Robert F. Mager.
See Robert F. Mager, *Measuring Instructional Intent or 'Got a Match'* Belmont, Calif.: Lear Siegler, Inc./Fearon Publishers, 1973, pp. v–vii.

*Figure 15.4* 'Dentonia': a case study in invalid assessment?

of NVQs may think. The competency procedures imply that performance criteria may always be specified so clearly that decisions can be dichotomous – they can or they can't do it. The net result is longer and longer lists of items to be assessed and justified. As lists increase, the reliability of individual markers decreases. MCQs become the favoured method of assessment outside of the workplace. Criterion validity is undertaken by the lead body who may not take account of local issues or differences in students. Intrinsic validity and the relationship between forms of assessment, teaching and learning are trivialised. The task of the assessor is to match the evidence collected against the pre-specified criteria. The criteria are established at sites remote from the teaching. The assessors have very little say in the development of criteria. Ownership is low and choice non-existent. All of these affect the reliability and validity of the NVQ approach.

However, competency approaches do highlight the importance of clarity and of specifying what one wants, or hopes, students will learn. The clarity is not only for the benefit of assessors but also for the benefit of students. Its weakness lies in its over-elaboration and its assumption that all knowledge and understanding can be placed within a tight hierarchy of practical skills. They do have their uses within courses where one wishes to set minimum thresholds of competence for particular tasks. The best approaches are to trial the tasks and invite a team of judges to make estimates of what is expected of students at a particular level within a course. These judgements are specific to a course, since courses differ in their emphases. For example, one would expect the performance of students on clinical tasks to be different in the third year of a traditional medical course than those in the third year of a problem-based course. Finally, it is almost always advisable for the team of judges to take the tests of competency that they are advocating. Whilst this approach does not provide criterion validity, it provides a useful corrective to unduly high expectations and workloads. Had all the lead bodies in the NVQ system adopted this approach we would probably have a better system of NVQs.

## THE ROLE OF THE EXTERNAL EXAMINER

The external examiner is essentially an instrument of reliability and validity. The two main tasks of external examiners are to protect students and to safeguard standards. Protecting students implies checking on the fairness and consistency of an assessment system through sampling and moderating. Safeguarding standards involves checking on the design of assessments, monitoring performance of students and making an estimate of comparability with other students following similar programmes. Criterion validity was regarded as the more important form of validity but the combination of mass higher education and modularity has led to greater concern with the intrinsic validity of courses or degree programmes. The demands on external examiners have consequently increased and changed and so, it is argued, the role of the external examiner should be re-evaluated (Silver and Williams, 1994).

One approach advocated is to increase the number of external examiners and partition their responsibilities into two tiers. Such a system requires careful coordination and it runs the risk of becoming heavily bureaucratic. An alternative approach is to abolish external examining. This would save money and align our system more closely with that of our American cousins. The

Answer all questions. This examination is un-timed. Consultation with others (including students) and reference to books and other sources *is recommended.*

1 What objectives do you assess?
2 Justify and criticise your choice of assessment methods. Refer to research in your answer.
3 Describe, justify and criticise your methods of grading.
4 With reference to research findings, describe, justify and criticise your marking techniques to overcome the following:

a) variations in standards on a single occasion;
b) variations in standards on different occasions;
c) variations between examiners;
d) differences in students' handwriting.

5 How do you ensure that your standards are similar to standards adopted in comparable assessments and examinations?
6 What values underlie your approach to assessment in higher education? How are they manifest in your practice?
7 Assess your answers to questions 1–6.

*Figure 15.5* A compulsory examination for all examiners

approach could be taken further. Double and second marking could be abolished and the module tutors be made solely responsible for the marks awarded. We would then have a fully fledged system that would be closely comparable to the perceived US system and which would save money, in the short term. The prospect is appealing to some senior managers but before taking that path it would be advisable to look more closely at the workings of systems in the United States (there is not, strictly speaking, a system of higher education in the United States). Reliability and validity are neglected even though they are central to the quality of student learning. Grades are more open to negotiation between students and tutors and, occasionally, corruption prevails. Other forms of assessment may have to be substituted for entry into professional courses and employment. Last but not least, there is great concern about variations in academic standards across and within American universities. It will be clear that of the two approaches we prefer the existing one. We recognise that some changes are necessary but we hold to the principle that some external measures of reliability and validity are necessary if one is committed to a fair and equitable system of assessment. The nub of the issue is how much the university system in Britain is willing to invest in the assessment of student learning. If the choice is left to universities then, as resources diminish, they will favour the approach that is cheapest for them. This issue is part of the wider debate about quality that is addressed in the final chapter.

## ACTIVITIES

15.1 Apply the following questions to a module or course:

1 Are the objectives of the course sufficiently clear to enable the assessment of the skills, knowledge and understanding that the course team value?

2 Are the assessment methods sufficiently clear for the students to know what is expected of them and usable by them when preparing their coursework or for examinations?

3 Are the criteria clear on what counts as different levels of performance within a learning task or assessment? Are the criteria known, understood and usable by students?

4 Are the methods of interpreting evidence by the tutors sufficiently clear to them?

15.2 How do you ensure that your marking of coursework and examination scripts is consistent?

15.3 How does your department or school moderate its marking of coursework and scripts? Could the system be improved without overburdening the tutors?

15.4 Is there a comparability across modules in the amount of work required? How are marks from different modules aggregated?

15.5 What are the mean scores for coursework and written papers across the modules of the course? What is the correlation between coursework and written papers? What is the correlation between part one and part two results or between level one and level three results? What implications do these results have for the assessment system?

15.6 Meet with a group of colleagues who teach modules on your course or related courses. Exchange questions used for coursework or written papers. Try to decide the rationale and objectives underlying a sample of the questions and compare your deductions with the intentions of the tutor who set the paper or assignment.

15.7 Match the objectives and coursework assignments in your module and in a friend's module. Swap opinions on the match/mismatch of objectives in assignments in the modules that you both chose.

15.8 Design three different answers to the same question. Ask colleagues to mark them independently using the existing marking procedure or one that you provide. Meet with the colleagues and discuss and compare the results.

15.9 What proportion of Firsts, 2.1s, 2.2s, 3s, Passes and Fails were awarded in each faculty in your university during the past two years? What are the usual entry requirements for the faculty? Draw up the tables of results and account for the differences across faculties.

15.10 Re-read 'Dentonia' (Figure 15.1). What implications does it have for validity and reliability of assessment of courses?

15.11 What counts as a First, a 2.1 and a 2.2 in your subject? List the criteria that you would expect a student to fulfil at each of these classifications.

15.12 The following broad principles of assessment are based on Rowntree's suggestions (Rowntree, 1987). Consider them in relation to your own courses and your own values.

1 We should aim to maximise the feedback from assessment procedures to students and where appropriate, involve the students actively in the assessment process. Where possible assessment procedures should be relevant learning experiences in themselves.

2 We should accept that in some areas, especially of attitudes and personality, different lecturers may hold different opinions about a student. They should caution us about being too dogmatic in our judgements of a student's character.

3 We should be prepared to design and adapt more imaginative assessment procedures if current or conventional measures do not relate well to the objectives of the course or scheme. We should be willing to risk using methods that provide valuable learning methods even if this reduces marginally the reliability of the approaches but we should, wherever possible, take the best examples of the students' learning as evidence.

4 We should make sure that employers and others in the community who use the assessments of our students are aware of the grounds on which these assessments are based. If possible we should ensure that our assessment results are not used inappropriately by others.

5 We should make sure that lecturers and employers have the necessary support and skills to develop appropriate assessment procedures and to interpret the results sensitively.

6 We should bear in mind that assessment is about values and that those values influence the content of what is assessed, the methods of assessment and the interpretation of the evidence provided by students.

# Chapter 16

# Quality, standards and underlying issues

This chapter examines the concern for quality, quality assessment, national standards and quality assurance that permeates higher education. It points to the links between the assessment of student learning and the assessment of educational provision. It discusses the notion of graduateness and the drive towards competence and it explores the purposes of higher education.

There are three approaches to quality that are manifest in higher education: quality assessment, the drive for national standards and quality audit. Underpinning these approaches are conflicting notions of quality. So before discussing the manifestations of the assessment of educational provision and audit it may be useful to consider what is meant by assessment and quality in the context of higher education.

## ASSESSMENT AND QUALITY ASSESSMENT

There are many similarities between the assessment of student learning and the assessment of 'quality'. Indeed Rowntree (1987, p. 1) opens his famous text on assessing student learning with the words, 'If we wish to discover the truth about an educational system, we must look into its assessment procedures. What student qualities and achievements are actively valued and rewarded by the system? How are its purposes and intentions realised?'

Both types of assessment influence the nature of learning and performance. Changing the mode of assessment changes the mode of student learning. Measuring the performance of a department on given criteria changes performance towards those criteria. If the criteria are not appropriate for the purposes of the task then one may end up fulfilling the criteria but not performing the task well. Assessment both of student learning and of educational provision is based upon the procedure of taking a sample, drawing inferences and estimating worth.

Common weaknesses are:

- the sample does not match the stated outcomes
- the sample is drawn from too narrow a domain
- the sample is too large or too small

- absence of well-defined criteria
- unduly specific criteria
- variations in the inferences drawn by different assessors of the sample
- variations in estimates of worth.

The purposes of assessment, whether of student learning or of the quality of education provided by a department, contain inherent conflicts. Assessment may be criterion-referenced or normative. The former relies on pre-determined standards that a student or a department is expected to achieve; the latter upon rank ordering according to some hidden or explicit criteria. Strictly speaking, if a department or student meets the criteria they should receive the appropriate grade. In practice, considerations of better and best affect decisions – particularly funding decisions. Assessment may be primarily formative: it may provide feedback that assists students or departments to reflect upon their goals and on ways of improving. It may be primarily summative: a series of judgements or recommendations. The distinction between formative and summative assessment is not clear-cut. Summative assessment can, if expressed appropriately, provide meaningful and useful feedback and thereby aid development. Formative feedback may involve multiple points of summative feedback. Both summative and formative assessments involve judgements and judgements are based on values – which may or may not be explicit to the assessors themselves or to the assessed. There are conflicts between the judgmental and developmental purposes of assessment. These conflicts are shot through student learning, staff appraisal, academic audit, the research selectivity exercise and quality assurance. Achieving a satisfactory balance that satisfies all those concerned is not easy.

There is, inevitably, debate about what counts as good assessment for both student learning and educational provision. Issues of fairness, reliability and validity predominate. Fairness implies equality of opportunity and treatment. Reliability implies consistency of approach and validity implies appropriateness of methods of truth-seeking. Purposes and context are central to estimates of what is good assessment. All of these are deep problems. None the less, most people agree that:

- The purposes, dimensions and criteria should be clear to the assessors and the assessed.
- They should be used consistently by the assessors.
- The sample of activities observed should be representative of all the major dimensions being assessed.
- The dimensions should be related to the purposes of the assessment.
- The inferences drawn should be consistent.
- The estimates of worth should be consistent with the inferences and the criteria.

Many of the criticisms of the quality assessment procedures of the Higher Education Funding Councils may be fitted into the model of assessment described above. Conflicts of purpose, variability across and within subject assessments, the sample of activities assessed, the methods of assessment and the grading system of worth in the English system of quality assessment have all been criticised in the Barnett Report (Barnett, 1994a). Similar criticisms have been made of many universities' procedures for assessing student learning (Atkins *et al.*, 1993).

The Barnett report advocated the use of profiles and the abolition of global categories of excellent, satisfactory and unsatisfactory. The label of satisfactory was very broad and the connotations of that label were hardly encouraging. Subsequently the words 'quality approved' were substituted for those who received a minimum score of two or more out of four on each of the six aspects of provision:

- Curriculum design, content and organisation.
- Teaching, learning and assessment.
- Student progression and achievement.
- Student support and guidance.
- Learning resources.
- Quality assurance and enhancement.

The HEFCE are coy about what they mean precisely by the term 'quality'. They indicate that 'The quality of teaching and learning in a diverse sector can only be understood in the context of an institution's own aims and objectives' (Circular 3/93, HEFCE, 1993, para. 11). The circular uses the terms 'quality of educational provision' and 'fitness for purpose'. Quality of educational provision can roughly be translated into the questions:

Is this a good learning experience for *these* students in *this* department?
Does this contribute to a good learning experience for *these* students in *this* department?

Fitness for purpose is concerned with the question:

How well does the educational experience of students match the claims of the department?

The method of quality assessment is based on evaluating the quality of the student learning experience and student achievement, measured against the aims and objectives set by the subject provider for each programme of study within the subject. Its key aspects are:

- Assessment against subject provider's aims and objectives.
- Assessment of student learning experience and student achievement.
- Assessment by peer review.
- Combination of internal and external processes – self-assessment and visit.

The HEFCE's new system is profile-based and criterion-referenced. Its circular warns against adding the scores of each aspect (HEFCE, 1994, 1996). In practice, others use and misuse the published results. The scores are added together. Over 20 is regarded as very good. It is not seen as goodness of fit between objectives and provision so much as the 'best in the country' by intending students, their parents, employers and by some academic departments. Comparisons across subjects and universities are made even though the purposes and contexts are supposed to be different. For example, in the first round of quality assessments, history departments received more 'excellents' than either chemistry or mechanical engineering. This finding was misinterpreted as meaning that history is taught better than chemistry or engineering. The variation across these subjects was not read as revealing goodness of fit of purpose and method so much as showing that teaching in history is better than in chemistry and mechanical engineering. Most of the higher grades go to departments in older universities. This is taken to mean that departments in older universities teach better than departments in newer universities. It might indicate that those departments with better qualified students on entry, better staff–student ratios and more library resources provide a better education. Certainly the statistical analyses of the league tables of universities published by *The Times* indicate that one can predict with almost complete accuracy the position in the league table from a regression analysis based on entry grades, research performance, student accommodation and number of postgraduates (Yorke, 1996). The recent claim by a government minister (*THES*, March 1996) that there is no evidence that existing levels of resources are affecting quality is based, spuriously, on the results of HEFCE assessments. No department or school has yet received a '1' for resources; therefore, it is claimed, resources are not an issue. But the aspect of resources in the HEFCE exercise is not concerned with the *level* of resource but with whether the resource matches the objectives of the programme. There is a further problem of conflict of loyalty facing peer assessors. Do they penalise a department with poor resources but which is struggling to provide a good education for its students? If they do, there is no guarantee that resources will be improved. On the contrary, the department might be closed. If they do not, then others will argue that resources are sufficient.

Such interpretations are not without controversy. They highlight how the results of an assessment intended, ostensibly, to be sensitive to diversity of mission and intake can be converted into a league table of national standards. The purpose, content and methods of a system of assessment always require regular scrutiny.

## QUALITY AND STANDARDS

In higher education quality is based usually on the notion of 'fitness for purpose' whereas standards are concerned with 'fitness of award'. There is an inherent conflict between concern for quality, as measured by fitness for purpose, and national standards. Fitness for purpose examines the links between particular students' experience and specific programme objectives. National standards implies that judgements are made against general criteria that are relatively independent of particular programmes and students. The conflict is deep. It is related to the issue of relatives and absolutes and so to the Platonic and Aristotelian notions of the 'good'. There are of course similarities as well as differences between Platonic and Aristotelian approaches but they are a convenient way of highlighting the conflicts in the assessment of quality and standards. For Plato there were ideal standards to which all human beings should aspire. National standards of degrees and rank ordering of departments and universities emanate from this concept. In a Platonic model of assessment, measures are matched to 'ideal' standards that are independent of context, resources, the nature of the subject or the abilities of the students. The present concern with 'graduateness' is an example of a Platonic approach. For Aristotle, the term 'good' raises the question 'good for what and for whom?' Aristotelian approaches begin with reflections upon experience. These may lead to differing notions of 'good' according to purposes, context and the shifting boundaries of experience. The approach of the HEFCE is Aristotelian, with a touch of Platonism. 'The quality of teaching and learning in a diverse sector can only be understood in the context of an institution's own aims and objectives' (Circular 3/93, para. 11, HEFCE, 1993). Platonic approaches begin with principles that are pre-determined by the 'guardians' of society. In managerial language, these may be expressed as performance indicators. They are potent: modes of measurement do change phenomena. But they may not produce the desired changes so much as align changes in performance to the indicators. There is the further difficulty that some aspects of quality or change are not easily captured in numbers. As Aristotle observed, 'the mark of the educated man (person) is that he brings to each subject only that measure of precision that is proper to the subject' (Aristotle, *Nicomachean Ethics*).

'Fitness for purpose' is concerned with matching students' experience against the objectives of a degree programme. Expressed in this way, one can see problems in the approach. In particular:

What are appropriate measures of students' experience?
How does one judge the appropriateness of the objectives of a degree programme?
Do free-choice modular systems preclude programme objectives and therefore measures of fitness for purpose?
If quality is wholly intrinsic, can one apply external standards?
Can this model of quality be used to compare students' experience across degree programmes?
Can this model be used to compare performance across degree programmes?

The Higher Education Funding Councils are concerned primarily with fitness for purpose and, with varying degrees of sophistication, the first four of the above problems. The Higher Education Quality Council, in its Graduate Studies Programme, is primarily concerned with academic standards which it defines as 'explicit levels of academic attainment that are used to measure academic requirements and achievements of individual students and groups of students' (HEQC, 1995, p. 2). The Graduate Studies Programme is particularly concerned with comparability. To this end, it has commissioned a survey of the proportions of honours degrees awarded and initiated the exploration of 'graduateness'. Evidence collected by Macfarlane (1992) and subsequently by Chapman (1996) indicate that about 20 years ago just over one third of all degrees awarded were firsts or upper seconds. By 1990 more than half of degree awards were firsts or upper seconds and by 1993, in the eight most popular subjects, just under 60 per cent of the degrees awarded were firsts or upper seconds. The modal class is now the upper second whereas previously it was the lower second. During roughly the same period higher education has expanded from 6 per cent of an age cohort to about 28 per cent. Resources per student have declined by 63 per cent since 1973. Not surprisingly, the increase in the number of good honours degrees awarded gives rise to the question whether standards are declining. The question is complicated by changes in A level syllabuses, changes in subjects, the shifting purposes of higher education and the definitions of 'standards' and 'decline' that are used. It could be argued that if standards have not changed in the past 20 years then there have been remarkable changes in the gene pool of the present generation of students or a dramatic shift in methods of teaching and learning. On the other hand, it could be argued that standards have not declined so much as changed towards greater emphasis on preparation for employment.

Concern for standards is not limited to the increase in the number of good honours degrees awarded. There are also variations in proportions of good honours degrees awarded in different subjects and different universities. Such differences have been remarked upon for over 30 years (Robbins, 1963). Broadly speaking, more good honours degrees are awarded in the sciences than in the arts. These results appear to be weakly related to entry qualifications and they are attributable to the range of marks customarily used in different subject areas (see Chapter 15). Overall there appear to be no major differences between newer and older universities but there are variations between universities. These findings lead to the issue of what counts as a degree and to the possible solution of 'graduateness'.

## Graduateness

The Graduate Studies Programme aims to identify what attributes are expected of graduates across all degree programmes and how these might be defined and assessed. The programme, to some extent, builds on the work of Otter (1992) on outcomes in design, environmental science, social science, engineering and English. The report (HEQC, 1995) suggests that an award of a degree signifies three kinds of achievement: field or subject specific, shared characteristics with cognate subjects, generic characteristics. These may be linked to the generalisations that:

- each subject has unique characteristics
- some subjects have some common characteristics
- all subjects share some characteristics.

The Graduate Studies Project focuses on the last two categories although the boundaries between the categories are far from clear.

The initial survey of views of graduateness by Atkins (1996) indicates that 'the concept of a minimum threshold standard has little meaning except on vocational courses' and 'Far from regarding a pass as a threshold standard, students and staff regard a second class degree as the real minimum required – even a third is seen as a failure' (Atkins, 1996, p. 25). The majority of respondents thought it would not be feasible to define precise threshold standards at the broad subject level. Four main reasons were given: lack of consensus on what constitutes the academic core or subject specific skills, the diversity of students, the prohibitive costs of defining, monitoring and reviewing and the limited usefulness of such definitions for employers or graduates. Modularity was seen as the biggest obstacle to defining standards. None the less, defining standards for single honours programmes was thought to be easier than designing standards for multi-subject programmes. Defining standards within a subject which has a core curriculum in every university might, it was thought, prove feasible. Despite these reservations, several respondents thought that threshold standards might be developed for general academic or employer-related skills. Whether such an initiative should be university-based or subject-based at the national level is open to debate.

Already some universities have begun to consider seriously the notion of graduateness. The task, at the university level, is challenging but not impossible providing one uses a broad-brush approach based upon aims and objectives of degree programmes. The suggestions given in Chapter 3 (see Figure 3.10) together with Appendix One of Atkins *et al.* (1993) provide a useful point of departure. The task of standardising degrees across subjects and universities will prove more challenging and, probably, not worthwhile.

The issue of graduateness leads naturally to considerations of levels within a degree and the relationship between Bachelor and Masters' degrees. The problems here are no less difficult than those of graduateness. Shaw (1995) offers a broad set of categories for performance in each level (year) of a degree. Beyond such a broad approach lurk some epistemological issues. The notion of levels of degrees assumes a strong hierarchy of knowledge which *may* fit physical sciences and mathematics but sits less comfortably in the framework of arts and social sciences where knowledge is more concatenated than hierarchical. Vectors, vector analysis and vector mechanics form a logical progression but, in English Literature, the sequence of topics is determined more by the particular purposes of the programme. The same questions could be asked in each year of a course but the responses of each year group, one hopes, would be different. None the less there would be overlap of responses between years. It would be extremely difficult to articulate precise, meaningful threshold standards across a range of levels and programmes. The net result might be a set of measurable but trivial indicators. Not all experience of assessing student learning can be articulated and communicated in the form of levels.

A further complication emerges when one considers the different types of postgraduate degrees. Some MSc courses in engineering overlap with the content and assessment of final-year BEng courses. Other conversion Masters' courses may contain material from early parts of an undergraduate course and some MA courses may study the 'same' materials that are tackled in undergraduate courses but at a greater depth. Again, articulating these differences might prove difficult and perhaps unnecessary. Time devoted to articulating and checking the *precise* differences between levels of different degree programmes might be better spent on teaching and research.

## National standards and competence

An alternative approach to national standards is provided by the competency framework of NVQs (National Vocational Qualifications) and similar approaches such as that of BTEC (Business and Technical Council) and SCOTVEC (Scottish Vocational Education Council). There is much to be said in favour of competency. Indeed, the development of intellectual competence could be regarded as one of the main purposes of higher education. There is less to be said in favour of the existing framework of NVQs which are based on an unduly narrow definition of competency as observable performance (see Chapter 15: 'The special case of competency').

NVQs grew out of a concern for occupational standards. They were intended to replace apprenticeship schemes but as the NVQ Council has grown so too has its ambitions. It has been supported strongly by the government's drive to have a better-qualified workforce. But better qualified is not necessarily better able. It is assumed that certificating people for the work that they do, or might do, will improve their performance. Competence in the NVQ model is defined as 'the ability to perform to recognised standards' (Jessup, 1991, p. 40). It is criterion-based rather than normative. NVQs are based primarily upon performance, or potential performance, in the workplace. Other measures are acceptable but only for reasons of cost and expediency. Knowledge and understanding are seen as merely supplementary to observable practice. Progression from lower to higher levels is 'measured' in terms not of understanding but of situational complexity. Each NVQ is structured in terms of levels, units, elements, and specified performance criteria. Methods of teaching and learning and their links with assessment are not considered.

All of the above features present obstacles for using the existing NVQ framework for all degrees. Either the NVQ framework will have to change or the higher education system move towards the culture of further education. Assessment based only on criterion referencing does not fit honours degrees yet class of degree is an important criterion of selection for employment and research. We need to know who is best as well as who is competent. Several academic subjects do not have a specific vocational bias. Graduates from most disciplines take posts in a wide range of industries and commerce where general ability and understanding are required rather than specific vocational performance.

The relationship between skills, knowledge and understanding is more complex than the simplistic notion built into NVQs (see Chapter 3; Atkins *et al.*, 1993 and Barnett, 1994b). Progression and levels of degrees are linked to depth of understanding, not situational complexity. Levels 4 and beyond do not match the content and purposes of many undergraduate and postgraduate programmes. Last but not least, there is more to higher education than preparing students for their first posts in industry and commerce (see the later section of this chapter on the purposes of higher education for further discussion of these issues).

As well as the conceptual difficulties of integrating NVQs with all degrees of all universities, there are more practical difficulties. Not least is the cumbersome, expensive bureaucratic procedure that underpins NVQs and the heavy burden of assessment imposed upon students and staff (Mitchell and Cuthbert, 1989). There is, despite the considerable investment in NVQs (or perhaps because of it), very little published independent research on the efficacy of NVQs. Methods of assessment in the workplace are subject to wide variability and the written papers are heavily biased towards recall and rote learning of key 'facts'. Informal reports suggest there are variations in standards at levels 1, 2 and 3. NVQs obtained in larger enterprises tend to be more rigorous than those of some small employers. There appear to be variations between, as well as within, occupational standards. If there are such differences at the lower levels, which are relatively easy to assess, then there are likely to be even greater differences at higher levels. The use of the existing NVQ framework to standardise degrees would be a costly failure.

Despite the weaknesses of the NVQ framework, there are aspects of competency-based approaches that are worth using on some courses for some purposes. Courses that are vocational in orientation or require reflection upon professional experience are obvious examples. Competency-based approaches can be used for some of the assessments in laboratory work, some aspects of IT, library searches, oral presentations and poster sessions. But one should avoid undue specificity and guard against converting a useful method for some purposes into an inappropriate national system for all purposes.

## Motives and standards

Before leaving the issues of standards it is worth considering the motivation for considering standards of degrees. Leaving aside the survival needs of national standard bearers, there are three strands of this motivation. One is that employers claim they need to know what they are getting. But a minimum threshold that encompasses University College, Stockton and University College, Oxford is hardly helpful. In practice, major employers opt for graduates from prestigious universities. The rhetoric of employers and their practice do not always match. The second strand is the government's expressed concern for obtaining value for money. The phrase has electoral appeal but its meaning, in the context of higher education, has not been addressed cogently. Beneath the phrase lie the implicit motives of control and cost-cutting. The third and most important strand is related to the university as a learning organisation. We need to reflect upon what counts as degrees in our academic subjects as knowledge-bases, ideologies and social structures change. The reasons are both intellectual and moral: they are part of the development of our subjects and our students. But we should recognise that glib general formulae will never capture the essence of degrees in different subjects.

## QUALITY ASSURANCE

Quality assurance is a misnomer. Quality is not assured by quality assurance procedures; consistency may be. The underlying approach is often described as quality audit. Its primary focus is upon mechanisms and procedures. Power (1994) suggests that audit is the most powerful form of control in education and health care. He argues that the remoteness of external audit is in conflict with participation and ownership. As such, it is likely to produce conformity to the indicators used by auditors rather than internalised commitment. He favours a more local approach that is facilitatory and developmental. Such an approach implies high trust between government and universities.

In Britain, the body responsible, at present, for quality assurance in higher education is the Higher Education Quality Council through its Quality Audit Group. It has no legal authority but its reports on the quality-assurance procedures in individual universities are influential. Its methods are documentary analysis supported by group interviews with staff and students. The remit of the Quality Audit Group is to explore the mechanisms of quality assurance within universities. In the words of its director:

> It describes, analyses and makes judgements on the effectiveness of quality assurance mechanisms and structures in respect of six main areas: design and review of courses; teaching, learning and the student experience; academic staff; student assessment and degree classification; promotion material and feedback and verification systems . . . Reports have both formative and judgmental elements but do not offer categorical judgements of the 'satisfactory/unsatisfactory' type.
>
> (HEQC, 1994, p. vii)

The report provides an analysis of the term 'quality assurance system' and an analysis based on the audit reports to 69 universities. It suggests that a system of quality assurance could be defined as something which:

- is clear in its specifications of roles, responsibilities and procedures
- enables institutional aims and objectives to be achieved

- informs decision-making
- is free from individual personal bias
- is repeatable over time
- involves all staff
- includes the specification of standards and acceptable evidence
- prompts continuous improvement.

The analysis of the reports provides a summary of areas for further consideration. Some of the findings are shown in Figure 16.1.

There is no doubt that the Quality Audit Group and its forebears have had a considerable impact upon quality assurance in universities. Procedures, mechanisms and lines of responsibility are clearer, particularly in older universities. However, the costs are not inconsiderable. First, the preparation for an audit probably exceeds 2,000 person-hours. Second, fulfilling internal quality demands now probably takes almost as much time as teaching students. Third, the system has induced an obsession with recording and maintaining records of trivial events. Fourth, smaller departments and colleges are 'persuaded' to adopt procedures that are expensive and probably less appropriate than informal approaches so as to meet the perceived demands of quality assurance. Last but not least, quality-assurance procedures are changing the role of a lecturer from a relatively independent professional to a managed team-member. The last point may appear to be a gain but, in the long run, may prove costly for the development of knowledge.

These changes are, of course, not solely due to audit. The quality-assessment procedures of the Higher Education Funding Councils and accreditation procedures of national bodies are also time-consuming. The conjoining of quality audit and quality assessment might shift the balance towards a less intensive system – but we are not optimistic.

## THE PURPOSES OF HIGHER EDUCATION?

Skills, knowledge and understanding are central to the debate about the purposes of higher education. Those concerned with vocationalism are likely to stress the importance of skills and their transferability and those concerned with truth-seeking are likely to stress the importance of understanding. Vocationalist perspectives neglect the fact that knowledge and understanding of different concepts and contexts are the pre-requisites of transfer. Those concerned with knowledge-seeking and understanding neglect the fact that the development of skills is necessary for improving the acquisition and management of knowledge and for deepening understanding. Concern with the development of higher-order skills is not only useful to students but also for the development of academic subjects.

The wider debate concerning the purposes of higher education is at least as old as Hippocrates. The question then posed was: is the learning of medicine an

'The extent to which teaching and learning is evaluated, both across and within institutions, remains variable and is sometimes absent.' (p. xv)

'There are serious concerns about the adequacy of provision of library services, due in the main to the great increase in student numbers.' (p. xix)

'In some cases the library is not involved in programme approval and review. This is one aspect of a wider problem; a lack of co-ordination between academic and resource issues was noted in some universities.' (p. xix)

'The training of lecturers to be effective teachers tends to be short, voluntary and concentrated at the start of a career, and is generally focused on full-time staff.' (p. xxi)

'Staff development activities are often not adequately monitored or reviewed to assess their effectiveness.' (p. xxi)

'Most universities have introduced staff appraisal schemes, yet these often require greater monitoring and oversight to assess their use and value and to determine staff development needs.' (p. xxi)

'There is concern that students (within and across universities) may not be receiving fair and equal treatment in terms of the marking scales used to assess performance, the criteria used, or the methods used to record achievement (e.g. degree classification).' (p. xxii)

'The methods used to monitor the effectiveness of assessment practices are, mostly, rudimentary.' (p. xxii)

'The duties of external examiners and their impact upon the operation of programmes within universities often vary considerably.' (p. xxii)

'There is variation in the distribution of external examiner reports, and in the mechanism for ensuring that appropriate and timely action is taken on the results.' (p. xxiii)

From HEQC (1994)

*Figure 16.1* Observations on quality-assurance systems in universities

education or a training? The debate has see-sawed between vocationalism and liberalism since then, but it is a false antithesis. There is a continuum of views from specific vocationalism through what might be called liberal vocationalism, to vocational liberalism to liberalism and beyond. As a rule of thumb, prestigious departments and universities are more likely to be liberal than vocational and less prestigious universities to be vocational rather than liberal – although it is likely that there is a whole spectrum of views from extreme vocationalism to post-modernism within a university.

These parts of the continuum provide different purposes for higher education. In their cogent and scholarly analysis of the assessment of student learning in higher education, Atkins *et al.* (1993) distinguish and discuss the evidence and assumptions underlying four broad overlapping purposes:

- specific vocational preparation
- preparation for general employment
- preparation for knowledge creation
- general educational experience.

They point to significant gaps in our knowledge of whether higher education is achieving its present purposes, to the shift towards specific or general employment-related outcomes in many courses and universities and to changes in the student population.

The purposes of higher education can not easily be separated from the people involved or from their other intentions and motives. As well as purposes, one needs to consider *whose* purposes. In times of unemployment, it is hardly surprising that students are likely to be more concerned with the relevance of their education to job-seeking. Only about half of the present graduates entered permanent employment within six months of completing their degree. 40 per cent of jobs advertised do not specify a subject. Major employers receive on average 90 applications per vacancy (AGR, 1994). Employers concerned for the future of their companies may look towards higher education for some solutions to their problems. But their claims to be concerned to recruit undergraduates with the requisite skills seem to be mingled with a concern to recruit from the most prestigious universities. A government eager to appear to be solving unemployment problems may prefer to keep a substantial group of young people out of its unemployment statistics. On the one hand it claims that it wishes to expand the system from an elitist system to a mass higher education system yet, on the other hand, it reduces student grants and thereby excludes potentially able students from the less prosperous sectors of society. A mass higher education system of 40 per cent of young people has been advocated recently by the Confederation of British Industries to increase brainpower, creativity and motivation (CBI, 1994). Given that organisation's commitment to no minimum wage for employees, to no maximum salary for directors and to dismantling the existing support structures for the unemployed one wonders whether expressed purposes belie some hidden intentions. It would seem that the conflict of vocationalism and liberalism together with expressed values and implicit values applies as much to employers and government as to academics.

Although instrumental purposes of higher education are in the ascendancy, it is worth repeating some cautionary notes. Narrow vocationalism is a naive goal for courses when so many graduates enter a diversity of occupations and may change careers. Even if they do not change jobs, their jobs may change. A sound basis of the skills involved in knowledge acquisition and understanding may serve them better than attempts to make an academic subject more vocational.

This is not to deny the value of some vocational influences. There is a role for transferable skills in all courses. Work-based learning can provide opportunities to develop and apply skills in different contexts that can enrich students' understanding of some subjects as well as of workplaces. Employers and past students can provide useful suggestions on course development.

The debate about the purposes of higher education impinges upon the purposes of teaching and assessment in universities. Whilst it would be rash to lay down a programme of purposes and methods for all departments to follow, the broad questions introduced in Chapter 14 should be considered by any department interested in the quality of its students' learning:

- What kinds of things do we want our students to learn?
- What opportunities are provided?
- What assessment tasks are set?
- What methods of assessment are used?
- Are they worthwhile?
- How much time is spent by students on assessment tasks?
- How much time is spent on setting, marking and managing assessment?

The answers to these questions are interlinked. They provide a sound basis for self-assessment and reflection. And just as reflection upon learning aids a student to deepen his or her approach to learning so too can reflection by departments lead to deeper approaches to teaching and assessing students.

## QUO VADIMUS?

This chapter has outlined the assessment of educational provision, the issues surrounding quality and standards, quality-assurance procedures and the purposes of higher education. It has pointed to the inherent conflicts between assessment for judgmental purposes and for developmental purposes and it has shown how the Platonic and Aristotelian notions of the 'good' permeate the debate on quality assessment. The weaknesses of the present quality-assessment system are more related to issues of reliability than validity. The funding councils have demonstrated their willingness to respond to criticisms and one suspects that they may have had vigorous debates behind closed doors with ministers and senior civil servants who were more concerned with the system's capacity for summary judgements and control than with the quality of the assessment process or of the educational provision itself.

So what does the future hold? Historians and, latterly, chaos theorists, warn of the dangers of predictions in complex systems. The task is approached cautiously.

The shift from an elitist to a mass higher education together with a marketing philosophy has brought in its wake a diminution of the collegial model of governance and an increase in managerialism. The boundaries between FE and HE will be blurred and perhaps the two sectors will be merged. A three-tier system of universities will emerge and perhaps be formalised. There will be pressure to abolish the existing honours degrees but this will be resisted, except perhaps in the lowest tier, which will be most vulnerable to this pressure. The purposes of higher education, as defined by government, will shift towards vocationalism. On the wider front, quality assurance will probably be an issue and a feature of higher education in all industrialised nations well into the next century.

In the immediate future in Britain, quality assurance and quality audit will be conjoined, ostensibly for efficiency gains. Whether the emphasis will be weighted more towards development and fitness for purpose or more towards summary judgement, national standards and payment by results depends upon wider political movements. Whether assessors of quality remain temporary, part-time contract staff or become a cadre of trained, full-time specialists who are able to offer professional expertise and judgement is again dependent upon wider issues. A commitment to the quality of the assessment process itself implies a commitment to fairness, and to improving the validity and the reliability of the system. These commitments raise issues of values in a democratic society and have implications for costs and for professional approaches to the provision of undergraduate education. Whether Britain remains as democratic as it has been since 1945 is open to question. Changes in the core values of the powerful will, as ever, be reflected in the myriad of systems of control and assessment that permeate our society, its culture and its educational provision.

# Appendix
## Examples of examination questions in arts, law and social sciences

We provide here a sample of questions drawn from arts, law and social sciences. The sample is not intended to be representative of each subject domain, but it does provide an indication of the range of topics and themes that are addressed. Nor is the sample intended as examples of 'good' questions so much as a range of questions which have been asked of students. Whether a question is good is determined, in large measure, by its intention as perceived by students and its relationship to the objectives of the course. The examples of questions may be of interest to lecturers in all academic fields. They show how similar structures of questions may be used for different purposes. You should bear in mind that the same question may have a different meaning in different subjects (see Chapter 4). Indeed, each subject has its own sub-culture and shared meanings.

The same and similar samples have been used by one of the authors (George Brown) in workshops and seminars on assessment. Participants' reactions to the range of questions have been intriguing. Some have been amazed at the intellectual challenge and diversity of the questions posed in other subject areas, some have been dismissive of other people's specialities and some apprehensive about the public exploration of values, particularly when the questions had a contemporary ring. Yet it may be argued that one of the purposes of higher education is to develop an understanding of past events, achievements and perspectives, and their relationships to contemporary problems and issues. There is also the deeper problem of freedom to choose what is taught and assessed – and how it is taught and assessed.

You might like to: (a) read the range of questions within each subject area which follows, (b) make your own notes on the purposes, structure and style of the questions, (c) note any improvements/amendments you might make to them for your own use and (d) use them and your notes as a basis for discussions with colleagues. As you read the questions you might wish to consider how the structures might be adapted for use in your subject. If you read actively then you will find yourself considering what each question means to you – but do not be deceived by the apparent simplicity of some of the questions. After all, even a fool can ask questions that wise people cannot answer to their own satisfaction.

## ARCHAEOLOGY, CLASSICS AND ANTHROPOLOGY

1 Discuss the deployment and interconnections of the themes of amor, militia and rus in Tibullus's *Elegies*, Book 1.
2 What kinds of information can be extracted from the study of human remains?
3 'Rivers do not make good frontiers' (J. J. Wilkes). Discuss with reference to the Danubian provinces of the Roman Empire.
4 Write short notes on three of the following:
   (a) South Mimms Castle
   (b) The sheel keep
   (c) The gatehouses at Exeter and Newark
   (d) The design of Flint Castle
   (e) Chateau Gaillard
5 Why do virgins give birth?
6 How can the computer assist in determining the authorship of natural language documents?
7 Comment on one of the following two passages:

(a) 'I honestly want to die!' As she left me, she wept profusely and said this too to me: 'Ah, how unfairly we are treated! I swear, Sappho, I leave you against my will.' I answered her in these words: 'Go, and good fortune attend you, and remember me; you know how we cherished you; if you do not, then I will now remind you . . .'

(Sappho fr. 94.1–10 L–P)

(b) 'We educated the men both physically and intellectually; we shall have to do the same for the women, and train them for war as well, and treat them in the same way.' 'It seems to follow from what you said', he agreed.
   'I dare say', I rejoined, 'that their novelty would make many of our proposals seem ridiculous if they were put into practice.'
   'There's no doubt about that', he said.

(Plato, *Republic* 5.452)

*Note*: the above question is an extract from a paper, 'Women in Antiquity', which required candidates to comment on three out of nine passages.

## ARCHITECTURE

1 In the UK, over the past 8 years, there has been a tendency for new buildings that would formerly have been fully air-conditioned to now be naturally ventilated or at most, partially mechanically ventilated. Concurrently, some new air-conditioned buildings have adopted extensive energy conserving/efficiency strategies in the form of heat recovery to achieve the same aim, viz., reduced purchased energy input. As a designer you may have to adopt one of these two trends. Argue a case for the co-existence of the two situations.

2 It is proposed to construct a hospital which will span a city inner ring road. How does one determine whether or not to mount the hospital on anti-vibration mountings? In choosing anti-vibration mountings one parameter is r, the ratio of actual resistance:critical resistance. How do variations in r affect the performance of the mounting?

3 The following terms have been used by architectural historians and theorists to describe particular developments in architectural form:
(a) Brutalism
(b) High Tech
(c) Neo-vernacular
(d) Historicism
(e) Post-modernism
Discuss these styles, the reasons for their emergence and your opinion of their true place in the long-term development of British architecture.

4 Lofty is employed by Bright Eyes Ltd to build an extension to Bright Eyes' factory at a cost of £40,000. The completion date of 1 October 1985 is made a term of the contract. The plans for the extension have been drawn up by Pingo, an architect. Bright Eyes Ltd makes luminous belts to be worn at night by cyclists and pedestrians. Bright Eyes Ltd is hoping to double its weekly production between the beginning and end of October 1985. Lofty employs Ace Cee to do the necessary electrical work for the extension but Ace Cee does such a poor job that Lofty is forced to employ a second electrical contractor, Dee Cee, to do the whole of the work again. As a result the completion is delayed by one month. Bright Eyes Ltd is concerned about the loss of antici-pated additional revenue during the month of October. On 1 November 1985 the extension is complete but one of Bright Eyes Ltd's employees is injured because of defective electrical wiring.
Discuss.

## ECONOMICS

1 What would be the effects in the UK of a fall in the value of sterling on:
(a) investment
(b) the rate of interest
(c) real income
(d) prices?
For the purposes of your answer you may assume that three million are unemployed.

2 The concept of 'value added' is central to understanding both how gross national product is measured and why agriculture's share of GNP declines with economic development.
Explain and amplify.

3 'Competition policy is irrelevant. In the first place monopolies aren't neces-sarily undesirable. Second, firms will always find ways of colluding whatever policies are imposed.' Discuss.

4 Why has inflation been so persistent since 1945?
5 A Chancellor of the Exchequer, new to his job, asks you for advice as follows: 'We have inflation and we want to control it. We intend to use monetary measures. But what monetary variables should we set out to control? How will we check on the results of what we are doing? And how does monetary control work anyway?'
Write him two different memos in reply, pretending in turn that you are:
(a) an extreme monetarist and
(b) an extreme post-Keynesian.
6 It is sometimes said that, 'from two economists, you will get at least three opinions'. Should not the econometricians have been able to ensure that all economists would be of the same opinion? Discuss with reference to the nature of economic data and your knowledge of econometric theory.

## ENGLISH

1 What are the grounds for distinguishing between an Occult and a Scientific mentality in the Renaissance?
2 'Larkin's Poetry involves the portrayal of contemporary life with a concern for traditional values.' Discuss.
3 Say what is meant by norm, foregrounding and deviation in stylistics and discuss the uses and limitations of these concepts in stylistics.
4 Write an essay on the importance of one of the following themes in Romantic writing: love; torture and pain; isolation; mountains; grief.
5 Write the opening paragraph of a new book for children. Specify the age range for which you intend it. Add a commentary on the linguistic difficulty of the text you have produced.
6 If you were given the task of revising the spelling system of the English language, what changes would you make and why?
7 Offer a critical reading of the following passage, assessing the effectiveness, the intention and the motivation apparent within its persuasiveness. Pay due attention to the operation of rhetorical 'proofs', and to the structural and figural aspects of the passage.

As war is the last of the remedies, cuncta prius tentanda, all lawful expedients must be used to avoid it. As war is the extremity of evil, it is surely the duty of those whose station intrusts them with the care of nations, to avert it from their charge. There are diseases of animal nature which nothing but amputation can remove; so there may, by the depravation of human passions, be sometimes a gangrene in collective life for which fire and the sword are the necessary remedies; but in what can skill or caution be better shewn than preventing such dreadful operations, while there is yet room for gentler methods?

It is wonderful with what coolness and indifference the greater part of mankind see war commenced. Those that hear of it at a distance, or read of it in books, but have never presented its evils to their minds, consider it as little more than a splendid game; a proclamation, an army, a battle, and a triumph. Some indeed must perish in the most successful field, but they die upon the bed of honour, 'resign their lives amidst the joys of conquest, and filled with England's glory, smile in death'.

The life of a modern soldier is ill represented by heroick fiction. War has means of destruction more formidable than the cannon and the sword. Of the thousands and tens of thousands that perished in our late contests with France and Spain, a very small part ever felt the stroke of an enemy; the rest languished in tents and ships, amidst damps and putrefaction; pale, torpid, spiritless, and helpless; gasping and groaning unpitied among men made obdurate by long continuance of hopeless misery, and whelmed in pits, or heaved into the ocean, without notice and without remembrance. By incommodious encampments and unwholesome stations, where courage is useless, and enterprise impracticable, fleets are silently dispeopled, and armies slugglishly melted away . . .

(From 'Thoughts on the late transactions respecting Falkland's Islands',
Samuel Johnson, 1777)

## FRENCH, SPANISH, GERMAN AND SLAVIC LITERATURE

1  How do we know that French is a romance language?
2  In what sense is *Le Mariage de Figaro* a revolutionary play?
3  A bas le patrotisme!
4  Discuss the various portrayals of Christ on the west front of Chartres Cathedral.
5  What have been the main implications of Spain's transition to democracy?
6  'The fictional world of J. L. Borges is a structuralist's paradise.' Discuss.
7  Discuss the problems posed to interpretation by Bunuel's first two films.
8  Is Nietzsche's concept of Übermensch sexist?
9  Discuss the importance of the concepts of original sin and unwitting sin for an assessment of Gregorious guilt.
10 For copyright reasons the title of Christoph Hein's *Der Fremde Freund* had to be changed to *Drachenblut* for the West German edition. Discuss the respective merits of the two titles.
11 Categorise and discuss the many forms of cruelty which appear in Kis's work, *Grobnica za Borisa Davidovica*.
12 Assess the cultural significance of the work of Ljudevit Gaj for the Croats.

## GEOGRAPHY

1  'Maps are more than merely mirrors of a society; they can also contribute to the shaping of society's behaviour or beliefs.'
Discuss with reference to specific maps or map genres.

2 Does man's impact on the hydrological cycle matter? Support your answer with appropriate examples.

3 Discuss the contention that the Inverse Case Law best explains the persistence of several profound disparities within the USA and UK.

4 'Change and decay in all around I see.'
How far is this quotation a fair assessment of current changes in the British rural landscape and what might be done to improve matters?

5 You are asked to design a programme of geomorphological work in association with a road building project in the Himalayas. Describe what you would include and why.

6 'Working with maps can seriously damage a behavioural geographer's imagination.' Do you agree?

7 Compare the facilities in an academic automated cartography research environment with those necessary in a commercial concern.

8 'Offices will soon cease to be a major feature of our city centres.' Discuss.

## HISTORY

1 'Both the First and the Second World Wars were caused by Germany's desire to break the encircling ring of potential enemies.'
Discuss.

2 Why was the Methodist movement so successful?

3 'Wishful thinking supported by conceptually deficient data.'
How far does this statement reflect the Bolshevik policy towards class differences in the Russian countryside during the 1920s?

4 What part did the friars play in the early history of the University of Oxford?

5 Did the Labour Government, during the period 1945–1951, make Britain a better place to live in, in terms of comfort and enjoyment of life?

6 'Major ambitions pursued with only limited success.'
Discuss this judgement of Colbert as a Finance Minister.

7 What accounts for the location and development of the textile manufacturers in the East Midlands?

8 Would you agree that the prevalence of muddle in human affairs makes conspiracy-theories untenable?

9 'The fever chart of a sick society.'
Is this a fair description of either the 1930s musical or that of the 1950s?

10 Does the history of France show that liberty and democracy were irreconcilable in the 1930s?

## LAW

1 Write a memorandum to the Lord Chancellor indicating the criteria you consider to be important in deciding which legal problems should receive

help from public funds. Compare your criteria with the present provision of civil legal aid and advice.

2 Either (a) 'The rules of civil procedure are not designed to encourage settlements. Settlements result from manipulation of the rules by cunning litigants.' Discuss.

Or (b) 'We should take small claims out of our elaborate court system altogether.' Discuss.

4 'In 1960 Rosso and Carmen, domiciled in and nationals of Italy, were married in Rome, the marriage being by Italian law indissoluble in any circumstances. In 1983 Rosso met Sophia, a Mexican tourist on holiday in Italy, and they decided to marry when Rosso was free to do so. A few months later Rosso obtained a divorce by proxy in Mexico. Neither he himself nor Carmen set foot in Mexico.

In 1984 Rosso was transferred by his employers from Rome to Caracas, Venezuela, where he acquired a domicile of choice. Earlier this year Rosso flew to Ireland on holiday to meet Sophia who was completing an educational course at Trinity College, Dublin. Three weeks later they married each other in Dublin with the intention of settling in England when Sophia had successfully completed her studies. Rosso returned to his job in Venezuela and obtained a transfer to London. Subsequently Rosso and Sophia cohabited intermittently in London.'

Assuming that by Italian and Irish law the Mexican decree of divorce would not be recognised, but the Venezuelan law would recognise the decree, advise Rosso who now wishes to petition for nullity of the Irish marriage on the ground that he had still been married to Carmen at the time of the ceremony.

## PHILOSOPHY

1 What has freedom to do with reason?
2 Do pink elephants confirm that 'All ravens are black'?
3 'Hegel was a flat-headed, insipid, nauseating, illiterate charlatan' (Schopenhauer). 'Hegel . . . that mighty thinker' (Marx).
On the whole, with whom do you agree?
4 Suppose that each of the following is false:
Karpov will win if and only if he has been training hard.
Short will win if Karpov has not been training hard.
What are the truth-values of the following propositions? Justify your answers.
(i) Karpov will win.
(ii) Short will win.
(iii) Karpov has been training hard.
(iv) Karpov has been training hard. If he doesn't win, then neither will Short.
5 Comment on three of the following:

(a) But in many orders of beauty, particularly those of the finer arts, it is requisite to employ much reasoning in order to feel the proper sentiment ... There are just grounds to conclude that moral beauty partakes much of the latter species.

(b) Men are necessarily born in a family-society at least.

(c) Thus two men pull the oars of a boat by common convention for common interest, without any promise or contract.

(d) Imitation has no place in morality.

(e) I can indeed will to lie, but I can by no means will a universal law of lying: for by such a law there could properly be no promises at all.

(f) Man is not a thing – not something to be used merely as a means.

6 Which of the following sentences follow from which others? Explain your answer.

(a) Jules must have told Jim.

(b) Jules can't have told Jim.

(c) Jules may have told Jim.

(d) Jules may not have told Jim.

(e) It must have been the case that Catherine or Jules told Jim.

(f) Catherine must have told Jim or Jules must have told Jim.

(g) Neither Catherine nor Jules can have told Jim.

7 What is truth?

8 Discuss our reasons for expecting that cats won't start barking tomorrow.

9 Is there a good argument for the non-existence of God?

## POLITICS

1 Explain the main differences between conservatism and liberalism.

2 What makes the UK a democracy?

3 Discuss critically Lord Devlin's view that there is no theoretical limit to the role of the state in regulating personal behaviour.

4 What does it mean to say that there is a powerful 'State tradition' in France?

5 'The Christian Democrats succeeded in the Federal Republic because they avoided the temptation to become a Conservative party.' Discuss.

6 What is meant by the national interest?

7 'The broad shape and the nature of the press is ultimately determined by no one but its readers.' Discuss.

## PSYCHOLOGY

1 What limits the amount of visual information that can be apprehended in a single glimpse?

2 Assess the adequacy of psychological accounts of how humans solve problems.

3 When do cognitive failures lead to accidents?

4  How can a student ensure that the information presented in a lecture will be remembered?
5  Is abnormal behaviour an illness?
6  Given the knowledge that exists about negotiation strategies, what advice would you offer trade union leaders?
7  Evaluate the proposition that the way in which adults talk to children influences the course of language acquisition.
8  Discuss the practical and theoretical difficulties which arise when we try to discover which part of the brain is responsible for a particular psychological function.

## SOCIAL POLICY

1  What do you understand by fraternity? How is it related, if at all, to liberty?
2  What are the principal arguments for and against increased selectivity in welfare provision?
3  How dangerous are the dangerous?
4  Lord Chief Justice Lane said in the House of Lords, in 1981, that crime statistics were 'mostly misleading and very largely unintelligible'. If this is so, why do we have them?
5  'Hunger is created and maintained by human decisions' (George and Paige). Discuss.
6  How can the bereaved be helped to bear the loss of a loved one?
7  'One way of looking at social policy would be to describe it as a set of structures created by men to shape the lives of women' (Wilson). Critically discuss this way of looking at social policy.
8  For these questions, each candidate is provided with a copy of the following:
   • Non-Means-Tested Benefits – The Legislation
   • Supplementary Benefit Act 1976 (as amended)
   • Supplementary Benefit (Conditions of Entitlement) Regulations 1981
   • Supplementary Benefit (Requirements) Regulations 1983
   • Supplementary Benefit (Single Payments) Regulations 1981

   (a) 'The extraordinary range of welfare benefits – contributory, non-contributory and means-tested – reveals a confused and incoherent approach to the provision of funds for those who are in need of State support. In particular, the insurance principle regarded as so significant by Beveridge is now largely ignored.'
      Discuss, with particular reference to the changes in entitlement to welfare benefits proposed in the recent White Paper, Reform of Social Security, Programme for Action (Cmnd. 9691, 1985).
   (b) 'Those rules of unemployment benefit originally intended to protect the fund against claims by people who chose to work for only part of the week or part of the year at a time of full employment, are now causing

injustice as working habits and patterns change in response to social and economic factors.' Discuss.

9 'Vince, aged 17 years, lives with his brother Wayne, aged 20 years. Their mother, with whom they lived, died recently. Their father, Rock, who is working, has not lived with the family for more than 10 years. Their parents were never divorced, but throughout their separation Rock agreed to pay for the maintenance of the boys until the age of 18. He is currently sending £7 per week for Vince. He has never paid maintenance for his wife. Vince has been unemployed since leaving school a year ago. At the beginning of this year he enrolled to do a course at the local FE college. The course is for a certificate in Computer Studies which he hopes will help him to get a job. He attends classes at the college for 16 hours a week and spends several hours each week practising and doing homework with his computer at home. The college authorities describe the course as a full-time course in Computer Operations. Vince says that he has always spent several hours a week 'playing' with his home computer and that he would do this whether or not he was on this course. Wayne is also at the FE college doing two A level subjects. These require classroom attendance for 11 hours each week. In addition he is doing a Computer Studies course in the evening for 2 hours per week. His teacher has recommended this as an adjunct to one of his A level courses. After his mother's death, Wayne arranged the funeral; he has recently got the bill for £400 and has insufficient money to pay.'

Advise Vince, Wayne and Rock on their respective entitlements to Supplementary Benefit and Child Benefit.

## SOCIOLOGY

1 'The essence of a market system is that no one has power over others.' Is this so?
2 Why is an ideological view of the world so often taken to be synonymous with a distorted view?
3 How would Marx have accounted for the collapse of East Germany?
4 Is social class outmoded?
5 What can discourse analysis tell us about the relationships between doctors and patients?

## THEOLOGY

1 'There is ample evidence that the exodus happened. It is much less easy to say what kind of event it was, about whose historicity we can be so categorical.' Discuss.
2 'The only important thing to know about the date of Ezra is that it doesn't matter.'
Discuss.

3  'Prophets are usually mistaken for predictors. The prophets of Israel unveiled not the future but the absolute.' Discuss.
4  In what sense, if any, did Jesus believe he was God's son?
5  What do you understand to be Calvin's teaching on the Lord's Supper?
6  What is the meaning of justification by faith?
7  'St Mark hates the Twelve.' Why should anyone think this?
8  Can a male Saviour effect complete salvation?

# Notes and comments on activities

## CHAPTER 1

**1.1** A common reason is to find some ideas that are usable in one's course. Other reasons are to confirm that what one is doing is OK, to get a rapid overview of the field of assessment or to find references to research or developmental work that might be useful. The reasons for reading the module may influence (and some would say should influence) your approach to the module.

**1.2** Most people choose bad experiences and that in itself is significant. The lessons to be drawn from these activities revolve around sensitivity and feedback. Some people apply what they have learnt to do or not do to their own approach to assessing students. Underlying the activity is the notion of reflective learning.

**1.3** We deliberately described the students in gender-free terms although if it helps you can call the first student, Di or Dai, and the second student, Andy or Mandy. (We have never met a gender-free student.) The thoughts and discussions are usually about giving feedback and estimating what would be appropriate feedback to give. How one gives feedback is determined by the context, the content one is giving feedback on, the person whom one is giving feedback to, the reason for giving the feedback and one's values and knowledge of communication strategies. Values may obtrude in the discussion of mini-problems so be prepared for disagreements.

**1.4** Some dislike telling students that an assignment is poor, others dislike failing a student. Some mention giving a viva to a student who one knows will fail. Some go outside the remit of the question and describe examiners' meetings as a sacrificial rite in which people argue irrationally about a student's marks.

**1.5** This activity often produces much discussion. Ultimately one's choice is determined by whether one prefers a pleasant personal relationship to the possibility of working with an expert. Most people reject the Head of Department, and most would prefer a mentor with some of the characteristics of A and C. The discussion often moves on to what counts as good mentoring and the analogies with research supervision.

**1.6** This activity is to start you thinking about your priorities and what you would want to get from a series of group meetings on assessment. You might also consider how the meetings might be organised.

# CHAPTER 2

2.1 This exercise is a useful way of stimulating discussion of assessment by colleagues.

2.2 Writing some notes *before* reading stimulates an active search of the material to pinpoint similarities between one's own thoughts and those of the writer. The activity is a straightforward example of active learning. A similar approach may be used with students. They might be asked to note what criteria they think should be used for assessing a particular task before the criteria are outlined. They might be asked to note what points a paper is likely to contain before reading it or listening to its presentation.

2.3 Feedback to improve learning and grading students are often high priorities although the former may be neglected. Selection and prediction for future employment are usually low priorities. If this activity is done in a group you might compile the group's rank order of priorities.

2.4 There are several features to consider. The main difficulty is establishing which features take priority. If the emphasis is upon developing learning then one might opt for a predominance of coursework. If one is concerned that a person should be capable of doing certain things independently and under pressure then one might opt for written examinations. As usual, it is the balance of methods that is important.

2.5 This activity can lead to uproar! Some colleagues in well-established universities are appalled at the demise of written examinations and the advent of self-assessment. Others are appalled at the narrowness and rigidity of the present system. Values and traditions are salient in the discussions. A note of the discussion might be made in your assessment log. This activity could be repeated after some of the alternative approaches have been explored.

# CHAPTER 3

3.1 This is a useful reflective activity for comparing and refreshing approaches to learning. The activity often leads to a discussion of the conditions of learning, its purpose and how assessment and assessment load can affect it. Occasionally, colleagues point out that the pressures on them can also induce a surface approach to their tasks.

3.2 Many colleagues are surprised at the similarities of the lists from different subject areas. There are differences but these are usually at the level of fine detail. For example, written communication has different emphases in science and literature. Problem-solving requires different approaches in medicine and mathematics. Arguments about these issues may be traced back to Platonic and Aristotelian notions of forms and content of knowledge.

Some colleagues are uncomfortable with the other questions in the activity. They recognise the importance of guidance and feedback – although some retreat to the argument about spoon-feeding students. Some are unsure if enough is provided. The items that are generated are not necessarily assessed directly and some people point to the difficulty of doing so. The pragmatists might say give it a try. Surprisingly few colleagues provided specific criteria to students although most claim to provide oral or written guidance.

The major items of learning that are suggested include oral and written communication, thinking including problem-solving and practical skills. All of these may of course be unpacked further. The model of skills provided in the chapter often prompts people to think of other important aspects of learning.

3.3 Self-assessment of one's style of learning provides a basis for reflection on learning and one can also pick up some useful suggestions from colleagues who may approach the same task differently. You could extend this activity by matching your self-assessed style against the style identified by an inventor such as Biggs, Entwistle, Kolb or Myers. See the references for sources.

3.4 Often colleagues begin with a discussion of the tactics of reading such as skimming, surveying and deep study. The discussion then often turns to how one's style of learning influences one's purposes and approach to reading. Some people will be looking for a theoretical framework, some for empirical evidence and some for practical hints and some for something that they could use next week. If your learning style is not consonant with the reasons for reading the text then there are only three possibilities. The reasons offered for reading were not the real reasons, your self-assessment of learning style was inaccurate or learning styles and approaches to reading are unrelated. The last reason is the most unlikely. Learning styles also influence one's attitudes to different types of discussion. Activists and theorists often irritate each other unless they understand the basis of their differences in approach.

3.5 In our workshops, some argued that higher and further are institutional labels rather than qualitative differences in learning. Others said that undergraduates have a more extensive knowledge, a deeper understanding and a more critical approach. Teaching methods in higher education were not usually regarded as more advanced than those in schools. The views on whether higher education promotes active learning were mixed. Assessment methods in secondary and higher education seem to be converging. Further education is influenced by BTEC which favours clear and tightly structured assessment procedures based on pass/fail criteria. Some pointed out that higher education in America is similar to sixth form and further education in Britain. The activity is also a useful entrée into the changing purposes and characteristics of higher education (see Atkins *et al.*, 1993).

3.6 If you have done the previous activities then you will have found this task was fairly easy. If you have not, then you will have to dig out what you value in subject expertise and in capable students. The characteristics that you identify are useful when reconsidering one's course design, teaching methods and modes of assessment.

# CHAPTER 4

4.1 It is usually a good idea to know where one is starting from. If you use 4.2 and 4.3 as a group activity then you may find that some people are reluctant initially to reveal all of their assessment methods. You may find a richer variety of approaches than you realised.

Several approaches are used to create questions. Some look at past papers – but not usually at last year's paper. Some choose a sprinkling of old chestnuts, fashionable topics and run of the mill questions. Some have an intensive brain-storming session, others note the questions as they emerge from their unconscious. Some create the questions and assignments as they are preparing or reviewing the course. The last is an efficient and good approach if you are experienced. Some less experienced lecturers worry about setting assignments or examinations on material that they have not taught. A mentor might help, discreetly, with the setting and the marking of assignments.

Outside of Oxford and Cambridge there is a demise of assignments that do not count towards Part I of the degree or the degree itself. The present calculative system is likely to produce calculative students.

Informal discussions with students about assessment can be revealing. Pairs of tutors can exchange students – even between departments, so that the students feel safer. The exchange can be mutually informative.

4.2    No comment.

4.3    This is an extension of Activity 4.1 and it is related to Activity 3.1. The task can be time-consuming but it may be timely. It will help you to clarify the assessment tasks of your course or module.

4.4    This activity may be done in conjunction with 4.3. The suggestions in the chapter may help you to generate new assessment tasks and some appropriate criteria. There are arguments for and against providing criteria to students. We take the view that broad criteria are useful and over-elaborate criteria are worse than no criteria. Incidentally, too detailed a set of criteria does not advance problem-solving skills.

4.5    The answer depends in part on what is meant by 'taught'. If little or no opportunities are provided for learning the content and skills then it is probably wrong to set such tasks. If there are opportunities to learn with some guidance and feedback then it is probably right. There are other issues lurking under the question. Amongst these are the changing role of the lecturer, the changing nature of courses, the promotion of independent learning and the purposes of higher education.

4.6    Several possibilities. Test anxiety – certainly. Rapid analytical, organisational and decision-making skills and speed of response – probably. Rote-learning skills – but the learning may be short term. Revision strategies – probably. It can be argued that some of these features are relevant to the everyday life of a professional or executive.

You might try the alternative question, 'What does coursework measure that examinations do not measure?' The term 'measure' is problematic. Some people prefer the term 'estimate'. Others distinguish between direct and indirect measures and between intended measures, consequential measures and unintended measures.

There is very little hard empirical evidence on this question.

4.7    The responses ranged from 'I would not reply. It could be dangerous' to a sympathetic response that thanked the student and acknowledged that neither the tutorial system nor the use of examinations was perfect but indicated that there was a renewed interest in these issues. The letter that you draft may provide you indirectly with your own value statements about teaching, assessment and students.

4.8    A common problem in modular courses is the variation in assessment requirements and, often, the overload of assessment in modular courses. The overload is demanding for students and it may lead to superficial learning. It is burdensome for academic staff and it may lead to superficial marking. The estimates of time can help planning of student and lecturer assessment schedules. You may wish to compare the estimates with those given in the chapter.

## CHAPTER 5

5.1 Most people rate Essay Two marginally better than Essay One because it contains less irrelevant information and it did provide evidence directly on economic and social impact. The variation in marks ranged from 2.1 to pass. If the same pattern was repeated across coursework and examinations then the degree awarded would owe as much to the examiner's predilections as to the student's capabilities Second marking is important! Many people write comments that are judgmental rather than helpful. We included fictional names of the students to remind people of the issues of anonymity and stereotyping.

5.2 The results may surprise you. Criteria marking may reduce variability but it does not abolish it. Unduly complex criteria can increase variability. Holistic marking based on pass/fail or degree classifications are the fastest form of marking but not the most useful for feedback purposes. If the criteria are simple and clear then time spent on marking and variability may be reduced. The criteria are useful for students as well as tutors.

5.3 The comments were provided by students. Not all of them are helpful. Some prefer the crisper versions. An alternative exercise is to ask people to recall some comments written on their work and their degree of helpfulness. Or one can invite colleagues to invent constructive comments in relation to various weaknesses.

5.4 Arguably, but probably it is better to spend more time on marking that will help the students to improve their next essay than on preparing beautifully polished lectures. Your answer, of course, depends upon your values.

5.6 A sample of views are:

1 b is more precise and so easier to mark than 1a.
2 A challenging question. Did you answer it? The assertion is questionable and the inferences do not necessarily follow.
3 is also challenging. This notion of a First is based upon personal knowledge rather than publicly available criteria. As one gains in knowledge and understanding the likelihood of awarding a First diminishes.
4 is uncomfortable? a and b are clear but a grid may not be a useful way of showing similarities and differences. In practice, publications are counted, not evaluated. Promotion committees assume that peer review of publications is adequate. We could go on but we won't.
5 Even without a knowledge of cardiology and radiology one can see the links between the sections of the question. It is thought to be a good question for assessing knowledge. Errors in a should not be penalised in b.

5.6 The first attempts are difficult. Ask the students in a tutorial how the MCQ could be made clearer (not easier). Most students enjoy using MCQs in tutorials because of the challenge, discussion and feedback. And one should use them in tutorials if they are to be used in summative assessment.

5.7 No further comment.

5.8 Already discussed in the chapter.

5.9 Answers vary across subjects as well as individuals. The stronger and more stable the paradigms that one is working in the more likely one is to opt for common standards. Anecdotal evidence suggests that scientists and engineers favour common standards. Historians tend to be marginally in favour of standards and linguists marginally in favour of freedom of choice. English literature specialists used to favour freedom and individuality within a broad framework but the advancement of critical theory may change this. The PC (politically correct) movement may increase dogmatism in some subjects.

5.10  Most people regard 1 as central but recognise the importance of 2 and 3. Some people regard 3 as outside of their responsibility. Is it only the student's responsibility? The argument that students will learn 2 and 3 from doing 1 is not borne out by evidence on transfer and generalisability. If you think 2 and 3 are important, then set and assess assignments on them.

5.11  We don't know. The few post-modernists that we have asked have been curiously reticent on the issue. There is bound to be a tension between, on the one hand, their theoretical perspectives on authorship, relative values, literary canons and subtexts and on the other, their marking and judging essays and dissertations.

## CHAPTER 6

6.1  Question 1 has an ambiguous stem so any of the alternative responses could be correct. The purpose of the question is unclear. Is the information required concerned with dates? locations?

Question 2 is incorrect. Great Britain does not have a capital. London is the best, but wrong, guess. The other items are too different to be good distractors. Incidentally this MCQ could be turned into a rather clever essay question along the lines of 'Argue the case that the seat of government in Britain is now in Belgium or the United States.'

Question 3 contains confusing negatives. It could be simplified by re-phrasing the item to read 'MCQs can measure high-level cognitive ability – true/false.'

Question 4 has plausible distractors. The key characteristic is given in alternative 4.

Question 5 requires thought – unless you have done it before. The correct alternative is false.

Question 6 is confusing because 1990 is so near to the present. The stem is ungrammatical. It does not make clear whether the responses are based on clothing in 1990 or in 1909. The alternatives are for different domains. Candidates are likely to choose item 4 because it is the most comprehensive.

6.2  No further comment.

6.3  The first example shows that A is the favoured wrong response and since it attracted a lower proportion of the top students compared with the bottom students it is unlikely to give cause for concern. But there would be cause for concern if analysis yielded the second matrix. More of the bottom students chose the correct response than the top students. An apparently incorrect response, A, attracted the greatest proportion of the top students. Further investigation of this item and response A is required. Responses D and C are superfluous so a three-choice item would have been as effective and, possibly, easier to prepare.

## CHAPTER 7

7.1  Weak links and overload are common weaknesses.

7.2  The range of assessment methods is often narrow.

7.3  Sometimes people want a finer classification system. The activity often generates discussion of the relative merits of recipe and enquiry approaches in different subjects. The argument hinges on what objectives one wishes to prioritise.

7.4 This is not quite as easy as it looks. It is a good introduction to task and error analysis. Even in this simple activity there are likely to be disagreements between colleagues on the correct procedures. Common criteria are temperature, flavour, strength. Note that scales of quality do not correspond to the scale of temperature. Good is optimum, not high. Very good is broader than perfection. Simple points but ones often neglected by designers of rating scales.

Several implications. Clarity of instruction and assessment involves estimating what the students already know, eliminating ambiguities and cueing the right actions. Pictures often communicate more clearly than words in instructions. Error analyses help one to develop better instructions and assessment tasks. To assess quality one needs an agreed set of criteria. All phenomena are assessable, from a painting by Rembrandt to a cup of tea. This assertion does not mean that everyone will agree upon criteria or that they will apply the criteria in the same way. But developing criteria and working together towards shared meanings can help to minimise inconsistencies between markers. Objectivity in the sense of 'right' or 'wrong' is not always possible to judge outside of a narrow domain of tasks. Some would say that even within those domains, objectivity merely means a group consensus within an existing strong paradigm that may change in emphases as the subject develops. What was a good answer on a finals paper in physics in 1940 may not be regarded as a good answer in 1992.

7.5, 7.6, 7.7 and 7.8 Useful and unexpected forms of feedback for students. The results may have implications for the organisation of laboratory work. The activities can increase student awareness of their laboratory organisation, their task allocations and team work.

7.9 Salutary but important!

7.10 You can use this activity to investigate student and staff workloads in your department or school. It could be a mini-project or one could use it as a discussion activity. Most people will probably only be able to provide rough estimates of time spent on different tasks.

7.11 The activity requires careful planning. It can provide a useful starting-point for reviewing and re-developing a laboratory. The information provided enables one to take decisions and design a course but in the 'real' world one should do an audit of objectives, assessment and levels of experiment. The activity has been used successfully with experienced lecturers on courses on laboratory work.

## CHAPTER 8

8.1 Useful starting-point for reappraising project work. Some people assume that projects are for assessment purposes only and that feedback should be minimal during the life of a project. Others drift to this position because of other commitments.

8.2 When we did this activity with final-year students, many of them agreed that supervisors should help and that the students' approach was sensible! Colleagues were a little uncomfortable, although some had used the same approach as students. However, some refused to believe Gabb's report. It was suggested that the views of the present final-year students should be collected by an unbiased and independent source after the projects had been marked.

8.3   This activity highlights the importance of planning in a context. Most students forget about Christmas and its attendant activities! They often neglect other commitments in their plans. They allow little time for slippage, for the supervisor to read the draft or for getting the dissertation bound. Often they only allocate time for writing towards the end of the project whereas drafts of sections of the report or dissertation should be produced during the early stages. Often they do not distinguish between time required to write in order to clarify one's thinking and time to write to communicate one's thoughts. The activity could be followed by a discussion of time management, its importance and, if it is being assessed, how it will be assessed.

8.4   A difficulty here is that some colleagues prefer to withhold criteria or to use a totally holistic approach (I know a First when I see one). The use of criteria does not eliminate disagreements but they do pinpoint the area of disagreement. The criteria do aid consistency in marking and they do help students to clarify their approach.

8.5   This activity is often salutary. People who anticipate it may involve a reappraisal of marking procedures may resist the activity on the grounds that it is not necessary or there is insufficient time. We leave you to answer these arguments. It is all a matter of priorities.

8.6   Just as we may ask students to reflect upon their learning and share it, so too it is useful for us to do the same. For in so doing we may obtain confirmation of our strategies or discover approaches that will help us to develop.

8.7   Students often complain of inconsistencies in vivas. The approach suggested increases fairness and yet it does not ignore individual differences in students.

8.8   The first poster sessions that you organise will take longer than you think! Second time round it is easier and faster.

8.9   You should decide what the purposes of the meeting are so that the discussion has a focus.

8.10   Naturally, opinions vary on what is the best approach. Several people opt for briefing and discussion with students, peer-assessment of processes and a small proportion of peer-assessment marks for the group project and the rest of the marks to be awarded by the tutor.

8.11   Another good starting-point for reviewing project work.

8.12   An audit of previous years' projects and dissertations can prompt guidelines and suggestions. The activity is best undertaken by a group of colleagues. It is time-consuming so only tackle it if you wish to improve the existing approach.

## CHAPTER 9

9.1 and 9.2   These activities provide a more meaningful and sharper focus for students than 'How do you solve problems?' Some students reported to us that this was the first time that they had been required to think systematically about how they solved problems. They found particularly useful the task of articulating precisely how to help others to solve problems.

9.3   This activity is best done after 9.1 and 9.2. Do include self-assessment, tutor assessment, tutor feedback and how problems are marked in examinations. Students are sometimes surprised at the complexity of marking some problems in examinations. Some do not use the feedback provided on solutions in course-work.

**9.4**   9.1, 9.2 and 9.3 provide the basis for this activity. Try to use a practical inter-active approach rather than a series of lectures followed by a question and answer session.

**9.5**   This activity is best done as a joint exercise so that the demonstrators are involved in the procedure and sampling of their marking. The activity should be repeated with each new group of demonstrators although, of course, you might wish to show them the approaches developed by earlier groups of demonstrators.

**9.6**   No further comment.

**9.7**   A useful way of stimulating discussion of marking schemes. Occasionally one should refresh one's approach and views. Sometimes departments discover that they are not using efficient (or effective) methods of designing problems. The discussion can lead to ways of saving time in designing and marking problems.

**9.8**   This problem is tricky because most people do not use all the information given. It combines trial and error with reasoning so it is not unlike many practical problems. The solution is that the verger's children are aged 1, 6 and 6. The process of solving first involves working out the eight combinations of numbers that yield 36 when multiplied together, that is, 3×3×4; 2×3×6; 1×6×6; 2×2×9; 1×4×9; 1×3×12; 1×2×18; and 1×1×36. At this point most people get stuck. If you re-read the problem you might note that the vicar still could not do the problem even though he knew the number on the verger's door. Why? Because two of the sets of numbers add up to the number on the verger's door. These sets are 1+6+6 and 2+2+9. The vicar still could not do the problem until the verger said the vicar's son was older than any of the verger's children. Given that the two possible solutions were 1, 6, 6 and 2, 2, 9 and the problem was solved then the vicar's son must be 7 or 8 and the verger's children 1, 6 and 6. If the vicar's son had been older than 9 the problem would still not have been solved.

   The problem and its solution are worth discussing thoroughly with students for they highlight many of the approaches required by problem-solving. It is also worth inviting demonstrators to write explanations of the solutions of problems along the lines of this note.

**9.9**   The answers are 31 and 2,047. The first part can easily be worked out as 16 matches in the first round, 8 in the second round and so on. A similar procedure can be used for 2,048 competitions but it is cumbersome so the students should be encouraged to experiment and develop a more elegant and general strategy. Experimenting with simple problems and looking for patterns and principles is important. So too is refocusing or recasting a problem. In this case it follows that if there are 32 competitors and 1 winner then there must be 31 losers so there must be 31 matches. Of course one should check that the general strategy works and under what conditions. Again the problem has many implications for solving more complex problems and for developing self-assessment of problem-solving strategies.

**9.10**   The nub of the problem is the difference between a hard-boiled egg and a raw egg. A hard egg is solid and a raw egg contains liquid, a yolk and a space. X rays could be used but that solution is expensive and inconvenient. So one might look for differences between a solid object and a shell container containing a liquid. One difference is spin or inertia. The solid egg will spin faster at a given force because the inside of a raw egg will not start to spin immediately, thereby slowing the outside down. Since seeing is believing the solution should be demonstrated.

The problem may be used to demonstrate the importance of looking for comparators and then working towards a simple solution. The problem also raises the issue of cost, reliability, ease of use, etc.

9.11   One solution would be to remove the doors from the furnace part way through the bonding process and let them cool before returning them to the furnace. During the cooling time the thinner sections would lose heat faster and cool more than the thicker sections. When returned to the furnace the thicker sections would would rise in temperature more quickly and the thin sections would take longer, thus preventing over-heating. An alternative would be to redesign the component parts so that the problem did not arise. However, a new design might not necessarily be a better design.

9.12   Some people tackle this problem holistically and others tackle it serially. The holistic approach is to check on prices of a comparable bridge today, check on the overall changes in prices since 1928 and adjust the estimate accordingly. The serial approach is to identify the material and machinery used, the labour needed, the cost of the land and so on and cost these individually. This procedure is much more time-consuming but probably more accurate. Each approach has underlying assumptions that should be teased out, including the practical question of how much time and money one is willing to invest to obtain a precise solution. The notion that solutions can only have two of the three characteristics of cheapness, speed and high quality is worth exploring. For example, if a solution is cheap and fast it is probably not of high quality.

## CHAPTER 10

10.1   It will help you to understand the processes involved in presenting, analysing and viewing presentations. You may learn a little (or more) about giving and receiving feedback. This will help you to prepare a sensible and sensitive approach to assessing presentations by students.

10.2   The course is a useful way of introducing self and peer feedback techniques as well as helping students to improve their presentation skills. The repeat of the task demonstrates to students that they can improve. The feedback from the first activity should be used to improve performance on the second activity.

10.3   This activity helps students to understand the processes of seminars and it usually improves their performance in seminars.

10.4   A useful way of involving colleagues and students in the development and understanding of the criteria used for assessing oral proficiency. Discussion might lead to a consideration of what counts as good feedback in oral proficiency.

10.5   A challenging task! But given the interest in student progression, it is one worth trying – even if, initially, the activity only raises awareness of the problems involved.

10.6   Vivas for borderline cases are often based on the assumption that they are a reliable way of upgrading – or worse, downgrading – students. The activity reveals the importance of clear criteria and consistency.

10.7   The activity is usually enjoyed by students and it increases their awareness of what is required in a consultation.

Note: Assessment during training in oral communication need not lead to formal marks and grades. One should distinguish between assessment for feedback purposes only and assessment of what has been learnt.

## CHAPTER 11

11.1   How have you done? If you scored more than 12 YES's than you are too good to be true! If you scored fewer than 4 YES's then perhaps you should reconsider your approach. Were you honest with yourself? Did you feel sufficiently confident to disclose your self-assessment to your peers? The assessment we hope was developmental, that is the judgements were made with a view to improving.

11.2   This an adaptation of a well-used question in selection interviews. It encourages one to reflect and to consider one's actions from the standpoint of others. Similar questions may be asked of students. For example, What do your friends think of the way you study and do coursework?

11.3   A good way of introducing self-assessment to students. It is seen as useful and non-threatening.

11.4   We leave you to decide what you think of self- and peer-assessment. If you do this activity as a group exercise then divide the group into smaller groups and ask each group to compile a list of reasons for using or not using self- and peer-assessment. Then compile a master list and decide as a group whether the methods are worth a try. You can use a similar approach with students. We suggest that you do 11.3 with them first so they have recent experience of self- and peer-assessment on which to base their views. Students' anxieties about peer-assessment are that it is time-consuming and unfair to ask students to make judgements that contribute to marks for a degree. Chapter 14 contains further suggestions on introducing different approaches to assessment.

11.5   This is a good reflective exercise that may be adapted for use in any subject. The discussion is related to styles of learning that were discussed in Chapter 3. The implications for teaching and course design are sometimes neglected in discussions and in practice. There is always a wide range of individual differences amongst students so it is better to have a wide range of methods of teaching, learning and assessment.

## CHAPTER 12

12.1   Ask them to reflect upon their learning experiences, to consider things that they are good at and not so good at. Use Kolb's or Entwistle's learning inventory or Belbin's inventory on team work (see Kemp and Race, 1992). Ask them to think and write about any significant learning experience or assessment that they completed at school. Ask them to keep a learning log for a few weeks to note down their thoughts or sudden insights and to be prepared to share their thoughts with their peers. If you are reluctant to devote a whole tutorial to APEL then use the first 15 minutes of a few tutorials for these exercises.

12.2   Here are a few suggestions.
   • Keep them simple and brief.
   • Use them for reflective learning not for formal assessment.
   • Use some tutorial time to discuss the purposes and some to discuss openly the student's reflections and evaluation of their usefulness.

- Make sure the activities are perceived as helpful rather than as a chore.
- Don't use them just because they are fashionable.

12.3  Ouch!! But if things are worth doing then sometimes they are worth doing badly rather than not at all. You might turn back to the suggestions given in Chapter 1 on keeping a learning log. Then review what you have read so far in this chapter and make a note of what you wish to explore further – and when. Put the dates in your diary.

12.4  Views differ and depend in part upon the definitions of the terms. Our views are:

1  Portfolios should not replace degree classifications but they should be used to encourage reflective learning, as a basis for compiling CVs and as a record for future private use. Few employers are going to wade through several thick dossiers of students' achievements so some form of crude indicator will always be necessary. Students should be encouraged to fit their applications to the particular demands of the job for which they are applying, not to offer the same document for every job.

2  It is not intended to do so. We remain unconvinced of its usefulness in its present form.

3  No. See remarks under 1. In addition, employers might be encouraged to consider the nature of assessment. Many of them seem to have a naive faith in expensive, franchised tests and a lack of understanding of the purposes and processes of learning and assessment in higher education.

12.5  To answer this question fully you would need to know what tasks the students will be tackling in their work placement and what tasks they tackle in their courses. However, your thoughts on these matters are a useful first approximation. The discussion may prompt you to explore more fully the nature of work placements and it may help you to clarify your expectations of work placements and mentors.

12.6  There are arguably no substantive differences between the processes of assessing work-based learning and those of assessing academic work. However, the quality of learning opportunities in some work settings and in some academic settings may be a problem. Work-based learning and projects are more likely to develop independent, active, reflective learning than written examinations.

12.7  This activity is designed to get you thinking about the skills that you want students to develop in courses and in work-based learning. It may also start you thinking about ways of assessing student learning on work placements. The allocation of marks is a signal of the value that you place upon the assessment of work-based learning. That signal will be received and interpreted by students. A simple but interesting exercise in a seminar or workshop on work-based learning is to ask participants to write down what proportion of marks they would allocate to work-based learning in their course. Then ask them to write down what marks the department or school would be likely to allocate. Follow this with a comparison and discussion. It not only reveals the values of members of the department with regard to work-based learning, it also provides an indirect estimate of their perceptions of the school or department of which they are members.

12.8  This simulation (or is it real for you?) is a good way of listing and evaluating strengths, weaknesses, opportunities and threats of such a change in the curriculum.

12.9  You may find it possible to use the same broad approaches across the options but within each option you may wish to use some criteria which are specific to it. If you are implementing either of these options for real, then do monitor the process of assessment of each option.

12.10 This is a deep and controversial question. Responses may obviously range from none to all. However, most of us value systematised knowledge, understanding and 'higher education' so we see work-based learning as just one of many possible learning opportunities rather than as a replacement. Even within this relatively narrow band there is still plenty of room for argument and disagreement!

## CHAPTER 13

13.1 Re-read the chapter, if you are unsure of what you can do.

13.2 Put the MCQs on transparencies. Ask students to hand in sheets with their names on and the coded responses (e.g. 1a, 2c, 3b, etc). Design a set of MCQs. Make sure they fit the format of the card. Ask students to mark the cards clearly. Be prepared to correct some cards before feeding them through the OMR.
   Several possibilities. Look through the chapter; it may trigger ideas.

13.3 The plan might include some peer marking as well as MCQs. It may be that the objectives of the course need changing as well as the assessment procedure. If a realistic estimate of the time required to develop and use the new approach exceeds 450 hours, think again.

13.4 An open activity that can provide a wide range of practical suggestions.

13.5 A SWOT (strengths, weaknesses, opportunities and threats) analysis is often a useful entrée into developing a new approach. It clears the air and it provides cues for developing and presenting an innovation.

13.6 There are some surprising inefficiencies and frustrations lurking here. Administrators and secretarial staff should be involved in this discussion. You should expect some resistance to change, particularly if their recent experience of computerisation has been frustrating.

## CHAPTER 14

14.1 Common arguments against self-assessment are that students will cheat or their assessments will be invalid. It is true that more able students tend to under-estimate and less able students tend to over-estimate. One can build in procedures that will none the less help participants to reflect accurately upon their own learning.

14.2 Students usually tackle this task with vigour. The discussion can be refreshing if somewhat overwhelming for tutors. Be sure to ask what they like as well as what they dislike, what they find useful as well as what they find unhelpful.

14.3 Ownership, choice and involvement, as indicated in this chapter, are important features of even a simple innovation such as a questionnaire. Hence it is better to feed the items in after students have become involved but before they have completed their draft. They may incorporate some of the suggested items and they may reject some. They may well have thought of some of them for themselves. The use of a questionnaire within the two-page format is a powerful discipline. It helps them to establish their priorities and it sharpens their perceptions of the issues involved.

14.4   A few lecturers are less enthusiastic about this task – perhaps they know the weaknesses in the system of assessment but they do not want to face them. Others find the exercise of looking at assessment from the standpoint of students valuable.

14.6 and 14.7   These activities often help colleagues to understand better the processes of change in their own department and institution.

14.8   This exercise gets the presenters and other participants to think about tactics and persuasive arguments. It can be role-played but we find it better done as a straightforward presentation followed by a discussion of the approaches to use. The activity may also be used with students.

14.9   This is a more open activity than 14.6 and 14.7. It often generates sets of guidelines not dissimilar from those in figures 14.1, 14.2, and 14.3 but which are the group's own products.

## CHAPTER 15

15.1   The activity goes to the heart of assessment. The answers provide you with clear guidelines for improving your approach.

15.2   People have different strategies for this. Some mark each question in turn, some skim-read and throw the scripts into five piles and then mark properly. Some look for the potential best and worst scripts and use these as the range. Some mark the whole set using one of the above methods and then re-mark a sample. Some people find they mark better if they have five initial categories and then within each category three sub-categories. The more detailed the categories or the wider the scale, the greater the probability of inconsistency. Perhaps this is the reason why some people mistakenly prefer pass/fail.

15.3   Second marking and an arbitrator if the first two markers disagree. Use of explicit criteria is important. Purists argue for totally independent marking. Small-scale experiments conducted by one of the authors suggest that totally independent marking based on a degree classification is no better than marking where the second marker knows the first marker's mark. The confirmation of the initial mark is obviously less time-consuming than independent (double blind) marking.

15.4   Often the assessment load is higher than realised. It is useful to mark the assignments, tests and examinations on to a time line. On the time line indicate when assignments are set and expected to be handed in. There may be wider variations in assessment loads and the range of marks awarded than is realised. Students who take difficult units may be penalised. If several assessments are combined the result is a large proportion of 2.2s. This phenomenum, regression to the mean, can be avoided if there is broad agreement on the likely proportion of Firsts and 2.1s to be awarded in a module. A more complicated way prepared by some statisticians is to standardise all marks to an agreed mean and standard deviation. However, relatively small shifts in the mean and standard deviation can produce quite dramatic changes in the proportions in each degree category.

15.5   The audits may be carried out quickly. The results obtained and their implications should be discussed at departmental meetings. If the analysis yields serious anomalies then a change in the system of assessment is required. This in part accounts for some of the resistance to the audit. More detailed analysis such as by gender or by entry qualifications may also yield interesting findings.

15.6   Tutors usually agree on the objectives of the questions and find the process of discussing the nature of questions and objectives useful. It is also good to get one's approach confirmed from time to time!

15.7   Again there is usually broad agreement but the exercise highlights ambiguities in the objectives of the course and the questions. Tutors often report that it is good to get confirmation of their approaches and the chance to discuss their approaches in a relatively non-threatening situation.

15.8   The degree of agreement is usually not as great as one would wish. Kendall's coefficient of concordants may be used to provide a statistical estimate of agreement (see Ebel and Frisbie, 1986). The more categories the greater the likelihood of disagreement. Detailed and complex marking schemes produce greater disagreement than simple guidelines. If you are feeling really bold ask a few students to mark the essays too and compare their results with those of members of staff.

15.9   Usually more Firsts are awarded in sciences than arts. The reasons are to do with the traditions of the subject and in particular the unwillingness in some subjects to use a wide range of marks. What is nominally a 0–100 scale is often a 45–75 scale and within that scale few marks are awarded below 50 and very few above 70. It is not surprising therefore that there are fewer Firsts awarded in the arts and social sciences even though the entry qualifications of such students can be higher than of those in sciences in some universities.

15.10   The consistency of judgements was high but the assessment tasks were inappropriate for the criterion task. Predictive validity was low and criterion validity was low. There are other implications for examining the assessment of courses using practical work.

15.11   The exercise of trying to decide what counts as a First, 2.1, etc., in one's own course is salutary.

15.12   Provides the basis for a gentle (?), reflective discussion which might lead to considerations of how one might use assessment to develop students whilst at the same time taking account of the constraints of the systems in which we operate. Perhaps too it might lead to consideration of how the system might be changed.


## CHAPTER 16

We leave you to reflect upon your approach to quality, standards and quality assurance.

# Some further reading

## ON ASSESSMENT IN HIGHER EDUCATION

Atkins, M., Beattie, J. and Dockrell, B. (1993) *Assessment Issues in higher education* Sheffield: Employment Department.
A substantial and scholarly commentary on assessment and the purposes of higher education.

Brown, G. and Pendlebury, M. (1992) *Assessing Active Learning* Sheffield: CVCP UCoSDA.
Part One provides hints, suggestions, activities and brief reviews of relevant research on assessment. Part Two contains articles and short pieces by colleagues in universities who describe their use of various types of assessment in different subjects. Part Three describes various approaches to workshops on assessment.

Elton, L.R.B. (1987) *Teaching in Higher Education: Appraisal and Training* London: Kogan Page.
A collection of thought-provoking articles on assessment and the evaluation of teaching.

Gibbs, G., Habeshaw, S. and Habeshaw, T. (1988) *53 Interesting Ways of Assessing Your Student* 2nd edn: Bristol: Technical and Educational Services.
A useful set of hints on different approaches to assessing student learning.

Gibbs, G. (1992) *Assessing More Students* London: PCFC.
A useful summary of approaches to assessment that focuses upon the problems of assessing larger numbers of students.

Heywood, J. (1989) *Assessment in higher education* 2nd edn, Chichester: John Wiley.
For a detailed review of the literature on assessment.

Rowntree, D. (1987) *Assessing Students – How Shall We Know Them?* London: Harper and Row.
A stimulating discussion of the ideas and assumptions underlying assessment.

## ON TEACHING AND LEARNING

Brown, G. and Atkins, M. (1988) *Effective Teaching in higher education* London: Methuen.
Provides outlines of research, guidelines, hints and suggestions on lecturing, small group teaching, laboratory work, research supervision and helping students learn.

Entwistle, N. (1987) *Styles of Learning and Teaching* 2nd edn, Chichester: Wiley.
Provides a thoughtful overview of the theories and research on student learning.

Entwistle, N.J. (1992) *The Impact of Teaching on Learning Outcomes*. Sheffield: Department of Employment, Higher Education Branch.
A thorough and scholarly review of student learning and cognate matters.

Entwistle, N., Thompson, S. and Tait, H. (1992) *Guidelines for Promoting Effective Learning in Higher Education* Edinburgh: Centre for Research on Learning and Instruction.
A readable and useful outline of approaches to improving learning through course design, teaching and assessment.

Laurillard, D. (1993) *Rethinking University Teaching* London: Routledge.
A thought-provoking and perceptive analysis of teaching and learning from the standpoint of a distinguished information technologist.

Macfarlane, A. (chmn) (1992) *Teaching and Learning in an Expanding Higher Education System* Edinburgh: Committee of Scottish University Principals.
Provides a survey of the literature and argues for greater use of information technology. It contains an excellent annotated bibliography on teaching and assessment.

Ramsden, P. (1992) *Learning to Teach in Higher Education* London: Routledge.
A thoughtful account of research and practice that takes as its starting-point the importance of developing the capacity for deep learning.

## ON ESSAY WRITING AND ASSESSING

Clanchy, J. and Ballard, B. (1992) *How to Write Essays* 3rd edn, London: Longman.
A practical guide to helping students to improve their essay writing. It is particularly useful for humanities and social science students although science students can also benefit from the exercises and suggestions.

Hounsell, D. and Murray, R. (1992) *Essay Writing for Active Learning* Sheffield: CVCP UCoSDA.
A comprehensive guide to designing and marking essays.

Hounsell, D. (1995) 'Marking and commenting on essays' in F. Forster, D. Hounsell and S. Thompson (eds) *Tutoring and Demonstrating: A Handbook* Sheffield: CVCP UCoSDA.
A useful practical guide for less experienced tutors.

## ON MULTIPLE CHOICE QUESTIONS

Gronlund, N.E. (1988) *How to Construct Achievement Tests* Englewood Cliffs, NJ: Prentice Hall.
A comprehensive text on designing assessments that focuses upon MCQs and allied methods.

## ON LABORATORY TEACHING

Boud, D., Dunn, J. and Hegarty-Hazel, E. *Teaching in Laboratories* London: SRHE/NFER-Nelson.
A set of readings on different aspects of the design and teaching of laboratory work.

Hegarty-Hazel, E. (ed.) *The Student Laboratory and the Science Curriculum* London: Routledge.
A useful collection of readings on teaching and assessing laboratory work.

## ON PROBLEM-SOLVING

De Bono, E. (1968) *The Five Day Course on Thinking* Harmondsworth: Penguin.
One of De Bono's earlier texts that is particularly useful on creative problem-solving.

Schoenfeld, A.H. (1985) *Mathematical Problem-solving* New York: Academic Press.
A text with a strong mathematical application.

## ON PEER- AND SELF-ASSESSMENT

Brown, S. and Dove, P. (eds) (1991) *Self and Peer-Assessment* Birmingham: SCED
Paper 63.
A collection of articles that provide hints and some research on self- and peer-
assessment.

Foot, H.C. Howe, C.J., Anderson, A., Tolmie, A.K. and Warder, D.A. (eds) (1994)
*Group and Interactive Learning* Southampton: Computational Mechanics Publications.
A useful collection of articles on different aspects of peer- and self-assessment.

## ON STATISTICAL AND EDUCATIONAL MEASUREMENT

Ebel, R.L. and Frisbie, D.A. (1986) *Essentials of Educational Measurement* Englewood
Cliffs, NJ: Prentice Hall.
This is a technical but readable text on all aspects of educational measurement.

## ON COMPETENCY-BASED APPROACHES

Jessup, G. (1991) *Outcomes: NVQs and the Emerging Model of Education and Training*
London: Falmer Press.
The essential text on NCVQs.

## ON EXTERNAL EXAMINING

Partington, J., Brown, G. and Gordon, G. (1993) *Handbook for External Examiners in
Higher Education* Sheffield: UCosDA.
Provides a practical guide to the work of external examiners at undergraduate
and doctoral level and a consideration of the role of the external examiner in quality
assurance.

Partington, J. (1995) *Improving Examiners Meetings: A Video-training Package* Sheffield:
CVCP UCoSDA.
An amusing but serious exploration of the work of boards of examiners.

## ON QUALITY AND STANDARDS

Ellis, R. (ed.) (1993) *Quality Assurance in Teaching* Milton Keynes: Open University
Press.
For a broader view of quality and quality issues. The chapter by Brown provides a review
of research on effective teaching and the chapter by Elton discusses quality and standards
in teaching.

Partington, P. and Elton, L. (1993) *Teaching Standards and Excellence in Higher Education: Developing a Culture for Quality* Sheffield: UCoSDA.
This policy document discusses the issues of quality and standards and suggests ways of estimating excellence in teaching.

Other useful publications are available from UCoSDA, University of Sheffield and the Staff and Educational Development Association (SEDA), Birmingham.

# Bibliography

AAC (1985) *Integrity in the College Curriculum* Washington DC: Association of American Colleges.

ABGDP (1992) *Self-Assessment Manual of Standards* London: Royal College of Surgeons.

Abouserie, R. (1995) 'Self esteem and achievement motivation' *Studies in Higher Education* 20: 19–26.

Adderly, K., Ashwin, L., Bradbury, P., Freeman, J., Goodlad, S., Green, J., Jenkins, D., Rao, J. and Uren, O. (1975) *Project Methods in Higher Education* London: Society for Research in Higher Education.

AGR (1994) *Graduate Salaries and Vacancies 1994* Cambridge: Association of Graduate Recruiters.

Albano, M.G., Cavallo, F., Hoogenboom, R., Magni, F., Majoor, G., Marenti, F., Schurwith, L., Stiegler, I. and van der Vleuten, C. (1996) 'An international comparison of knowledge levels of medical students: the Maastricht progress test' *Medical Education*, 30: 239–45.

Alexander, S. (1995) 'Review of interactive assessor' *Monitor, Newsletter of CTI Centre for Computing, Oxford.* Summer, 1995.

Allison, I. (1995) 'Demonstrating' in F. Forster, D. Hounsell and S. Thompson (eds) *Tutoring and Demonstrating: A Handbook* Sheffield: CVCP UCoSDA.

Andreson, L., Nightingale, P., Boud, D. and Magin, D. (1993) *Strategies For Assessing Students* Birmingham: SEDA Paper 78.

Annett, J. and Sparrow, J. (1989) 'Transfer of training: a review of research and practical implications' *APLET Journal* 22: 116–24.

Aristotle *The Nicomachean Ethics* Translated by D. Ross and revised by J.L. Ackrill and J.O. Urmson, Oxford: Oxford University Press, 1980.

Arnold, P., O'Conell, C. and Meudell, P. (1994) 'A practical experiment' *The New Academic* 3 (2): 4–5.

Ashbury, J.E., Fletcher, B.M. and Birtwhistle, R.V. (1993) 'Personal journal writing in a communication course for first year medical students', *Medical Education* 27: 196–204.

Ashworth, P. and Morisson, P. (1989) 'Some ambiguities of the student's role in undergraduate nurse training' *Journal of Advanced Nursing*, 14: 1009–15.

Ashworth, P. and Saxton, J. (1992) *Managing Work Experience* London: Routledge.

ASSHE (1996) *Assessing Student Learning in Scotland: The Database* Sheffield: UCoSDA/University of Edinburgh.

Assiter, A. and Fenwick, A. (1992) *Profiling in Higher Education* London: CNAA.

Assiter, A., Fenwick, A. and Nixon, N. (1992) *Profiling in Higher Education: Guidelines for the Development and Use of Profiling Schemes.* HMSO/CNAA.

Assiter, A. and Shaw, E. (eds) (1993) *Using Records of Achievement in Higher Education* London: Kogan Page.

Atkins, M.J. (1993) 'Theories of learning and multi-media applications: an overview' *Research Papers in Education* 8: 251–71.

Atkins, M.J. (1996) 'Threshold and other academic standards: the views of four subject groups' London: HEQC.

Atkins, M.J., Beattie, J. and Dockrell, B. (1993) *Assessment Issues in Higher Education* Sheffield: Employment Department.

Atkins, M.J. and O'Halloran, C. (1995) AMEE Medical Education Guide No. 6. Evaluating multi-media applications for medical education *Medical Teacher*, 17: 149–60.

Ausubel, D. (1978) *Educational Psychology: A Cognitive view.* 2nd edn, New York: Holt, Rinehart & Winston.

Balla, J., Stephanou, A. and Biggs, J. (1996) 'Development of a methodology for assessing medical students' ability to integrate practical and theoretical knowledge' (in preparation).

Barnett, R. (1994a) *Assessment of the Quality of Higher Education: A Review and An Evaluation* London: Centre for Higher Education Studies, University of London Institute of Education.

Barnett, R. (1994b) *The Limits of Competence* Milton Keynes: Open University/SRHE.

Barrass, R. (1978) *Scientists Must Write* London: Chapman & Hall.

Bayne, R. (1995) *The Myers–Briggs Type Indicator: A Critical Review and Practical Guide* London: Chapman & Hall.

Begg, D., Fischer, S. and Dornbusch, R. (1991) *Economics*, 3rd edn, London: McGraw Hill.

Bell, J. (1994) *Doing your Research Project: A Guide for First time Researchers in Educational and Social Science*, 2nd edn, Milton Keynes: Open University Press.

Bell, R.C. (1980) 'Problems in improving the reliability of essay marks' *Assessment and Evaluation in Higher Education* 5: 254–63.

Benford, S., Burke, E. and Foxley, E. (1992) 'Automatic assessment of computer programs in the Ceilidh system' *IEEE-CS International Software Metrics Symposium, 1992.*

Berg, B. and Ostergren, B. (1977) *Innovations and Innovation Processes in Higher Education.* Stockholm: National Board of Universities and Colleges.

Berliner, D. (ed.) (1996) *Handbook of Educational Psychology* New York: Macmillan.

Biggs, J. (1987) *Student Approaches in Learning and Studying* Melbourne: Australian Council for Educational Research; Hawthorn, Victoria: Australian Council for Educational Research.

Biggs, J. (1996) 'Enhancing teaching through constructive alignment' *Higher Education* 32: 347–64.

Black, J. (1975) 'Allocation and assessment of project work in the first year of the engineering degree course at the University of Bath' *Assessment in Higher Education* 1: 35–53.

Bliss, J. (1990) 'Student reactions to undergraduate science' in E. Hegarty-Hazel (ed.) *The Student Laboratory and the Science Curriculum* London: Routledge.

Bliss, J. and Ogborn, J. (eds) (1977) *Students' Reactions to Undergraduate Science* London: Heinemann.

Bloom, B.S. (1965) *A Taxonomy of Educational Objectives Handbook I: Cognitive Domain* 2nd edn, New York: McKay.

Bloor, M. and Butterworth, C. (1990) 'The accreditation of prior learning on in-service education courses for teachers' *Aspects of Educational Technology* 22: 77–82.

Booth, A. and Hyland, P. (eds) (1995) *Teaching History in Higher Education* Oxford: Blackwell.

Boscolo, C. (1996) *Assessing Oral Proficiency* Department of Italian, University of Birmingham, England.

Boshuizer, H.P.A., Norman, G.R. and Schmidt, H.G. (1990) 'A cognitive perspective on medical expertise: theory and implications' *Academic Medicine* 65: 611–21.

Boud, D. (1987) *Implementing Student Self-assessment* Sydney: HERDSA.

Boud, D., Keogh, R. and Walker, M. (1985) *Reflection: Turning Experience into Learning.* London: Kogan Page.

Boud, D., Dunne, J. and Hegarty-Hazel, E. (1986) *Teaching in Laboratories* London: SRHE/NFER-Nelson.

Boud, D. and Brew, A. (1995) *Enhancing Learning through Self-Assessment* London: Kogan Page.

Bowden, J., D'all' Alba, G., Martin, E., Laurillard, D., Marton, F., Masters, G., Ramsden, P., Stephanou, A. and Walsh, E. (1992) 'Displacement velocity and frames of reference' *American Journal of Physics* 60: 262–9.

Brew, A. (1995a) 'What is the scope of self-assessment?' in D. Boud and A. Brew (1995) *Enhancing Learning through Self-Assessment* London: Kogan Page.

Brew, A. (1995b) 'Self-Assessment in different domains' in D. Boud and A. Brew (1995) *Enhancing Learning through Self-Assessment* London: Kogan Page.

Brewer, I.M. (1985) *Learning More and Teaching Less* London: SRHE.

Brown, G. (1968) 'Role of examinations in society' *Conference Proceedings on Examinations,* Queens University, Belfast.

Brown, G. (1978) *Lecturing and Explaining* London: Methuen.

Brown, G. (1982) 'Two days on explaining and lecturing' *Studies in Higher Education* 2: 93–104.

Brown, G. (1992) 'How does self-assessment work?' Unpublished paper, University of Nottingham.

Brown, G. (1994a) 'Effective teaching' in R. Ellis (ed.) *Quality Assurance in University Teaching* Milton Keynes: Open University Press.

Brown, G. (1994b) *Professional Development Materials for Engineering Tutors* Sheffield: CVCP UCoSDA.

Brown, G. (1995) 'Learning enterprise or enterprising learning' in H. Gray (ed.) *Changing Higher Education: Going with the Grain* Sheffield: UCoSDA and Peat Marwick.

Brown, G. and Atkins, M. (1988) *Effective Teaching in Higher Education* London: Routledge.

Brown, G. and Atkins, M. (1996) 'Explaining' in O. Hargie (ed.) *Handbook of Communication Skills* London: Routledge.

Brown, G., Neerinck, D. and Lapiere, D. (1991) *Supervision of Science Research: An International Study* Brussels: Ministry of Education and Science.

Brown, G. and Pendlebury, M. (1992a) *Assessing Active Learning Vol. 1* Sheffield: CVCP UCoSDA.

Brown, G. and Pendlebury, M. (eds) (1992b) *Assessing Active Learning Vol. 2* Sheffield: CVCP UCoSDA.

Brown, G. and Pendlebury, M. (1992c) 'Audit in general medical and dental practice' in Frostick, S. and Wallace, A. (1992) (eds) *Medical Audit* Cambridge: Cambridge University Press.

Brown, G. and Pendlebury, M. (1996) *Effective Teaching in Dentistry* London: Royal College of Surgeons of England.

Brown, J.S. and van Lehn, K. (1980) 'Repair theory: A generative theory of bugs in procedural skills' *Cognitive Science* 4: 379–426.

Brown, S. and Dove, P. (eds) (1991) *Self and Peer-Assessment* Birmingham: SCED Paper 63.

Brown, S. and Knight, P. (1994) *Assessing Learners in Higher Education* London: Kogan Page.

Bruner, J. (1992) 'Another look at New Look 1' *American Psychologist* 47: 780–3.

Bull, J. (1993) *Using Technology to Assess Student Learning* Sheffield: TLTP Project ALTER, CVCP UCoSDA.

Bull, J. (1994) 'Computer-based assessment: some issues for consideration' *Active Learning* 1: 18–21.

Bull, J. and Otter, S. (1994) *Recording Achievement: Potential for Higher Education* Sheffield: CVCP UCoSDA.

Bull, J. and Stephens, D. (1996) 'The Use of Questionmark software to enhance learning through assessment in two UK universities' Paper presented at the 16th Annual Conference on Teaching and Learning in Higher Education, University of Ottawa, June 1996.

Burgess, R. and Lee, B. (1989) *Good Practice in Assessment: Criteria and Procedures for CNAA Undergraduate Courses* London: Council for National Academic Awards.

Butcher, V. and Ball, B. (1995) *Developing Students' Career Planning Skills: The Impact of the Enterprise in Higher Education Initiative.* Sheffield: Employment Department.

Butterworth, C. (1992) 'More than one bite at the APEL' *Journal of Further and Higher Education* 16: 39–51.

Candy, P., Crebert, G. and O'Leary, J. (1994) *Developing Lifelong Learners through Undergraduate Education* Canberra: Australian Government Publishing Service.

Carter, R., (1985) 'A taxonomy of objectives for professional education' *Studies in Higher Education* 10: 135–49.

CBI (1994) *Thinking Ahead: Ensuring the Expansion of Higher Education in the 21st Century* London: Confederation of British Industries.

Challis, M. (1993) *Introducing APEL* London: Routledge.

Chapman, K. (1996) *An Analysis of Inter-institutional Variability of Degree Results for UK Universities* London: Higher Education Quality Council.

Clanchy, J. and Ballard, B. (1992) *How to Write Essays* 3rd edn, London: Longman.

CNAA (1989) *How Shall We Assess Them?* London: Council for National Academic Awards.

Coates, H. and Wright, J. (1991) *The Integration of Work-based Learning into Academic Courses* Coventry: Coventry University.

Cockroft, R. and Cockcroft, S. (1992) *Persuading People: An Introduction to Rhetoric* London: Macmillan.

Cohen, L. (1971) 'Anxiety, ambiguity and supervisory style in relation to students' evaluation of their thin sandwich course experience' *Bulletin of Mechanical Engineering Education* 10: 297–302.

Collins, M. (1991) *Adult Education as Vocation* London: Routledge.

Colliver, J.A., Verhuist, S.J., Williams, R.G. and Norcini, J.J. (1989) 'Reliability of performance on standardised patient cases' *Teaching and Learning in Medicine* 1: 31–7.

Cornford, F.M. (1908) *Microcosmographica Academica* Cambridge: Mainsail Press. Reprinted 1993.

Cornwall, M., Schmitals, F. and Jaques, D. (eds) (1978) *Project Orientation in Higher Education* London: (now Centre for Studies in Higher Education, University of London Institute of Education).

Cox, R. (1967) 'Examinations and higher education' *Universities Quarterly* 21: 292–317.

Cox, R. (1986) 'Higher education assessment of students' in T. Husen and T.N. Postlethwaite (eds) *International Encyclopaedia of Education* Oxford: Pergamon Press.

Cryer, P. (ed.) (1992) *Effective Teaching and Learning in Higher Education* Sheffield: CVCP UCoSDA (12 modules).

Daines, J.M. (1986) 'Self-assessment in a laboratory course on dispensing' unpublished PhD, University of Nottingham.

Darby, J. and Gardner, N. (1991) *CTI Annual Report* Oxford: Computers in Teaching Initiative Support Service.

Davidson, G. (1992) *Modular Courses in Universities* Canterbury: University of Kent.

Davies, L. (1991) *Experience-based Learning in the Curriculum: A Synthesis Study.* Sheffield: Sheffield Hallam University.

Davis, H., Hutchings, G. and Hall, W. (1993) *Microcosm: A Hypermedia Platform for the Delivery of Learning Materials* CSTR, 93, 10.

De Bono, E. (1968) *The Five-day Course on Thinking* Harmondsworth: Penguin.

De Bono, E. (1973) *PO: Beyond Yes and No* Harmondsworth: Penguin.

Dempster, J. (1993) 'Question Mark for Windows, Life Sciences' *Educational Computing,* December: 37–43.

Dempster, J. (1994) 'Review: Question Mark Designer for Windows' *Active Learning* 1, December: 47–50.

Denicolo, P., Hounsell, D. and Entwistle, N.J. (1992) *What is Active Learning?* Sheffield: CVCP/UCoSDA.

Dewey, J. (1933) *How to Think* New York: Heath Publishers.

Diederich, P. (1957) *The Improvement of Essay Examinations* Princeton: Educational Testing Service.

Donald, J.G. (1986) 'Knowledge and the university curriculum' *Higher Education* 15: 267–82.

Dorsman, M. (1984) 'Experiential learning in undergraduate study' *Assessment and Evaluation in Higher Education,* 9: 57–61.

Dowdeswell, W.H. and Harris, W.D.C. (1979) 'Project work in university science' in D. McNally (ed.) *Learning Strategies in Science,* Cardiff: University of Cardiff Press.

Duckenfield, M. and Stirner, P. (1992) *Learning Through Work* London: HMSO.

Dunster, D.F. (1982) 'An instrument for the control of sandwich courses' *Vocational Aspects of Education* 34: 67–75.

Ebel, R.L. and Frisbie, D.A. (1986) *Essentials of Educational Measurement* Englewood Cliffs, NJ: Prentice Hall.

ED (1982) *Glossary of Terms in Employment and Education* Sheffield: Department of Employment.

ED (1990) *Higher Education Development: The Skills Link* Sheffield: Employment Department.

ED (1991) *Enterprise in Higher Education* Sheffield: Employment Department.

ED (1992a) *Working for Degrees* Sheffield: Employment Department.

ED (1992b) *The REAL Initiative on Assessment* Further information available from the Higher Education Branch, ED, Sheffield S1 4PQ.

ED (1993) *Higher Education and Employment: The HE Projects Fund Guidance for Applicants 1993/4* Sheffield: Employment Department.

Edgeworth, F.Y. (1890) 'The elements of chance in competitive examinations' *Journal of the Royal Statistical Society* 400–75, 644–63.

Eliot, T.S. (1958) *Collected Poems 1909–1935* London: Faber.

Elton, L.R.B. (1983) 'Improving the cost-effectiveness of laboratory teaching' *Studies in Higher Education* 8: 79–85.

Elton, L.R.B. (1987) *Teaching in Higher Education: Appraisal and Training* London: Kogan Page.

Entwistle A. and Entwistle, N.J. (1991) 'Contrasting forms of understanding in degree examinations: the student experience and its implications *Higher Education* 22: 205–27.

Entwistle, N.J. (1987) *Styles of Learning and Teaching* 2nd edn, Chichester: Wiley.

Entwistle, N.J. (1988) 'Motivational factors in students' approaches to learning' in R.R. Schmeck (ed.) *Learning Strategies and Learning Styles* New York: Plenum Press.

Entwistle, N.J. (1991) *The Impact of Teaching on Learning Outcomes* Sheffield: Department of Employment, higher education Branch.

Entwistle, N.J. (1992) *The Impact of Teaching on Learning Outcomes* (rev. edn). Sheffield: CVCP UCoSDA.

Entwistle, N.J. (1995) 'Frameworks for understanding as experienced in essay writing and in preparing for examinations' *Educational Psychologist* 30: 47–54.

Entwistle, N.J. (1996) 'Motivational factors in students' approach to learning' in R. Schmeck (ed.) *Learning Strategies and Learning Styles* New York: Plenum Press.

Entwistle, N.J., Hounsell, D.J., Macaulay, C., Siturayake, G. and Tait, H. (1989) *The Performance of Electrical Engineers in Scottish Higher Education* Edinburgh: Centre for Research in Learning and Instruction, University of Edinburgh.

Entwistle, N.J. and Marton, F. (1994) 'Knowledge objects: understanding constituted through intensive academic study' *British Journal of Educational Psychology* 62: 161–78.

Entwistle, N.J. and Ramsden, P. (1983) *Understanding Student Learning* London: Croom Helm.

Entwistle, N.J. and Tait, H. (1990) Approaches to learning, evaluation of teaching and preferences for contrasting academic environments' *Higher Education* 19: 169–94.

Entwistle, N.J. and Tait, H. (1992) *Learning Actively on One's Own* Sheffield: CVCP UCoSDA.

Entwistle, N.J., Wall, D., Macaulay, C., Tait, H. and Entwistle, D. (1991) *School to Higher Education: Bridging the Gap* Edinburgh: Centre for Research on Learning and Instruction, University of Edinburgh.

Eraut, M. (1985) 'Knowledge creation and knowledge use in professional contexts' *Studies in Higher Education* 10: 117–33.

Evans, N. (1988) *The Assessment of Prior Experiential Learning* London: CNAA.

Evans, N. (1992) *Experiential Learning: Assessment and Accreditation* London: Routledge.

Evans, N. and Turner, A. (1993) *The Potential of the Assessment of Experiential Learning in Universities* London: HMSO.

Exley, K. and Dennick, R. (eds) (1996) *Innovations in Teaching in Medical Sciences* Birmingham: SEDA.

Exley, K. and Moore, I. (eds) (1992) *Innovations in Science Teaching* Birmingham: SEDA.

Fabb, W.E. and Marshall, J.R. (1983) *The Assessment of Clinical Competence in General Family Practice* Lancaster: MIT Press.

Falchikov, N. (1991) 'Group process analysis' in S. Brown and P. Dove (eds) *Self and Peer-Assessment* Birmingham: SCED Paper 63.

Falchikov, N. (1994) 'Learning from peer feedback marking: student and teacher perspectives' in H.C. Foot, C.J. Howe, A. Anderson, A.K. Tolmie and D.A. Warder (eds) *Group and Interactive Learning* Southampton: Computational Mechanics Publications.

Falchikov, N. (1995a) 'Peer feedback marking: developing peer-assessment' *Innovations in Education and Training International* 32: 175–87.

Falchikov, N. (1995b) 'Improving feedback to and from students' in P. Knight (ed.) *Assessment for Learning in Higher Education* London: Kogan Page.

Falchikov, N. (1996a) 'Involving students in feedback and assessment' in D. Hounsell (ed.) (1996) *Rethinking Assessment* London: Kogan Page (in press).

Falchikov, N. (1996b) 'Improving learning through critical peer feedback and reflection' HERDSA conference papers, Perth, Western Australia.

Falchikov, N. and Boud, D. (1989) 'Student self-assessment in higher education: a meta-analysis' *Review of Educational Research* 59: 395–430.

FitzGerald, J., Burnett, M., Hughes, E., Manning, J., Shatto, S. and Thompson, J. (1994) 'Small group project work: making English work' in I. Sneddon and J. Kramer (eds) *An Enterprising Curriculum* Belfast: HMSO.

Freeman, J. (ed.) (1982) *The Influence of Trainers on Trainees in General Practice* London: Royal College of General Practitioners.

Fuller, A. and Saunders, M. (1990) 'Open learning in action: a case study of open learning in a large retailing company' in R. Farmer (ed.) *Making Learning Systems Work* London: Kogan Page.

Gabb, R. (1981) 'Playing the project game' *Assessment in Higher Education* 6: 26–48.

Garratt, R.M. and Roberts, I.F. (1982) 'Demonstration versus practical work in science. A critical review of studies since 1906' *Studies in Science Education* 9: 109–46.

Gibbs, G. (1990) *Improving Student Learning: Briefing Paper* Oxford: Oxford Centre for Staff Development.

Gibbs, G. (1992) *Discussion with more students* London: Polytechnic & Colleges Funding Council

Gibbs, G., Habeshaw, S. and Habeshaw, T. (1988) *53 Interesting Ways of Assessing Your Student* 2nd edn, Bristol: Technical and Educational Services.

Gibbs, G., Jenkins, A. and Wisker, G. (1992) *Assessing More Students* London: Polytechnic and College Funding Council (Teaching More Students series).

Glover, L. (1994) *Using IT for Assessment: Going Forward* Coventry: National Council for Educational Technology.

Gold, J.R., Jenkins, A., Lee, R., Monk, J., Riley, J., Shepherd, I. and Unwin, D. (1991) *Teaching Geography in Higher Education* Oxford: Blackwell.

Goldfinch, J. (1994) 'Further developments in peer-assessment of group projects' *Assessment and Evaluation in Higher Education* 9: 21–35.

Gray, H. (ed.) (1995) *Changing Higher Education: Going with the Grain* Sheffield: UCoSDA and Peat Marwick.

Gretton, R. (1992) *Admissions to Higher Education Project Report.* Sheffield: Employment Department and University of Sussex.

Griffiths, S. and Partington, P. (1992) *Enabling Active Learning in Small Groups* Sheffield: CVCP UCoSDA (this module includes a video tape of small-group discussions in a wide range of subjects).

Gronlund, N.E. (1988) *How to Construct Achievement Tests* Englewood Cliffs, NJ: Prentice Hall.

Halsey, A.H. (1992) *The Decline of Donnish Dominion* Oxford: Oxford University Press.

Halstead, P. (1994) 'Computer aided learning and assessment for programming skills' *Monitor*, CTI Centre for Computing, 4: 76–81.

Hammar, M.L., Forsberg, P.M.W. and Loftas, P.I. (1995) 'An innovative examination ending the medical curriculum' *Medical Education* 29: 452–7.

Harden, R. and Gleeson, F. (1979) 'Assessment of clinical competence using an objective structured clinical examination (OSCE)' *Medical Education* 13: 41–54.

Harden, R. and Cairncross, C. (1980) 'Assessment of practical skills' *Studies in Higher Education* 5: 187–96.

Harden, R.M. and Dunn, W.G. (1981) *Assessment: A Work Manual* Dundee: Centre of Medical Education.

Hargie, O. (ed.) (1996) *Handbook of Communication Skills* London: Routledge.

Harper, C. and Kember, D. (1989) 'Interpretation of factor analyses from the approaches to studying inventory' *British Journal of Educational Psychology* 59: 66–74.

Harris, N. and Bell, C. (1989) *Evaluating and Assessing for Learning* London: Kogan Page.

Hart, J. and Smith, M. (1994) *Innovations in Computing Teaching* Birmingham: SEDA Vol. 1.

Hart, J. and Smith, M. (1996) *Innovations in Computing Teaching* Birmingham: SEDA Vol. 2.

Harter, S. (1978) 'Effective motivation reconsidered' *Human Development* 26: 34–64.

Hartley, J.R. (ed.) (1991) *Technology and Writing: Readings in the Psychology of Written Communication* London: Kogan Page.

Hartog, P. and Rhodes, E.C. (1935) *An Examination of Examinations* London: Macmillan.

Hartog, P. and Rhodes, E.C. (1936) *The Marks of Examiners* London: Macmillan.

Hatton, N. and Smith, D. (1995) 'Reflection in teacher education: towards definition and implementation' *Teaching and Teacher Education* 11: 33–51.

Hedges, P.D. (1993) 'The assessment of individuals in a group-based simulated enquiry' Paper presented at the Higher Education for Capability Conference: Using Assessment to Develop Student Capability, University College London.

HEFCE (1993) *Assessment of the Quality of Education* Circular 3/93. Bristol: Higher Education Funding Council.

HEFCE (1994) *The Assessment of Educational Provision* Circular 39/94 Bristol: Higher Education Funding Council.

HEFCE (1996) *Assessors Handbook* Bristol: Higher Education Funding Council.

Hegarty-Hazel, E. (1979) 'The role of laboratory work in teaching microbiology at university level' Unpublished PhD, University of New South Wales, Sydney, Australia.

Hegarty-Hazel, E. (1982) 'The role of laboratory work in science courses', in M.B. Rowe (ed.) *Education in the 80s: Science* Washington, DC: National Education Association.

Hegarty-Hazel, E. (1989) 'Research on laboratory work' in D. Boud, J. Dunn and E. Hegarty-Hazel (eds) *Teaching in Laboratories* London: SRHE/NFER-Nelson.

Hegarty-Hazel, E. (ed.) (1990) *The Student Laboratory and the Science Curriculum* London: Routledge.

Henry, J. (1994) *Teaching through Projects* London: Kogan Page.

HEQC (1994) *Learning from Audit* London: Higher Education Quality Council.

HEQC (1995a) *Graduate Standards Programme: An Interim Report* London: Higher Education Quality Council.

HEQC (1995b) *Thresholds and Other Academic Standards: The Views of Four Subject Groups* London: Higher Education Quality Council.

HEQC (1996) *Academic Standards in the Approval, Review and Classification of Degrees* London: Higher Education Quality Council.

Herbert, M. (1990) *Planning a Research Project: A Guide for Practitioners and Trainees* London: Cassells.

Herron, M. (1971) 'The nature of scientific enquiry' *School Review* 79: 171–212.

Heywood, J. (1977; 2nd edn 1989) *Assessment in Higher Education* Chichester: John Wiley.

Hindle, B.P. (1993) 'The "Project" putting student-controlled, small group work and transferable skills at the heart of a geography course' *Journal of Geography in Higher Education* 17: 11–20.

Holland, S. (1987) 'New cognitive theories of harmony applied to direct manipulation tools for novices' *CITE Technical Report 17*, IET Open University, Milton Keynes.

Honey, P. and Mumford, A. (1983) *Using your Learning Styles* Maidenhead: Peter Honey.

Hopson, B. and Scally, M. (1992) *Time Management: Conquering the Clock* London: Mercury Publications.

Horobin, R. and Williams, M. (1992a) *Active Learning in Field Work and Project Work* Sheffield: CVCP UCoSDA.

Horobin, R. and Williams, M. (1992b) *Active Learning in Practical Classes* Sheffield: CVCP UCoSDA.

Hounsell, D. (1984) 'Learning and essay writing' in F. Marton, N.J. Entwistle and D. Hounsell (eds) (1984) *The Experience of Learning* Edinburgh: Scottish University Press.

Hounsell, D. (1995) 'Marking and commenting on essays' in F. Forster, D. Hounsell and S. Thompson (eds) *Tutoring and Demonstrating: A Handbook* Sheffield: CVCP UCoSDA.

Hounsell, D. (ed.) (1997) *Rethinking Assessment* London: Kogan Page (in press).

Hounsell, D. and Murray, R. (1992) *Essay Writing for Active Learning* Sheffield: CVCP UCoSDA.

Hounsell, D. and Thompson, S. (eds) (1995) *Tutoring and Demonstrating: A Handbook* Sheffield: CVCP UCoSDA.

Hubbard, R. (1991) *53 Interesting Ways of Teaching Mathematics* Bristol: Technical and Educational Services.

Hudson, L. (1996) *Contrary Imaginations* London: Methuen (repr. Penguin Books).

Hunter, R. and Cook, M. (1996) 'Learning to learn'. Paper given at 16th Annual Conference on Teaching and Learning in Higher Education, University of Ottawa, Canada. (Available from Learning Development Unit, University of Humberside, Hull HU6 7RT.)

Husbands, C.T. (1976) 'Ideological bias in the marking of examinations: a method of testing for its presence and its implications' *Research in Education* 15: 17–38.

Jackson, N. (1995) 'The road to universal modularity' *HEQC Update* 8: i–iv.

Jenkins, A. and Walker, L. (eds) (1994) *Developing Student Capability through Modular Courses* London: Kogan Page.

Jenkins, A. and Ward, A. (eds) (1995) *Developing Skill-based Curricula through the Disciplines: Case Studies of Good Practice in Geography* Birmingham: SEDA.

Jessup, G. (1991) *Outcomes: NVQs and the Emerging Model of Education and Training* London: Falmer Press.

Johnson-Laird, P.N. (1988) *The Computer and the Mind* London: Fontana.

Kemp, R. and Race, P. (1992) *Enabling the Development of Personal and Professional Skills* Sheffield: CVCP UCoSDA.

King, T. (1994) 'Using an optical mark reader for continuous student assessment: a case study in higher education' *Active Learning* 1: 23–5.

Klemp, G.O. (1977) 'Three factors of success' in D.W. Vermilly (ed.) *Relating Work and Education* San Francisco: Jossey Bass.

Klug, B. (1974) *Pro Profile* London: NUS Publications.

Klug, B. (1977) *The Grading Game* London: NUS Publications.

Kolb, D. (1976) *Learning Style Inventory: Technical Manual* Boston: McBer.

Kolb, D. (1984) *Experiential Learning: Experience as a Source of Learning* Englewood Cliffs, NJ: Prentice Hall.

Kulik, J.J. and Kulik, C.C. (1979) 'College teaching' in R.L. Peterson and H.J. Waldberg (eds) *Research on Teaching: Concepts, Findings and Implications* Berkeley: McCutchan.

Kulik, J.J. and Kulik, C.C. (1991) 'Effectiveness of computer-based instruction: an updated analysis' *Computers in Human Behaviour* 7: 75–95.

Landeen, J., Byrne, C. and Brown, B. (1992) 'Journal keeping as an educational strategy in teaching psychiatric nursing' *Journal of Advanced Nursing* 17: 347–55.

LMU (1996) *The Student Assessment Project* Internal document.

Laurillard, D. (1993) *Rethinking University Teaching* London: Routledge.

Laurillard, D., Swift, B. and Darby, J. (1993) 'Academics' use of courseware materials: a survey' *Association of Learning Technology Journal* 1: 4–14.

Lawson, A.E., Abraham, M.R. and Renner, J.W. (1989) *A Theory of Instruction: Using the Learning Cycle to Teach Scientific Concepts and Thinking Skills* Cincinnati: National Association for Research in Science Teaching.

Lee, B.S. (1995) 'Encouraging computing students to become reflective and autonomous learners through self-assessment' in J. Hart and M. Smith, *Innovations in Computing Teaching 2: Improving the Quality of Teaching and Learning*. SEDA Paper 91. Birmingham: Staff and Educational Development Association.

Lee, B.S., Benett, Y. and Potter, J. (1991) *Development of Placement and Assessment Procedures in Supervised Work Experience* London: CNAA.

Lee, B.S. and Tuck, R. (1992) *Workbased Learning and Self-Assessment* Huddersfield: Huddersfield Polytechnic.

Leigh, A. (1991) 'The assessment of vocational and academic competence' *Competence and Assessment* 17: 18–20. Sheffield: Employment Department publication.

Lewin, K. (1951) *Field Theory in Social Science* New York: Appleton Century Croft.

Lewis, R. (1984) *How to Help Learners Assess their Progress* London: Council for Educational Technology.

Lloyd, D., Martin, J.G., McCaffery, K. (1996) 'The introduction of computer-based testing on an engineering technology course' *Assessment and Evaluation in Higher Education* 21 (1): 83–91.

Loughlin, M. (1995) 'Brief encounter: a dialogue between a philosopher and an NHS manager on the subject of "quality"' *Journal of Evaluation in Clinical Practice* 1 (2): 81–5.

Lucas, J. (1994) 'Computer aided salvation virtually relief in four parts: a review of Question Mark Professional' *Geocal*, CTI Centre for Geography, June 1994: 25–8.

Lueddeke, G. (1995) *Perspectives on Change and Innovation in Higher Education* SRHE Annual Conference 'The Changing University' Edinburgh, December 1995. Available from the Teaching and Learning Development Unit, University of Bradford.

Lyons, F. (1994) *The Partnership Project and the Partnership Programme: Executive Summary.* Employment Department and University of Portsmouth.

MacDonald-Ross, G. (1992) 'The Hospers test' in G. Brown, and M. Pendlebury (eds) *Assessing Active Learning Vol. 2* Sheffield: CVCP UCoSDA.

MacDonald-Ross, G., Parry, J. and Cohen, M. (1992) *Philosophy and Enterprise in Higher Education* Leeds: University of Leeds.

Macfarlane, B. (1992) 'The Thatcherite Generation and Degree Results' *Journal of Further and Higher Education* 16: 107–13.

Mack, D., Partington, P., Simmons, C., von Hentz, M. and Wilson, A. (1996) *Making the Grade* Sheffield: CVCP UCoSDA. (This module contains several examples of video-recorded excerpts from lectures and seminars.)

Mager, R.F (1973) *Preparing Instructional Objectives* Palo Alto, Calif.: Fearon.

Maguire, P., Fairbairn, S. and Fletcher, C. (1986) 'Consultation skills of young doctors' *British Medical Journal* 292: 1573–8.

Mandel, S. (1988) *Effective Presentation Skills* London: Kogan Page.

Manogue, M. and Brown, G. (1995) 'Ten questions on assessment: some views of staff and students' Conference Proceedings of Association of Teachers of Restorative Dentistry, 1995.

Marton, F. and Booth, S. (1996) 'The learner's experience of learning' in D.R. Olsen and N. Torrance (eds) *The Handbook of Educational and Human Development* Oxford: Blackwell.

Marton, F., Hounsell, D. and Entwistle, N.J. (1984) (eds) *The Experience of Learning* Edinburgh: Scottish Academic Press.

Matthews, J. (1981) *The Use of Objective Tests* rev. edn, Lancaster: University of Lancaster Press.

Mayer, R.E. (1992) *Thinking, Problem-solving, Cognition* New York: Freeman.

McCabe, M. (1994) 'Computing practical exams for over-forties (large student numbers)' in *Monitor*, CTI Centre for Computing, 4: 82–8.

McGuiness, C. (1984) 'Staff and student development: a mixed model' in I. Sneddon and J. Kramer (eds) *An Enterprising Curriculum* Belfast: HMSO.

Meester, M.A.M and Maskill, R. (1993) *First Year Practical Classes in Undergraduate Chemistry Courses in England and Wales* London: Royal Society of Chemistry.

Mellor, A. (1991) 'Experiential learning through integrated project work: an example from soil science' *Journal of Geography in Higher Education* 15: 135–49.

Michaels, S. and Kierans, T.R. (1973) 'An investigation of open and closed book examinations in mathematics' *Alberta Journal of Educational Research* 19: 202–7.

Miller, Beth (1992) 'Peer and self-assessment' in G. Brown and M. Pendlebury (eds) *Asessing Active Learning Part 2* Sheffield: CVCP UCoSDA.

Miller, C. and Parlett, M. (1974) *Up to the Mark* London: SRHE.

Mitchell, K. and Anderson, J. (1986) 'Reliability of holistic scoring for the MCAT essay' *Educational and Psychological Measurement* 46: 771–5.

Mitchell, L. and Cuthbert, T. (1989) *Insufficient Evidence: The Final Report of the Competency Testing Project* Glasgow: SCOTVEC Project.

Power, M. (1994) *The Audit Explosion* London: Demos, Paper 7.

Montgomery, B.M. (1986) 'An interactionist analysis of peer-assessment' *Small Group Behaviour* 17: 19–37.

Moore, I. and Exley, K. (eds) (1994) *Alternative Approaches to Teaching Engineering* Sheffield: CVCP UCoSDA.

Morgan, A. (1983) 'Theoretical-based aspects of project-based learning in higher education' *British Journal of Educational Technology* 14: 66–79.

Morton-Cooper, A. and Palmer, A. (1993) *Mentoring and Preceptorship* Oxford: Blackwell.

Mowl, G. and Pain, R. (1995) 'Using self and peer-assessment to improve students' essay writing: a case study from geography' *Innovations in Education and Training International* 32: 324–55.

Moyse, R. (1992) 'A structure and design method for multiple viewpoints' *Journal of Artificial Intelligence in Education* 3: 207–33.

Murphy, R.J.L. (1979) 'Removing the marks from examination scripts before re-marking them. Does it make any difference?' *British Journal of Educational Psychology* 49: 73–8.

Myers, J.B. (1991) *Introduction to Type* Palo Alto, Calif.: Consulting Psychological Press.

Neill, N.T. (1993) 'Computer-based testing with Question Mark Professional' *Computer Education*, June: 23–6.

Nelson-Jones, R. (1986) *Human Relationship Skills: Training and Self Help* London: Holt, Rinehart & Winston.

Nelson-Jones, R. (1988) *Practical Counselling and Helping Skills* London: Holt, Rinehart & Winston.

Newble, D.I. (1992) 'Assessing clinical competence at the undergraduate level' *Medical Education* 26: 504–11.

Newble, D.I. and Jaeger, K. (1983) 'The effects of assessment and examinations on the learning of medical students' *Medical Education* 17: 25–31.

Newble, D.I. and Clarke, R. (1987) 'Approaches to learning in a traditional and an innovative medical school' in J.T.E. Richardson, M.W. Eysenck and D.W. Piper *Student Learning, Research in Education and Cognitive Psychology*, Milton Keynes: SRHE and Open University.

Newman, J.H. (1853) (1947 edn) *The Idea of a University* London: Longman Green.

Newstead, S. and Dennis, I. (1994) 'Examiners examined: The reliability of exam marking in psychology' *The Psychologist* 7: 216–19.

Newton, P.E. (1996) 'The reliability of marking of General Certificate of Secondary Education scripts: Mathematics and English' *British Educational Research Journal* 22: 405–20.

Nicholls, D. (1992) 'Making history students enterprising: "independent study" at Manchester Polytechnic' *Studies in Higher Education* 17: 167–80.

Nisbet, J. and Shouksmith, J. (1984) *The Seventh Sense* Edinburgh: Scottish Council for Research in Education.

Norman, D. (1977) *Teaching Learning Strategies* San Diego: California University Press.

Norman, D. (1980) 'Cognitive engineering in education' in D.J. Tumo and S. Reis (eds) *Problem-solving and Education* Hillsdale: Lawrence Erlbaum.

Norman, D. (1982) *Learning and Memory* San Francisco: Freeman.

Norman, G.R., Van Der Vleuten, C.P.M. and Graaf, E. de (1991) 'Pitfalls in the pursuit of objectivity: issues of validity, efficiency and acceptability' *Medical Education* 25: 119–26.

November, P. (1993) 'Journals for the journey into deep learning' *Research and Development in Higher Education* 16: 299–303.

Ogborn, J. (1977) *Practical Work in Undergraduate Science* London: Heinemann.

Otter, S. (1992) *Learning Outcomes in Higher Education* London: UDACE/HMSO.

Owen, S.V. and Freeman, R.D. (1987) 'What's wrong with three-option multiple items?' *Educational and Psychological Measurement* 47: 513–22.

Owers-Bradley, J. and Exley, K. (1993) 'Physics laboratory projects' in K. Exley and I. Moore (eds) *Innovations in Science Teaching* Birmingham: SEDA; Oxford: Blackwell.

Papert, S. (1980) *Mindstorms: Children, Computers and Powerful Ideas* Brighton: Harvester Press.

Partington, J. (1995) *Improving Examiners' Meetings: A Video-training Package* Sheffield: CVCP UCoSDA.

Partington, J., Brown, G. and Gordon, G. (1993) *Handbook for External Examiners in Higher Education* Sheffield: CVCP UCoSDA.

Pask, G. (1976) 'Styles and Strategies of Learning' *British Journal of Educational Psychology* 46: 12–23.

Perry, W.G. (1970) *Forms of Intellectual and Ethical Development in the College Years* New York: Holt, Rinehart & Winston.

Piaget, J. and Inhelder, B. (1969) *The Psychology of The Child* London: Routledge.

Pickering, M. and Crabtree, R.H. (1979) 'How students cope with a laboratory procedures class' *Journal of Chemical Education* 56: 487–8.

Pieron, H. (1963) 'Examens et docimologie: Paris', cited in R.J. Cox (1967) 'Examinations and higher education' *University Quarterly*, June: 292–340.

Plants, H.L., Dean, R.K., Sears, J.T. and Venable, W.S. (1980) 'A taxonomy of problem-solving activities and its implications for teaching' in J.L. Lubkin (ed.) *The Teaching of Elementary Problem-solving in Engineering and Related Fields* Washington, DC: American Society for Engineering Education.

Polya, G. (1957) *How to Solve It* 2nd edn, New York: Doubleday.

Polya, G. (1962) *Mathematical Discovery Vol. I: On Understanding, Learning and Teaching Problem-solving* New York: John Wiley.

Power, M. (1994) *The Audit Explosion* London: Demos, Paper 7.

Pritchett, N. and Zakrzeswki, S. (1996) 'Interactive computer assessment of large groups: student responses' *Innovation in Education and Training International* 33: 242–7.

Proctor, A. and Donoghue, D. (1994) 'Computer-based assessment: a case study in geography', *Active Learning* 1: 29–34.

Prosser, M. and Millar, R. (1989) 'The how and why of learning physics' *European Journal of Psychology of Education* 4: 513–28.

Ramsden, P. (1988) (ed.) *Improving Student Learning* London: Kogan Page.

Ramsden, P. (1992) *Learning to Teach in Higher Education* London: Routledge.

Ramsden, P. and Entwistle, N.J. (1981) 'Effects of academic departments on students' approach to studying' *British Journal of Educational Psychology* 51: 368–83.

Rankin, J. (1972) 'The future of the integrated sandwich course' *Industrial Training International 1972* 60–2.

Reason, J. (1990) *Human Error* Cambridge: Cambridge University Press.

Resnick, L. and Omanson, S. (1987) 'Learning to understand arithmetic' in R. Glaser (ed.) *Advances in Instructional Psychology Vol. 3* Hillsdale, NJ: Lawrence Erlbaum.

Richardson, J.T.E. (1995) 'Approaches to studying of mature students' *Studies in Higher Education* 20: 5–12.

RISE (1985) *An Assessment of the Costs and Benefits of Sandwich Education* Research into Sandwich Education Committee. London: Department of Education and Science.

Robbins, Lord (chmn) (1963) *Higher Education* London: HMSO Committee on Higher Education Command 2154.

Robertson, D. (1994) *Choosing to Change: Extending Access, Choice and Mobility in Higher Education* London: Higher Education Quality Council.

Rowntree, D. (1987) *Assessing Students – How Shall We Know Them?* London: Harper & Row.

Rudd, E. (1985) *A New Look at Postgraduate Failure* London: SRHE.

Ryans, D.G. (1960) *Characteristics of Teachers* Washington, DC: American Council on Education.

Saljo, R. (1979) *Learning in the Learners' Perspective: Some Common-sense Conceptions* Gothenberg Institute of Education, University of Gothenburg.

Saunders, M. (1995) 'The integrative principle: higher education and work-based learning in the UK' *European Journal of Education* 30: 203–16.

Saxton, J. and Ashworth, P. (1990) 'The workplace supervision of sandwich degree placement students' *Management Education and Development* 21: 133–49.

Schmidt, H.G. Norman, G.R. and Boshuzen, H.P.A. (1990) 'A cognitive perspective on medical expertise: theory and implications' *Academic Medicine* 65: 611–21.

Schoenfeld, A.H. (1985) *Mathematical Problem-solving* New York: Academic Press.

Schon, D.A. (1983) *The Reflective Practitioner* London: Temple Smith.

Schon, D.A. (1988) *Educating the Reflective Practitioner* San Francisco: Josscy-Bass.

Sellman, R. (1991) 'Hooks for tutorial agents: a note on discovery learning environments' *CITE Technical Report 145*, IET, Open University, Milton Keynes.

Shaw, M. (1987) 'The tutorial: an analysis of skills'. Unpublished PhD thesis, University of Nottingham.

Shaw, M. (1992) 'Monitoring the acquisition of enterprise skills: a novel approach' in G. Brown and M. Pendlebury (eds) *Assessing Active Learning Vol 2* Sheffield: CVCP UCoSDA.

Shaw, M. (1995) 'Assuring quality and standards in a large modular scheme' *Innovations in Education* 3: 1–20.

Shaw, M. (1996) *Developing Capabilities* Internal document, Leeds Metropolitan University.

Shymansky, J.A., Kyle W.C. and Pennick, J.E. (1980) 'How do science laboratory assistants teach?' *Journal of College Science Teaching* 9: 24–7.

Silver, H. and Williams, R. (1994) *Using External Examiners: A Report to Open University Validation Services* Milton Keynes: Open University Quality Support Centre.

Simon, R. (1988) 'For a pedagogy of possibility' *Critical Pedagogy Networker* 1: 1–4.

Simosko, S. (1991) *Accreditation of Prior Learning: A Practical Guide for Professionals* London: Kogan Page.

Slavin, R.E. (1990) 'Mastery learning reconsidered' *Educational Research* 60: 300–2.

Smith, J.K. (1982) 'Converging on correct answers: a peculiarity of multiple choice items' *Journal of Educational Measurement* 3: 211–20.

Smithers, A. (1976) *Sandwich Course: An Integrated Education?* Slough: NFER.

SRHE (1995) 'Illuminating mentoring' *SRHE News* 8: 7–8 London: Society for the Study of Higher Education.

Stalenhoef-Halling, B.F., van der Vleuten, C., Jaspers, J. and Fiolet, J. (1990) 'The feasibility, acceptability and reliability of open-ended questions in problem-based learning curricula' in W. Bender, R. Hiemstra, A. Scherpbier and R. Zwiestra (eds) *Teaching and Assessing Clinical Competence* Groningen: Boekwerk.

Starfield, A.M., Smith, K.A. and Bleloch, A.L. (1990) *How to Model It: Problem-solving for the Computer Age* New York: McGraw Hill.

Steffe, L. and Gale, J. (1995) (eds) *Constructivism in Education* Hillsdale, NJ: Erlbaum.

Stephens, D. (1994) 'Using computer-assisted assessment: time saver or sophisticated distraction? *Active Learning* 1: 11–15.

Stephens, D. (1995) Results of a survey of the use of computer-assisted assessment in higher education in the UK. Available from Dept of Library and Information Studies, University of Loughborough. Paper presented at Association of Learning Technology Conference, September 1995.

Stephenson, J. and Weil, S. (1992) *Quality in Learning* London: Kogan Page.

Stoney, C. and Shaw, M. (1996) 'Assuring standards in a large modular scheme – two years on' *Innovations and Learning in Education* 2: 23–7.

Swanson, D.B. (1987) 'A measurement framework for performance-based tests' in J.R. Hart and R.M. Harden *Further Developments in Assessing Clinical Competence* Montreal: Can-Heal Publications.

Tennyson, R.D., Elmore, R.L. and Snyder, L. (1990) 'Advancements in instructional design theory: contextual module analysis and integrated instructional strategies' *Educational Technology Research and Development* 40 (2): 9–22.

Tisher, R.P. and White, R.T. (1986) 'Research on natural science' in M.C. Wittrock (ed.) (1986) *Handbook of Research on Teaching* 3rd edn, New York: MacMillan, 874–905.

Thomas, P. and Bain, G. (1984) 'Contextual differences of learning approaches: the effects of assessment' *Human Learning* 3: 227–40.

Thompson, R.A. (1973) 'Assessment of industrial training' *Education in Chemistry* 10: 138–9.

Thyne, J.M. (1966) *The Psychology of Learning and Techniques of Teaching* 2nd edn, London: University of London Press.

Tomlinson, P. and Kilner, S. (1991) *The Flexible Learning Framework and Educational Theory* Sheffield: Employment Department.

Tolley, G. (1985) 'Learning and assessment' *Education Today* 35: 20.

Topping, J. (1975) 'Sandwich courses' *Physics Education* 10: 141–3.

Trowler, P. (1996) 'Angels in marble? Accrediting prior experiential learning in higher education' *Studies in Higher Education* 21: 17–30.

Turney, C. (ed.) (1984) *Skills of Supervision* Sydney: University of Sydney Press.

Usher, R.S. and Bryant, I. (1989) *Adult Education as Theory, Practice and Research: The Captive Triangle*. London: Routledge.

Van der Vleuten, C.P.M., Norman, G.R. and de Graaf, E. (1991) 'Pitfalls in the pursuit of objectivity: issues of reliability' *Medical Education* 25: 110–18.

Vernon, D.T.A. and Blake, R.L. (1994) 'Does problem-based learning work? A meta-analysis of evaluative research' *Academic Medicine* 69: 550–63.

Wagenaar, T.C. (1984) 'Using student journals in sociology courses' *Teaching Sociology* 11: 419–37.

Walker, D. (1995) 'Writing and reflection' in D. Boud, R. Keogh and D. Walker (eds) *Reflection: Turning Experience into Learning* London: Kogan Page.

Wankat, P.C. and Oreovicz, F.S. (1993) *Teaching Engineering* New York: McGraw-Hill.

Watkins, D. (1982) 'Identifying the study process dimensions of Australian university students' *Australian Journal of Education* 26 (1): 76–85.

Watkins, D. and Hattie, J. (1985) 'A longitudinal study of the approaches to learning of Australian tertiary students' *Human Learning* 4: 127–41.

Watson, G. (1989) *Writing a Thesis: A Guide to Long Essays and Dissertations* London: Longman.

Welsh, J. (1981) 'The PhD student at work' *Studies in Higher Education* 6: 159–62.

Wertheimer, M. (1957) *Productive Thinking* London: Associated Book Publishers.

Wetherall, J. and Mullins, G. (1996) 'The use of student journals in problem-based learning' *Medical Education* 30: 105–11.

Whelan, G. (1988) 'Improving medical students' clinical problem-solving' in P. Ramsden (ed.) *Improving Learning: New Perspectives* London: Kogan Page.

Wickelgren, W.A. (1974) *How to Solve Problems* rev. edn, San Francisco: Freeman.

Wills, S. and McNaught, C. (1996) 'Evaluation of computer-based learning in higher education' *Journal of Computing in Higher Education* 7: 106–28.

Wilson, L.R. (1969) 'A research approach to the introductory laboratory' *Journal of Chemical Education* 46: 447–50.

Wittrock, M. (1986) 'Students' Thought Processes' in M. Wittrock (1986) (ed.) *Handbook of Research on Teaching* New York: Macmillan.

Woods, D.R. (1987) 'How might I teach problem-solving?' in J.E. Stice (ed.) *Developing Critical Thinking and Problem-solving Abilities* San Francisco: Jossey-Bass.

Wright, J. (1991) 'Studies of research supervision' Unpublished PhD thesis, University of Nottingham.

Wright, J. and Lodwick, R. (1989) 'The process of the PhD: a study of the first years of doctoral study' *Research Papers in Education* 4: 22–56.

Yager, R., Engen, H.B. and Snider, B.C.F. (1969) 'Effects of the laboratory and demonstration methods upon the outcomes of instruction' *Journal of Research in Science Teaching* 6: 76–86.

Yorke, M (1996) 'Rating the rankings.' Paper presented at the 36th AIR Forum, Albuquerque, New Mexico, 5–8 May 1996.

Zimbardo, P., Erbeson, E. and Maslach, C. (1977) *Influencing Attitudes and Changing Behaviour* Massachusetts: Addison-Wesley.

# Index

A levels 18–19
Abouserie, R. 27
accountability: peer-assessment 171; self-assessment 185
accreditation of prior achievements (APA) 190
accreditation of prior assessed learning (APAL) 19, 190
accreditation of prior experiential learning (APEL) 19, 190–2
accreditation of prior learning (APL) 19, 190–92
accreditation of prior learning achievements (APLA) 190
achievement motivation 23–4
Adderly, K. 121
Albano, M.G. 212
Alexander, S. 215
Allison, I. 113
Anderson, J. 73
Andreson, L. 93
Annett, J. 35
anthropology 266
archaeology 266
architecture 266–7
Aristotle 156, 254
Arnold, P. 121
artefacts 127
Ashbury, J.E. 186
Ashworth, P. 193, 199
ASKIT analysis 163
assessment: changing procedures see change; criteria see criteria; criteria-graded 12; criterion-referenced 10–11, 244–6, 251; designing 49–55; developmental 9; effect on learning 7–8; essays see essays; formative 12, 251; group 3–4; importance of 7–8, 24; instruments 41–2; judgmental 9; marking see marking; methods/strategies 40–58; modular see modular assessment; normative 251; norm-referenced 11–12; objectives/outcomes 17, 25; peer-assessment see peer-assessment; practical work see practical work; product-process 16–17; publications 40–1; purposes 10; quality assessment 250–3; self-assessment see self-assessment; sources 41–2; summative 12, 251; systems 8–9; terminology 10–13; time management see time management; trends 13–19; tutor-led–student-led 15–16
Assessment Strategies in Scottish Higher Education (ASSHE) 40
Assiter, A. 189
Atkins, M.J. 23, 36, 59, 109, 130, 142, 154, 157, 164, 166, 205–6, 252, 256, 258, 262
audience 109
Authorware Professional 215–16

Bain, G. 7
Ball, B. 189
Balla, J. 143
Ballard, B. 59, 72
Barnett, R. 18, 252, 258
Barnett Report (1994) 252
Barrass, R. 72
Begg, D. 215
Bell, J. 121
Bell, R.C. 234
Benford, S. 217
Berg, B. 223, 225, 231
Berliner, D. 27

BIAS interaction system 162
Biggs, J. 7, 23, 25
Black, J. 130
Blake, R.L. 7–8, 141
Bliss, J. 99
Bloom, B.S. 36, 144
Bloor, M. 192
Booth, A. 41
Booth, S. 122
Boscolo, C. 161
Boshuizer, H.P.A. 181
Boud, D. 3, 32, 109, 116, 174, 178,
    179, 180
Bowden, J. 143
Brew, A. 170
Brewer, I.M. 109
Brown, G. 3, 15, 23, 40, 50, 59, 86,
    104, 109, 121, 130, 142, 154, 157,
    160, 164, 166, 178, 226, 233, 238,
    265
Brown, J.S. 143
Brown, S. 7, 31, 170, 181
Bruner, J. 35
Bryant, I. 192
Bull, J. 3, 40, 189, 204, 205, 212,
    217–18, 219, 220
Burgess, R. 44
Burke, E. 217
Business and Technical Council (BTEC)
    17, 257
Butcher, C. 105, 111
Butcher, V. 189
Butterworth, C. 191, 192

Cairncross, C. 103
Candy, P. 36, 37
capabilities 18, 36
Carter, R. 36
cases/open problems 46
CEILIDH (Computer Environment for
    Interactive Learning in Diverse
    Habitats) 217
Challis, M. 186
change 222–32; approaches 223–31;
    resistance to 222–3
Chapman, K. 255
checklists 42, 53; projects 127–30
Clanchy, J. 59, 72
Clarke, R. 7
classics 266
Coates, H. 199
Cohen, L. 193
Cohen, M. 53

collaborative learning 17
Collins, M. 192
Colliver, J.A. 36
competencies 17–18, 244–6; clinical
    35–6; and national standards 257–8;
    self-assessment 185–6
competition–collaboration 17
computer-aided instruction (CAI) 206
Computer Aided Learning Mathematics
    (CALM) 207
computer-assisted assessment (CAA)
    204–21
computer-assisted learning (CAL)
    204–18
computer-based learning (CBL) 206
computer-based teaching (CBT) 206
computers 202–21
concept maps 150
concurrency 242
consistency 236–8
consultations 166–8
Cook, M. 31
coping strategies 55–7
Cornford, F.M. 223
courses: assessment 18; design 53–4
coursework: assessment 12, 13–14;
    concurrency 242; varying 44
Cowper, William 66
Cox, R. 13
Crabtree, R.H. 100
credit exchange system 191
criteria 16, 41–2, 53; essay marking
    67–9; projects 127–30; validity 243
criteria-graded assessment 12
criterion-referenced assessment 10–11,
    244–6, 251
Cryer, P. 40
curriculum planning 198
Cuthbert, T. 258

Daines, J.M. 99
Darby, J. 204, 219
Davies, L. 194
Davis, H. 215
De Bono, E. 142
deep learning 27
Deering Report on Higher Education 231
Denicolo, P. 21
Dennick, R. 40, 109, 121, 170
Dennis, I. 171, 234
developmental assessment 9
Dewey, J. 3, 30
DIADS system 216–17

diaries, learning *see* logs
Diederich, P. 234
discussion: assessing management
    157–60; assessing quality 160–1
dissertations 47; assessing 127–30;
    reading 130–1; *see also* projects
Donald, J.G. 35
Donoghue, D. 213
Dorsman, M. 193
Dove, P. 31, 170, 181
Dowdeswell, W.H. 121
drill and practice 207
Duckenfield, M. 193
Dunn, W.G. 88
Dunne, J. 109, 116
Dunster, D.F. 197

Ebel, R.L. 85, 233, 244
economics 267–8
Edgeworth, F.Y. 234
Effective Engineering Education Project
    3, 40
effectiveness 1–2, 50–1, 229
efficiency 1, 229
Eliot, T.S. 208–9
Elton, L.R.B. 98
enablement 2, 229
Engen, H.B. 98
English literature 268–9
Enterprise in Higher Education
    Programme 3
Enterprise Learning 31
Entwistle, A. 25
Entwistle, N.J. 8, 18, 19, 21, 23, 24, 25,
    26, 27, 146
EQL interactive assessor 215
Eraut, M. 36–7
essays 46, 59–83; conversion of grades to
    marks 74; feedback 69–72; marking
    64–74; model answers 73; modified
    essay questions (MEQs) 77–80,
    150–1; question-design 61–4; single
    essay examinations 47; structured
    marking 73; varying methods 74–81;
    versus MCQs 76–7, 95–6; writing
    59–60
ethos 157
Evans, N. 186, 190, 191, 194
examinations: 168-hour 43; external
    examiner 246–7; open-book 42–3,
    150; orals 44, 47; prior-notice topics
    43; questions 265–75; single essay 47;
    varying 42–4; written 13–14

Examine 214–15
Exley, K. 40, 41, 109, 121, 170
experiential learning 19, 190–2
explanations 154–7
external examiners 246–7

Fabb, W.E. 80
Falchikov, N. 31, 32, 170, 171, 173, 180
feedback 4–5, 21, 51–5; essays 69–72;
    global reports 73–4; learning journals
    187; marking for 51, 69–72, 73–4;
    peer-assessment 171–3; practicals 108,
    113; presentations 154–7;
    problem-solving 146–8; projects
    123–4, 137–8; self-assessment 178;
    time management 52–3; video *see*
    video feedback
Fenwick, A. 189
Filemaker Pro 74
FitzGerald, J. 121
formative assessment 12, 251
Foxley, E. 217
Freeman, J. 80
Freeman, R.D. 84, 94
French literature 269
Freudian psychology 178
Frisbie, D.A. 85, 233, 244
Fuller, A. 193

Gabb, R. 122
Gale, J. 122
Gapmaster 218
Gardner, N. 204
Garratt, R.M. 99
geography 269–70
German literature 269
Gestalt psychology 142
Gibbs, G. 24, 40, 43, 69, 177
Gleeson, F. 103
Glover, L. 205
Gold, J.R. 86
Goldfinch, J. 174
Gordon, G. 40, 233, 238
grades: conversion into marks 74; as
    incentive 54
Graduate Studies Programme 254–7
graduateness 255–7
Gray, H. 3
Gretton, R. 189
Griffiths, S. 160
Gronlund, N.E. 85, 233
group assessment 3–4
group projects 47, 136–7

Habeshaw, S. 43
Habeshaw, T. 43
Halsey, A.H. 222
Halstead, P. 217
Hammar, M.L. 43
Harden, R. 103
Harden, R.M. 88
Hargie, O. 33
Harper, C. 7
Harris, W.D.C. 121
Hart, J. 41, 204, 218
Harter, S. 54
Hartley, J.R. 206
Hartog, P. 234
Hattie, J. 7
Hatton, N. 3, 30, 180–1
Hedges, P.D. 175
Hegarty-Hazel, E. 99, 109, 116
Henry, J. 121
Herbert, M. 121
Heywood, J. 239
higher education, purposes of 260–3
Higher Education Funding Councils
    (HEFCs) 223, 251–3, 254–5
Higher Education Quality Council
    (HEQC) 254–5; Quality Audit Group
    259–60
Hindle, B.P. 121
history 270
holistic learning 32
Holland, S. 209
Honey, P. 31
Hopson, B. 124
Horobin, R. 109, 121
Hounsell, D. 40, 55, 59, 60, 69, 72
Hubbard, R. 142, 150
Hudson, L. 142
Hunter, R. 31
Hyland, P. 41
hypermedia 207–9
hypertext 207–9

Inhelder, B. 30
interaction analysis 162
Internet 203

Jackson, N. 18
Jaeger, K. 7
Jenkins, A. 18, 41
Jessup, G. 17, 35, 244, 257
Johnson-Laird, P.N. 142
journals, learning see logs
judgmental assessment 9

Kember, D. 7
Kemp, R. 124, 142, 157
Kierans, T.R. 43
Kilner, S. 33
King, T. 220
Klemp, G.O. 37
Klug, B. 13
Knight, P. 7
knowledge-seeking 23–7
Knox, J.D.E. 79
Kolb, D. 3, 23, 30–1, 186
Kulik, C.C. 51, 205
Kulik, J.J. 51, 205
Kyle, W.C. 99

laboratory work see practical work
Landeen, J. 186
language: assessing 161–4; learning 32
Laurillard, D. 23, 122, 142, 143, 207,
    208, 219
law 270–1
Lawson, A.E. 116
learning 21–39; academic 23–7;
    collaborative 17; computer-assisted
    204–18; contract assessment 195; cycle
    (Kolb) 30–2; deep 27; definition 21;
    diaries see logs; environment 26;
    experiential 19, 190–2; holistic 32;
    knowledge-seeking 23–7; learning to
    learn (meta-cognition) 178, 181; logs
    see logs; motivation see motivation;
    orientations 23–7; outcomes 17, 25,
    31–2; and personality 27;
    portfolio-based 187, 192;
    problem-centred approaches 27 (see
    also problem-solving); processes 21–2;
    in professional contexts 29–32;
    reflective see reflective learning;
    reproductive 7–8, 24–5, 27; serial 32;
    skills see skills; stages of development
    28–9; studies of 22–33; styles 7–8,
    23–4, 30–2, 99–100; surface 27;
    taxonomies 36–8; understanding-
    seeking 23–7; verbal 33; visual 33;
    work-based 192–9
Learning from Experience Trust 194
Lee, B.S. 44, 194
Leigh, A. 17
Lewin, K. 30, 223
Lewis, R. 170
Lloyd, D. 205
Lodwick, R. 121
logos 156

logs 151, 186–7, 196; assessment 3;
  practicals 46, 102–3, 108; projects 134
Loughlin, M. 63
Lucas, J. 213
Lueddeke, G. 223
LUISA 218
Lyons, F. 194

McCabe, M. 217
MacDonald-Ross, G. 53, 87
Macfarlane, B. 255
McGuiness, C. 121
Mack, D. 160
Mackenzie, D.M. 217
McNaught, C. 220
McPherson, J. 77
Mager, R.F. 245
Maguire, P. 166
Mandel, S. 157
Manogue, M. 226
marking 49–55; anonymous 235;
  computer-aided 210–12; computer
  recording/transmitting 218;
  consistency 236–8; criteria 67–9;
  delegation 53; essays 64–74; feedback
  51, 69–72, 73–4; multiple choice
  questions 84; peer feedback marking
  171–2; peer marking 171, 174–6;
  problem-solving 145–6; projects
  136–7; reducing variability 66–7;
  reliability 234–6; schemes 42;
  structured 73; for summative purposes
  73; time management 52–3, 72–4
Marshall, J.R. 80
Marton, F. 22, 23, 25, 122
Maskill, R. 100
Matthews, J. 92, 95
Mayer, R.E. 142, 143
medical students: assessment 43–4;
  clinical competence 35–6, 43; oral
  examination 44
Meester, M.A.M. 100
Mellor, A. 121
memorising 32
mentors 4–5
meta-cognition 178, 181
Michaels, S. 43
microworlds 209
Millar, R. 23, 143
Miller, B. 174
Miller, C. 226
Millican, P. 236
mini-practicals 46–7, 103–5

Mitchell, K. 73
Mitchell, L. 258
modelling 209
modified essay questions (MEQs) 77–80,
  150–1
modular assessment 18; tactics 54
modularity 230–1, 256
Montgomery, B.M. 174
Moore, I. 40, 41, 109, 121, 170
Morgan, A. 122
Morrision, P. 193
Morton-Cooper, A. 4
motivation 27; achievement motivation
  23–4; and standards 258–9
Mowl, G. 171
Moyse, R. 209
Mullins, G. 186
multi-media 111
multiple choice questions 46, 84–97;
  alternatives per item 93–4; analyses
  94–5; assertion-reason 92; best answers
  89–91; computer-assisted learning 205;
  computer marking 210–12;
  construction 85; design 84;
  discrimination 94–5; exceptions-based
  88–9; extending 85–93; facility 94;
  guessing corrections 93; guidelines 86;
  item arrangement 94; and learning
  styles 7–8; marking 84; matching
  items 91–2; medicine 211–12; peer
  marking 171, 174–6; pooling 95;
  pre-tests/post-tests 94–5; preparation
  time 93; problem-solving 150;
  reliability 235–6; self-assessment 86;
  standard MCQs 87; technical aspects
  93–6; terminology 85; true/false 87–8;
  versus essays 76–7, 95–6
Mumford, A. 31
Murphy, R.J.L. 234
Murray, R. 59, 69, 72
Myers, J.B. 23

National Council of Vocational
  Qualifications (NCVQ) 186
National Record of Achievement 189
national standards 257–8
National Vocational Qualifications
  (NVQs): competencies 17, 244–6;
  standards 257–8
Neill, N.T. 213
Nelson-Jones, R. 5
Newble, D.I. 7, 36
Newman, J.H. 35

Newstead, S. 171, 234
Newton, P.E. 234
Nicholls, D. 121
Nisbet, J. 181
Nixon, N. 189
Norman, D. 27, 28, 32
Norman, G.R. 42, 96, 181
normative assessment 251
norm-referenced assessment 11
November, P. 186

Objective Structured Clinical
    Examinations (OSCE) 103–4
objectives 17, 25
Ogborn, J. 99, 109
O'Halloran, C. 206
Omanson, S. 143
open-book examination 42–3, 150
optimal mark readers (OMRs) 204, 210
oral communication 154–69
oral presentations see presentations
orals (vivas) 44, 47, 164–6; projects
    131–3
Oreovicz, F.S. 23, 144
Östergren, B. 223, 225, 231
Otter, S. 3, 17, 21, 37, 40, 189, 255
outcomes 17, 25, 31–2
Owen, S.V. 84, 94
Owers-Bradley, J. 121

Pain, R. 171
Palmer, A. 4
papers 81
Papert, S. 209
Parlett, M. 226
Parry, J. 53
Partington, J. 40, 233, 238
Partington, P. 160
Partnership Project 194
partnerships, work-based learning 198
Pask, G. 32
pathos 156
peer-assessment 15–16, 42, 53, 170,
    171–6, 181–2; criteria 174–5;
    feedback 171–3; introducing 181–2;
    research 173–4; using 174–6
peer feedback marking 171–2
peer marking 171, 174–6
Pendlebury, M. 40, 50, 86, 104
Pennick, J.E. 99
Performance Evaluation Guides (PEG)
    104–5
Perry, W.G. 5, 23, 28–9

personality 27
philosophy 271–2
Piaget, J. 30
Pickering, M. 100
Pieron, H. 234
placements 193–5; matching students
    198
Plants, H.L. 144
Plato 254
politics 272
Polya, G. 142
portfolio-based learning 187, 192
poster sessions 47; practicals 109;
    projects 133; work-based learning
    196–7
Power, M. 259
practical work 98–119; alternative
    approaches 109–12; audience 109;
    auditing 100–2; draft reports 108;
    feedback 108, 113; goals 98–9;
    laboratory report sheets 103; learning
    styles 99–100; method menus 110–11;
    mini-practicals 46–7, 103–5;
    multi-media 111; objectives 100;
    observation 112–13; poster sessions
    109; reports/notebooks 46, 102–3,
    108; research labs 110; seminars 109;
    students as teachers 108; task-
    orientated 109–10; theory–practice
    111–12; usefulness 115–16; versus
    written tests 113–14
predictability 242–3
presentations 47, 81; assessment 154–7;
    feedback 154–7; projects 134;
    work-based learning 197
prior learning: assessment 190–2;
    competency approaches 186
Pritchett, N. 214
problem-solving 35, 46, 141–53;
    designing problems 145; feedback
    146–8; marking 145–6;
    misconceptions 143–4; multiple choice
    questions 150; publications 142;
    strategies 143; strategy development
    146–9; studies of 142–4; taxonomy
    144
Proctor, A. 213
product-process assessment 16–17
profiles 189–90
Project ALTER 40
projects 47, 120–40; assessing 122–3,
    127–35; checklists 127–30; criteria
    127–30; feedback 123–4, 137–8;

group projects 47, 136–7; guidelines
121; logbooks 134; marking 136–7;
objectives 122–3; poster sessions/
exhibitions 133; presentations 134;
reports 196; research on 121–2;
structured approaches 124–6;
supervisors 122, 130; time
management 124, 137–8; timetabling
125; tutorials 123–4; vivas 131–3;
weighting difficulty 130; and written
examinations 134–5
Prosser, M. 23, 143
psychology: examination questions
272–3; Freudian 178; Gestalt 142

quality: assessment 250–3; assurance
259–60; and standards 253–9
Question Mark 213–14, 217–18
Quizmaker 215

Race, P. 124, 142, 157
Ramsden, P. 7, 8, 21, 23, 26, 28, 122,
142, 143
Rankin, J. 193, 197
Reason, J. 146
records of achievement 189–90
reflective learning 3, 29–30; self-
assessment 185–6; self-assessment tasks
180–1
reflective practice assignments 47
reliability 233–8; competencies 244–6;
external examiners 246–7
reproductive learning 7–8, 24–5, 27
Resnick, L. 143
rhetoric 156–7
Rhodes, E.C. 234
Richardson, J.T.E. 19
Robbins, Lord 255
Roberts, I.F. 99
Robertson, D. 191
role play 166–8
Rowntree, D. 66, 249, 250
Rudd, E. 121
Ryans, D.G. 157

Saljo, R. 21, 143
sampling 8
sandwich placements see placements
Saunders, M. 193, 194
Saxton, J. 193, 199
Scally, M. 124
Schmidt, H.G. 21, 181
Schoenfeld, A.H. 142

Schon, D.A. 3, 29
scientific learning cycle 115–16
Scottish Vocational Education Council
(SCOTVEC) 257
self-assessment 15–16, 31–2, 42, 170,
176–84; competencies 185–6;
computerised 212; criteria 174–5, 179,
182–4; development approach 185–6;
feedback 178; introducing 181–2;
MCQs 86; related approaches
185–201; research 180–1; tasks,
designing 182–4; time management
174; uses 178–9; work-based learning
194
Sellman, R. 209
seminars 109
serial learning 32
Shaw, E. 189
Shaw, M. 31, 36, 123, 256
short answer questions 46, 76–7
Shouksmith, J. 181
Shymansky, J.A. 99
Silver, H. 246
Simon, R. 192
Simosko, S. 191
simulations 209
single essay examinations 47
skills: cognitive 33–5; definitions 33; and
learning 33–6; perceptual 33–4;
presentation skills 154–7; required of
graduates 36–7; social 35; taxonomies
36–8; transferable 18, 35–6; writing
74, 80–81
Slavin, R.E. 41
Smith, D. 3, 30, 180–1
Smith, J.K. 85
Smith, M. 41, 204, 218
Smithers, A. 193, 194
Snider, B.C.F. 98
social policy 273–4
sociology 274
software 212–17
SOLO 25, 143
Spanish literature 269
Sparrow, J. 35
spreadsheets 203
Stalenhoef-Halling, B.F. 93
standards 244; and motives 258–9;
national 257–8; and quality 253–9
Starfield, A.M. 142
Steffe, L. 122
Stephens, D. 205, 219, 220
Stephenson, J. 18

Stirner, P. 193
Stoney, C. 36
Structure of Observed Learning Outcome
    (SOLO) 25, 143
student learning *see* learning
subject expertise/subject knowledge 18
summative assessment 12, 251
surface learning 27
Swanson, D.B. 36
Swift, B. 219

Tait, H. 26
teaching: computer-assisted 206–10;
    effective 157
Teaching Learning and Technology
    Programme 204
terminology 10–13
Thatcher, M. 61
theology 274–5
Thomas, K. 74
Thomas, P. 7
Thompson, E.P. 61
Thompson, R.A. 197
Thyne, J.M. 32
time management 48–9, 52–3; feedback
    52–3; marking 52–3, 72–4;
    peer-assessment 174; projects 124,
    137–8; self-assessment 174
Tisher, R.P. 99
Tolley, G. 197
Tomlinson, P. 33
Topping, J. 193
Trowler, P. 191
Tuck, R. 194
Turner, A. 190, 194
Turney, C. 51
tutorial programs 209–10

understanding-seeking 23–7
unemployment 262
universities: APEL 190–1; changing
    assessment approaches 229–31;
    consistency 236–8; Graduate
    Studies Programme 254–7; predictive
    validity 242–3; profiles 190; standards
    254–7
University of Derby Interactive
    Assessment Delivery System (DIADS)
    216–17
Usher, R.S. 192

validity 233, 239–44; competencies
    244–6; consequential 239; construct
    241; criterion 243; external examiners
    246–7; face 239; intrinsic 241;
    predictive 242–3
Van der Vleuten, C.P.M. 42, 236
Van Lehn, K. 143
verbal learning 33
Vernon, D.T.A. 7–8, 141
video feedback: consultations 166–8;
    discussions 160–1; presentations
    154–6
visual learning 33
vivas *see* orals
vocational training 192–3

Wagennar, T.C. 186
Walker, D. 186
Walker, L. 18
Wankat, P.C. 23, 144
Ward, A. 41
Watkins, D. 7
Watson, G. 121
Weil, S. 18
Welsh, J. 121
Wertheimer, M. 142
Wetherall, J. 186
Whelan, G. 143
White, R.T. 99
Wickelgren, W.A. 142
Wilkinson, E. 77
Williams, M. 109, 121
Williams, R. 246
Wills, S. 220
Wilson, A. 65
Wilson, L.R. 102
Wittrock, M. 27, 180
Woods, D.R. 143
work-based learning 192–9
work experience 193
Working for Degrees 194
world-wide web 204
Wright, J. 121, 122, 199
writing skills 74, 80–1

Yager, R. 98
Yorke, M. 253

Zakrzeswki, S. 214
Zimbardo, P. 223